Juan García

AI-MANAGER

Building the future with Artificial Intelligence

DEEP ATHENA

For reasons of better readability, the simultaneous use of masculine, feminine, and diverse (m/f/d) language forms, or man, woman, and diverse (m/w/d), is omitted. All designations of people apply equally to all genders.

Published by DEEP ATHENA
(an Imprint of SMART &PRO AI Juan García)
Revised Edition 2025

https://deepathena.com
https://smartandpro.de
ES Version Proofreader: Juan García
DE Version Proofreader: Juan García / Lisa García
EN Version Proofreader: Juan García / Lisa García
Cover Design: Juan García
Cover Images: © Juan García @Midjourney
Photography: Juan García, freepik
Graphics: Juan García
Other images:
https://k3no.medium.com/the-chinese-room-experiment-2c0d6848f05
https://www.mdpi.com/2227-7390/11/14/3074
Notebooks: Juan García

Hardcover ISBN: 9783912099041
Softcover ISBN: 9783912099065

DEEP ATHENA

the Artificial Intelligence Publishing House

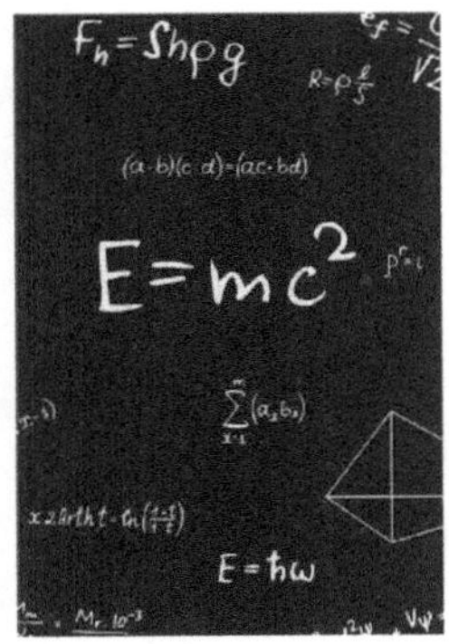

You can download all the example codes included in the book in ".py" and ".ipynb" files in a single .zip archive from the following link:
https://deepathena.com/assets/downloads/8k0M6s.zip

Index

Prologue

On the threshold of a new technological era, we find ourselves in a moment of unprecedented transformation. Artificial Intelligence (AI) has ceased to be mere science fiction fantasy and has become a tangible reality that is redefining the business, social, and cultural landscape. In an era where technology advances by leaps and bounds and the world is in constant evolution, Artificial Intelligence has emerged as one of the most revolutionary and promising tools for transforming how businesses, governments, and society in general operate. However, for this transformation to be effective and beneficial, trained professionals capable of leading and managing these changes are required: the AI-Managers.

The role of an AI-Manager is not simply an evolution of previous roles in technology or management. It is the response to an emerging need: to guide companies through the vast and sometimes bewildering ocean of possibilities that AI offers. Implementing Artificial Intelligence is not a simple task. It requires a deep understanding not only of the technology itself but also of the ethical, social, and business implications it entails.

This book is a compass for those venturing into the fascinating world of AI. With this book, the reader will discover step by step what it means to be an AI-Manager. From understanding the fundamentals of Artificial Intelligence to learning the most advanced strategies for its application in different business sectors, this manual offers a comprehensive tour of all the aspects necessary to master this trade.

Juan García offers much more than just a technical manual with this book. It is a reflection on the impact of AI on our society and how AI-Managers can be agents of positive change. In an era where technology advances rapidly, it is essential that we have leaders who not only understand these tools but also comprehend their potential and limitations, and are capable of guiding organizations towards a future where AI is used responsibly and beneficially for everyone.

For those considering embarking on the profession of AI-Manager, this book is an invaluable investment. And for those who simply wish to better understand the crucial role that Artificial Intelligence will play in our future, Juan García offers a clear and concise vision of the challenges and opportunities that await us.

The book you hold in your hands is not simply a technical guide, but a complete roadmap for those pioneers seeking to understand, implement, and lead projects related to Artificial Intelligence in various sectors and areas. "AI-Manager - The AI-Manager's Manual" is more than a name; it's a philosophy that encompasses the strategic, technical, and human vision necessary to successfully carry out the integration of AI in any organization.

The book begins by immersing us in the fascinating world of AI and Machine Learning, unraveling its definitions, classifications, and real-life applications. It explores not only the types of learning and algorithm categories but also provides a detailed view of the essential tools, software, and libraries in the field.

The book delves into the methods and techniques that allow companies to leverage the potential of AI. From Big Data to the Internet of Things (IoT), and Natural Language Processing (NLP), this module is essential to understanding how data are collected, stored, and processed to feed AI systems.

This manual takes us on a journey through different sectors, showing practical cases and real applications of AI. From human resource management to marketing, and from the banking to the automotive industry, examples and scenarios are presented where AI has proven to be a valuable tool for optimizing and improving processes.

The book also focuses on one of the most crucial aspects: the management of AI projects. Implementing Artificial Intelligence in an organization is not a simple task, and it requires meticulous management and direction to ensure that projects are carried out efficiently and effectively.

This book is the result of years of experience, research, and practice in the field of AI. It is designed to be an invaluable tool for both those just beginning their journey in the world of Artificial Intelligence and for experienced professionals looking to expand their horizons. As we advance in the intelligent revolution, it is essential that we have reliable guides to help us navigate these unexplored waters. With this book, the author offers precisely that: a roadmap to understand, implement, and make the most of the transformative power of Artificial Intelligence.

The revolution of Artificial Intelligence is underway, and with "AI-Manager: The AI-Manager's Manual," you have a compass to navigate this exciting and challenging terrain. I invite you to dive into its pages, to learn, to question, and above all, to dream of the infinite possibilities that AI offers for the future.

Welcome to the era of the AI-Managers. Let the journey begin!

Introduction

What is Artificial Intelligence? What is "intelligence"? And how is the definition of "intelligence" understood in practice among people, both inside and outside the world of Artificial Intelligence?

These are very complex questions that, although they are part of our day-to-day lives and seem to be assimilated and understood among people, the truth is that they are not at all clear yet, especially in the minds of those who are just beginning in the world of Artificial Intelligence, taking advantage of the boom we are experiencing especially in the past year 2022 and currently in 2023, so they continue to be complex questions with complex and therefore subjective answers.

Every day new news is published about new artificial intelligences, about new improvements for existing ones, about new applications for Artificial Intelligence. Day-to-day life in the world of Artificial Intelligence can be as stressful as it is exciting. Meta presents an agreement with Microsoft, Google presents an AI in its new Google Pixel 8, OpenAI announces that ChatGPT will regain "freedom" thanks to Bing.

Isn't it a coincidence that because Microsoft has an agreement with OpenAI, Bing receives updates before ChatGPT?! Artificial Intelligence offers us the future today!

The world of Artificial Intelligence is tremendously active, however, most people are not aware of the amount of news that happens every day in the world of Artificial Intelligence, and the truth is that they cannot be blamed, since traditional media do not cover these news, and people themselves do not inform themselves through forums and magazines available. The world of intelligence is very active and is always in constant evolution. Artificial Intelligence is opening doors in fields as important as medicine, road safety, drug development, surveillance, teaching, communication, and countless fields, as Artificial Intelligence is applicable to practically any field and task you can imagine. However, people confuse all this world and categorize it into groups called "ChatGPT", "Midjourney", etc., something that, although understandable, is still sad.

Although many topics can be discussed, in this book, I do not want to talk to you about ChatGPT, Bard, Alexa, ChatBots, etc.; instead, I want to teach and convey to you everything related to the management of Artificial Intelligence projects, from answering the questions I began writing the book with, through the different algorithms needed to program Artificial Intelligence, including what are "data" for those who are still not clear, what data is needed and how they are worked on a day-to-day basis as a Manager of Artificial Intelligence project management (AI-Manager, as I will call it from now on). We will see its use cases in the most important departments of a company with some examples, and we will finish with the management of such projects. We will also see aspects as important as "Bias" and legal in relation to AI.

In addition, you will have the opportunity to acquire twenty books that add up to a total of two hundred projects (ten projects per book), which complement this book and I professionally recommend them. They are a compilation of projects and ideas of my own that I have gathered and developed personally, for a total of twenty departments within a company, one book per department and in each book, I have included ten projects for that department, and that, after reading and learning the content of this book, you yourself will be able to apply in your company. They are fully schematized and detailed projects that guide you step by step so that you can guide and develop them yourself once you finish reading this book. In addition, you will also find various Cheat-Sheets on my website that will help you, if you are starting, in the field of programming and data analysis.

A long and very intense life and everything that my experience and all the training I have received have provided me with a lot of knowledge, knowledge that of course I want to convey to you. Both my most sincere and open way of seeing things, of understanding the meaning of the term "optimization", as in the best possible way I want to convey my knowledge in this field of Artificial Intelligence and project management for its implementation in companies. But you must be very clear that theory is not everything, not because you have a certificate does it mean that you are better than another. In practice and what counts, is how you manage your knowledge, and this skill is only given to you by experience. Think that because you obtain the title of AI-Manager does not mean that you are really a good AI-Manager, if you are not really interested in this world and are not informed of the latest news, advances, and events of this technology. Not because you have seen the latest presentation video of Marc Zuckerberg of the latest Ray-Ban Meta glasses does it qualify you as an AI-Manager.
It is very important that you understand the importance of being well-trained, of having a clear and broad understanding of what Artificial Intelligence is and the possibilities it offers us, as well as the situations in which you can implement it. We are living in the age of transition, "from the stone age to the future", and the role that the AI-Manager plays is of vital importance, since it depends on us a successful and good change for everyone. Since AI is a field that influences the whole society, and by this, I mean the whole world. The only thing that matters in the end is not how much you know, but your understanding of this world and its importance when applying this technology. Since you can show up for a job interview and be well prepared for the interview and pass it, but once you are working on a project among professionals, your capabilities will be noticeably seen and therefore at the end of the project your results will be decisive for the company.

A good AI-Manager is one who knows the field of Artificial Intelligence, who masters development methods, and has a broad understanding and vision of this technology. If you don't even agree with AI, can you even call yourself an AI-Manager? This implies many more things, starting with interest and vision for the future.

I have more than 25 years of experience working in the industrial sector and I know all the departments within a company, whether small or multinational. In addition, I have worked with companies in eleven different sectors and with clients in various countries. I have several degrees in different sectors and am certified in Spain and Germany as a professional trainer, to
finally take advantage of all this knowledge and experience and my passion for optimization and technologies and train as an AI-Manager. For these and other reasons, I see myself perfectly qualified, in the most humble way, to convey all this knowledge to you and also to share with this book some of my ideas, thoughts, and opinions about this world of Artificial Intelligence.

I want in this book to summarize in the best possible way, but without skipping any detail, all my knowledge and ideas both in project management and what Artificial Intelligence refers to. Unfortunately, it is inevitable for me to have to summarize the topics as much as possible. Along the way, I have worked with and met people who really did not have a clear idea of what Artificial Intelligence is. Something that personally I think is very sad. They weren't even very in agreement with its implementation. So many times very strange situations are presented. This last even occurred in IA-Manager trainings. In some AI-Manager training, there were even some who did not know at all what to expect in the course, and on the contrary, they believed that the job of AI-Manager was something like learning to write Prompts for ChatGPT, Midjourney, etc, and that they would be in charge of this within companies. Believing that being an AI-Manager is being in charge of the use of ChatGPT and these types of AI within the company is truly sad. If you are one of those, and you are reading this book, then I am sorry to have disappointed you. This is not about Prompt-Engineering, nor about writing texts with ChatGPT for the Instagram posts of the company account, this is about learning the profession of Manager of Artificial Intelligence project management. It is about understanding what Artificial Intelligence is and its importance in our day-to-day life, as well as visualizing the possibilities it offers us. Here you will learn what Artificial Intelligence really is, how it works, how it is built, how it is kept alive, how to keep it optimized, and of course, how to advise companies and manage projects, whether you work in a company or are self-employed. At the beginning of the paragraph, I said that my intention is to summarize in the best possible way, but without leaving out any important detail, and that is because Artificial Intelligence is a very complex topic, there are many algorithms that can be used, many questions arise depending on the project and the goal to be achieved, for that reason I will focus on those that for me are without a doubt the best algorithms to acquire the necessary knowledge to take control of this type of projects, manage and direct the team of professionals and finally deliver the best results to the company.

In Spain, it is said that "each master writes his own book", this means nothing more or less than that in the end it is one with the experience who, when doing something, follows his own experience as if it were a book, and in the same way, transmits it to others. The profession of AI-Manager covers many fields that individually can be deepened, such as programming of Artificial Intelligence, data analysis, etc., but here I am going to focus on the most important points and topics for the AI-Manager. At least the ones I consider are the most important.

I am going to divide the syllabus into nine modules: Classification, methods, diagrams in Machine Learning, software, TinyML, use cases, Project management, Bias, ethics, and laws, as this is the order that has convinced me the most and personally I believe it is the best for the teaching of this syllabus. Finally, I make available to you a series of questions and answers for your training, as well as What is Artificial Intelligence? What is "intelligence"? And how is the definition of "intelligence" understood in practice among people, both inside and outside the world of Artificial Intelligence?

I will divide the syllabus into nine modules: Classification, Methods, Diagrams in Machine Learning, Software, TinyML, Use Cases, Project Management, Bias, Ethics, and Laws, as this is the order that has convinced me the most and I personally believe it is the best for teaching this subject. Finally, I provide you with a series of questions and answers for your training, as well as a glossary with two thousand three hundred and eighty-eight terms and their respective definitions, which I have carefully gathered and chosen. Remember that as a supplement to this book, you also have access to twenty other project books (one book per department within a company), which you can acquire separately and which offer you ten detailed projects per department, thus having a total of two hundred projects available as ideas to implement in your company.

Before getting into detail, and to avoid confusion later on, you should be clear about where you stand within the world of Artificial Intelligence. Artificial Intelligence is not just an emotional conversation with ChatGPT. Behind every Artificial Intelligence, there is programming; with this programming, algorithms are generated, mathematical and logical algorithms. These algorithms are fed with data containing a lot of information, and to achieve Artificial Intelligence, these data are analyzed. After these analyses, the algorithms return a result and based on these results, the Artificial Intelligence is trained, finally offering you a response that you perceive as intelligent. That is why from the beginning you have to be very clear about these concepts, and above all, not be scared by the terms "programming" and "algorithms". This is part of the knowledge that an AI-Manager must have, otherwise, it would not make sense for them to lead the team working on these projects. Then they would be an expert in the field, but in this case, since you have the knowledge, you are the expert managing and directing the Artificial Intelligence project. That's why I strongly recommend that you learn as much as you can, do not fall behind, an AI-Manager must be in continuous updating, if you don't, you can only report bad results and this will have a very negative impact on a company that trusts you to position it in the market as the best and toughest competition. Keep in mind that an Artificial Intelligence implementation process is developed to optimize, improve, and also save.

Keep in mind that we are going to work as much as possible with terms in English, for example, Machine Learning, Data Science, etc. This will help you, if you are not already, to familiarize yourself with the terminology of the AI-Manager profession and Artificial Intelligence. I will also try, to avoid being repetitive, to change the terms so as not to overwhelm you when reading. Also, keep in mind that in programming the English language is used, so when programming, the "." is used to mark decimals in mathematical operations and/or results. For example, in Europe, the "," is used to mark decimals. So, both when reading the data and when programming, it is better to use the "." for decimals. Knowing this in advance will help you greatly if you are starting and will save you many headaches. Believe me, you wouldn't be the first one to experience this.

I sincerely hope that this book helps you and you manage to learn the trade of AI-Manager, that it helps you to know AI in a clearer and deeper way, and that you enjoy, above all.

MODULE 1

Classification

Module 1 – Classification

1. Definition and Classification of Artificial Intelligence

Within the field of Artificial Intelligence, there are various fields, which contribute their potential to obtain Artificial Intelligence, and likewise, Artificial Intelligence is within another even larger field, this is Data Science. Let's see it with a simple drawing.

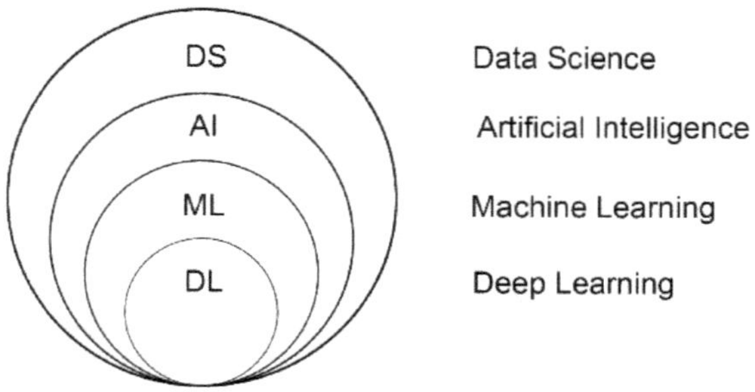

The drawing shows you what fields exist and how they integrate with each other. Thus, you can get a visual idea of where you stand as an IA-Manager within the Data Science globe. However, this drawing is very standardized and is the version or "vision" that is usually taught. The field of artificial intelligence is in continuous advancement and evolution, so in practice and as this happens, this classification may become subjective.
You, as an IA-Manager, must come to know and understand the fields of Deep Learning, Machine Learning, and Artificial Intelligence, and for this, you inevitably must develop your understanding of various concepts and aspects of Data Science, as well as data analysis.

To delve into the concept of Artificial Intelligence, I am going to offer you my most personal view, risking that scientists and professionals in the field will bombard me with comments while they tear their hair out and scream to the heavens about my words. There are two types of Artificial Intelligence systems, traditional and intelligent. I am going to clarify this right away. The traditional one is what we all know as a calculator or, for example, Excel; while an intelligent system is what we know as ChatGPT. What are the differences? The traditional system is programmed to perform a task, you tell it what you want and it does it for you, just as you could do yourself. The intelligent system, on the other hand, is programmed to learn to learn to perform it and to improve its result, just as you do throughout your life.

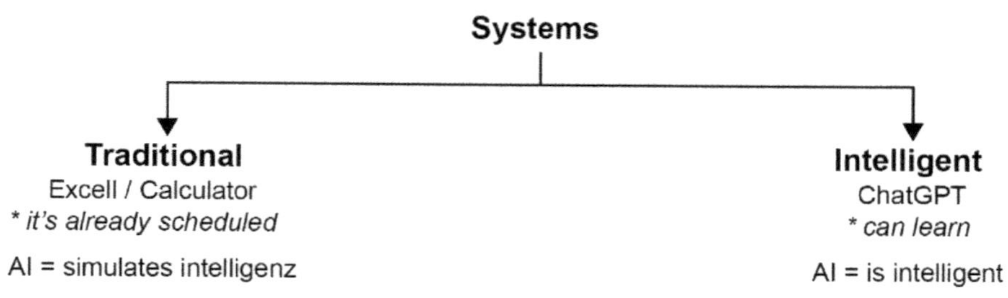

This is known as "weak Artificial Intelligence" and "strong artificial intelligence". Weak Artificial Intelligence simulates having intelligence or being intelligent, while strong Artificial Intelligence is intelligent because it learns.

AI weak ← **AI** → *AI strong*

These concepts of Artificial Intelligence should not be confused at all with what I am going to explain next, as we are going to delve deeper into the concept of "intelligence," and this is where, in relation to these concepts, opinions diverge. Due to the confusion it generates among those unfamiliar with the basics of Artificial Intelligence, I will try to explain it to you in the clearest and simplest way possible, since not only should everyone already understand it, but you specifically, as an AI-Manager, must have these ideas absolutely clear, as you as an AI-Manager are the expert in Artificial Intelligence within a company, and you must, necessarily, be able to explain these concepts to each of your colleagues and/or bosses.

Within the world of the science of Artificial Intelligence, opinions are divided among the scientific community. Since the 1930s, concepts and theses about what is and what is understood as Artificial Intelligence began to develop. Today there are two theses in the scientific community that explain and argue their opinions, and both are right and very convincing, so in the end the question "What is Artificial Intelligence?" remains very subjective and without a clear and unique answer. However, it is their acceptance within the scientific community that differentiates them. These theses are called "Weak AI-Thesis" and "Strong AI-Thesis." Do not let these terms confuse you with "Weak AI" and "Strong AI," as we are now talking about the thesis itself, and the adjectives "weak" and "strong" refer only to how widespread/accepted these theories are in the scientific community. I will explain it to you in detail next.

The two points within this topic of AI that use the same terms, "Weak AI and Strong AI" and "Weak AI-Thesis and Strong AI-Thesis," can be extremely confusing if you do not know them and know how to differentiate them. One thing is Artificial Intelligence itself, as we have seen there is a Weak Artificial Intelligence (simulates) and another Strong (learns), and another completely different thing is the conception of what Artificial Intelligence is within the scientific community, "Weak AI-Thesis and Strong AI-Thesis." This conception of Artificial Intelligence within the scientific community is called "thesis," and this thesis is divided into two points of view or opinions within the scientific community, which are called "weak thesis" and "strong thesis." If you manage to understand this point, believe me, you will undoubtedly be able, with just a little effort, to master the profession of AI-Manager.

Why are these two opinions within the thesis called "weak" and "strong"? Does it have anything to do with Weak and Strong Artificial Intelligence? Well, actually no. Pay close attention to this. It is called "weak thesis" and "strong thesis" only because each of these two opinions has a "strength," a "weight," within the scientific community, which means that the "weak thesis" is less accepted by the arguments it offers about what Artificial Intelligence is, so it is less recognized or less widespread within the scientific community than the "strong thesis," which (the strong thesis) is a very recognized thesis within the scientific community for the arguments it presents, so it is more widespread and therefore more generally accepted by scientists who explore and develop this field.

The "Weak AI-Thesis" and the less accepted by the scientific community explains and expresses that in Artificial Intelligence intelligence manifests itself in the interaction with the system. This thesis indicates that AI does what it does without understanding it. If we think about it, I know people who know the multiplication tables, but when you ask them what is the purpose of the multiplication tables, you realize that they do not understand the concept and therefore are not able to react to your question to offer you a clarification spontaneously or quickly, however, they are able to solve mathematical problems since they have stored in their memory the multiplication tables, so "intelligence manifests itself in the interaction with the system."

The "Strong AI-Thesis" and the most accepted by the scientific community explains and expresses that people are "equal to machines" in terms of intelligence. This thesis explains that consciousness and intelligence is nothing more than information processing and this is no more and no less than what we all do every day in our daily lives, and ChatGPT can, in fact, do what I do, whether it feels, understands or not. The truth is that if we think deeply about it we have all learned throughout our lives, you are doing it right now reading this book, and with that information that we store in our "database," we solve the problems that arise in our day to day life. We learn, memorize, and only when we need it we access that information, we process it and take the necessary measures to solve our problems, overcome barriers, improve ourselves, relate, choose our food each day, choose our clothing depending on the weather etc. This involves learning from information previously acquired, and depending on previous results, we make one decision or another. Haven't you ever heard the saying "learn from your mistakes"?

Still a little confused? I will try to make it clearer with the following image.These concepts of Artificial Intelligence should not be confused at all with what I am going to explain next, as we are going to delve deeper into the concept of "intelligence," and this is where, in relation to these concepts, opinions diverge. Due to the confusion it generates among those unfamiliar with the basics of Artificial Intelligence, I will try to explain it to you in the clearest and simplest way possible, since not only should everyone already understand it, but you specifically, as an AI-Manager, must have these ideas absolutely clear, as you as an AI-Manager are the expert in Artificial Intelligence within a company, and you must, necessarily, be able to explain these concepts to each of your colleagues and/or bosses.

Within the world of the science of Artificial Intelligence, opinions are divided among the scientific community. Since the 1930s, concepts and theses about what is and what is understood as Artificial Intelligence began to develop. Today there are two theses in the scientific community that explain and argue their opinions, and both are right and very convincing, so in the end the question "What is Artificial Intelligence?" remains very subjective and without a clear and unique answer. However, it is their acceptance within the scientific community that differentiates them. These theses are called "Weak AI-Thesis" and "Strong AI-Thesis." Do not let these terms confuse you with "Weak AI" and "Strong AI," as we are now talking about the thesis itself, and the adjectives "weak" and "strong" refer only to how widespread/accepted these theories are in the scientific community. I will explain it to you in detail next.

The two points within this topic of AI that use the same terms, "Weak AI and Strong AI" and "Weak AI-Thesis and Strong AI-Thesis," can be extremely confusing if you do not know them and know how to differentiate them. One thing is Artificial Intelligence itself, as we have seen there is a Weak Artificial Intelligence (simulates) and another Strong (learns), and another completely different thing is the conception of what Artificial Intelligence is within the scientific community, "Weak AI-Thesis and Strong AI-Thesis." This conception of Artificial Intelligence within the scientific community is called "thesis," and this thesis is divided into two points of view or opinions within the scientific community, which are called "weak thesis" and "strong thesis." If you manage to understand this point, believe me, you will undoubtedly be able, with just a little effort, to master the profession of AI-Manager.

Why are these two opinions within the thesis called "weak" and "strong"? Does it have anything to do with Weak and Strong Artificial Intelligence? Well, actually no. Pay close attention to this.

It is called "weak thesis" and "strong thesis" only because each of these two opinions has a "strength," a "weight," within the scientific community, which means that the "weak thesis" is less accepted by the arguments it offers about what Artificial Intelligence is, so it is less recognized or less widespread within the scientific community than the "strong thesis," which (the strong thesis) is a very recognized thesis within the scientific community for the arguments it presents, so it is more widespread and therefore more generally accepted by scientists who explore and develop this field.

The "Weak AI-Thesis" and the less accepted by the scientific community explains and expresses that in Artificial Intelligence intelligence manifests itself in the interaction with the system. This thesis indicates that AI does what it does without understanding it. If we think about it, I know people who know the multiplication tables, but when you ask them what is the purpose of the multiplication tables, you realize that they do not understand the concept and therefore are not able to react to your question to offer you a clarification spontaneously or quickly, however, they are able to solve mathematical problems since they have stored in their memory the multiplication tables, so "intelligence manifests itself in the interaction with the system."

The "Strong AI-Thesis" and the most accepted by the scientific community explains and expresses that people are "equal to machines" in terms of intelligence. This thesis explains that consciousness and intelligence is nothing more than information processing and this is no more and no less than what we all do every day in our daily lives, and ChatGPT can, in fact, do what I do, whether it feels, understands or not. The truth is that if we think deeply about it we have all learned throughout our lives, you are doing it right now reading this book, and with that information that we store in our "database," we solve the problems that arise in our day to day life. We learn, memorize, and only when we need it we access that information, we process it and take the necessary measures to solve our problems, overcome barriers, improve ourselves, relate, choose our food each day, choose our clothing depending on the weather etc. This involves learning from information previously acquired, and depending on previous results, we make one decision or another. Haven't you ever heard the saying "learn from your mistakes"?

Still a little confused? I will try to make it clearer with the following image.

Acceptance of the AI thesis

Strong AI Thesis:
People = Machines

Consciousness and intelligence are nothing more than information processing.

ChaGPT can, in fact, do what I do.

I have learned throughout my life and solve problems with the information stored in my "database" based on my experience.

Weak AI Thesis:
The intelligence is manifested in the interaction with the system.

AI does it without understanding it.

To make sense of all the theory you are going to learn in this book, I am going to take a few lines to delve into the concept of intelligence, and we are going to immerse ourselves in our deepest thoughts. And here is the question: what is intelligence?

Intelligence is a complex and multifaceted concept that has been the subject of study and debate throughout human history in various disciplines, such as psychology, neuroscience, philosophy, and for a few decades now, Artificial Intelligence. Although there is no single and widely accepted definition, there are some perspectives on intelligence, and as you will see, they all basically express the same thing.

Psychological perspective: In psychology, intelligence has traditionally been defined as the ability to learn, reason, and solve problems. Intelligence quotient tests (IQ tests) have been used to measure this ability in people and animals since they were invented in 1905 by the Frenchmen Alfred Binet and Théodore Simon.

Biological perspective: From a biological standpoint, intelligence can be seen as the result of neural processes in the brain. The structure and function of the brain, as well as the interaction between genes and environment, play a crucial role in determining an individual's intelligence.

Philosophical perspective: Philosophers have debated the nature of intelligence for centuries. Some see intelligence as a purely rational quality, while others consider it a combination of reason, emotion, and will. Aristotle refers to the rational part of the human soul as the intellect. Thus, it has the ability to acquire knowledge of abstract universals as opposed to knowledge obtained through perception.

Artificial Intelligence perspective: In the field of Artificial Intelligence, intelligence refers to the capacity of a machine or system to perform tasks that, when performed by humans, require intelligence. This includes tasks such as learning, reasoning, and adapting to new situations. For example, a calculator, Excel, ChatGPT, a chess-playing program, a vehicle that drives and decides completely on its own, etc.

Multiple intelligences: Howard Gardner, an American education scientist, proposed the theory of multiple intelligences, suggesting that intelligence is not a single ability, but that there are different types of intelligence, such as logical-mathematical, linguistic, musical, spatial, among others.

Social perspective: Some theorists argue that intelligence is not only an individual capacity but also a social one. This refers to a person's ability to interact and function effectively in a social context. This perspective is often included and interpreted by many as one of the multiple intelligences.

If everyone has a different perspective on intelligence, then how can we expect the scientific community to agree on a definition of Artificial Intelligence?

Now I am going to give you my most sincere and open opinion on this topic, and with this, I want to close the discussion. Humans have evolved, developed, and advanced over the centuries with the thought and idea that they are the most intelligent beings that exist. For this reason, we understand as intelligent, something that we all know as our own intelligence, the ability to learn, solve problems, perform analysis, and make decisions, all this added to our ability to feel, taking into account the factor of "consciousness." It is because of this last point, feeling, that I firmly believe we are mistaken in what we refer to as the definition of Artificial Intelligence. Humans blindly insist on comparing Artificial Intelligence with human intelligence. We have not learned, nor accepted, that intelligence is not only what we know as intelligence but that other intelligences can be developed, such as Artificial Intelligence, an intelligence that, like us, can perform the same tasks and make decisions and even interact with us without the factor of the soul, without that "factor" that makes us human, "rational," and "better" than other beings and which affects decision-making. We strive to be unique, and intelligence is what makes us different and "better" than other living beings, so we don't want to accept that there are more intelligences than ours, because we don't want to lose our throne as unique and "intelligent" beings. Today, and this is, as I say, my most personal opinion, there are two clear intelligences, human and artificial. For this reason, we should stop thinking of the word "intelligence" as a single intelligence, and we should start to give a plural and multifaceted sense to its definition, and accept that we are facing two intelligences, which, although they do the same, are different. A person is guided by their feelings and reason when making a decision, the machine analyzes probabilities and makes a decision, without feelings involved, but with a logic, just like the human one, but previously programmed. If both make the decision based on the same criteria, aren't they both intelligent? On the other hand, if both are guided differently, although with the same bases, aren't they both intelligent? So we should stop associating intelligence with humans as the supreme intelligent being and accept that there are two intelligences, that of human beings (or living beings, let's not now take animals for fools), and artificial intelligence.

Only when you have knowledge about the definition of the word "intelligence" are you truly prepared to be a true IA-Manager, a professional capable of creating intelligence for the benefit of the company, and you will have taken the first step towards truly becoming a manager of Artificial Intelligence projects.

What is intelligent behavior?

In 1950, the British mathematician and logician Alan Turing developed the so-called "Turing Test," a test aimed at evaluating a machine's ability to exhibit intelligent behavior comparable to that of humans. In the original procedure of the test, a human interrogator interacts with a human and a machine, not knowing which is which, through a text interface. The interrogator asks questions and receives answers from both participants, trying to determine which one is the machine. If the interrogator cannot distinguish between the human's and the machine's responses, the machine is considered to have passed the test.

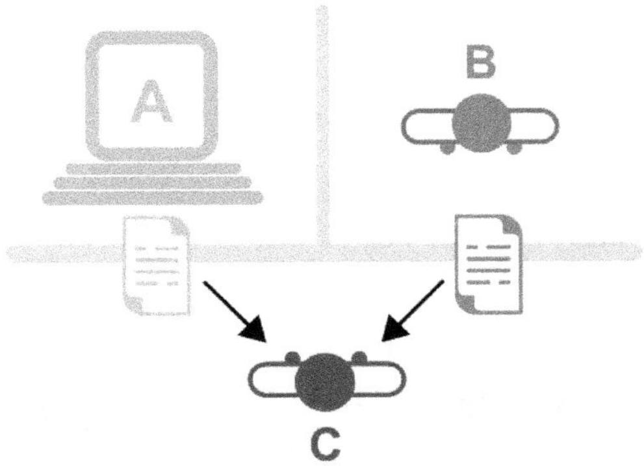

Turing predicted that by the year 2000, machines would be capable of answering questions as convincingly as a human for at least five minutes in 30% of interrogation sessions. The Turing Test has been a significant influence in the field of Artificial Intelligence, sparking much debate about the nature of intelligence and the possibility of replicating human intelligence in machines. It has also driven research in AI, leading to significant developments in the field. However, it has faced criticism for not being a suitable measure of all forms of intelligence, as it primarily focuses on the ability to deceive and superficial similarity to human behavior. Additionally, it is argued that the test does not address fundamental aspects of human intelligence such as understanding or consciousness. Despite these criticisms, the Turing Test continues to be a central concept in the debate about Artificial Intelligence, although there are other metrics and tests that are also used to evaluate machine intelligence.

2. Machine Learning (ML)

Machine Learning (ML) emerges as an intriguing subset of Artificial Intelligence, offering the promise of machines that improve and learn from experience, rather than relying solely on pre-defined code. In other words, Machine Learning is a branch of Artificial Intelligence that focuses on developing algorithms and techniques that enable computers to learn and make predictions or decisions based on data, without being explicitly programmed to do so. At its core, ML relies on models, which are mathematical representations of a specific process or phenomenon. These models, unlike traditional systems, have the ability to adapt and evolve based on the data they are fed.

The heart of the learning process in ML is the algorithm. These algorithms, acting like recipes, guide and adjust the model through a process called training. During this training, the model processes data, adjusts its parameters, and seeks to improve its predictions or decisions.

There are different approaches or typologies in ML, each with its own goals and techniques. Supervised learning, for example, is akin to a classroom where a teacher (labeled data) guides the student (the model) towards the correct answer. On the other hand, in unsupervised learning, the model is presented with a set of unlabeled data, aiming to discover patterns or hidden structures on its own. Finally, reinforcement learning is similar to a game: an agent interacts with its environment, learning from the rewards and penalties it receives for its actions.

The machine must learn patterns based on data.
Input: Data
According to the ML algorithm, a different representation is obtained. This provides insights into patterns or enables predictions.
Output: Model

"Machine Learning models are only as good as the data with which they were created."

ML is behind many of the innovations we see today. From recommendation systems on streaming platforms to advanced medical diagnostics, its presence is ubiquitous. However, this power brings responsibilities and challenges. Data quality is crucial; a model is only as accurate as the data it is trained on. Additionally, there are technical challenges such as Overfitting, where a model adapts too much to the training data and loses its ability to generalize. Interpretability and the need for robust infrastructure are other important considerations.

Machine Learning represents one of the most powerful and transformative tools of our era, opening countless possibilities in various fields. But, like all powerful tools, its use must be informed, ethical, and responsible.

2.1. Patterns

In the context of Machine Learning, "patterns" refer to identifiable structures or relationships in data that can be learned and used by models to make predictions or decisions. Patterns are essential for understanding the underlying information in the data and how these relationships can be leveraged to solve specific problems. Let's look more closely at the mentioned patterns and how they relate to ML:

Regressions (Correlations)
Correlations indicate a linear relationship between two variables. In ML, identifying correlations can be fundamental in understanding the relationships between features and the prediction target. For example, in a regression model, the aim is to understand how various features are correlated with the target variable.
Example: In an e-commerce platform, it is observed that as site visits increase, sales also increase. This correlation pattern can help the company understand the relationship between web traffic and sales, and plan marketing strategies.

Classification
Classification is a type of task in ML where the goal is to assign labels to new instances based on the learning of previously labeled data. For example, a classification model can be trained to identify spam emails based on certain patterns in the data.
Example: A bank may classify credit applicants as 'high risk' or 'low risk' based on various factors such as credit history, income, and debt level. This assignment process helps the bank decide whom to grant credit.

Clustering
Clustering is an unsupervised ML technique where the goal is to discover inherently existing groups in the data. For example, a clustering algorithm can identify customer segments in a dataset based on their purchasing behaviors.
Example: An online music store could use clustering algorithms to classify songs into different musical genres based on attributes like tempo, key, instrumentation, and lyrics. This allows the platform to offer genre-based playlists to its users.

Association rules
Association rules aim to identify relationships between variables in a dataset. For example, an association rule algorithm might discover that customers who buy a particular product also tend to buy another, which can be useful for product recommendations.
Example: In a supermarket, data analysis reveals that customers who buy diapers often also buy beer. Based on this rule, the supermarket could place these products near each other to increase

cross-selling. Although it may not seem like a very logical strategy, the data does not lie, making it a very important strategy to consider if looking to increase sales.
These patterns and techniques are fundamental in ML, as they provide the mechanism for models to learn from data and perform tasks such as prediction, classification, and knowledge discovery in databases. These patterns identified through Machine Learning techniques can be extremely useful for businesses and organizations, allowing them to better understand the relationships between different variables, effectively classify data, identify natural groups within their data, and discover rules that can help improve sales and marketing strategies, among other applications.

2.2. Key Features of Machine Learning

Learning from data: The platform collects data about users' preferences and viewing behaviors. Through ML, the system learns and adapts recommendations based on these data. For example, if user A watches many comedies, the system will learn to recommend more of this type of content to user A.
Algorithms: Algorithms like collaborative filtering are used to analyze user data and find patterns. For example, if user A and user B have watched the same comedies, it's likely that user A will also like other shows that user B has watched, and vice versa.
Prediction and decision-making: Based on the identified patterns, the system makes predictions about what other content might interest users and decides what to recommend next.
Models: Mathematical and logical models are created and trained using the collected data to make more accurate predictions about users' preferences.

2.3. Uses of Machine Learning

Predictive Analysis: Predicts viewing trends to plan the acquisition of new content.
Pattern Recognition: Identifies patterns in users' viewing habits to improve recommendations.
Personalized Recommendations: Provides personalized content suggestions for each user based on their viewing history.
Process Optimization: Optimizes the content supply chain, identifying which types of content are most popular and where resources should be invested.
Development of Smart Products and Services: Develops new features, such as a virtual assistant that can help users find content they will like.
Health: Although not directly applicable in this example, ML can be used in health contexts, such as computer-assisted medical diagnosis.
Scientific Research and Development: Also outside this example, ML assists in research, such as analyzing large data sets to discover new materials.

The role of the AI-Manager in this scenario would be crucial in coordinating efforts among data, engineering, and business teams, ensuring that the project goals are aligned, resources are well-managed, and ML solutions are implemented ethically, legally, and effectively to enhance user experience and achieve company objectives.

Let's graphically see two examples of its application that may be familiar to us.

Detecting unwanted emails:

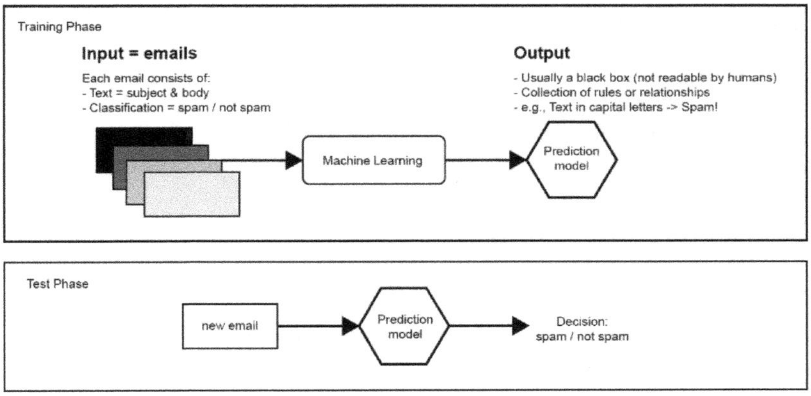

Customer segmentation:

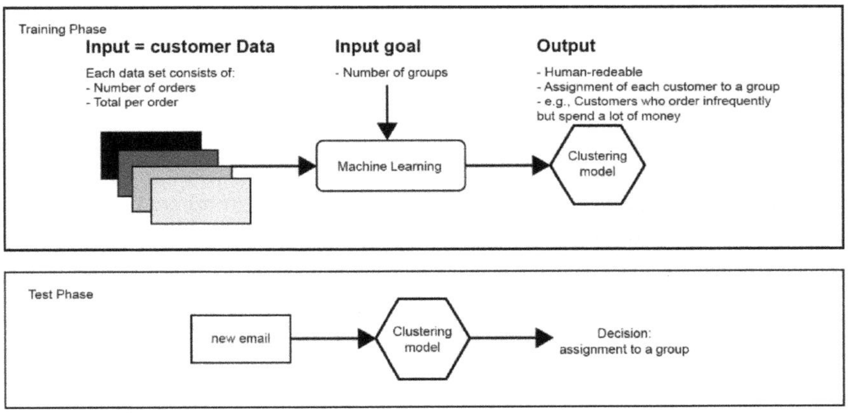

3. Categories of algorithms in ML

In the context of Machine Learning, "learning" refers to the process by which a computational model improves its performance in a specific task with the experience gained from being exposed to more data. In Machine Learning, "learning" implies that an algorithm improves its ability to predict, classify, or perform some other task by processing data, adjusting its parameters and internal structures to minimize error or the difference between its predictions and the actual values. Through this learning process, the algorithm is able to generalize its acquired knowledge to new data, thus enabling it to make predictions or take informed decisions in previously unseen situations.

In Machine Learning, algorithms can be classified into various categories based on the type of learning they perform and the type of task they address. Here are the main categories of algorithms in ML:

Supervised learning:

- **Regression:** These algorithms predict continuous values, such as the price of a house.
Examples: Linear regression, polynomial regression.

- **Classification:** These algorithms predict categorical labels.
Examples: Logistic regression, support vector machines (SVM), decision trees, k-nearest neighbors (k-NN).

Unsupervised learning:

- **Clustering:** These algorithms group similar data into clusters or groups.
Examples: k-Means, DBSCAN, hierarchical.

- **Dimensionality reduction:** These algorithms reduce the number of variables in a dataset.
Examples: Principal Component Analysis (PCA), t-SNE.

- **Association:** These algorithms find rules that describe large portions of data.
Example: Apriori algorithm.

Reinforcement learning:
These algorithms allow an agent to learn how to behave in an environment by performing actions and receiving rewards or penalties.
Examples: Q-learning, Deep Q Network (DQN), Policy Gradients.

Semi-supervised learning:
These algorithms are located between supervised and unsupervised learning, using both labeled and unlabeled data to improve learning performance. They are useful when there are few labeled data and many unlabeled data.

Multi-instance learning:
In this type of learning, there is a bag of instances and a label for the bag instead of each instance. The task is to predict a new bag instead of a single instance.

Multi-Label learning:
Instead of assigning a single label to each instance, these algorithms assign a set of labels. It is useful in situations like text classification where a document may belong to multiple categories.

These are the main categories, but the field of ML is broad and constantly evolving, with new types of algorithms and approaches continually emerging. Additionally, with the rise of Deep Learning, there is a variety of neural network architectures designed for specific tasks, such as convolutional networks for image processing or recurrent networks for temporal sequences.
Each category and algorithm has its own strengths, weaknesses, and ideal applications, so choosing the right algorithm largely depends on the specific problem being addressed and especially on your ability to recognize the project's needs and relate them to the project's objectives.

To learn what learning is in ML we will mainly focus on these five types:

1. Supervised Learning
2. Semi-supervised Learning
3. Unsupervised Learning
4. Reinforcement Learning
5. Deep Learning (DL)

These categories represent different approaches and techniques within the field of Machine Learning, each with its specificities and applications depending on the nature of the data and the problem to be solved.
For each category, there is a different data structure and different algorithm models. We will look at them separately in more detail.

3.1. Supervised Learning

In supervised learning, algorithms learn from a set of labeled data, where each training example has an associated label or outcome. The objective is to learn a function that maps inputs to outputs so that it can make accurate predictions about previously unseen data.
There are different types of supervised learning:

Classification:
- Assignment to categories (classes). This is done through labels.
- The prediction model is only as good as the input data
- Challenges: Overfitting / Underfitting

Regression:
- Learning a mathematical function f(x) = ...
- Outliers can affect the outcome
- Challenges: Overfitting / Underfitting

Supervised learning is a vast field with many models and algorithms. Here I present a list of some of the most well-known and used models: (the most recommended for beginners are the k-NN algorithm (Classification) and the Linear Regression algorithm (Regression).

Linear Regression
Used to predict a continuous value based on one or more independent variables.

Logistic Regression
Used for binary classification, that is, to predict the probability that an instance belongs to one of two classes.

Decision Trees
Used for classification and regression, they divide the feature space into disjoint regions.

Random Forests
An extension of decision trees that constructs multiple trees and aggregates their predictions.

Support Vector Machines (SVM)
Used for binary and multiclass classification, seeks to find the hyperplane that best separates the classes in the feature space.

k-Nearest Neighbors (k-NN)
An instance-based algorithm that classifies new instances based on the majority votes of its k nearest neighbors. Where "k" is a previously given number, and better if odd.

Artificial Neural Networks (ANN)
Deep learning models that can be used for classification and regression in complex and high-dimensional data sets.

Naive Bayes
A set of algorithms based on the application of Bayes' theorem for classification.

Boosting (e.g., AdaBoost, Gradient Boosting)
Techniques that build a series of models, usually decision trees, where each one tries to correct the errors of the previous one.

Ridge Regression
A variant of linear regression that includes an L2 penalty to avoid overfitting.

Lasso Regression
Similar to Ridge regression but with an L1 penalty that can lead to feature selection.

Convolutional Neural Networks (CNN)
Specially designed for image processing, but also used in other types of structured data.

Recurrent Neural Networks (RNN)
Designed to work with sequential data, such as time series or text sequences.

These models and algorithms offer a variety of tools for tackling different types of supervised learning problems, from simple to complex, and each has its own strengths and weaknesses depending on the type of data and the problem in question.

3.1.1. k-Nearest-Neighbours-Algorithm (k-N-N)

Possibly the most commonly used algorithm is "k-Nearest-Neighbors-Algorithm" (k-N-N), due to its simplicity and effectiveness. Of course, for each situation, there are different algorithms, and therefore, each case will require or recommend a different algorithm. Likewise, k-N-N is the most recommended algorithm to start with in supervised learning. Let's take a closer look at the k-N-N algorithm to perform classification.

Algorithm: k-N-N (k-Nearest-Neighbours) – (Classification)

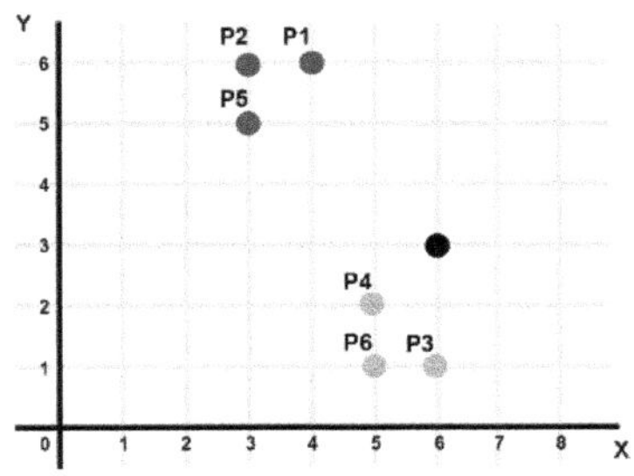

Point	X	Y	Class
P1	4	6	dark grey
P2	3	6	dark grey
P3	6	1	light grey
P4	5	2	light grey
P5	3	5	dark grey
P6	5	1	light grey

Idea: Tell me who your neighbors are, and I'll tell you who you are.

Concept: Lazy Learning
It does not generate a model, but rather stores training data in a database (DB).

Procedure:
1. Enter training data (with labels).
2. Enter test data (without labels).
3. The algorithm searches for the k nearest neighbors (for example, using Euclidean distance).
4. Output: The label that is most represented among the k neighbors.

Attention: As I mentioned before, the value for "k" should preferably be odd (to avoid a 50:50 tie), in order to classify new data under an exact label.

Basically, Supervised Learning is a category within Machine Learning where algorithms learn from a previously labeled dataset. In this set, each training example is associated with a label or a specific output value. The main goal of supervised learning is to develop a model that can make accurate predictions or decisions on new unseen data based on the learning acquired from the training data.

1. Data collection: A set of labeled data is collected to train the model.
2. Data preparation: Data is cleaned and prepared, generally divided into training and testing sets.
3. Model selection: A suitable supervised learning algorithm is chosen for the problem.
4. Model training: The model is trained using the training set, adjusting its parameters to minimize the error between the model's predictions and the actual labels.
5. Model evaluation: The model's performance is evaluated using the test set to ensure that the model has learned correctly.
6. Model tuning: If necessary, the model is adjusted and retrained until acceptable performance is achieved.

7. Model deployment: Once trained and successfully evaluated, the model is deployed to make predictions on new and unseen data.

Example:

Email classification as "spam" or "non-spam":
- **Data collection:** Emails labeled as spam or non-spam are collected.
- **Objective:** Classify new emails into spam or non-spam categories.
- **Model:** A classification model like Naive Bayes can be used to learn patterns that distinguish spam from legitimate email.

In these examples, supervised learning allows for the development of models that can generalize well from training data and make accurate predictions on new data, thus helping to solve practical problems in various fields.

Now let's look at the Linear Regression algorithm more closely for making a prediction.

3.1.2. Linear Regression

Linear regression is one of the most basic and widely used techniques in supervised learning. It is mainly used for regression problems where the goal is to predict a continuous value.

Algorithm: Linear Regression

Concept: Relates independent variables to a dependent variable through a linear equation.
Idea: An increase in X results in an increase/decrease in Y.
Model: Linear regression assumes a linear relationship between the inputs and the output. The relationship is modeled as:

$$y = \beta_0 + \beta_1 x_1 + \beta_2 x_2 + \dots + \beta_n x_n + \epsilon$$

where:
- y is the dependent variable or the output.
- $x_1, x_2, \dots, x_n$ are the independent variables or inputs.
- $\beta_0, \beta_1, \dots, \beta_n$ are the coefficients.
- ϵ is the error or residue.

Procedure:
1. Data Collection: A data set with independent variables and a dependent variable is needed.
2. Data Preparation: The data must be cleaned and often normalized or standardized.
3. Model Training: A training data set is used to estimate the β coefficients that minimize the mean squared error (MSE).
4. Model Evaluation: The model's performance is evaluated on a test data set to ensure the model generalizes well.

5. Prediction: The trained model is used to make predictions on new data.

Attention:
- Linear Regression assumes a linear relationship between the inputs and the output. If the relationship is nonlinear, the model may not fit well.
- It is susceptible to outliers, which can affect the quality of the model.
- Multicollinearity (high correlation among independent variables) can be problematic and should be addressed.

Examples:

Prediction of Housing Prices:
- **Data Collection:** Data from past housing sales are collected, including features like size, location, and number of rooms.
- **Objective:** Predict the selling price of new homes based on their features.
- **Model:** A linear regression model is used to learn the relationship between the features of the homes and their selling price.

Prediction of Automobile Fuel Consumption:
- **Context:** Automotive companies are constantly seeking ways to improve the fuel efficiency of their vehicles due to environmental regulations, market demand, and competition. For this, it's essential to understand how different vehicle features affect fuel consumption.
- **Data Collection:** Data from various car models produced in recent years are collected. These data include features like the vehicle's weight, engine power, transmission type, aerodynamics, and the type of fuel used.
- **Objective:** Predict the fuel consumption (e.g., miles per gallon or liters per 100 km) of a new car model based on its features.
- **Model:** A linear regression model is used to learn the relationship between the car's features (independent variables) and its fuel consumption (dependent variable).

- **Procedure:**
1. Model Training: With the collected data from existing models, a linear regression model is trained to understand how different features impact fuel consumption.
2. Model Evaluation: A separate data set (not used in training) is used to evaluate how well the model predicts fuel consumption.
3. Prediction: With the trained model, predictions can be made about the fuel consumption of new models or prototypes of cars based on their features.

- **Results and Uses:** With this model, engineers and designers can make adjustments to the vehicle's features during the design phase to achieve specific fuel efficiency goals. Additionally, it can help the company make informed decisions about which technologies or innovations to prioritize for improving fuel efficiency in future models.

This last example illustrates how linear regression can be a valuable tool in the automotive industry for predicting and optimizing fuel consumption, which in turn can have significant impacts in terms of costs, compliance with regulations, and customer satisfaction.

Linear regression is a powerful and versatile tool used in a variety of applications. Although simple, it is fundamental in statistics and Machine Learning and serves as a basis for more advanced techniques.

3.2. Unsupervised Learning

In unsupervised learning, algorithms work with unlabeled data sets, seeking to find structures, patterns, or inherent relationships in the data without any prior supervision. Common tasks include clustering, dimensionality reduction, and association rules.

Features of unsupervised learning are:
- There are no labels!
- The goal is to recognize patterns in the data.
- This should lead to grouping the data sets. (Making different groups with them).
- It can be used to generate labels.
- Attention: Labels are only mathematical assignments!
- It can be completely wrong.
- Output: Assignment to a group for each data set.
- Clusters or associations.

Unsupervised learning encompasses a variety of techniques and models. Below I name some of the most well-known models and algorithms in this category:

Clustering Algorithms
- k-Means
- Hierarchical Clustering
- DBSCAN (Density-Based Spatial Clustering of Applications with Noise)
- Agglomerative Clustering
- Gaussian Mixture Model

Dimensionality Reduction Algorithms
- Principal Component Analysis (PCA)
- Linear Discriminant Analysis (LDA)
- t-SNE (t-Distributed Stochastic Neighbor Embedding)
- UMAP (Uniform Manifold Approximation and Projection)

Association Algorithms
- Apriori
- Eclat
- FP-Growth (Frequent Pattern Growth)

Anomaly Detection Algorithms
- Isolation Forest
- One-Class SVM (Support Vector Machine)
- Local Outlier Factor (LOF)

- Autoencoders (especially when used for anomaly detection)

Generative Models
- Autoencoders
- Variational Autoencoders
- Generative Adversarial Networks (GANs)

Self-Organizing Neural Networks
- Self-Organizing Maps (SOM)

Matrix Factorization
- Non-negative Matrix Factorization (NMF)

These models and algorithms cover a variety of tasks within unsupervised learning, including clustering, dimensionality reduction, association rules, anomaly detection, and generation of new data. Each has its own strengths, weaknesses, and applications in different domains and data sets. Among all these forms of unsupervised learning, we will focus on "clustering" and "dependency analysis" or "association rule", as they are the most recommended for starting in unsupervised learning.

3.2.1. Clustering

Data sets are divided into groups:
Disjoint groups: group A has different characteristics than group B.
Hierarchical groups: groups A, B, C describe different manifestations of the same characteristic.

Challenges: How is similarity defined? How are outliers handled?
Algorithm: k-Means

Clustering:
- Classification of data sets into groups (disjoint or hierarchical)
- The groups are previously unknown! (unsupervised learning)

Cluster = Group of data sets

Objective:
- Discover groups
- Data sets in the same cluster are as homogeneous as possible
- Clusters are as heterogeneous as possible among themselves.

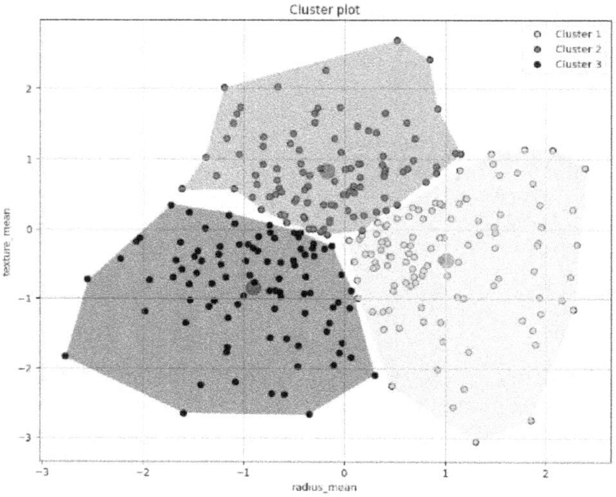

Idea: Data should be classified into k groups.

Procedure:

1. Place k random centroids.
2. Assign each data set to the nearest centroid.
3. Calculate the position of the centroids again.

- The centroids should then be at the center of all points in the respective group.

4. Return to step 2 or stop here if step 2 does not generate a new assignment.

Distance between 2 points: P (x_1, y_1) y Q (x_2, y_2)

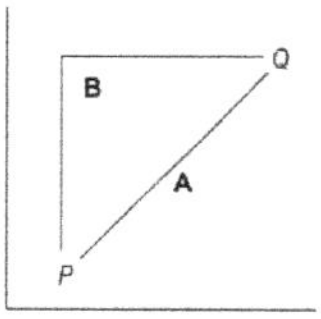

a) $d(P,Q) = \sqrt{(x_2 - x_1)^2 + (y_2 - y_1)^2}$

b) $d(P,Q) = |x_1 - x_2| + |y_1 - y_2|$

Example of the k-Means Algorithm:
People from a database must be assigned to different groups. In this case, people have already been initially assigned to one of the 3 centroids.

Person	Age	Weight	Initial assignment
P1	25	70	C1
P2	32	82	C1
P3	45	90	C3
P4	51	85	C2
P5	29	76	C1

The k-Means algorithm is a common clustering technique used to divide a dataset into k groups based on their characteristics. Assuming we have a database of products and we want to group them into two categories based on their characteristics (such as price, quality, type, etc.), the process would be something like this:

1. Initialization
Select 2 centroids initially, either randomly or based on some logic, and assign each product to one of the 2 centroids based on similarity or distance.

2. Assignment
Assign each product to the nearest centroid based on a distance metric (such as Euclidean distance): P (x_1, y_1) y Q (x_2, y_2)

$$d(P, Q) = \sqrt{(x_2 - x_1)^2 + (y_2 - y_1)^2}$$

3. Updating centroids
Calculate the new centroids by finding the average of all features of the products assigned to each centroid.

4. Iteration
Repeat steps 2 and 3 until the assignments of products to the centroids no longer change or until a maximum number of iterations is reached.

5. Evaluation
Once the assignments stabilize or the maximum number of iterations is reached, you will have the products grouped into 2 clusters, each with a centroid.

With this process, similar products will be grouped together, allowing for more effective organization and analysis of the product database. For example, this could help a company better understand the variety of products it has and make decisions about marketing strategies or inventory.

Examples:

Customer segmentation for marketing strategies:
- **Data collection:** Data is collected on purchasing behavior, transaction history, preferences, and feedback from customers of an online store.
- **Objective:** Segment customers into different groups with similar purchasing patterns to personalize marketing strategies.
- **Model:** A clustering algorithm, such as k-Means, can be used to group customers into clusters based on their purchasing patterns and behavior.

Gene analysis in biology:
- **Data collection:** Gene expression data is collected from different biological samples.
- **Objective:** Identify groups of genes that are expressed similarly and may be involved in related biological functions.
- **Model:** A hierarchical clustering algorithm can be used to group genes based on similar expression patterns.

3.2.2. Dependency Analysis or Association Rule

The main objective of dependency analysis, or association rules, is to discover interesting relationships or hidden patterns among different items in large data sets. A classic example of its application is in the analysis of shopping baskets in supermarkets: Which products tend to be bought together?

Learning an association rule: "If x, then y".

The given association problem:
- **Set J of items:** for example, products of an assortment; no duplicates!
- **List D of transactions t:** where t is a subset of J

Example:
J = `{"Folder", "Dividers", "Paper"}`
D = `[{"Paper"}, {"Folder", "Dividers"}, {"Paper", "Dividers"}]`
t is, for example, `{"Folder", "Dividers"}` (Note: the order does not matter)

Association rule: X → Y
- Body of the rule X (set of items)
- Head of the rule Y (set of items)
- A transaction t satisfies an X → Y if X and Y are in t

To evaluate the relevance and reliability of these rules, metrics such as support, confidence, and lift are used.

Measures:
Support: Proportion of transactions containing a specific item or set of items.
= Frequency of occurrence (How often do "x" and "y" occur in total?)
Confidence: Probability that, given item A has been purchased, item B will also be purchased.
= Strength of the rule (How often does the rule apply?)
Lift: Measure of how much more often A and B occur together than we would expect if they were statistically independent.

The most well-known algorithm for generating association rules is the Apriori, which reduces the complexity of searching for combinations by eliminating sets of items with low support.

This type of analysis has found applications in multiple areas, from marketing to bioinformatics, providing valuable insights and helping to make decisions based on underlying patterns in the data.

Example:
X = `{"Folder"}`
Y = `{"Dividers"};`
The transaction from D satisfies X → Y

support
Proportion of transactions from D that satisfy the association rule:

$$support(X \rightarrow Y) = \frac{|\{t \in D | (X \cup Y) \subseteq t\}|}{|D|}$$

Simpler: Number of transactions containing both X and Y, divided by the total number of transactions

Example:
J = {"Folder", "Dividers", "Paper"}
D = [{"Paper"}, {"Folder", "Paper"}, {"Dividers", "Folder"}, {"Folder", "Paper"}]
support ("Folder" → "Dividers") $= \frac{1}{4}$
support ("Folder" → "Paper") $= \frac{2}{4} = \frac{1}{2}$

confidence
Proportion of transactions that satisfy the association rule, relative to all transactions that satisfy the body of the rule (X):

$$confidence(X \rightarrow Y) = \frac{|\{t \in D | (X \cup Y) \subseteq t\}|}{|\{t \in D | (X \subseteq t\}|} = \frac{support(X \rightarrow Y)}{support(X)}$$

Example:
J = {"Folder", "Dividers", "Paper"}
D = [{"Paper"}, {"Folder", "Paper"}, {"Dividers", "Folder"}, {"Folder", "Paper"}]
confidence ("Folder" → "Dividers") $= \frac{\frac{1}{4}}{\frac{3}{4}} = \frac{1}{3}$
confidence ("Folder" → "Paper") $= \frac{\frac{2}{4}}{\frac{3}{4}} = \frac{\frac{1}{2}}{\frac{3}{4}} = \frac{2}{3}$

Unsupervised learning (Unsupervised Learning) is a category of Machine Learning algorithms where models are trained on unlabeled data. Unlike supervised learning, where each training data comes with a corresponding label, in unsupervised learning, the model works with unlabeled data, seeking to identify inherent structures and patterns in the data by itself.

Discovery of structures: Algorithms seek to discover structures and relationships in data without the guidance of predefined labels.
Feature extraction: Helps in the extraction and selection of relevant features from the data.
Pattern identification: Identifies patterns and groups similar data together.
Dimensionality reduction: Reduce the dimensionality of the data while maintaining the essential structure.
No prior supervision: Does not require a labeled dataset, which can be an advantage in situations where labeling data is expensive or impractical.

Examples:

Shopping cart analysis in supermarkets:
- **Data collection:** Data on customer transactions in a supermarket are collected, recording the products each customer buys on a visit.
- **Objective:** Discover combinations of products that tend to be frequently purchased together.
- **Model:** The Apriori algorithm can be used to find association rules that indicate common product combinations, such as "If a customer buys diapers, they are also likely to buy beer."

Content recommendation on streaming platforms:
- **Data collection:** Data on the movies and series that users watch on a streaming platform are collected.
- **Objective:** Suggest new content to users based on what other users with similar tastes have watched.
- **Model:** The FP-Growth algorithm can be used to discover association rules that suggest, for example, "Users who watched 'Stranger Things' and 'The Witcher' also tend to watch 'Dark'".

These examples illustrate how clustering techniques and association rules can be applied in different contexts to discover patterns and relationships in unlabeled data sets.

Other examples of unsupervised learning applications:

Clustering in marketing

Suppose a company has a large customer database but has no information about these customers' purchasing preferences. A clustering algorithm, like k-Means, can be used to segment customers into different groups based on their demographic characteristics and purchasing behaviors. For example, it may discover a group of young customers who buy technology products and another group of older customers who buy health products. This allows the company to target specific marketing campaigns to each segment, thus improving the effectiveness of its marketing strategies.

Dimensionality reduction in genomic data analysis

In genomics, researchers often work with high-dimensional data, where they have thousands of genes and genetic variants to consider. A dimensionality reduction algorithm, such as Principal Component Analysis (PCA), can be used to reduce the dimensionality of these data, maintaining the essential structure and relationships between genes. This facilitates the visualization and analysis of the data, allowing researchers to identify genetic relationships and potential disease markers more easily.

These examples illustrate how unsupervised learning can discover valuable information in data without the need for predefined labels, making it especially useful in situations where obtaining precise labels is difficult or expensive.

3.3. Semi-supervised Learning

Semi-supervised learning sits between supervised and unsupervised learning, where algorithms use a partially labeled dataset for training. This allows for leveraging the large amount of unlabeled data available, improving model performance without the need for complete manual labeling.

Basically, semi-supervised learning is a Machine Learning technique that sits between supervised and unsupervised learning. It is used when there is a large dataset available, but only a small part of it is labeled. The main idea behind semi-supervised learning is to use information from both labeled and unlabeled data to build a more robust and accurate predictive model. This technique is very useful in scenarios where labeling data is costly or time-consuming.

Examples:

Text Classification
Suppose a Bookstore wants to classify a large collection of documents into different categories (e.g., fiction, non-fiction, science, art, etc.). Manually labeling each document would be an extremely tedious and time-consuming task. However, if they have a small sample of already labeled documents, they can use semi-supervised learning.
In this case, a semi-supervised learning algorithm could use the small amount of labeled data to learn basic features about each category. Then, it could explore the unlabeled data to discover additional structures and patterns that help improve classification, such as keywords or common themes in each category, and thus assign labels to the unlabeled documents.

Fraud Detection
In a bank, detecting fraudulent transactions is crucial for financial security. However, fraudulent transactions are rare, and therefore the labeled data (transactions identified as legitimate or fraudulent) may be scarce. Nevertheless, the bank has a large volume of unlabeled transactions.

In this scenario, a semi-supervised learning model could be trained with the small set of labeled data available, learning features of fraudulent and legitimate transactions. Then, the model could explore the unlabeled transactions, identifying those that resemble known fraudulent transactions, thereby improving fraud detection by incorporating this additional information.
In both examples, semi-supervised learning allows for leveraging a combination of labeled and unlabeled data to build more effective and precise models, despite the scarcity of labels.

In semi-supervised learning, there are various models and techniques used, some of which include:

Self-training (Iterative Learning): A model is initially trained with labeled data, then used to label the unlabeled data. This process is repeated iteratively.
Generative models: These models attempt to learn the joint probability distribution of the data and labels, aiding in classification.
Graph-based methods: Represent data as nodes in a graph, where edges reflect similarity between data, propagating labels through the graph.
Vector-based techniques: Transform data into vector representations and use geometry to infer labels for unlabeled data.
Deep Neural Networks (DNN): For extracting data features using a multi-layer model.

They use multiple layers of processing to extract features and learn hierarchical representations of the data, benefiting semi-supervised learning by extracting useful features.

Each of these models or techniques has a unique approach to leveraging both labeled and unlabeled data to improve model performance in specific tasks.

3.4. Reinforcement Learning

In reinforcement learning, an agent learns how to interact with an environment to maximize cumulative reward over time. The agent makes decisions, the environment responds, and the agent receives a reward or penalty, thus learning an optimal behavior strategy.

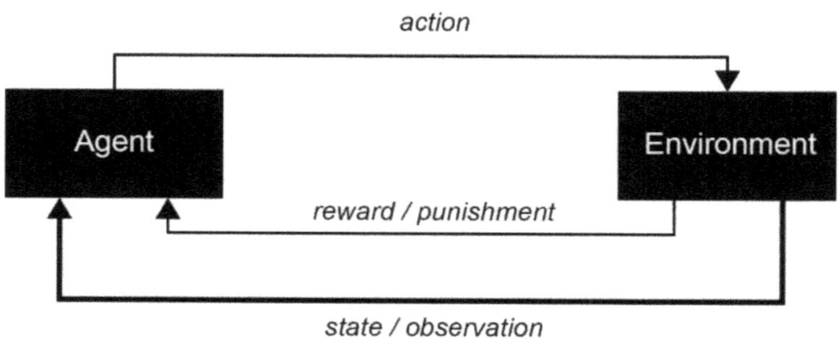

Reinforcement Learning is a branch of Machine Learning where an agent learns how to act in an environment to maximize a cumulative reward signal. Unlike supervised learning, where the model receives direct feedback on the correctness of its predictions, in RL, the agent only receives a reward signal indicating how well it is performing its task, but does not receive explicit indications about which actions are correct or incorrect.

The basic structure of RL includes the following components:

Agent: It is the model that is learning to make decisions. It is the entity that makes decisions. It can be imagined as a robot, a software, or any system that can interact with an environment.
Environment: It is the context in which the agent operates. It is everything that the agent interacts with. The environment presents certain states, and the agent performs actions that can modify those states.
Action: It is a decision made by the agent that affects the environment.
Reward: It is a signal received by the agent after performing each action in a particular state of the environment, indicating how well it is doing. This signal can be positive (beneficial) or negative (harmful). The reward indicates how good the action taken by the agent was in that specific state.
State: It is a description of the environment that the agent uses to make decisions.
Policy: It is the strategy that the agent uses to determine which action to take in each state.

Learning process:
1. The agent observes the state of the environment.
2. Based on that observation, the agent decides and performs an action.
3. The environment responds by changing its state.
4. The agent receives a reward (or penalty) based on the action it took.
5. The agent uses this reward to update its knowledge and improve its future decisions.

Objective: The agent's goal is to maximize cumulative reward over time. This does not simply mean seeking immediate rewards but often involves learning to perform actions that may not have an immediate reward but will lead to greater rewards in the future.

Illustrative Example
Imagine a robot in a maze. The robot's goal is to find the exit. Every time the robot moves in a direction, it is an action. If it moves and hits a wall, it might receive a penalty (negative reward). If it finds the exit, it receives a large positive reward. Through multiple attempts and errors, the robot will learn the optimal path to exit the maze, avoiding crashing into walls and seeking the exit to obtain the maximum reward.

Below, I show you two examples to illustrate how Reinforcement Learning works:

Example 1: Chess Game
In a chess game where an AI system is trained to play against human or computerized opponents, RL can be applied as follows:

Agent: The AI system.
Environment: The chessboard and the pieces.
Action: Each move that the agent decides to make.
Reward: Can be positive if the agent captures an opponent's piece or achieves a strategic position, or negative if it loses an important piece.
State: The current arrangement of the board.
Policy: The strategy that the agent uses to decide its next move.
Example 2: Navigating Robot
Consider a robot designed to navigate through a maze to find an exit:

Agent: The robot.
Environment: The maze.
Action: Movements the robot can make (forward, back, left, right).
Reward: Can be positive as it gets closer to the exit, and negative if it crashes into a wall or moves away from the exit.
State: The robot's current position and the structure of the maze.
Policy: The strategy that the robot uses to decide which movement to make in each position to maximize its probability of finding the exit.

Through an iterative process of trial and error, and receiving rewards for their actions, agents in these examples can learn optimal policies for playing chess or navigating through a maze, respectively. Reinforcement Learning allows agents to learn and improve over time, adapting their policies to maximize total accumulated reward.
In the field of Reinforcement Learning, there are several models and algorithms that help agents learn how to interact with the environment to maximize a cumulative reward. Here are some well-known models and algorithms in the field of Reinforcement Learning:

Q-Learning
Q-Learning is a fundamental technique in reinforcement learning that helps an agent learn a value function for each action-state pair in an environment. The value function, represented as Q, indicates the quality of performing an action \(a\) in a state \(s\). Over time, the agent learns to estimate these values accurately and uses this information to make decisions that maximize accumulated reward.

Deep Q Networks (DQN)
DQN is an extension of Q-Learning that uses neural networks to approximate the Q function. This allows the agent to handle environments with a continuous or high-dimensional state space, which would be intractable with traditional tabular methods.

Policy Gradients
Policy Gradient methods seek to directly optimize the agent's policy (the strategy it uses to choose actions) instead of learning a value function. This is achieved through gradients that indicate how the policy should change to increase accumulated reward.

Actor-Critic
Actor-Critic methods combine ideas from both value and policy methods. The "actor" updates the policy in a direction that increases the reward, while the "critic" evaluates the current policy and provides feedback to the actor.

Proximal Policy Optimization (PPO)
PPO is a policy optimization method that seeks to make efficient and stable policy updates, limiting the change in policy during each update to ensure stable learning.

SARSA (State-Action-Reward-State-Action)
SARSA is a reinforcement learning algorithm that, like Q-Learning, learns the action value function, but differs in how the Q function is updated, using the actual action taken in the next state instead of the action that maximizes the reward.

Monte Carlo methods
Monte Carlo methods in Reinforcement Learning estimate the value of a state or action-state pair through sampling, calculating the average accumulated reward over multiple episodes.

Temporal Difference Learning (TDL)
Temporal Difference Learning is a class of methods that combine ideas from Monte Carlo methods and dynamic programming to learn the value function.

Double Q-Learning
Double Q-Learning addresses the problem of Q function overestimation in traditional Q-Learning by using two Q functions and alternating between selecting actions and updating values between them.

Deep Deterministic Policy Gradients (DDPG)
DDPG is an algorithm that combines ideas from DQN and policy gradient methods to learn deterministic policies in continuous environments.

These models and algorithms provide a wide variety of tools that RL practitioners can use to tackle different types of reinforcement learning problems.

3.5. Deep Learning (DL)

Deep learning is a subcategory of ML that focuses on algorithms with multiple layers of processing (deep neural networks) to extract and transform features from data in a hierarchical manner and learn complex representations. It is especially useful for tasks like image and voice recognition, where processing large amounts of high-dimensional data is required.

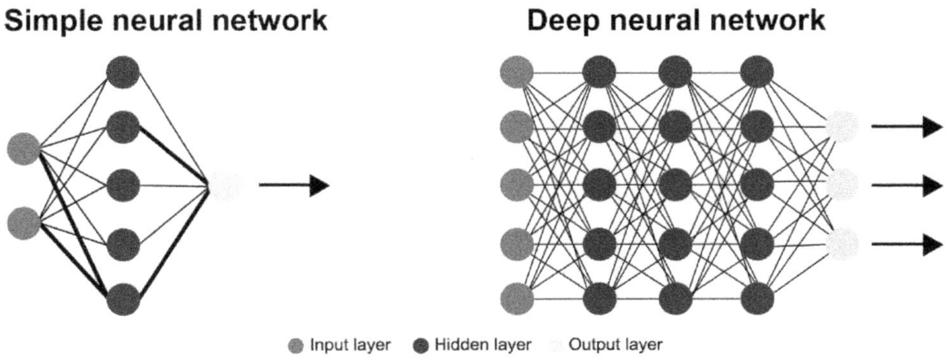

Essentially, Deep Learning is a branch of Machine Learning that relies on neural networks with many layers, also known as deep neural networks. These networks are capable of learning directly from data, extracting features and useful representations for specific tasks. Deep learning has proven to be very effective in a variety of complex tasks, especially those involved with large amounts of data and high dimensionality.

Characteristics of deep learning:

Automatic feature extraction: Unlike other ML methods, deep learning can automatically extract relevant features from data without the need for manual feature engineering.
Hierarchy of representations: Deep neural networks learn a hierarchy of representations, where lower layers capture low-level features (such as edges in images) and higher layers capture high-level features (such as objects).
Generalization ability: Through regularization and other techniques, deep learning models can generalize their learning to new data, which is crucial for real-world performance.
Processing of unstructured data: They are especially effective for processing unstructured data such as images, sound, and text, where they can capture complex structures and relationships.

Examples:

Image recognition:
A common application of deep learning is image recognition. For example, convolutional neural networks (CNNs) can be trained to identify objects in images. In a practical case, a CNN can be used in a surveillance system to identify and alert about suspicious activities detected in real-time video.

Automatic translation:
Deep learning is also applied in automatic text translation. Recurrent neural networks (RNNs) or attention networks, like Transformer models, can be trained on pairs of texts in different languages to learn to translate text from one language to another. For example, a system like Google Translate uses deep learning to provide automatic translations between many different languages.

These examples demonstrate how deep learning can be used to solve complex and practical problems in various fields, leveraging its ability to learn rich and useful representations directly from raw data.

4. Data

4.1. What is data?

Data are representations of information in a specific format. Essentially, they are raw or unprocessed facts that, when interpreted and processed, become information. Data can be presented in various forms, such as numbers, words, images, sounds, etc. In the context of computing and, more specifically, in ML and AI, data usually refer to the information that can be processed with a computer.
Let's delve into these aspects.

Data attempts to represent reality:
Indeed, data are a representation of facts, observations, or perceptions of the real world. They capture events, states, features, and other properties of the environment. However, it is essential to understand that data in themselves are not reality, but representations of it. Just as a map is not the territory it represents, data capture aspects of reality, but do not reproduce it in its entirety.

Data are units of information:
Data represent information in its crudest form. When these data are processed, analyzed, or interpreted, they turn into information that can be useful for making decisions, generating knowledge, or understanding phenomena. It is the transformation and analysis of these data that generates value and knowledge.

Three different approaches according to Ballsun Stanton:
1. Data as facts:
These data are objective and, in theory, independent of the observer. They represent quantitative or qualitative properties that can be measured consistently and reproduced in different circumstances or by different observers.

For example:
- The population of a city: can be measured and verified through censuses.
- The speeds of different cars on a highway: Can be measured using speed radars.
- Weight analysis of a group of people: These data are objective and measurable.
- A person's height: can be measured with a tape measure.
- Analysis of ambient temperature over a week: can be measured with a thermometer.

Suppose you have a dataset that records the ambient temperature of a specific city for seven consecutive days. These data are objective and measurable using standardized thermometers.
Task: Determine the warmest and coldest day of the week.

2. Data as observations:
These data are subjective and depend on the context and the observer. They are often the result of human perceptions and can vary depending on who or how they are collected.

Examples:
- The notes of a song may be interpreted differently by different people, depending on their musical or cultural experience.
- The perception of flavors in a wine tasting: Different individuals may identify different nuances or flavors in the same wine, based on their palate and previous experience.
- Sentiment analysis of reviews: Suppose you have a set of reviews of a product and want to determine if they are positive or negative. Reviews are subjective and based on individual perceptions.
- An audio recording may capture a conversation, but the interpretation and meaning of that conversation may vary according to the listener.
- Interpretation of works of art.

Imagine you have descriptions of several paintings from a museum. The interpretation of these paintings can be subjective and vary from one individual to another, depending on their cultural, educational, or personal background.

Task: Classify paintings according to perceived emotions: happiness, sadness, anger, etc.

3. Data as messages:
These data are designed to communicate information. They are created with the purpose of transmitting knowledge or understanding to a receiver.

Examples:
- A diagram showing the relationships between different variables.
- A table comparing the prices of different products.
- An infographic showing the demographic distribution of a population by age, gender, and occupation. This infographic is meant to quickly and visually communicate the composition of a population to a general audience.
- Interpretation of a sales table: Suppose you have a table showing the monthly sales of a product over a year. This table is created to communicate sales performance over time.
- Interpretation of a bar graph of a company's annual growth.

Imagine you have a graph showing the annual growth percentage of a company over the past five years. This graph is designed to communicate the growth trajectory of the company to shareholders or stakeholders.

Task: Identify the year with the highest growth and the year with the lowest growth.

Data are multifaceted representations of reality, and their nature and meaning can vary depending on the context and purpose for which they are collected and used. It is crucial to keep these nuances in mind when working with data in any capacity, especially in fields like AI and ML, where data are the basis of learning and decision-making.

4.2. Why are Data important in ML and AI?

Algorithm Fuel: ML and AI algorithms are trained using data. These data provide examples from which algorithms learn patterns, relationships, and structures. Without data, there is no learning.
Accuracy Improvement: The more (high-quality) data we have, the more accurate and generalizable our models will be. Having a large amount of data makes it more likely that our model captures the variability and underlying features of the information.
Validation and Testing: Data is not only used to train models but also to validate and test their performance. This allows us to know how well a model performs on previously unseen data.
Decision Making: In AI applications, data supports decision-making by providing evidence and patterns that can be interpreted by algorithms.
Innovation: Data can reveal previously unknown patterns or trends, leading to new ideas or solutions in various fields.

Data is the fuel for ML and AI systems. They are the foundation upon which models are built and validated, and they largely determine the effectiveness and applicability of an AI solution. Imagine trying to learn to recognize objects without ever having seen examples of them; it would be impossible. Similarly, ML and AI algorithms need data to learn, adapt, and improve.

If I show you the data as in the following image, it will probably be more familiar to you:

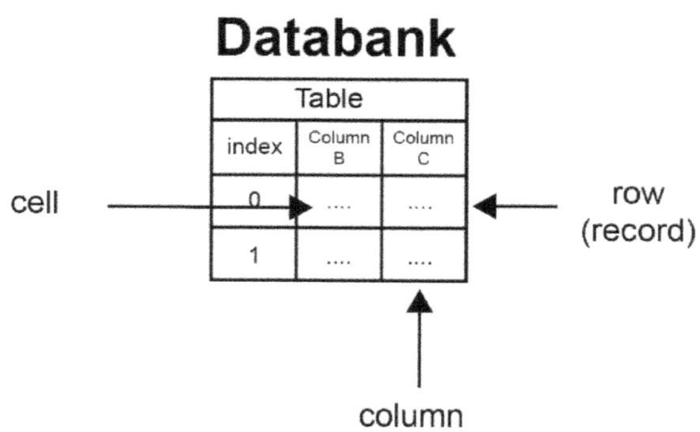

4.3. Data Structures

Data structures are essential in the world of computing and, in particular, in the field of Artificial Intelligence and Machine Learning. These structures determine how data is organized, related, and stored in a computer system's memory. Choosing the right data structure for a particular task can significantly influence the efficiency and effectiveness of an algorithm or analysis process. Thus, a deep understanding of these structures is fundamental for optimally working with large volumes of data.

Types of data structure:
- Structured data:
These are data that are organized following a predefined schema or model, typically in tabular form with columns and rows.
Examples: Relational databases where tables have specific fields (like SQL), spreadsheets, and CSV files.

- Unstructured data:
These data do not follow a specific model or schema, making them more difficult to analyze and process than structured data.
Examples: Text documents, emails, images, audios, videos, and social media.

- Semi-structured data:
While not organized into rigid structures like structured data, they have certain elements that facilitate their processing and analysis, such as tags or hierarchies.
Examples: JSON files, which use tags to identify fields, and XML files.

- Metadata:
Refers to data that describes other data, providing additional or contextual information about that data, such as its origin, creation date, author, among others.

Data Structures in ML and AI
Data structures not only refer to how data is classified (structured, unstructured, etc.), but also to how they are represented and stored in memory for processing.

Vectors: These one-dimensional lists of numbers are essential for representing data in many ML algorithms. For example, a vector might represent individual features of a house, such as its number of rooms, square meters, and year of construction.
Matrices: They are two-dimensional tables of numbers, and are fundamental in operations such as matrix multiplication in ML algorithms.
Tensors: They are generalizations of matrices to more dimensions and are essential in areas such as deep learning, where data such as images are represented as three-dimensional tensors (height, width, and color channels).
Dataframes or data tables: These tabular structures, where each column can have a different type of data, are popular in data analysis and are fundamental in libraries like Pandas in Python.
Trees and graphs: These hierarchical and relational structures are vital in algorithms such as Decission Trees, knowledge graphs, and Bayesian networks.

Understanding and appropriately choosing among these data structures is crucial for efficiency and effectiveness in data management and analysis in Artificial Intelligence.

4.4. Types of Data

Before delving into the theory of the different types of data, I consider it very important to first take a look at the following diagram. This describes a classification of data types, dividing them into metric and categorical, and then providing subcategories within each main type.

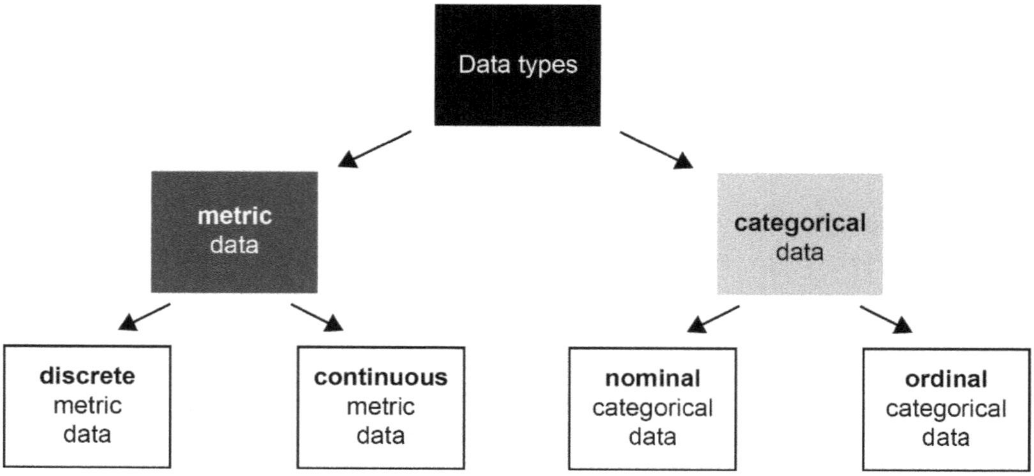

Metric Data: These data are quantitative and represent measurements. They are numerical data that can be subjected to mathematical operations.

a. Discrete Metric Data: These data are numerical and represent a finite or countable set of values.
Example: the number of rooms in a house or the number of students in a class. You can't have, for example, 2.5 students or 3.7 rooms.

b. Continuous Metric Data: These data can take any value within a specific range. They are infinite within certain limits.
Examples: height, weight, temperature, or the time it takes to run a distance. These data can have values like 20.5 degrees, 75.32 kilograms, etc. They are values that can be divided and subdivided and so on.

Categorical Data: These data represent categories or labels and do not have an inherent order or measurement.

a. Nominal Categorical Data: These are data that are divided into mutually exclusive categories that do not have a specific order or hierarchy.
Examples: the color of a car (red, blue, green) or the type of animal (dog, cat, bird). You cannot say that one color or type of animal is "greater" or "better" than another based on nominal data.

b. Ordinal Categorical Data: Although these data also represent categories, there is a clear order or hierarchy among the categories.
Examples: levels of education (elementary, secondary, university) or ranks in the military (soldier, sergeant, lieutenant). In these cases, it can be said that one level or rank is "greater" or "prior" than another.

This classification is essential in statistics and data analysis, as the type of data determines what type of analysis is appropriate and what statistical techniques can be applied. For example, metric data allow calculations such as mean and standard deviation, while categorical data could be analyzed using frequencies or modes.

Let's look at these data from a practical context with four different situations.

Situation 1:
You are at the airport waiting for your flight which is delayed. You are very bored and start thinking about how you can pass the time until you can board the plane. There are many people walking back and forth through the airport. You come up with some ideas to pass the time and finally decide to start counting how many people board a specific plane.

Context: You are counting how many people board a specific plane.
Type of data: Discrete Metric Data.
Explanation: The data you are collecting are whole numbers representing people. These data are "discrete" because you cannot have, for example, 1.5 people. Discrete data are those that take finite values or an infinite countable set, and cannot be subdivided into smaller units in their context.

Flight number	Number of people who have boarded
DC 6487	183
NM 3154	149
TL 9142	62

Situation 2:
You are at the airport waiting for your delayed flight. You are very bored and start thinking about how you can pass the time until you can board the plane. There are many people walking around the airport. You come up with some ideas to pass the time, and finally, you decide to ask people about their age.

Context: Asking people about their age.
Data Type: Continuous Metric Data.
Explanation: Age can be measured in years, but also in months, days, hours, minutes, seconds, etc. Therefore, it is "continuous" data. Continuous data is data that can take any value within a specific range and can be subdivided into infinitely smaller units.

Person	Age
Heiko Schmidt	24
Yuto Kawa	63
Martina Torres Barados	54

Situation 3:
You are at the airport waiting for your delayed flight. You are very bored and start thinking about how you can pass the time until you can board the plane. There are many people walking around the airport. You come up with some ideas to pass the time and finally decide to group the flights by destination.

Context: You group the flights by their destination.
Data Type: Nominal categorical data
Explanation: The flight destinations are categories. They are "nominal" because there is no inherent order in the destinations; that is, you cannot objectively say that one destination is "greater" or "better" than another. Nominal data is used to label variables that do not have an order or hierarchy.

Flight	Destiny
DC 6487	New York
NM 3154	Miami
TL 9142	New York

Situation 4:
You are at the airport waiting for your delayed flight. You are very bored and start thinking about how to pass the time until you can board the plane. There are many people walking around the airport. You come up with some ideas to pass the time, and finally, you decide to assess the cleanliness of different boarding gates.

Context: You are evaluating the cleanliness of different boarding gates.
Data Type: Ordinal Categorical Data
Explanation: You are classifying the boarding gates into categories based on their cleanliness, but these categories have an order: "clean" is better than "dirty." Ordinal data is categorical, but the categories have a sense of order.

Boarding gate	Cleaning
B7	Clear
C32	Dirty
G30	Clear

These scenarios illustrate the importance of understanding the type and nature of the data you're working with, as this will affect the analysis methods and tools you will have to use.

While the previous classification focuses on more traditional and fundamental aspects of data (metric vs. categorical), the following list is a more detailed and diverse classification of data types, especially adapted for the modern context of data analysis and machine learning. This list addresses specific types of data that are common in current applications of technology and analysis.

- **Numerical data:** Quantitative values, such as ages, salaries, temperatures, etc.
- **Categorical data:** Non-numeric values that fall into predefined categories, such as gender, product type, color, etc.
- **Ordinal data:** They are categorical, but with a specific order, such as levels of education (primary, secondary, university).
- **Temporal data:** Represent dates and times.
- **Text data:** Strings of characters, such as tweets, reviews, etc.
- **Image data:** Pixelated representations of images.
- **Sound data:** Representations of audio signals.
- **Sequential data:** Time series or sequences of events.

Let's look at each type in a little more detail:
- **Numerical data:** This is another way of referring to the "metric data" mentioned earlier. They represent quantitative values and can be both discrete and continuous.

- **Categorical data:** Match the previous description. They are non-numeric values that fall into specific categories without an inherent order.
- **Ordinal data:** As mentioned earlier, they are categorical, but with a defined order or hierarchy.
- **Temporal data:** These data are related to time. They can be dates (for example, October 10, 2023) or specific timestamps (for example, 10:30 am, May 5, 2022).
- **Text data:** They are strings of characters and often require special processing techniques, such as natural language processing, to be analyzed.
- **Image data:** These data refer to visual information and are usually represented as pixel matrices. They are fundamental in areas such as deep learning and computer vision.
- **Sound data:** Digital representations of audio signals. Like images, sound data can also be processed with deep learning techniques, such as convolutional neural networks.
- **Sequential data:** These data have a specific order, such as time series (data recorded at regular time intervals) or event sequences (for example, click sequences on a website).

The variety in this list reflects the diversity of data that data professionals work with today. Correctly identifying the type of data being worked with is crucial, as it determines the most appropriate analysis and processing techniques for each case.

4.5. Data Processing

Data processing is an essential and preliminary stage in any Artificial Intelligence project involving Machine Learning. Before a model can be trained and validated, the data that will feed that model must be carefully processed and prepared to ensure the accuracy, efficiency, and effectiveness of the learning process. In many cases, the quality and meticulousness of data processing can determine the success or failure of an AI project. This is where the adage "garbage in, garbage out" comes into play: a model fed with poorly processed or poorly prepared data is likely to produce inaccurate or useless results.

Let's look in detail at the steps necessary for data processing:
1. Cleaning: Real-world data is often messy. They may contain errors, outliers, or missing values. Cleaning involves identifying and correcting (or eliminating) these problems, ensuring that the data is consistent and reliable.
2. Transformation: Depending on the nature of the data and the type of model to be used, it may be necessary to change the scale or format of the data. A common example is normalization, where data is scaled to have a mean value of 0 and a standard deviation of 1. This can help improve convergence and performance of many ML algorithms.
3. Dimensionality reduction: Data sets with a large number of features can be difficult to analyze and can lead to overfitting (overfitted models). By reducing dimensionality, the most important features can be identified and preserved, while discarding redundant or less significant ones. Techniques such as PCA (Principal Component Analysis) are used for this.
4. Encoding: ML models work with numbers, so it is crucial to convert categorical features (such as "red", "green", "blue") into a numerical form, often using techniques such as one-hot encoding.
5. Segmentation: To train and evaluate a model effectively, it is necessary to divide the data set into specific subsets. Typically, the data is divided into a training set (to train the model), a

validation set (to adjust hyperparameters and prevent overfitting), and a test set (to evaluate the model's performance on data never seen before).

Data processing is a crucial phase that sets the stage for effective training and evaluation of ML models in AI projects. Meticulous and considered preparation of the data can make the difference between a successful model and one that is not.

"The Machine Learning models are only as good as the data with which they were created."

4.6. Data Quality and Criteria

Data quality is a fundamental pillar in any Artificial Intelligence and Machine Learning project. A model, regardless of its sophistication or design, is as good as the data it is fed with. If the data is of low quality, the results generated by the model will be inaccurate or unreliable. Therefore, it is essential to ensure that the data used meets certain quality criteria. These criteria help identify and correct problems in the data, ensuring that subsequent analysis or modeling is based on a solid and reliable foundation.

To ensure the quality of results in ML and AI, the following criteria must be respected:
Completeness: Are there missing values in the data?
Coherence: Are there contradictions in the data?
Quantity: What amount of data is available?
Currency: How current are the data?
Relevance: Are the data relevant to the problem?
Precision: Are the data accurate and precise?

Let's look at the criteria in more detail:
Completeness: This criterion refers to the integrity of a data set. If values are missing or there are gaps in the data, it may be difficult to perform meaningful analysis or effectively train models. It is crucial to identify and, if possible, impute or handle these missing values appropriately.

Coherence: Coherence refers to the logic and consistency in the data. If there are contradictions, such as a client with two different birth dates recorded, this may indicate errors in data collection or storage. These errors must be identified and corrected to ensure the reliability of the analysis.

Quantity: While data quality is essential, quantity also matters, especially in machine learning. Enough data is needed to effectively train a model and ensure that it can generalize well to unseen data.

Currency: In many contexts, especially in rapidly evolving business or technological environments, the freshness of data is essential. Outdated data may not reflect the current situation and therefore lead to incorrect conclusions or decisions.

Relevance: Not all available data may be relevant to a specific problem. It is fundamental to identify which data are relevant and which are not. Using irrelevant data can introduce noise into the analysis and make the models less accurate.

Precision: This criterion refers to the accuracy and correctness of the data. If the data contains errors, either due to problems in collection, transcription, or other sources, the results of the analysis or modeling will be inaccurate. It is essential to validate the accuracy of the data against reliable sources and correct any inaccuracies identified. Redundancy in the data, such as duplicate entries, can skew results and cause the model to give more weight to certain observations simply because they appear multiple times.

Ensuring data quality is an essential step in any AI project. By evaluating and ensuring quality based on these criteria, a solid foundation can be established for reliable analyses and effective machine learning models.

To consider:
- For data analysis, metric data is preferable
They allow various operations: average, maximum, minimum, etc.
However, categorical data can be converted into metric data.
Determine the total sum of the values for a specific category.
Example: 78 flights to Bogota, 12 flights to Buenos Aires.

- Ordinal data is subject to the error of subjectivity
Example: Rating flight destinations based on the local typical food.
Person 1 opinion: The spicier, the better.
Person 2 opinion: The less spicy, the better.
There is no objective truth!

4.7. Determining Data Quality

To explain in a simple and clear way how to determine the quality of the data before using it, I will give you an example.
Example: The results of a survey on the topic of cell phone use were recorded in a table.
The question was: "How often do you use your cell phone every day?"

ID	Name	Date of birth	E-Mail	Answer
106	Alfred Zunder	29.03.1954	a.zun@gmail.com	"3 hours"
107	Gundel Thomsen	01.01.1900	gund.thomsen@live.de	"sometimes"
107	Beate Müller	01.01.1900		"Hmm... good question"
109		21.09.1975		"5 hours"
110	Christian Haubitz	01.01.1900	test@gmx.de	"3 hours"
107	Emil Johansson	18.06.1996	emil.the.k1ng@gmail.com	"7 hours"
112	Daria Klemens	01.12.1987	daria_klemens@gmx.de	"I don't know"

What problems do you see in the data sets?

Let's analyze the response:
Based on the survey results table on mobile phone usage, we can identify several problems related to data quality.

Inconsistencies in responses: The answers to the question "How much time do you use your mobile each day?" vary in format. Some responded with a specific amount of time (e.g., "3 hours"), while others gave vague answers like "From time to time" or "Hmm... good question". This makes analyzing the responses more complicated, as not all data is quantitative.

Missing data: There are empty cells in the table, indicating missing information. For example, ID 109 has no name or email address associated with it.

Duplicate data: ID 107 appears three times in the table, suggesting there are duplicate entries. Additionally, two of the entries with this ID have the same birth date but different names and email addresses.

Suspicious or unusual data: Several entries have the birth date as "01.01.1900". It is unlikely that several surveyed individuals were born on that exact date, suggesting a placeholder or default value was used.

Inconsistency in email format: While most email addresses seem valid, there is one (test@gmx.de) that, although it could be valid, seems generic and might not be a real address of a respondent.

These problems highlight the importance of having a well-defined and structured data collection process, and of conducting a review and data cleaning before any further analysis. The presence of these issues can affect the validity and reliability of any conclusions derived from these data.

4.8. Important Data Quality Criteria

As we have seen and verified, data quality is a fundamental pillar in any Artificial Intelligence and Machine Learning project, and it has been shown that a model, regardless of its complexity, is as effective as the quality of the data it is fed. It is essential to ensure that the data meet certain quality criteria to obtain accurate and reliable results.

Finally, it is important not to confuse data quality criteria with data integrity criteria. While both are essential for ensuring the reliability and accuracy of systems, data integrity criteria are mainly applied in database systems to ensure the consistency and correctness of stored data. In contrast, data quality criteria focus on ensuring that the data are adequate and optimal for analysis and modeling in Artificial Intelligence.

Let's look at these criteria in more detail using the example of the table shown in section 5.7:

ID	Name	Date of birth	E-Mail	Answer
106	Alfred Zunder	29.03.1954	a.zun@gmail.com	"3 hours"
107	Gundel Thomsen	01.01.1900	gund.thomsen@live.de	"sometimes"
107	Beate Müller	01.01.1900		"Hmm...good question"
109		21.09.1975		"5 hours"
110	Christian Haubitz	01.01.1900	test@gmx.de	"3 hours"
107	Emil Johansson	18.06.1996	emil.the.k1ng@gmail.com	"7 hours"
112	Daria Klemens	01.12.1987	daria_klemens@gmx.de	"I don´t know"

Completeness

- Definition:

a) A data record must contain values for all necessary attributes.

b) Values for an attribute must always be provided.

Percentage indication: from 0% to 100%

- Calculation:

$$\frac{(\#records\ - \#incomplete)}{\#records} * 100$$

Example:

- For Def a: A complete record consists of ID, Name, Response.

- Calculation: There are 7 records, 1 of them is not complete.

$$\frac{(7-1)}{7} * 100 = 85.71\%$$

- For Def b: The email address is a mandatory field.

- Calculation: There are 7 records, 2 of them are not complete.

$$\frac{(7-2)}{7} * 100 = 71.43\%$$

Coherence

- Definition: Data must be realistic.

- Percentage indication: from 0% to 100%

- Calculation:

$$\frac{(\#records\ - \#implauseble)}{\#records} * 100$$

- Example: The value "01.01.1900" often appears as a date of birth.

- Assumption: It is unlikely that many people are 121 years old.

- Calculation:

$$\frac{(7-3)}{7} * 100 = 57.14\%$$

Quantity

- Definition: Sufficiently complete data records must be available.

- Percentage indication: from 0% to ∞% including subjective evaluation.

- Calculation:

$$\frac{\#complete\ records}{\#required\ records} * 100$$

- Example: A complete record consists of ID, Name, Response. There must be at least 5 complete records available.

- Calculation:

$$\frac{6}{5} * 100 = 120\%$$

Note: Evaluation is subjective!

Precision
- Definition: There should be no duplicates for an attribute.
- Percentage indication: from 0% to 100%
- Calculation: (#Records - #Redundant) / #Records * 100)

$$\frac{(\#records - \#redundant)}{\#records} * 100$$

- Example: "Each ID must be unique."
- Calculation:

$$\frac{(7-2)}{7} * 100 = 71.43\%$$

4.9. Structured Data

As we have already seen in section 4.3, in the world of data analysis and Machine Learning, data is generally classified as structured or unstructured. While unstructured data refers to data that does not have a predefined format or an organized structure, such as texts, images, and videos, structured data has a clear and organized arrangement, generally in rows and columns. The latter are essential for many tasks in Machine Learning and Artificial Intelligence due to their organized nature and easy interpretability.
Next, we will delve into structured data.

Characteristics of structured data
Organization in rows and columns: Just like a table in a database or a CSV file, structured data is usually organized in rows, where each row represents an entry or instance, and columns, which represent attributes or characteristics of those entries.
Homogeneity: Generally, each column in a set of structured data has a specific data type. For example, a column representing a person's age would have numerical values, while a column representing gender might have categorical values such as "male" or "female".
Ease of query: Thanks to its organized structure, structured data can be easily queried and manipulated using structured query languages, like SQL.

Importance in Machine Learning and AI
Direct modeling: Since structured data is already in an organized format, it can directly feed many machine learning algorithms without the need for extensive prior processing.
Ease of interpretation: The characteristics and relationships in structured data are easier to understand and visualize. This is essential for tasks such as exploratory data analysis, where the goal is to understand the trends and patterns in the data before modeling.
Statistical analysis: Structured data lends itself well to statistical analysis, allowing for the identification of correlations, calculation of means, medians, modes, and other important metrics before applying Machine Learning algorithms.

Challenges and considerations

Despite its advantages, working with structured data also presents challenges. The presence of missing data, the need for transformations (such as normalization or encoding of categorical variables), and handling imbalanced data are aspects that professionals must consider.

Structured data is a cornerstone in many Machine Learning and Artificial Intelligence projects. Its organized and predictable nature makes it ideal for many analytical tasks. However, it is essential to understand its characteristics and challenges to make the most of it in any AI project.

4.9.1. .csv files

.csv (Comma-Separated Values) files represent one of the most popular and established formats for storing and exchanging structured data. They are often used to export data from a program like Excel and prepare it for Artificial Intelligence and Machine Learning processes.

Main characteristics of .csv files

Established format: .csv files are an industry-recognized standard for saving and sharing data.

Common use: These files are typically used to export data from a program or system and then prepare it for an Artificial Intelligence process.

File nature: Although it is a text format file, its structure allows it to represent tabular information.

Rules in .csv files

These files follow simple but essential rules:

First line: Usually contains the names of the columns, which represent the attributes or characteristics.

Subsequent lines: From the second line onwards, the data or values corresponding to those attributes are found.

Information separation: The different data (whether column names or values) are separated by a delimiter.

Conventional delimiter: Although "CSV" suggests the use of commas, in reality, any character can be used as a delimiter. The most common include the comma (,), semicolon (;), tabulator (represented as \t or simply a wide space), and colon (:).

Note: When the delimiter is a tabulator, the .tsv (Tab-Separated Values) format is usually used instead of .csv.

Structure of a .csv File

The tabular structure of a .csv file is easily interpretable, making it ideal for analysis and processing. Each row represents an entry or instance, and each column an attribute or characteristic of that entry. This clear organization facilitates the import of data into analytical tools and Machine Learning systems.

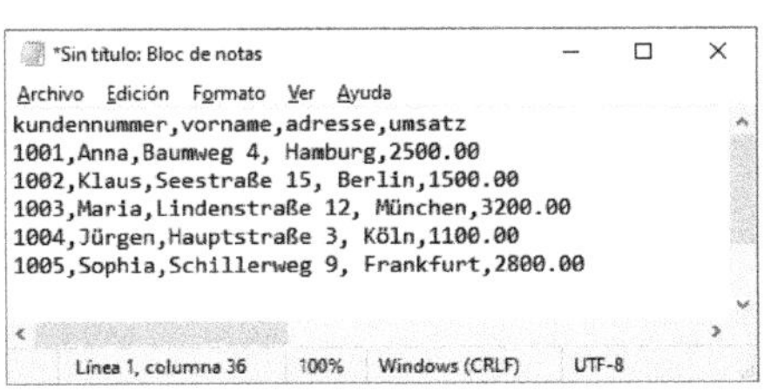
*Sin título: Bloc de notas
Archivo Edición Formato Ver Ayuda

```
kundennummer,vorname,adresse,umsatz
1001,Anna,Baumweg 4, Hamburg,2500.00
1002,Klaus,Seestraße 15, Berlin,1500.00
1003,Maria,Lindenstraße 12, München,3200.00
1004,Jürgen,Hauptstraße 3, Köln,1100.00
1005,Sophia,Schillerweg 9, Frankfurt,2800.00
```

Línea 1, columna 36 100% Windows (CRLF) UTF-8

id	name	surname	age
0	Sandra	Jimenez	37
1	Boris	Müller	40
2	Melanie	Lambert	28

CSV files are an essential tool in the world of structured data, offering a simple and efficient way to store and share information in a tabular and organized format.
You can view CSV files using Excel (Data/import/import from file/text/CSV).
And you can also create and save CSV files from Excel by simply saving as / .csv.

Caution!
- CSV files do not handle nested data well.
- CSV files do not recognize data types (only metric and categorical).

Clarification:
Nested data: Refers to data structures where some fields contain subfields or lists of data. For example, in formats like JSON, a field can contain a list of values or even another object with its own fields. CSV files are not designed to represent this type of complex structure.

Metric and categorical: In the context of data, "metric" generally refers to numerical data that can be measured and quantified, while "categorical" refers to data that describes categories or labels. In a .csv file, everything is saved as text, so there is no inherent distinction between numbers and text. It is the user's or the program reading the CSV file's task to interpret and manage this data appropriately.

.csv file

```
person_id,name,kinder_ids
0,georg,1,2
1,petra,
2,paul,
```

Zeile 4, Spalte 8 | 100% | Windows (CRLF) | UTF-8

Excel

person_id	name	kinder_ids	Column1
0	georg	1	2
1	petra		
2	paul		

Pandas

	person_id	name	kinder_ids
0	georg	1.0	2.0
1	petra	NaN	NaN
2	paul	NaN	NaN

Note: NaN --> "Is Not a Number" (Not a Number)
No value (does not mean "is not a figure"!). It means that the cell is basically empty.
More information: https://pandas.pydata.org/docs/user_guide/missing_data.html

4.10. Semi-structured Data

In the context of data analysis, between the extremes of structured and unstructured data, we find an intermediate category known as semi-structured data. These data are not organized in a rigid tabular structure, but contain labels, annotations, or elements that facilitate their processing and analysis. Common examples are .json and .xml files, which, although not organized in traditional tables, have labels and hierarchies that help identify and access different elements of the data.

Characteristics of semi-structured data
Tagged elements: Semi-structured data usually have labels that help identify different segments of the data, facilitating their interpretation and analysis.
Flexible format: Although they have a defined structure, this structure is much more flexible compared to structured data. For example, in a .json file, not all records need to have the same fields.
Interoperability: These data are particularly useful for exchanges between applications due to their flexibility and the ability to represent complex data structures.

Importance in Machine Learning and AI
Feature extraction: Semi-structured data, having labels, facilitate the extraction of relevant features to feed Machine Learning models.
Data integration: Due to their flexibility, semi-structured data are ideal for integrating data from multiple sources, which is common in Big Data projects.
Hierarchical data: Structures like XML allow representing hierarchical relationships and connections between different data segments, which can be crucial for certain analytical applications.

Challenges and considerations
Processing: Although semi-structured data are easier to process than unstructured data, they still require specialized tools and techniques for manipulation.
Consistency: Given their flexibility, there may be inconsistencies in the data, such as missing records or varied formats for the same information.
Conversion: In many cases, to feed Machine Learning models, semi-structured data must be converted into a more structured format, such as tables.

Semi-structured data occupy an intermediate space in the world of data analysis, offering a combination of flexibility and structure. Although they present their own challenges, their ability to represent complex and related information makes them valuable in many Artificial Intelligence contexts. To make the most of these data, it is essential to approach them with a clear understanding of their characteristics and the right tools.

4.10.1. .json File

JSON, which stands for "JavaScript Object Notation", is a lightweight data interchange format that is easy to read and write for humans and easy to parse and generate for machines. It is widely used on the web and in various applications due to its simplicity and versatility. This type of file, if you have already done some programming or have knowledge, will be very easy to understand. Below are the types of data that JSON offers to represent information:

1. String
- **Type:** Categorical or general text (e.g., names).
- **Definition:** Sequences of characters with at least 0 characters.

- **Notation:** Starts and ends with double quotes (`"`).
Example: `"name": "Juan Pérez"`

```
{
"first_name": "John",
"middle_name": "",
"last_name": "Connor"
}
```

2. Number
- **Type:** Metric
- **Classification:**
    - **Discrete:** Without decimals (integer).
    - **Continuous:** With decimals (use a dot instead of a comma, for example, 3.14 instead of 3,14).
Note: Can be positive or negative.
Example: `"age": 30`

```
{
"x_value": 100,
"y_value": -300,
"factor": 2.98
}
```

3. Bool
- **Type:** Categorical with only two possible states.
- **Represents:** True/False, Yes/No.
- **Possible values:** `true` (true) or `false` (false).
- **Note:** Not used in quotes.
Example: `"married": false`

```
{
"passed_exam": true,
"finished_lecture": false
}
```

4. Null (Empty)
Represents the absence of information.
Should not be confused with the number 0.
Example: `"children": null`

```
{
"something": null
}
```

5. Object
Objects can contain other objects in their values.
Nesting increases the amount of information, but also the complexity.
Should be used cautiously to avoid overly complicating the structure.
Example:

```
"address":{
        "street": "Avenida Central",
        "number": "123",
        "city": "Madrid"
        }
```

An object starts with {
contains key-value pairs
• key = Attribute name (in quotes! Example: "street")
• value = Attribute value (Representation according to the data type)
• Separate pairs with commas
• Keys must be unique
Ends with }
Group multiple objects with [{...}, {...}, ...] (Array)

```
{
"first_name": "Michelle",
"children":{
        "child_1": "Sara",
        "child_2": "Pedro"
        }
}
```

The following example shows an error. What not to do!

```
{
"first_name": "Michelle",
        "children":{
                "child_1":{
                        "first_name": "Sara",
                        "children":{
                                "first_name": "Clara",
                                "children": {…}
                                },
                "child_2":{
                        "first_name": "Pedro",
                        "children": null
                        }
                }
}
```

6. Array
Represents a collection of values.
Notation: Starts with `[` and ends with `]`.
Values are separated by commas.
Example: `"hobbies": ["read", "run", "cook"]`

```
{
"first_name": "Michelle",
        "children": ["Sara", "Enrique"]
}
{
"first_name": "Michelle",
        "children": [
                {"first_name": "Carlos"},
                {"first_name": "Lisa"}
        ]
}
```

It is essential to understand these data types and how they are represented in JSON, especially when working with semi-structured data in Machine Learning and Artificial Intelligence contexts. The correct representation and structuring of information will facilitate its subsequent processing and analysis, as well as the understanding of the information contained by other colleagues or participants in your Artificial Intelligence projects.

Characteristics and applications of the .json format in data management:
- JSON = JavaScript Object Notation
- Established format for data storage/exchange: .json
- Common use cases:
  - Semi-structured data (as in banks)
  - Configuration files
  - API (Application Programming Interface)
- Essentially, it is a text file
  - However, its structure allows for tabular representation of information
  - Offers data nesting
  - Supports more precise data types than csv

The last point mentions that JSON "supports more precise data types than csv". Let's break this down to understand it better:

CSV (Comma-Separated Values) is a simple file format that stores tabular data such as numbers and text in plain text, separated by commas. It does not distinguish between different types of data; everything is stored as text. When you read a CSV file, you must infer or have prior knowledge of what type of data each value is (for example, text, number, date).

On the other hand, JSON (JavaScript Object Notation) is a lightweight data interchange format that is structured and has a specific syntax that allows identifying different types of data. For example, in JSON:

- Strings are enclosed in double quotes: `"this is a string"`.
- Numbers are written without quotes: `1234` or `12.34`.
- Booleans are `true` or `false`.
- Objects are delimited with curly braces `{ }` and can contain multiple key-value pairs.
- Lists or arrays are delimited with square brackets `[ ]`.

Due to this defined structure, when working with data in JSON format, you can determine more precisely the type of data for each value, unlike CSV. This means that, for example, you would not confuse a string that looks like a number ("1234") with an actual number (1234) when working with JSON, but this could be ambiguous in CSV.

Therefore, the advantage of JSON over CSV in terms of data type precision is that JSON allows for a clearer and more structured representation of different types of data, while CSV makes no distinctions and treats everything as text.

4.11. Unstructured Data

In the field of data analysis and machine learning, in addition to structured data, and as we have already seen, there is an equally crucial category: unstructured data. These data do not follow a predefined schema or format and are generally not organized in a tabular manner. Common examples include texts, images, audios, videos, and social network records, among others. Their diverse and complex nature presents both opportunities and challenges in the world of Artificial Intelligence and Machine Learning.

Characteristics of unstructured data:
Diversity of formats: Unlike structured data, unstructured data can come in a wide variety of formats, from text to images and audio recordings.
Large volume: Unstructured data is often more voluminous. For example, a collection of images or videos can take up significant space in terms of storage. This requires greater storage capacity, as well as more expensive preparation for storage.
Complexity: They may require specialized processing tools and techniques to extract useful information from them.

Importance in Machine Learning and AI
Sentiment Analysis: Unstructured data, such as product reviews or comments on social networks, can be used for sentiment analysis, identifying how customers feel about a product or service.
Image Recognition: Images, another type of unstructured data, are essential in applications of facial or object recognition.
Natural Language Processing (NLP): Free text, such as articles or transcripts, is crucial for tasks such as automatic translation or text generation.

Challenges and Considerations
Preprocessing: Unstructured data often require significant preprocessing steps to convert them into a usable format for machine learning.
Storage: Given their nature, these data are often larger and may require specialized storage solutions.
Feature Extraction: It is crucial to identify and extract relevant features from unstructured data to feed Machine Learning models.

Unstructured data represents a vast source of information that, when handled properly, can provide deep insights and improve the accuracy of AI models. While they present unique challenges compared to structured data, the opportunities they offer in terms of analysis and modeling are immense. It is essential to address them with the appropriate tools and techniques to take full advantage of their potential in Artificial Intelligence projects.

Let's look at unstructured data in more detail.

4.11.1. Understanding Text

Unstructured data, especially free text, presents a particular challenge due to the peculiarities and flexibilities inherent in human language. Unlike structured or semi-structured data, natural languages do not always follow a fixed pattern, although they tend to have grammatical and syntactic structures.

Consider the following example:

"Marco is 39 years old and lives in Madrid."

Name: Marco
Age: 39
Place of residence: Madrid

Is there a structure?
<Name> is <age> years old and lives in <place of residence>.

"Alice is 47 years old and lives in Barcelona."
"Ernesto lives in Valencia and is 21 years old."

Alternative structure or search strategy?

The challenge lies in the fact that, although there is an underlying structure, the sentences can vary and do not always follow the same order or pattern.

Do natural languages have structures?

Definitely yes, natural languages have structures, but these are not rigid and can vary:

Subject-Verb-Object
Example: "The boy eats the apple."
Conjugation:
First person singular: Walk --> "I walk.", Run --> "I run."

However, structures are not always present or may vary according to context, which makes the processing and analysis of unstructured data, especially text, a challenge in the field of Machine Learning and Artificial Intelligence. It is fundamental to understand these variations and flexibilities to develop effective algorithms that can correctly interpret and analyze human language. It is in this field where, for example, artificial intelligences like ChatGPT break new ground. Let's see an example where we ask ChatGPT about this topic.

Can a sentence be converted into a structured form of data?
Definitely yes. For example, the sentence: "Marco is 18 years old and lives in Miami". Can be converted into a structured form of data and a structured representation could be as follows:

```
{
"Name": "Marco",
"Age": 18,
"Place of residence": "Miami"
}
```

This structure, in JSON format, organizes the information of the sentence into attributes and values, facilitating its processing and analysis.

How can this be understood?
Understanding the sentence “Marco is 18 years old and lives in Miami” and converting it into a structured form of data is a process that involves understanding natural language and extracting relevant information from it.

To do this, the following conceptual steps are followed:

1. Identify entities and attributes:
- “Marco” is an entity that can be associated with an attribute “Name”.
- “18 years” indicates an age, so “18” can be associated with an attribute “Age”.
- “Miami” is an entity that can be associated with an attribute “Place of residence”.

2. Relate verbs and prepositions to attributes:
- The verb “is” gives us a clue that the information that follows belongs to the previously mentioned entity. In this case, “18 years” belongs to “Marco”.
- The preposition “in” before “Miami” gives us a clue that it is a place of residence.

3. Construct a structure:
- With the identified information, a structure is constructed that represents the information in an organized way, as in the previous case, a JSON object.

This example is what we see in AIs like ChatGPT, Google Bard, Jasper Chat, etc., where their ability to understand and structure the sentence comes from training on large amounts of text and examples in various contexts, which allows them to process and understand natural language effectively. However, it is important to mention that this is a simplified task and in more complex contexts, natural language processing can present more challenges.

This process also works in reverse.
Name: Marco
Age: 18
Place of residence: Miami

Phrase: "Marco is 18 years old and lives in Miami".

Now, if you think about it, this phrase can be presented in different ways when speaking colloquially. One of them, for example, would be "the 18-year-old who lives in Miami is called Marco" or also "Marco, who lives in Miami, is 18". This is when the challenges arise when training an Artificial Intelligence for these purposes.

Natural Language Processing (NLP) is a fascinating branch of Artificial Intelligence that seeks to understand and process human language, allowing machines to interact more intuitively with us. Within NLP, there are various techniques and methods used to analyze texts. Next, we will delve into some of them, although the topic itself will be seen later in topic number 7. Some of the main methods for text analysis are:

4.11.1.1. Pattern Recognition

This technique focuses on identifying and extracting specific patterns within large volumes of text. For example, it could be as simple as identifying every second term of a sentence or looking for certain phenomena, such as particularly long or short sentences. However, it is crucial to understand that pattern recognition does not imply a deep understanding of the content of the text. Instead, it operates on a more superficial level, detecting specific sequences or structures without necessarily understanding their underlying meaning. It's like identifying the rhythm in a song without paying attention to its lyrics.

Features:
- It refers to the identification of specific patterns within texts, such as every second term of a sentence.
- It is used to search for certain phenomena, like long or short sentences.
- It is important to note that this method does not comprehend the semantic content of the text, but rather looks for specific patterns or sequences. In other words, it does not understand the underlying message of the text but focuses on its structure and form.

4.11.1.2. Sentiment Analysis

Much deeper than simple pattern recognition, sentiment analysis seeks to understand the emotions and opinions underlying a text. It is widely used in areas such as social media analysis or product review evaluation, where companies want to understand the perceptions and feelings of their customers. It works by identifying words and combinations of words that have a positive or negative emotional charge. For example, words like “lovely” or “amazing” usually have positive connotations, while “disappointing” or “terrible” indicate negative feelings. Through sentiment analysis, we can get a quick insight into whether a text expresses happiness, sadness, anger, surprise, or other emotions.

Features:
- This method is used to determine the tone or emotion conveyed in a text, identifying whether it is positive, negative, or neutral.
- It relies on the presence and combination of certain words that, when found together, can indicate a specific feeling.
- For example, words like “wonderful”, “excellent”, or “great” usually indicate a positive reaction, while words like “terrible”, “horrible”, or “disastrous” indicate a negative reaction.
- It is widely used in product review analysis, opinions on social media, and any other place where people express their opinions and feelings.

Both techniques, although different in their approach and depth, are valuable tools in the vast field of NLP. They allow machines to get a little closer to understanding the complexity and richness of human language, opening doors to applications and solutions that were previously unthinkable. These methods are just two of the many techniques used in NLP to better analyze and understand human language, allowing machines to process and generate language in a way that is meaningful for human users.

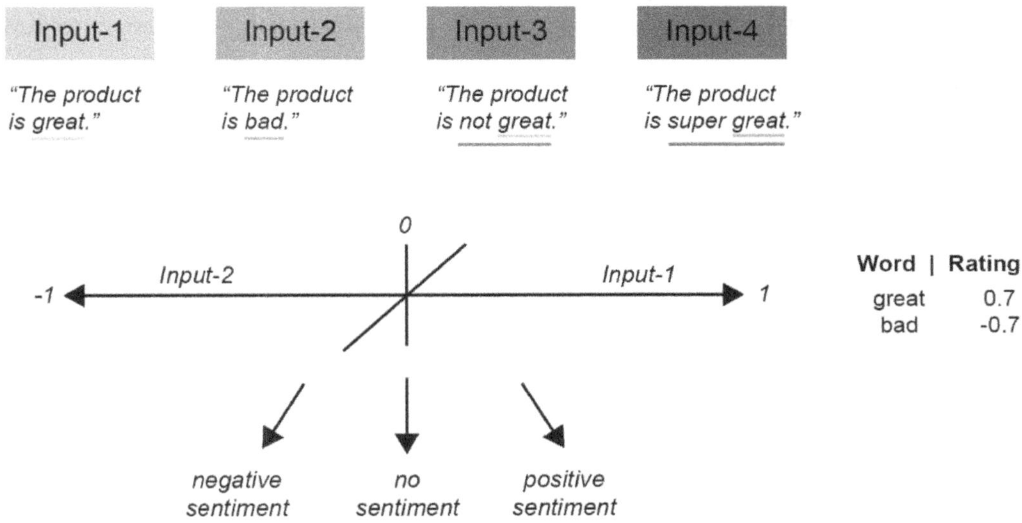

4.11.1.3. Text Mining / Text Analytics

Text mining, also known as Text Mining or Text Analytics (text mining or text analysis), refers to the process of extracting structural information and content from a text. This may involve identifying and categorizing themes, main ideas, or recurring patterns within a document or set of documents.

Working with text data presents its own challenges: it is a complicated process and can require a lot of time and effort. Texts, being linguistic representations of ideas, contain multiple layers of meaning, contexts, and nuances that must be understood and processed correctly. However, despite these complexities, textual data are a gold mine of information. They can offer deep insights into behaviors, opinions, trends, and much more.

In conclusion, if you have the right skills and quality textual data, it is highly beneficial to devote time, effort, and budget to NLP and text analysis for our Artificial Intelligence implementation projects in companies. These techniques not only provide a deeper understanding of the data but can also unlock valuable insights that can be essential for decision-making, research, and other critical applications.

Features:
Information extraction: Identifies and extracts structural and content information from a text, such as entities, relationships, and patterns.
Data diversity: Can handle a wide variety of texts, from formal documents to social media posts.
Complexity: Dealing with texts is inherently complex due to the multiple layers of meaning, contexts, and nuances present in human language.
Analytical depth: Goes beyond simple word or term counts and seeks to understand the underlying meaning and relationships in the text.
Theme identification: Detects and categorizes themes or topics present in a set of documents.
Sentiment Analysis: Capable of identifying and categorizing opinions and emotions expressed in the text.
Valuable: Despite the challenges, textual data contain extremely valuable information that can offer deep insights.

Integration with NLP: Often combined with natural language processing techniques to improve the accuracy and efficacy of the analysis.
Visualization: Provides tools and techniques to visualize patterns, relationships, and trends in large sets of textual data.
Automation: With the right tools, text mining can automate the extraction and analysis of information, resulting in time and resource savings.
Adaptability: Can be used in a wide range of applications and sectors, from social network analysis to academic research and business analysis.

4.11.2. Images

To start studying Artificial Intelligence and machine learning and their relationship with images, let's first take a look at the following image closely.

It doesn't seem anything out of the ordinary. The image shows a simple representation in .png format of a happy face. Basically, two dots and a small curve that represent the smiling face.

Now let's see what happens when we inspect the image from the inside.

In this case, we see a textual representation of the same file, which is what we would see if we opened the PNG file in a text editor instead of an image viewer. But why does this happen?

The image displays text representing binary data of a PNG image because image files like PNG contain binary data that is not intended to be read as text, and that's why they appear as a series of alphanumeric characters and symbols that make no sense in a text editor. This is because text editors are designed to interpret and display files containing text encoded in formats like ASCII or Unicode, not binary image data.

Now, let's see what happens if I extract the binary information from the file using Python.

```
def read_image_binary(file_path):
    # Reading the binary data of the file
    with open(file_path, 'rb') as file:
        binary_data = file.read()
    return binary_data[:64]  # returning the first 64 bytes for brevity

binary_data = read_image_binary('/mnt/data/smiley.png')
binary_data.hex()  # Convert to hexadecimal for compact representation
```

Here is the result:

```
89504e470d0a1a0a0000000d49484452000000af0000008908060000005a67685e0000000097048597300003
5d4000035d4015e65e5080000001974455874536f
```

Unstructured data refers to information that does not have a predefined format or is not easy to handle using conventional methods. The visual content of the image (the smiling face) is an example of unstructured data, as images do not have a clear tabular structure like databases or spreadsheets. However, the text representation of the PNG file (binary data) is a more "fixed" structure, but it is still difficult to interpret and analyze without the appropriate tools, therefore, it is also not suitable for data analysis.

In Machine Learning, we often work with unstructured data, such as images, text, and sound. For a machine to interpret and learn from an image, it needs to transform that image into a form that the machine can understand, generally in the form of numerical vectors. These numerical vectors are obtained through image processing techniques and can then be fed into machine learning algorithms to train models, such as image classifiers.

AI uses Machine Learning algorithms to interpret, analyze, and learn from data. In the context of the provided image, an AI application could be a model that recognizes and labels emotions in faces. If we train a model with enough images of faces showing different emotions, that model could be able to identify that the image on the left shows a "happy" or "smiling" face. However, to reach that point, a large amount of preprocessing and data transformation is needed, from its original unstructured representation to a structured form that the machine can understand. The image illustrates the difference between the human and machine representation of the same information. While humans see a smiling face, machines see a series of bytes and codes, and transforming that visual information into something that machines can interpret and learn is fundamental in the field of AI and Machine Learning.

Data as observations: "Subjective interpretation → different information."

In the context of images and the field of unstructured data in Machine Learning and Artificial Intelligence, this phrase, "Data as observations," reflects the idea that data, in this case images, act as observations of the real world that are captured and stored in digital format. These observations are essential for ML and AI systems to learn and generalize from past examples.

The second part, "Subjective interpretation → different information," suggests that although data act as objective observations, the interpretation of those data can be subjective. That is, different people (or even different AI systems) may interpret the same image in different ways.

In more concrete terms, imagine an image of a landscape. While one person might see it and think of the beauty of nature, another might focus on the technical aspects of the photograph, such as lighting or composition. Similarly, an AI model trained to recognize plants might identify the species of trees in the image, while another model trained to evaluate the quality of images might judge whether the photo is well framed or has good contrast.

This concept is fundamental in ML and AI because it highlights the importance of having a clear objective when training a model and interpreting its results. Data, by themselves, do not have inherent meaning; their value lies in how we interpret and use them. In the world of unstructured data, such as images, this interpretation becomes even more crucial, as there is no predefined structure to guide our understanding. Therefore, it is essential to be aware that different interpretations can lead to different conclusions, even when working with the same set of data or images.

4.11.3. Image Recognition & Object Detection

Image recognition and object detection, being subfields of Machine Learning and Artificial Intelligence, focus on the processing and analysis of visual data such as images and videos. These data are classified as unstructured because they do not conform to a tabular format or a defined structure, unlike structured data. The complexity of these data lies in their variability and the richness of the information they contain, which represents a significant challenge for ML and AI algorithms.

To address these challenges, techniques such as convolutional neural networks (CNNs) are used, which are particularly effective for image analysis. These networks learn visual patterns through processing layers that mimic the way the human brain interprets images. This ability allows them to identify and classify objects within an image, as well as understand the context and spatial relationships between elements.

Another important aspect is the training of these models, which requires large amounts of annotated data. Data annotation involves manually labeling images with relevant information, such as the location and type of objects present. This process is crucial for supervised learning, where the model learns from labeled examples to later make predictions about new data.

1. Image recognition:
- **Definition:** It is the ability of a model to identify and classify what is contained in an image.
- **Applications:** Facial identification, image classification (for example, distinguishing whether an image is a dog or a cat), medical diagnosis through images, among others.
- **Challenges:** Variations in lighting, perspective, scale, and occlusions can make image recognition complex.

** "Occlusions" refer to situations where part of an object or entity is covered or blocked by another object, preventing it from being seen completely. In the context of image recognition and object detection, occlusions can present a significant challenge, as parts of the object of interest might be hidden, making it difficult to properly identify or locate them.*

For example, in an image where there is a group of people, if one person is standing behind another, only part of the person in the back can be seen. This partially hidden person is an example of occlusion in the image. Specifically, in the image we observe a group of people among whom we can see that some are partially hidden behind others, and behind these people, more are also partially hidden.

2. Object detection:
- **Definition:** Goes a step further than simple image recognition. It not only identifies what is in an image but also locates these objects within the image, generally providing a "bounding box" (as we can see in the image) around each detected object.
- **Applications:** Surveillance systems, autonomous vehicles (to detect pedestrians, other vehicles, traffic signs), crowd analysis, among others.
- **Challenges:** Detecting multiple objects in congested or overlapping scenes and differentiating similar objects are challenging tasks in object detection. (See the previous image).

Relation to unstructured data
Unstructured nature: Images and videos, not following a tabular schema or clearly defined structure, are considered unstructured data. However, they contain rich visual details that, once processed and understood, can provide deep and valuable insights.
Preprocessing: Unlike structured data, which can often be fed directly into a machine learning algorithm, unstructured data like images generally require extensive preprocessing. This may include normalization, resizing, image enhancement, and feature extraction.
Feature extraction: Images are often converted into a set of numerical features that capture the essence of the image (such as edges, textures, colors) before being fed into an ML model.
Specific models: Convolutional Neural Networks (CNN) are a type of model that has proven particularly effective for image recognition and object detection tasks due to their ability to handle and process unstructured visual data.

Image recognition and object detection are clear examples of how AI and ML can work with unstructured data to achieve complex and advanced tasks. As technologies and algorithms advance, the ability of machines to "see" and "understand" the visual world becomes increasingly sophisticated and precise.

4.11.4. Optical Character Recognition (OCR)

Optical Character Recognition, commonly known as OCR, is a technology that enables the conversion of different types of documents, such as paper scans, images of text, or even photographs, into editable and searchable data. This capability is especially useful for digitizing printed documents, converting books into electronic formats, automating data entry processes, and many other applications.

TotalEnergies Station - M. Henschel
Binderslebener Landstr. 98
99092 Erfurt
Tankstellen-Nr.: 0000033496
Tel.: 0361 / 2229393
Fax.: 0361 / 2229394

* 33,17 Liter # 01 *
Super E10 * € 60,00*A
1,809 € / Liter

Summe € 60,00
EC Karte € 60,00

19,00 % MWST. A € 9,58
Summe Netto € 50,42

Terminal-ID 54706571/ND03349801
Datum/Uhrzeit 12.11.2023 06:26:54
AID A0000003591010028001

Historically, the first implementations of OCR were based on rules and fixed patterns to recognize characters. However, with the evolution of Artificial Intelligence and machine learning, OCR has undergone a revolution in terms of accuracy and applicability.
Machine Learning, and more specifically Deep Learning, has changed the way OCR systems work. Instead of strictly relying on predefined rules, modern OCR systems use neural networks, particularly Convolutional Neural Networks (CNN), to learn and recognize patterns in visual data. These systems are trained with large datasets containing examples of characters in different fonts, sizes, and lighting conditions, allowing them to recognize text in a wide variety of contexts and environments.

The relationship between OCR and Artificial Intelligence is symbiotic. On one hand, advancements in AI and ML techniques have greatly improved the accuracy and efficiency of OCR systems. On the other hand, the need to convert vast amounts of printed information into digital formats has driven research and development in the field of OCR, leading to innovations and advancements in the domain of AI.

Today, thanks to Artificial Intelligence, OCR systems can not only recognize text in standard documents but also in noisy images, handwritten documents, and even in scenarios where the text is partially hidden or distorted. Furthermore, the combination of OCR with other AI technologies, such as NLP, allows not only the extraction of text from images but also the understanding and processing of the extracted content, opening doors to applications such as automatic translation, advanced document search, and the automation of administrative tasks.

4.11.5. Facial Recognition

Facial recognition is one of the most prominent and, at the same time, controversial applications of Artificial Intelligence today. It is a technology that has the capability to identify or verify a person from an image or video by comparing and analyzing facial patterns.

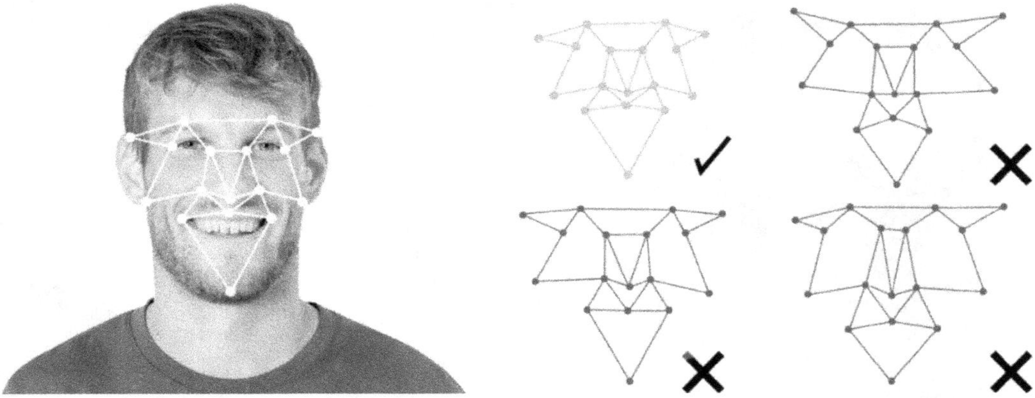

The rise and sophistication of facial recognition in recent years is directly linked to advances in Machine Learning and, more specifically, in deep learning. Previously, facial recognition systems were based on simpler techniques, identifying key facial features, such as the distance between the eyes or the shape of the nose. However, these systems were limited in terms of accuracy and flexibility.

With the introduction of Convolutional Neuronal Networks and other deep learning models, facial recognition has undergone a transformation. These models, trained with large datasets containing millions of faces, learn to identify subtle facial patterns and features with a high degree of accuracy. They can recognize faces in various lighting conditions, postures, expressions, and even when they are partially hidden or at different ages.

Machine Learning has not only improved the accuracy of facial recognition but also expanded its applicability. From unlocking smartphones and security systems in buildings to finding missing people, to applications in airports for security checks or even in advertising to tailor content based on the reaction of viewers.

However, along with its potential, facial recognition also poses serious ethical challenges and concerns about privacy. The misuse of this technology can lead to mass surveillance and human rights violations. That is why, parallel to its technical development, it is essential to reflect on its regulation and ethical use.

Facial recognition is a testament to the power and possibilities offered by the combination of ML and AI. However, like any powerful tool, its use must be measured and responsible, weighing its benefits and risks in society. In fact, I remember that one of my Use Cases professors had in each of his presentations an image of Spiderman that said "With great power comes great responsibility". And I completely agree!

4.11.6. Color Analysis

Color analysis is a technique widely used in Machine Learning and Artificial Intelligence to process and understand information in images and videos. Through color analysis, machines can identify, classify, and process objects, scenes, and activities based on color patterns and distributions.

What is color analysis?
Color analysis refers to the process of quantifying and categorizing the colors present in an image. In simple terms, it is about determining what colors and in what quantity are present. This information can be vital for various applications, from detecting diseases in medical images to classifying images on social networks.

How is color analysis performed in ML and AI?
1. Color feature extraction: Images are broken down into their basic color components, usually in RGB (Red, Green, Blue) or HSV (Hue, Saturation, Value) color spaces. Features such as color histograms, color moments, and descriptive statistics are extracted.

2. Classification and clustering: Once the features are extracted, ML algorithms can be trained to recognize and classify objects or scenes based on their color profiles. Clustering techniques can also be used to group similar images based on colors.

3. Advanced applications: With more sophisticated techniques, color analysis can be used in image segmentation (dividing an image into regions based on similar colors) or in the detection of patterns and anomalies.

Why are they considered unstructured data?
Images, as we have already seen in previous points, unlike tabular or structured data, do not follow a fixed schema or a predefined structure. Although they can be represented in pixel matrices, the information they contain, such as colors, shapes, and textures, does not have an inherent organization that facilitates direct interpretation. Each image is unique in its composition and presents challenges in terms of interpretation and processing.

Color itself is a complex property. Although we can decompose it into basic components (like RGB), the perception and interpretation of color are influenced by factors such as lighting, shadows, and the context in which it is found. Therefore, although color can be quantified to a certain extent, it remains a form of unstructured data that requires advanced ML and AI techniques to be processed and understood adequately.

Color analysis is essential in the field of image processing and has a wide range of applications in ML and AI. Despite its unstructured nature, technological advancements have enabled machines to process and understand images accurately, making color analysis a powerful tool in the AI toolkit.

4.11.7. Image Segmentation

Image segmentation is a technique in Machine Learning that allows dividing an image into multiple segments or regions, where each segment corresponds to an object or part of an object in the image. This technique allows machines to understand and process images at a more detailed level, identifying and differentiating specific objects and structures within them.

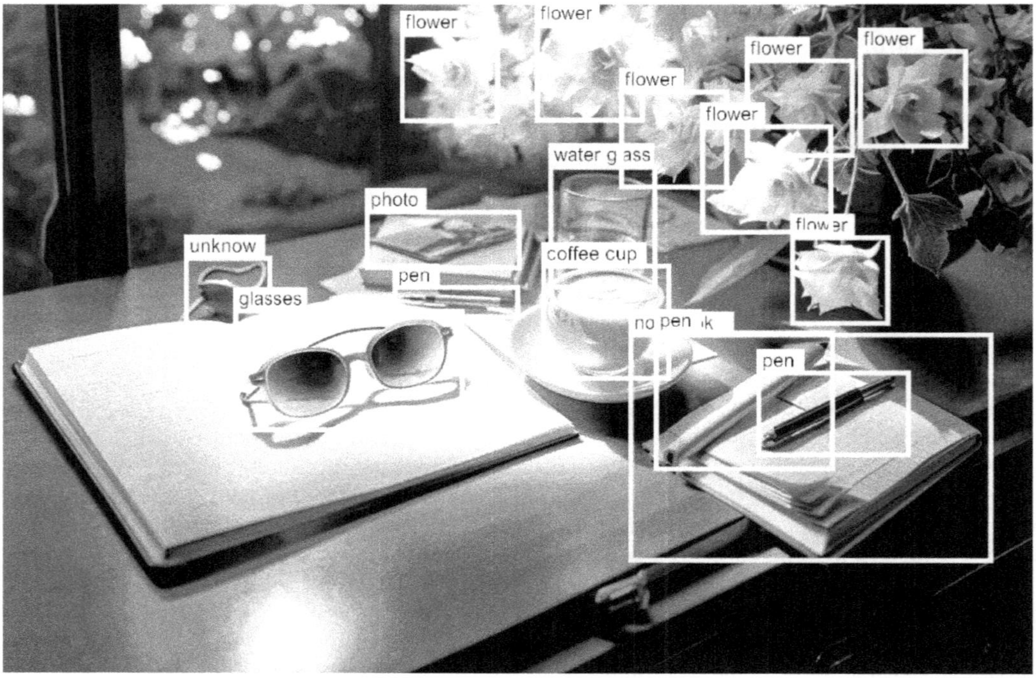

What is image segmentation?
Image segmentation refers to the process of dividing an image into sets of pixels that belong to the same object or category. In other words, the aim is to assign a label to each pixel in the image so that pixels with the same label share certain visual characteristics.

How is image segmentation done in ML and AI?
1. Traditional techniques: These include methods based on thresholds, edges, and region growing. For example, threshold-based segmentation involves selecting a threshold value and classifying all the pixels in the image into two categories based on whether their value is higher or lower than the threshold.

2. Deep Learning-based techniques: With the emergence of Convolutional Neural Networks, image segmentation has reached new levels of accuracy. Networks like U-Net or Mask R-CNN have proven to be particularly effective in segmentation tasks, being able to identify and outline objects in images in great detail.

3. Post-processing: After segmentation, it is often necessary to perform post-processing to refine segments, eliminate noise, or combine similar regions.

Why are they considered unstructured data?
Again, as we have seen before, images, just like in the case of color analysis, are inherently unstructured. Although they can be represented as matrices of pixels, they do not have a fixed organization or structure that indicates how pixels relate to each other. Segmentation seeks to impose a structure on these unstructured data, grouping pixels based on their visual and semantic characteristics.

The relationship between pixels, proximity, color, texture, and other characteristics form a complexity that cannot be easily interpreted without advanced techniques. Segmentation seeks to decipher this complexity and provide a more structured representation of the image, identifying distinct objects and features.

Image segmentation is fundamental in various ML and AI applications, from medicine, where it is used to identify areas of interest in medical images, to autonomous driving, where it helps identify and track objects in the vehicle's environment. Despite the challenge of working with unstructured data, modern Deep Learning techniques have revolutionized segmentation, allowing for detailed and accurate image analysis.

4.11.8. Image Classification

Image classification is also, like the previous ones, an essential task in ML and AI that involves assigning a label to an entire image based on its visual content. This technique allows machines to interpret and categorize visual content, facilitating a wide variety of applications, from object recognition to disease detection in medical images.

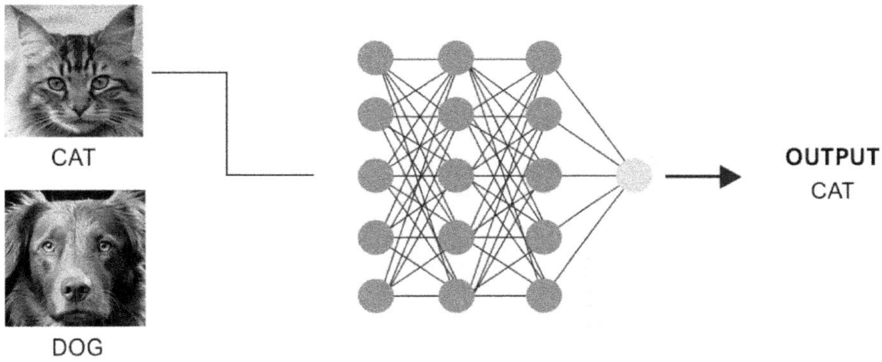

What is image classification?
Image classification is the process of identifying and assigning one or more categories to an image, based on the visual information it contains. For example, when viewing an image of a dog, the classification system should be able to identify it and label it as "dog". In the previous image you have it as an example. You can observe how the MLP algorithm is fed with images, and after processing the information, the algorithm, based on the results, decides whether the image belongs to a cat or a dog, in the example a cat.

How is image classification carried out in ML and AI?
1. Traditional techniques: These techniques include methods based on manual features, such as texture descriptors, edges, and key points. These features are extracted and then used to train classic Machine Learning models, like Support Vector Machines (SVM) or Decision Trees.

2. Deep Learning-based techniques: Convolutional Neural Networks have revolutionized image classification, providing superior accuracy and generalization capabilities. CNNs automatically learn relevant features from images through multiple layers of convolution and pooling, making them particularly suitable for visual tasks.

3. Transfer learning: This is a technique where a model pre-trained on a large dataset (like ImageNet) is adapted for a specific classification task with less data. This allows leveraging knowledge acquired in general tasks and applying it to specific problems.

Why are they considered unstructured data?
Again, we have to answer the question. Images, although they can be represented as two-dimensional matrices of pixels (or three-dimensional if we consider color channels), do not have an organized structure or fixed pattern that describes their content. The relationship between pixels, their arrangement, colors, shapes, and textures form a rich tapestry of information that does not follow a predefined scheme. At this point, you are able to clearly differentiate, and I hope also, and be able to explain to your colleagues, as well as the members of your project team why images are unstructured data and what are their preprocessing methods in ML.

Image classification is a cornerstone in the world of AI, with applications ranging from social networks to medical diagnostics. Despite the challenges presented by unstructured data, modern techniques, especially those based on Deep Learning, have allowed significant advances in this area, enabling systems that can interpret and classify images with an accuracy that often rivals human perception.

4.11.9. Video

Video, like images, is a form of unstructured data, but is even more complex due to its temporal nature and the massive amount of information it contains. A video is essentially a series of images (frames) that are displayed in rapid succession to create the illusion of movement.

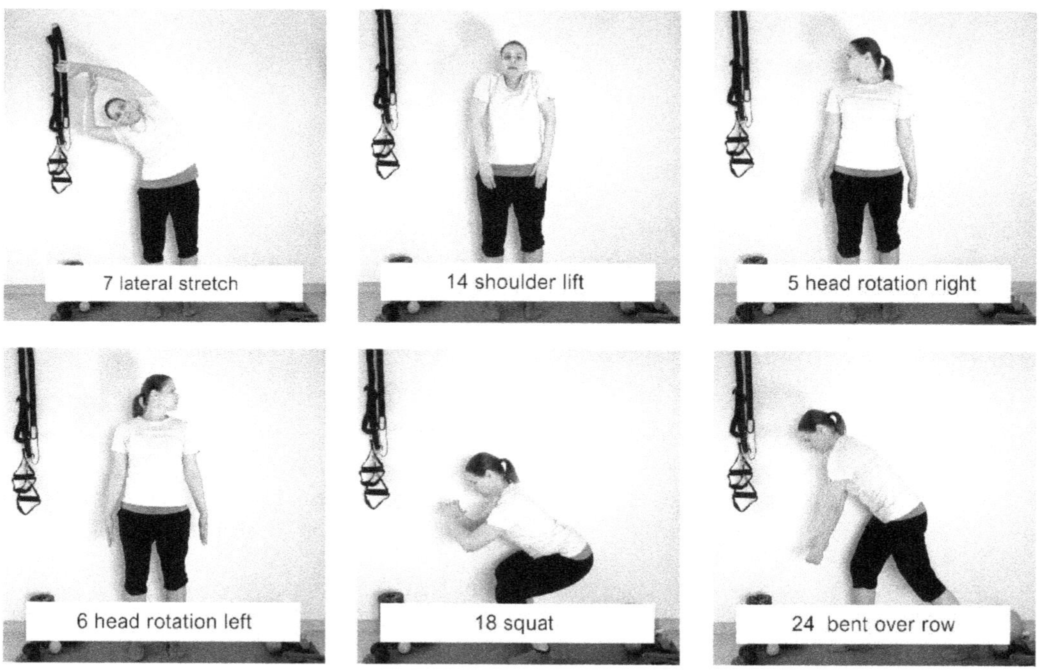

Why is it considered unstructured?
The video does not have a fixed structure or inherent pattern in terms of its content. Although technically it is a sequence of images, the temporal and spatial relationships between these

frames, as well as the associated sound, create an additional dimension of complexity that is not present in a static image. Each frame itself is an image and, therefore, is also unstructured data, but when combined in a sequence, the relationship between the frames adds another layer of unstructuring.

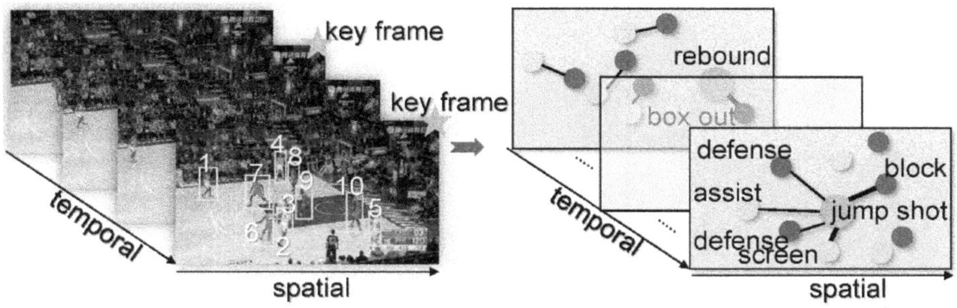

Image: https://www.mdpi.com/2227-7390/11/14/3074

Applications in ML and AI:
Activity Recognition: Detecting and classifying actions or events in videos, such as identifying if someone is running, jumping, or dancing.
Security Analysis: In surveillance systems, video is analyzed to detect suspicious or unauthorized activities.
Interactive Content: In streaming platforms, video analysis is used to provide recommendations based on the visual content a user has previously viewed.
Real-Time Facial and Object Recognition: Applications like social networks use video analysis to automatically tag people in live or recorded videos.
Traffic Analysis: Monitoring traffic flows, identifying congestion, and predicting traffic patterns.
Augmented Reality: Overlaying digital information on the real world through the lens of a camera in real-time. Check out this video from the appliance manufacturer Philips, presenting virtual reality glasses applied in emergency situations: https://youtu.be/z3owLTiEGJ4?si=V_Ml1ne-byARHyPFi

Challenges in Video Analysis:
Data Volume: A video generates a significant amount of data, requiring more computational power and storage capacity.
Occlusions: In a video, objects or people may block each other, making identification difficult.
Content Variety: Different videos may have different resolutions, orientations, lighting conditions, among other factors that can affect analysis.
Temporal Relationships: Unlike images, videos have a temporal dimension that must be considered when analyzing actions or events that unfold over time.

Video, as a form of unstructured data, presents unique opportunities and challenges in the field of ML and AI. Modern techniques, especially those based on Deep Learning, are beginning to unravel the complexity of video, opening doors to innovative applications and enhancing our ability to understand and interact with the visual world around us.

4.11.10. Audio

Audio is a representation of sound waves in digital or analog form. Like video and images, audio is considered a type of unstructured data because it does not follow a tabular or fixed structure. Instead, it is composed of time series of amplitudes that represent the variation of sound pressure over time.

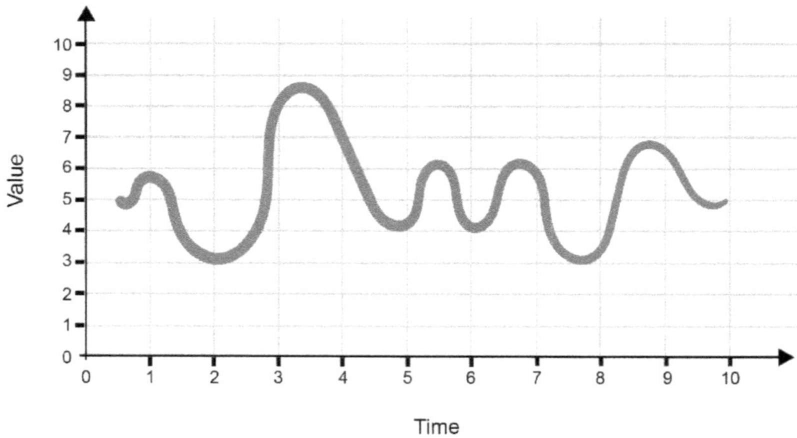

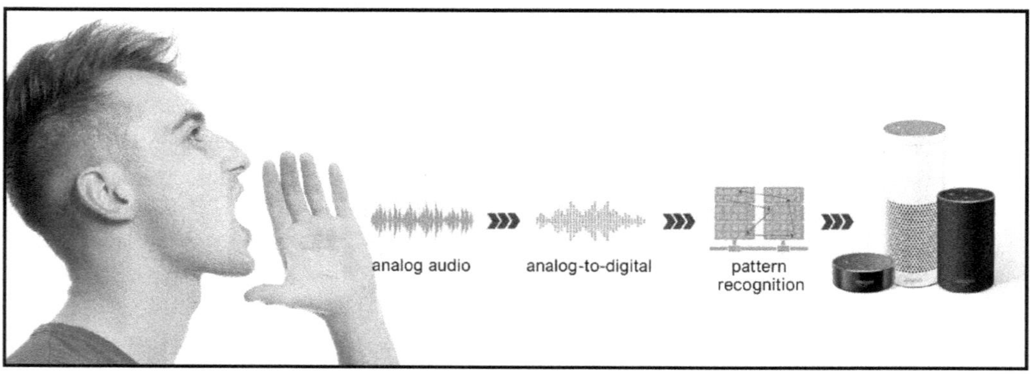

Why is it considered unstructured?
Audio does not have a fixed structure or inherent pattern in terms of content. It is composed of a variety of frequencies, amplitudes, and times, and the information contained in an audio file can vary widely depending on the sound source, the environment, and other factors.

Applications in ML and AI
Voice Recognition: Converting speech into text. This is fundamental in virtual assistants, automatic transcriptions, and more.
Music Identification: Applications that can identify a song based on an audio snippet, such as the well-known Shazam.
Sentiment Analysis: Determining the emotional state or sentiment of a speaker from their vocal characteristics.

Environmental Sound Detection: Identifying specific sounds in an environment, such as alarms, glass breaking, etc., used in security systems.
Voice Synthesis: Converting text into speech, used in text readers and virtual assistants, among others.
Medical Diagnosis: Analyzing body sounds, such as heartbeats or breathing, to detect abnormalities.

Challenges in Audio Analysis
Variety of Sources: Sounds can come from various sources and may overlap, making individual identification difficult.
Background Noise: Recorded audio may contain unwanted noises that can interfere with analysis.
Accents and Dialects: In voice recognition, different accents and dialects can present challenges in the correct transcription of speech. For example, German is not the same as Swabian, just as Spanish is not the same as Galician, nor is a Galician speaking Spanish the same as a Spaniard speaking Spanish. Both are legitimately Spanish, but the accent when speaking Spanish is very different, and therefore, more difficult to recognize by the algorithm.
Temporal Variability: The speed and rhythm of speech or music can vary, which can influence analysis.
Audio analysis in the context of ML and AI has opened a wide range of practical applications, from improving human-machine interaction to providing medical diagnoses. While audio data presents unique challenges due to its unstructured nature, advanced machine learning techniques, particularly those based on Deep Learning, are making great strides in this field, allowing machines to "listen" and "interpret" the sound world in previously unimaginable ways.

4.12. Metadata

Metadata is essentially data about data, not because they are above them, but because they provide descriptive information about the content, quality, condition, and other characteristics of the data. In the context of ML and AI, metadata play a crucial role in helping professionals understand and manage large data sets.

Importance of Metadata in ML and AI
Organization and Management: Metadata allows for effective organization and management of large data sets, facilitating the search, access, and reuse of specific data.
Quality and Provenance: They provide information about the data source, its change history, quality, and accuracy. This is vital for trusting the data and the results obtained from them.
Compatibility: They help ensure that data from different sources are compatible and can be integrated or compared correctly.
Security and Privacy: Metadata can contain information about who has access to the data, when and how it was accessed, and what actions were taken. This is essential for protection and compliance with regulations.
Training Efficiency: By having a clear view of the data through metadata, more informed decisions can be made about which data to use to train ML models, optimizing time and resources.

Applications of Metadata in ML and AI

Data Preprocessing: Before training a model, it is essential to understand the characteristics of the data set. Metadata facilitates this task by providing information about variables, data type, missing values, among others.

Model Versioning: When training and retraining models, it is crucial to have a record of what data and parameters were used. Metadata help to track these versions.

Interoperability: In complex systems where data come from multiple sources, metadata ensure that these data can be integrated and used consistently.

Challenges with Metadata

Complexity: As the quantity and variety of data grow, managing and maintaining up-to-date metadata can be a challenge.

Standards: There are different standards and practices for creating metadata, which can lead to inconsistencies.

Privacy: If not handled properly, metadata can reveal sensitive or private information.

Metadata is an essential tool in the arsenal of any ML and AI professional. Although often overlooked compared to raw data, their importance in managing, understanding, and effectively using that data cannot be underestimated. In a world where data is the new oil, metadata could be considered the map that allows us to navigate this vast and valuable resource.

MODULE 2

Methods

Module 2 - Methods

5. Big Data

In today's digital era, the amount of data produced and collected is astonishing. From social media and online transactions to sensors and devices connected all over the world, we generate a constant flow of information. This massive volume, variety, and velocity of data is what we know as Big Data.

Big Data is not just a matter of volume. It refers to data sets that are so large and complex that traditional database management tools and systems fall short in handling them.

Douglas Laney is widely known in the information technology world for coining the term "**3Vs**" or the "**3-V-Modell**" to describe the challenge and opportunity associated with managing large amounts of data. These three Vs are:

1. Volume: Refers to the amount of data. With the proliferation of devices like mobile phones, sensors, and cameras, as well as social media platforms and electronic transactions, huge amounts of data are generated every day.

2. Velocity: Refers to the speed at which data is generated, processed, and made available. Consider, for example, social networks, where thousands of tweets or posts are published per second.

3. Variety: Refers to the different types of data, which can be structured (like relational databases), semi-structured (like JSON or XML), or unstructured (like images, videos, or texts).

Laney proposed this concept in a research report by META Group (now Gartner) in 2001.

In relation to Machine Learning and Artificial Intelligence we can see that:

Volume: ML and AI benefit from large amounts of data. The more data available to train a model, generally, the better its performance, as it can capture more complex and subtle patterns.

Velocity: Real-time ML and AI systems need to process data quickly to provide real-time results. For example, a fraud detection system needs to evaluate transactions in milliseconds to decide whether they are legitimate or not.

Variety: ML and AI algorithms can process and learn from a wide variety of data. From image processing to text analysis, the ability to work with different types of data allows AI to address a wide range of problems.

Laney's 3Vs describe fundamental characteristics of Big Data, and these characteristics are essential for many modern applications of ML and AI. The tools and techniques developed to handle Big Data have facilitated the rise and expansion of ML and AI capabilities.

Over time and with the ongoing development of the Big Data field, Laney's original 3Vs concept has expanded to include up to six dimensions (or Vs) that characterize the challenges and opportunities of Big Data. In total, these are the 6Vs:

1. Volume: As mentioned earlier, it refers to the massive amount of data generated.
2. Velocity: Related to the speed at which data is generated, processed, and consumed.
3. Variety: Refers to the different types of data, whether structured, semi-structured, or unstructured.
4. Veracity: This dimension refers to the quality of the data. Not all generated data is useful or accurate. Veracity deals with data uncertainty, which can be due to data inconsistency, structure, availability, and accuracy.
5. Value: It's about the usefulness of the data. Refers to the ability to turn our data into value. It's the final V resulting from the proper treatment of the other dimensions. It's about the data's ability to benefit an organization or individual.
6. Validity: Refers to the inconsistency that data can sometimes show, which can make processing and analysis difficult. Variability can arise due to the seasonal or cyclical nature of some data, or due to the presence of outliers.

The recognition of these additional dimensions reflects the growing understanding that effective Big Data management is not just about handling large volumes of data quickly and in various formats, but also ensuring that the data is reliable and valuable for decision-making. These 6Vs are especially relevant for ML and AI, as the quality and usefulness of the models and solutions depend heavily on the quality and usefulness of the data with which they are trained and fed.

Artificial Intelligence, and particularly Machine Learning, have found fertile ground in Big Data. Machines can now learn patterns, gain insights, and make predictions or decisions based on these huge data sets. But, for AI and ML to be effective, the management and handling of these data is essential.

5.1. Data Management and Handling

1. Data Collection: Before training models or gaining insights, it's necessary to collect data. This involves defining what data is relevant and how it will be acquired, whether through sensors, online logs, databases, among others.

2. Data Preprocessing: Once collected, data is rarely ready to be used. There may be missing values, errors, or inconsistencies. Preprocessing involves cleaning and transforming these data to be useful.

3. Storage: Big Data requires robust storage solutions. It's not just about where to store data, but how to structure it, how to access it quickly, and how to ensure its integrity and security.

4. Analysis: With the data at hand, analyses are carried out to discover patterns and trends. These analyses can feed ML models or simply provide valuable insights.

5. Model Training: In ML, data is used to train models. This training requires proper data management, dividing it into training, validation, and testing sets.

6. Deployment: Once trained, models are deployed in production systems where they continue to interact with real-time data.

7. Updating and Maintenance: Data changes over time. Therefore, it's essential to keep databases updated and regularly retrain ML models.

8. Privacy and Security: Data management also involves ensuring compliance with privacy regulations and protecting data against unauthorized access or loss.
Big Data has revolutionized the way we understand and use data. It has opened doors to insights and capabilities that were previously unimaginable. However, its true potential can only be unlocked with effective data management and handling, especially in the field of Machine Learning and Artificial Intelligence. Proper management ensures that the data is not only abundant but also useful, accurate, and secure.

Companies and organizations have a huge amount of data. Let's look at them in more detail.

5.1.1. Operational Data

These data reflect the daily transactions and operations of a company. They are dynamic and constantly change as transactions are carried out. These data are essential for the daily operation of an organization. Here are some examples:

Goods Management Systems:
These systems manage and monitor the flow of goods within a company, from the acquisition of products to the sale to the customer. They help businesses maintain control over their inventory, orders, deliveries, etc.

Accounting Programs:
These programs handle the finances of the company, recording all financial transactions, such as income, expenses, accounts payable, and receivable.

ERP Systems (Enterprise Resource Planning):
ERP systems integrate different departments and functions of a company into a single system. This can include inventory management, accounting, human resources, customer management, among others. The purpose is to have an integrated and efficient view of the company's operations.

Others:
Depending on the nature and industry of the company, there may be other transactional systems, such as Customer Relationship Management (CRM) systems, Supply Chain Management (SCM) systems, among others.

5.1.2. Device Data

These data refer to consolidated and processed information that is stored long-term for analysis and decision-making. They do not reflect daily operations, but rather trends, patterns, and summaries. Let's look at their characteristics:

Consolidated and Preprocessed:
The data is cleaned, transformed, and consolidated to eliminate redundancies and errors before storage.

Highly Aggregated:
These data are not stored at the transaction detail level but are aggregated at higher levels. For example, instead of having daily sales, we might have monthly or annual sales by region or product.

Used for Analysis and Control (Steuerung):
These data are used for strategic analysis and decision-making. They can feed Business Intelligence (BI) tools and decision support systems. They help business leaders identify trends, assess performance, and plan for the future.

As you can see, it is easy to differentiate operational data from device data. While operational or transactional data reflect the day-to-day of the company and are essential for its daily operation, device data offers a consolidated and long-term view that is essential for analysis, planning, and strategic decision-making.

In summary, Big Data is:
A Complex Concept:
- Large volumes of data.
- The technologies that support these data.
- Analysis and use of data.

Opportunities:
- Identify patterns -> Explain complex situations.
- Provide objective recommendations for action.
- Anticipate problems.

Challenges:
- Unstructured and semi-structured data.
- Where to store data? Locally vs. in the cloud.
- The larger the amount of data, the greater the effort required.

5.2. Business Intelligence & Analytics (BI & BA)

In the current era of digitalization, companies are inundated with a deluge of data from various sources. If handled and analyzed correctly, these data have the potential to transform the way organizations make decisions and design their strategies. Within this context, two key concepts have emerged as pillars in the world of business data analysis: Business Intelligence (BI) and Business Analytics (BA). Although often used interchangeably, these terms refer to different approaches and objectives in the treatment and analysis of information. Below, we will explore in detail these two areas, their relationship with Big Data, and how each contributes value to the business world. Let's look at these terms as reflected in an image.

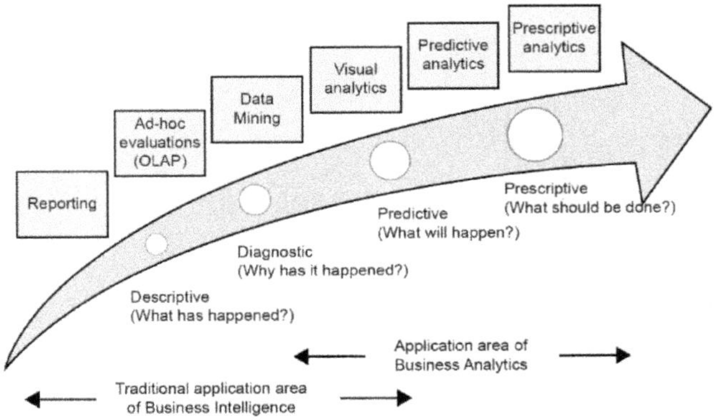

Inspired on: Gluchowski, P., & Gabriel, R. (2022). Business Intelligence-Begriff, Architektur und Entwicklungstendenzen. Handbuch Digitalisierung, 463.

Let's delve into these concepts and their relationship with Big Data.

5.2.1. Business Intelligence (BI)

Business Intelligence refers to the set of techniques, technologies, applications, and practices used to collect, integrate, analyze, and present business data. BI allows organizations to access and examine accumulated information with the goal of improving decision-making, identifying trends and patterns, and gaining a clear and comprehensive view of the company's status and performance.

Main features:
Data integration: BI integrates data from different sources, such as ERP systems, CRM, databases, among others, into a centralized repository, like a data warehouse.
Data presentation: BI tools offer visualization capabilities, allowing users to create reports, graphs, and dashboards.
Historical analysis: BI focuses on analyzing historical data to identify trends and evaluate past performance.

Examples:
- A company that uses a BI tool to monitor its sales over time, identifying seasons of high and low demand.
- A hospital that uses BI to analyze patient waiting times, identifying peak hours and areas for improvement.

5.2.2. Business Analytics (BA)

Business Analytics refers to the use of statistical analysis, predictive modeling, optimization, and similar techniques to identify patterns and predict future events. While BI focuses on historical analysis, BA looks to the future and seeks to anticipate trends and behaviors.

Main features:
Predictive and prescriptive approach: BA not only predicts what might happen but can also recommend specific actions to take advantage of opportunities or mitigate risks.
Modeling and simulation: BA uses algorithms and mathematical models to analyze data and make predictions.
Integration with Big Data: BA is often combined with Big Data to analyze large data sets and extract deeper insights.

Examples:
- A chain of stores that uses BA to predict which products will be popular in the upcoming season and adjust its inventory accordingly.
- An insurance company that uses BA to predict which customers are more likely to file a claim in the future, based on behavioral patterns and historical data.

5.2.3. Relation with Big Data

Both BI and BA greatly benefit from Big Data. Big Data provides the volume, velocity, and variety of data that can be analyzed to gain insights. BI uses Big Data to provide more detailed reports and dashboards and cover the entire organization, while BA uses Big Data to feed its models and make more accurate predictions.

While BI focuses on the "what" and "how" of past events, BA focuses on the "why" and predicting the "what" of future events. Both are essential for informed and effective business management.

Now let's address the relationship between BI, BA, ML, and AI, and how they differ from each other, to finally analyze the advantages of AI over BI and BA.

In the constantly evolving world of data, the intersection between Business Intelligence, Business Analytics, Machine Learning, and Artificial Intelligence has created a technological landscape rich in opportunities and complexities. To understand these interrelations, it is crucial to distinguish between these terms and understand how they complement and differ from each other. As an AI-Manager, you will be responsible for advising companies and showing them that AI goes far beyond BI and BA, and that therefore, the investment not only in economics and time, but also in the motivation to take the step and open the doors to change, will be clearly rewarded in the future.

BI and BA, as we have already discussed, focus on data analysis to inform business decisions. While BI tends to look at historical data to inform about the current or past state of a company, BA seeks to predict the future and propose actions based on those forecasts.

Now, let's introduce Machine Learning into the equation. ML is a sub-discipline of AI that focuses on algorithms and statistical models that allow computers to improve at a specific task without being explicitly programmed for it. This is where BA and ML begin to intertwine. While BA uses statistical techniques to foresee future trends, ML can automate and improve these forecasts by training models with large data sets and continuously adjusting them as new data becomes available.

On the other hand, Artificial Intelligence (AI) is a broader field that seeks to create machines that can simulate human capabilities such as learning, reasoning, and perception. ML is just one of the many techniques under the umbrella of AI.

So, how does AI differ from BI and BA? While BI and BA rely on analysis and predefined models to extract insights from data, AI, and particularly ML, allows the creation of systems that learn and adapt automatically from the data they process. AI can go beyond simple predictions, performing tasks such as image recognition, natural language processing, and autonomous decision-making.

5.2.4. The advantages of AI over BI and BA

Adaptability: AI can learn and adapt to new data or situations without human intervention.
Automation: AI can automate tasks that previously required manual analysis, freeing humans for more complex or strategic tasks.
Advanced analysis: With techniques like Deep Learning, AI can analyze data at a depth that goes beyond the traditional capabilities of BI and BA, such as interpreting images or understanding human language.
Personalization: AI can personalize experiences for individual users based on behavioral patterns, something that goes beyond the general analysis capability of BI and BA.

While BI and BA offer valuable tools for data-based analysis and prediction, AI and ML offer the promise of systems that not only analyze but also learn, adapt, and act. Together, these fields offer a comprehensive set of tools that can transform the way businesses operate and serve their customers. And here, dear reader, as an AI-Manager, you must manage the project that will lead the company to optimize, adapt, change, and be a competitive company today and in the future.

5.3. Modern Data Storage: Understanding Data Warehouse and Data Lake

In the era of Big Data, where companies manage increasingly large and complex volumes of data, it is essential to have adequate structures for storing, processing, and analyzing this information. Two central concepts that have emerged in response to this need are the Data Warehouse and the Data Lake. While both serve as repositories for storing large amounts of data, they differ significantly in their design, purpose, and functionality. A Data Warehouse is a structured solution, optimized for analysis and quick query, storing processed and organized data. On the other hand, a Data Lake is a vast repository that stores data in its original format, whether structured, semi-structured, or unstructured. While the former offers an optimized environment for data analysis with defined schemas, the latter provides unprecedented flexibility for storing any type of data in its natural state. Together, these two concepts form the basis of many modern data management strategies, allowing organizations to make the most of their information assets. Let's look at them in detail.

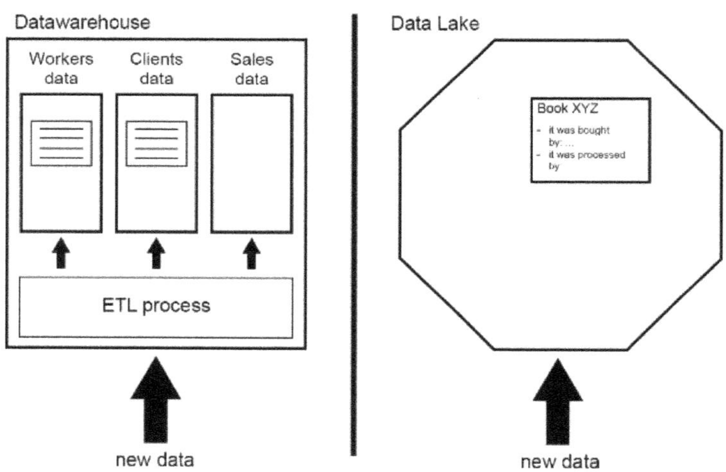

"I will try to explain them to you in more detail and provide several examples so that you can understand each of these types of data storage and thus make the most accurate decisions in your projects as an AI-Manager.

5.3.1. Data Warehouse

Characteristics:
Structured: The data in a Data Warehouse is structured and organized in defined schemas, such as star or snowflake schemas.
Optimized for queries: Designed to support complex queries and data analysis, allowing for quick responses for reports and dashboards.
Historical data: Data Warehouses usually store long-term data, providing a historical view of the information.
ETL process: Before entering the Data Warehouse, data usually undergoes an Extraction, Transformation, and Loading (ETL) process to ensure quality and consistency.
Data consistency: Having a defined schema ensures the consistency and quality of the stored data.
Integration: Can integrate data from multiple sources and systems into a single coherent platform.
Security: Data Warehouses usually have robust layers of security to protect sensitive information.

Clarification 1: A Data Warehouse is a centralized system that collects structured and processable data from different sources for business analysis. It is designed to maintain long-term historical data and provide accurate and consistent information.
Clarification 2: A Data Warehouse is a centralized database used to store large amounts of structured and hierarchically organized data. It is designed to support the generation of reports, analysis, and complex queries.

Use: Data warehouses are ideal for storing historical data and integrating information from multiple sources in a consistent format. They are primarily used for business analysis, strategic decision-making, and report generation.

Examples:
Example 1: A retail company uses a Data Warehouse to store information about daily sales of its products in all its stores. This allows for long-term trend analysis and data-based decision-making.
Example 2: A bank uses a Data Warehouse to store customer financial transactions over several years. This allows identifying fraudulent patterns or detecting business opportunities based on past customer behavior.
Example 3: A telecommunications company uses a Data Warehouse to store detailed records of calls made by customers. This helps analyze usage patterns, identify areas with higher demand, or improve customer service quality.
Example 4: A retail company may use a data warehouse to consolidate daily sales records, customer demographic data, and inventory stocks to analyze historical patterns, identify seasonal trends, or make decisions about inventory management.
Example 5: A financial company may use a data warehouse to consolidate transactional records from different branches or internal systems with the goal of conducting financial analysis or complying with legal regulations related to periodic reporting.

Example 6: A hospital may use a data warehouse to store electronic medical records (EMR), information about previously treated patients, and clinical results to improve care quality through comparative analysis.

5.3.2. Data Lake

Characteristics:
Raw format: Data is stored in its original, unprocessed, or untransformed format.
Data diversity: Can store structured, semi-structured, and unstructured data, such as images, logs, JSON documents, etc.
Scalability: Designed to scale and store petabytes of data without performance issues.
Schema flexibility: Unlike the Data Warehouse, Data Lakes do not require a defined schema at the time of data ingestion. The schema is defined when reading (often called "schema on read").
Exploratory analysis: Ideal for exploratory analysis and discovering patterns in large data sets.
Integration with Big Data technologies: Data Lakes are often compatible with Big Data tools and platforms, such as Hadoop and Spark.
Cost-effectiveness: By using object-based storage and open-source solutions, Data Lakes are often more cost-effective for storing large volumes of data compared to traditional solutions.

Clarification 1: A Data Lake is a centralized repository that stores large volumes of unprocessed data (structured, semi-structured, or unstructured) from various sources. The data is kept without prior transformations until needed for analysis.
Clarification 2: A Data Lake is a centralized repository where large volumes of data in their original, unstructured format are stored. It is a flexible and scalable system that allows storing any type of data and then processing it as needed.

Use: Data Lakes are used to store large amounts of unstructured or semi-structured data, such as text files, images, videos, or raw records. They are primarily used for exploratory analysis and discovering hidden patterns in data.

Examples:
Example 1: A technology company stores all records generated by its web applications (server logs, user data, events) in a Data Lake. This allows for advanced analysis to improve user experience and solve technical issues.
Example 2: A social media company stores all messages and posts generated by users in a Data Lake. This facilitates sentiment analysis, trend detection, and identifying patterns for personalized recommendations or advertisements.
Example 3: A hospital stores unstructured data such as medical images, clinical reports, and electronic patient records in a Data Lake. This allows researchers to access large volumes of data for epidemiological studies or medical discoveries.
Example 4: A social media company may use a Data Lake to store all messages posted by its users in order to analyze emerging trends, detect spam, or conduct large-scale sentimental analysis.

Example 5: An automotive company may use a Data Lake to store all records generated by sensors installed in its vehicles with the goal of analyzing engine performance, identifying potential failures, or predicting future maintenance needs.
Example 6: A scientific team may use a Data Lake to store large volumes of information about the climate (temperatures, precipitation), geography (satellite maps), ecology (biological records) for research related to climate change or environmental conservation.

While a Data Warehouse focuses on storing structured and processable data for specific business analysis, the concept of a Data Lake is more flexible, storing large volumes of unprocessed data from various sources until needed for analysis. In other words, a Data Warehouse focuses on the integration and structured organization of historical data from various sources for business analysis; a Data Lake focuses on the massive and raw ingestion of both structured and unstructured data without prior organization, allowing more free exploration and research."

6. Data Acquisition in 6 Steps

In today's digitalized world, proper data acquisition and management have become an essential component for any project, especially those related to Artificial Intelligence. If this process is carried out in a structured and methodical way, it can be the difference between the success and failure of an initiative. Below, I present a guide in 6 steps to ensure effective data acquisition.

Data Acquisition in 6 Steps:
1. Definition of objectives:
- What is my goal?
- What questions need to be answered?

2. Requirements analysis:
- What data is needed?
- What structure(s) should the data have?
- What types of data? What attributes? Metadata?

3. Internal sources:
- Search for suitable data within the company.
Examples: customer data, transaction data, or employee data.

4. External sources:
- Search for publicly accessible data.
Examples: market research reports, data providers, APIs.

5. Data acquisition plan:
- How do I obtain the data? Cost/effort? Legal requirements?
- Verify the quality or suitability of the data.

6. Data integration:
- Convert data to a uniform format.
- Regularly update the data.

However, while some of these steps, such as the specific search for data or technical integration, can be carried out by specialists such as data scientists or engineers, it is essential that the AI-Manager supervises and understands the entire process. This ensures that the project runs smoothly, that informed decisions are made, and that the team involved is managed effectively.

Key points for an AI-Manager and why:

Definition of objectives: Before starting any project, it is essential to have clarity on the objectives and key questions. This will guide the entire data acquisition process and ensure that efforts are aligned with the company's goals.

Requirements analysis: Determining exactly what data is needed, its structure, and attributes is fundamental. This ensures that no time or resources are wasted on irrelevant data.

Data acquisition plan: This step involves practical and logistical considerations on how to obtain the data. It is crucial for an AI-Manager because it involves aspects of costs, effort, and possible legal barriers. Additionally, ensuring the quality of the data is essential for any AI project.

Data integration: Artificial Intelligence requires clean and well-structured data. Proper integration ensures that data from different sources is in a coherent format and ready for processing and analysis. Although as an AI-Manager you are not in charge of carrying out this operation, you are responsible for checking that the data has the required quality and meets the requirements for the demands and needs of the project.

7. Natural Language Processing (NLP)

Language is one of the most powerful tools that human beings have for communication, sharing ideas, and building societies. From the earliest times, humans have sought ways to store, share, and process information in natural language, from the invention of writing to the creation of libraries and encyclopedias. Humans, to ensure they can communicate and preserve the valuable information, developed languages, both spoken and written, invented machines to capture information in written words, feelings, ideas, and convictions, from writing by hand to the pen, typewriters to computers.

With the rise of digital technologies, and particularly computing, there emerged a need and desire to make machines understand and generate human language. From this aspiration, Natural Language Processing was born.

NLP is a branch of Artificial Intelligence (AI) that focuses on the interaction between computers and human language. Its goal is to enable machines to understand, interpret, and generate text and speech in a language that people use naturally. This has applications in a wide variety of fields, from recommendation systems and search engines to virtual assistants and automatic translation.

To achieve these objectives, NLP employs a combination of computational linguistics and machine learning techniques. As technology advances and more data becomes available, NLP solutions become more sophisticated and accurate.

Currently, NLP is an essential tool for many companies looking to extract value from the large volumes of text data they generate or acquire. Additionally, with increasing global interconnection and the need to communicate in multiple languages, NLP plays a crucial role in breaking down language barriers.

As you continue your study in this fascinating field, you will discover the techniques, challenges, and opportunities that NLP has to offer in the modern era of Artificial Intelligence.

7.1. Chinese Room Argument

The "Chinese Room Argument" is a famous thought experiment proposed by philosopher John Searle in 1980. The argument seeks to question the idea that a machine or computer can truly "understand" language or have "consciousness" simply by being able to process and generate linguistic responses. Let's examine the experiment in detail:

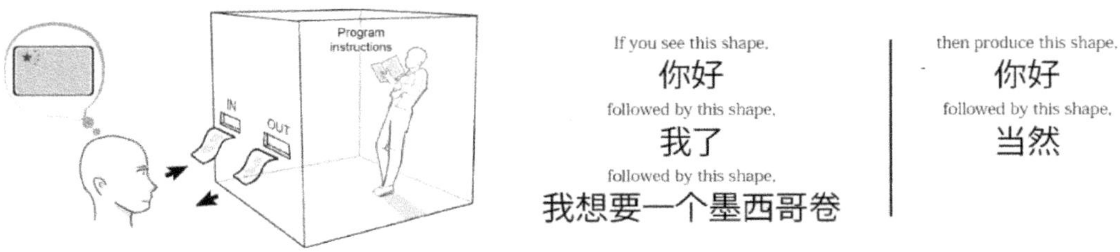

Inspired on: https://k3no.medium.com/the-chinese-room-experiment-2c0d6848f05

Chinese Room Argument
Imagine that you are in a closed room and have an instruction book that tells you how to respond to a series of Chinese symbols passed to you through a slot. You do not understand or speak Chinese, but by following the book's instructions, you can take the symbols that come to you, look in the book what to do with them, and return another set of Chinese symbols as a response. To someone outside the room who does speak Chinese, it might seem that you (or the room) understand the language because the responses are coherent and appropriate. However, in reality, you do not understand Chinese at all; you are simply following instructions without any awareness or understanding of the content.

John Searle proposed this argument to refute the idea that merely processing information, as a computer does, is equivalent to understanding it or having consciousness. According to Searle, even though a machine may process language and give coherent responses, this does not mean it truly "understands" the language or has a "mind" or "consciousness".

This argument has been the subject of much debate in the philosophy of mind and Artificial Intelligence. While some agree with Searle that processing does not equate to understanding, others argue that the analogy is not valid or that "understanding" and "consciousness" are more complex concepts and cannot be simply reduced to the Chinese Room argument.

"*A computer cannot understand and does not have consciousness.*"
- John Searle, 1980.

7.2. Symbolic NLP (Natural Language Processing)

Symbolic NLP is based on the idea that computers can understand human language through the application of predefined rules. Instead of learning from large amounts of data, as is the case with modern methods based on machine learning, symbolic NLP focuses on the use of grammatical rules, dictionaries, and other data structures to analyze and generate language.

A historical and significant example of this approach is the Georgetown-IBM experiment of 1954. This experiment introduced the first automatic translation program, specifically designed to translate from Russian to English. Although the capabilities of this program were limited and based on a restricted set of rules and vocabulary, it represented an important milestone in the early days of NLP.

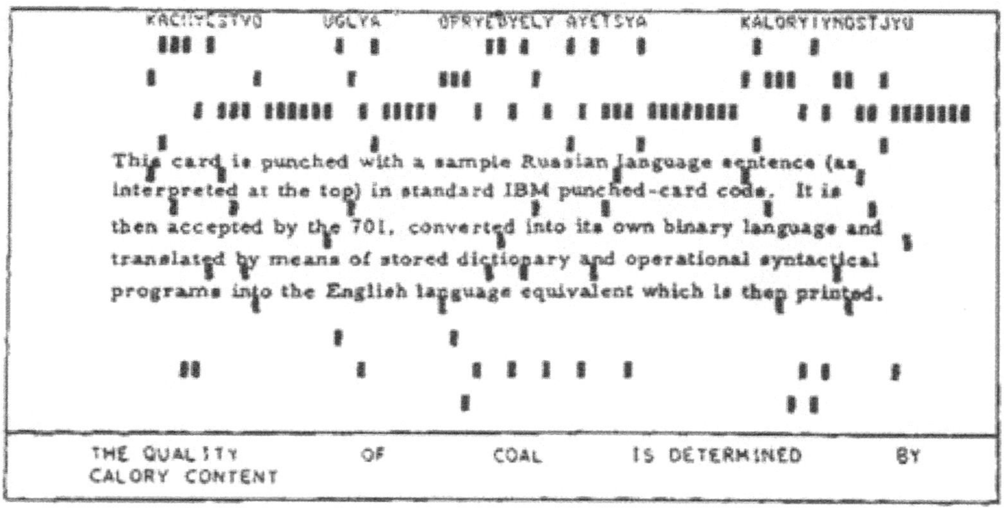

Specimen punched card and below a strip with translation, printed within a few seconds

Image: https://content.teldap.tw/index/?p=422

The experiment demonstrated the possibility of machines performing translation tasks using rules and logic, instead of an intrinsic understanding of the language. However, over time, it was recognized that the purely symbolic approach had its limitations, especially when dealing with rich and complex languages with numerous exceptions and nuances. Despite its limitations, symbolic NLP laid the foundation for future advances in the field, and rule-based methods still find application in certain areas of natural language processing today.

7.3. Statistical NLP (Statistical Natural Language Processing)

Statistical NLP relies on identifying and learning linguistic patterns using ML techniques. Unlike the symbolic approach, which focuses on predefined rules, statistical NLP learns directly from the data, allowing it to adapt and handle the variability and complexity of human language.

NLP can be understood as the intersection between computer science and linguistics. It combines computational algorithms and mathematical models with the study of language, enabling it to process, analyze, and generate text in a way that is coherent and meaningful to human users.

An essential component in many statistical NLP systems is the feature extractor. This component has several functions:

Preprocessing of the text: Before the text can be analyzed or used to train a model, it often needs to be cleaned and transformed. This may include removing punctuation, converting all text to lowercase, and other tasks that facilitate subsequent analysis.

Extraction of relevant terms: Once the text has been preprocessed, relevant terms or features that will be useful for the analysis or task at hand are identified and extracted.

Representation as a vector: For machine learning models to work with text, it must be converted into a numerical form. A common technique is to represent the text as a vector of numbers. For example, the sentence "the ball is round." might be represented by the vector (23, 345, 29, 104), and the sentence "The tree is big." by the vector (23, 943, 29, 430). Each number in the vector represents a feature or term of the text, allowing algorithms and mathematical models to process and analyze the linguistic content.

Statistical NLP has proven to be particularly powerful in a variety of applications, from automatic translation to text classification, and continues to be an active area of research and development in the field of Artificial Intelligence.

ML process taking sentiment analysis as an example:

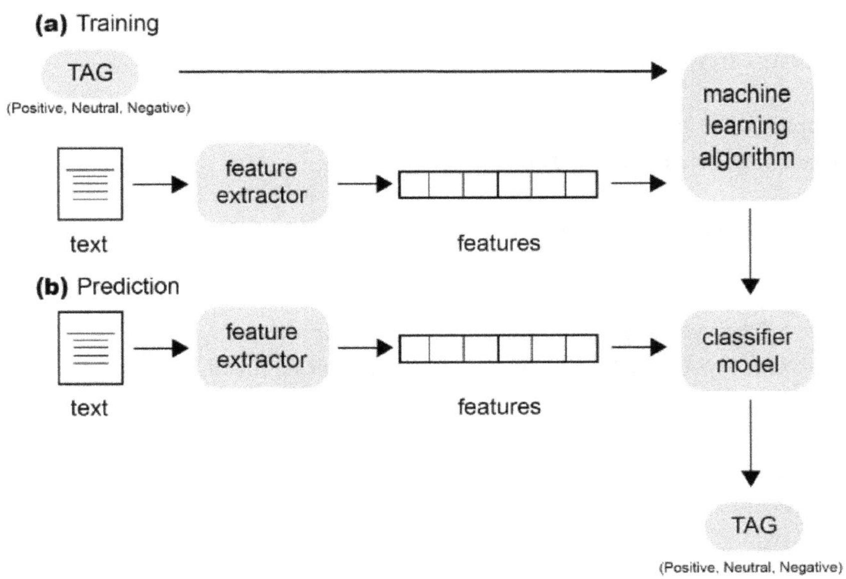

7.4. Main Components of NLP

From what we have learned so far, we can assert that NLP is a discipline that combines computer science, Artificial Intelligence, and linguistics with the aim of enabling machines to understand, interpret, and generate human language. Within NLP, there are two main components that are essential for most applications: Natural Language Generation (NLG) and Natural Language Understanding (NLU).

Natural Language Generation (NLG):
Objective: To generate text autonomously.
Method: Convert numerical representations (such as vectors) into coherent sentences.
Foundation: It relies on sets of rules, relating to symbolic NLP. However, it can also employ statistical NLP techniques.
Characteristics: Although it is a relatively simple process, it has great power and capacity to generate text that appears natural.

Natural Language Understanding (NLU):
Objective: To enable machines to understand human language.
Method: Determine or calculate the underlying meaning of a text.
Meaning: Refers to concepts, entities, emotions, among other aspects of linguistic content.
Characteristics: It is a more complex process compared to NLG, but also has great power and depth in its capacity to interpret and understand language.

It is important to mention that, although Natural Language Generation is a valuable tool, it is rarely used on its own. Often, it is combined with other techniques and processes within NLP to achieve broader objectives, such as the creation of virtual assistants or automatic response systems.

7.5. Examples of Application of Natural Language Generation (NLG) and Natural Language Understanding (NLU)

NLP encompasses various applications in the digital world, especially through NLG and NLU. Below are some notable examples of these applications.

Examples of NLG application (including NLU):

Language Translators:
- Translate text from one language (Language A) to another (Language B).
- Ideally, consider aspects such as sayings, slang, and other linguistic nuances.

Customer Service Chatbots:
- Provide customer support, among other functions. ChatGPT could be considered an evolution of a ChatBot after being massively trained.

Voice Virtual Assistants:
- Control smart home applications (Smart Home) and other functionalities through voice commands.
- Generate responses to inform the user about what has happened or to provide feedback.

Examples of NLU application:

Spam Detection:
- NLU is capable of identifying the purpose of an email, determining whether it is spam or not.

Sentiment Analysis:
- Also known as "Opinion Mining".
- NLU detects the emotion or sentiment conveyed in a text, such as positive, neutral, or negative.
- Additionally, it can identify the feeling towards a specific topic within the text.

Spelling Error Detection:
- NLU primarily identifies grammatical errors in the text.
- It focuses on linguistic rules rather than the actual meaning.
- For example, it detects errors like "The bid fly." and suggests corrections like "The bird fly.".

These examples illustrate the versatility and capability of NLP to enhance and automate language-related tasks in various fields and applications.

7.6. Text Preprocessing

Text, in its natural form, is considered a type of unstructured data. This makes it practically impossible to be processed directly by ML models and algorithms. Therefore, one of the most crucial steps before performing any ML operation with text is preprocessing.

The main objective of preprocessing is to transform these unstructured data into a structured form. That is, to convert text into a format that is easily interpretable and usable by ML models.

Advantages of Preprocessing
Improvement in accuracy: Generally, having well-structured and clean data increases the accuracy and performance of ML models.
Optimization of training time: With preprocessed data, the training of models tends to be faster.
Reduction of data size: By eliminating non-essential or redundant information, it is possible to reduce the amount of data being worked with, which facilitates and speeds up processing.

Disadvantages of Preprocessing
Need for implementation: It is not an automatic process, so it needs to be implemented properly.
Processing time in large data volumes: Although the goal is to speed up subsequent work, preprocessing can take time, especially when dealing with large data sets.

Potential loss of information: If not done correctly, preprocessing can lead to the elimination of important data, resulting in a loss of information that could have been valuable for the model.

Preprocessing is a very important stage in any workflow related to text analysis through machine learning. Although it has its challenges, the potential benefits in terms of model performance and accuracy usually outweigh the drawbacks.

7.7. Sentence Segmentation & Word Tokenization Part 1

Natural language analysis often requires breaking down the text into smaller and more manageable units, but that still retain a coherent meaning. This process is known as sentence segmentation and word tokenization. Both at this point (7.7 and in the next one, 7.8) you must pay close attention not to be confused by the similarity of the cases.

In this case, we will focus on converting text into a sentence.

Main idea: Convert text into the smallest possible form but still make sense.
Procedure:
1. From text to sentence: Sentences in a text are identified and separated.
Sentences are usually separated at points where there are typical punctuation marks of the end of a sentence, such as periods (.), question marks (?) or exclamation marks (!).
Example: From the text "What swims in the sea? A fish.", the sentences ["What swims in the sea?", "A fish."] are obtained.

2. Potential problems: Some text contents may contain periods that do not necessarily indicate the end of a sentence.
Example: In the sentence " The report drafted by Dr. González was presented at the conference.", the point after "Dr." does not indicate the end of a sentence since this is an abbreviation of "Doctor", but it could be misinterpreted as such, resulting in segments like ["The report drafted by Dr", "González was presented at the conference"].

Solutions:
Simple: Ignore these cases, given that a smaller proportion of sentences in most texts will contain periods that do not signal the end of a sentence.
More complex: Perform additional preprocessing, transforming common abbreviations into their full form before segmenting the text. For example, convert "Dr." to "Doctor" before performing the segmentation.

Sentence segmentation and word tokenization are essential steps in text preprocessing for natural language analysis. Although there are associated challenges, especially with punctuation and abbreviations, there are solutions and techniques to address these problems and ensure accurate analysis.

7.8. Sentence Segmentation & Word Tokenization Part 2

In the previous case, we have seen that in-depth text analysis often involves dividing it into more manageable units, which facilitates its processing and subsequent analysis. This is achieved, as in the previous case, through sentence segmentation and word tokenization.

In this case, we will focus on converting sentences into words.

Main idea: Transform text into the smallest possible form, but still retain its meaning.

Procedure:
3. From the sentence to the word: Once the sentences have been identified, the next step is to divide them into individual words.
Words are usually separated at places where there are white spaces.
Example: From the sentence ["The fish swims in the sea"], the words ["The", "fish", "swims", "in", "the", "sea"] are obtained.
4. Potential problems: Some phrases or names may consist of several words that have a joint meaning, despite being separated by white spaces. These are known as collocations.
Example: In the phrase ["We have a meeting in Las Vegas tomorrow"], the words "Las" and "Vegas" together refer to a single place, but they could be misinterpreted as two separate words, resulting in ["We", "have", "a", "meeting", "in", "Las", "Vegas", "tomorrow"]. However, "Las Vegas" is the name of a city and should be treated as a single entity in the analysis of the phrase.

Solutions:
Additional preprocessing: Convert collocations into a single entity. For example, change "Las Vegas" to "Las_Vegas".
Use lists of collocations: containing the most common word combinations. These lists can help identify and properly treat these combinations during tokenization.

While word tokenization is a fundamental step in natural language processing, it is essential to take into account the peculiarities and challenges of language, such as collocations, to ensure accurate and coherent text analysis.

7.9. Word Normalization Generally

The main idea behind this concept is to convert, as far as possible, each word to a standard or unified form to facilitate its analysis and processing.

Main idea: Transform each word into a unified or standard form.

Procedures:
Removal of unnecessary characters
It refers to the elimination of characters that do not contribute meaning to the text or that may interfere with the analysis, such as quotation marks, parentheses, and other punctuation marks.

Case Normalization (Normalization of uppercase and lowercase)
Convert all letters of a word to lowercase to maintain uniformity and prevent similar words from being treated as different due to differences in capitalization. For example, "Pony" becomes "pony".

Stop-word removal (Removal of stop words)
Stop words are common terms that, although essential for the structure of a sentence, often lack meaning on their own in text analysis. Examples of these words include "a", "and", "but", among others. The idea is to remove these words to focus on the more significant terms of the text.

Specific Normalization
In some cases, it is necessary to make specific adjustments to certain words to bring them to a standard form. For example, changing "teléfono" to "telefono" or "corazón" to "corazon". These adjustments often relate to the removal or modification of special characters or accents.

Word normalization is an essential step to ensure that the text is consistent and ready for analysis or any other operation in the field of NLP. This initial preparation can significantly improve the accuracy and effectiveness of the models and algorithms that process the text.

7.9.1. Word Normalization - Stemming

Stemming is a process within word normalization that seeks to reduce words to their root or base form. This method is especially useful for grouping variants of a word, which facilitates their analysis and processing in the field of NLP.

Main idea: Reduce words to their root or base form (also known as "word stem").

Porter Stemmer Algorithm:
- It is one of the most known and used stemming algorithms.
- It works iteratively and is based on rules to reduce words.
- You can get more information about the algorithm on the following website:
https://tartarus.org/martin/PorterStemmer

Examples of stemming with the Porter algorithm:
- "run" remains as "run".
- "running" is reduced to "run".
- "runner" is reduced to "run".

Problems with stemming
One of the challenges of stemming is that, in some cases, it can result in words that do not exist or lack meaning on their own. This is because the process seeks to reduce words without necessarily considering the context or meaning.
For example, "university" can be reduced to "univers".
"electricity" can be reduced to "electr".

Stemming is a valuable technique for word normalization, especially when the goal is to identify and group variants of a word. However, it is essential to be aware of its limitations and consider other techniques, such as lemmatization, if greater accuracy in normalization is sought.

7.9.2. Word Normalization – Lemmatization

Lemmatization is another approach within word normalization that, unlike "stemming" or derivation, seeks to reduce words to their canonical form or lemma. The lemma is the base form of a word, the one we would find, for example, in a dictionary, basically the root.

Main idea: Reduce words to their canonical or base form (also known as "word lemma" or lemma or root).

Algorithm
Lemmatization is based on a list of words (often derived from a dictionary or a lexical database) to transform each word into its corresponding lemma.

Examples of lemmatization:
- "run" remains as "run".
- "runner" remains as "runner" (unlike stemming, which would reduce it to "run").
- "running" is reduced to "run".

Solution to the problems of stemming with Porter
Lemmatization addresses some of the problems associated with derivation, such as the crea-tion of non-existent or meaningless words.
For example, "university" remains as "university" with lemmatization, while stemming would reduce it to "univers".
Similarly, "electricity" remains as "electricity" with lemmatization, but stemming would reduce it to "electr".

Lemmatization offers a more accurate and consistent alternative to derivation in many ca-ses. By being based on a set of known words and their canonical forms, lemmatization ensures that the reduced words are valid and recognizable terms in the language. However, its accuracy usually comes with greater computational complexity compared to stemming.

7.9.3. Word Normalization - Frequently Asked Questions (FAQs)

Word normalization is an essential process in Natural Language Processing, but confusion can arise as to which method to use and how to apply it properly. Below, some of the most common questions about this topic and their answers are presented.

Stemming or Lemmatization?
Stemming: It is a faster process, but it can generate fictitious or non-existent words in the language. It is based on rules and does not take into account the context of the use of a word.
Lemmatization: Although it is a slower process compared to stemming, it is more accurate. The quality of lemmatization largely depends on the quality of the underlying dictionary or lexical database.

Is it possible to overdo word normalization?
Yes! While normalization is essential for many NLP processes, an excess in its applica-tion can strip words or phrases of their original meaning. It is essential to balance normalization with the preservation of the content and meaning of the text.
To determine the appropriate level of normalization, it is useful to carry out tests and adjustments, for example, deciding whether or not to apply case normalization (Case Normaliza-tion) or the removal of stop words (Stop word removal).

Both derivation and lemmatization have their advantages and disadvantages, and the choice between them will depend on the specific use case and the goals of the analysis. In addition, it is crucial to apply normalization carefully to ensure that the text maintains its meaning and relevance.

8. Internet of Things (IoT) (Internet of Things)

In today's digital era, the connection between devices has transcended simple interactions between computers and smartphones. Today, a countless number of devices, from home appliances to vehicles and industrial machinery, are connected to the network, generating, sen-ding, and receiving data in real-time. This technological revolution is known as the "In-ternet of Things" or Internet of Things (IoT).

The concept of IoT refers to the digital interconnection of everyday objects with the internet, allowing these objects to collect and share data without direct human inter-vention. This extended connectivity offers unprecedented opportunities to improve effi-ciency, innovation, and comfort in various areas, from managing smart homes to optimizing supply chains in the industry.

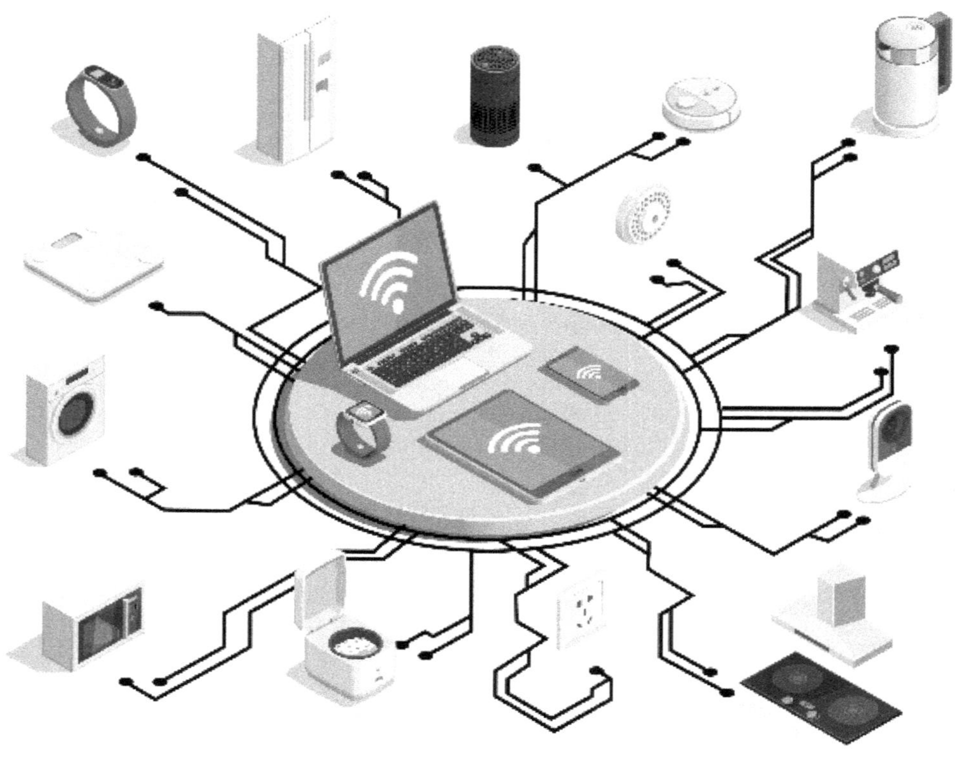

Some key benefits of IoT include:
Automation and control: The ability of devices to communicate with each other facilitates the automation of tasks and processes, leading to greater efficiency and time savings.
Data collection: IoT devices can collect a large amount of real-time data, allowing businesses to make informed decisions based on up-to-date data.
Real-time monitoring: With IoT connectivity, it is possible to monitor the status and performance of devices in real time, which can be crucial in situations like healthcare or fleet management.
Energy efficiency: Many IoT devices, especially those designed for home and industrial environments, can optimize energy use. For example, a smart thermostat can learn user preferences and adjust heating or cooling efficiently, saving energy.
Improvement in quality of life: Devices like wearables can continuously monitor an individual's health, alerting to potential problems before they become emergencies. Also, in smart homes, devices can adapt to the needs of residents to create more comfortable and safe environments.
Resource optimization: In the agricultural sector, for example, IoT sensors can monitor soil and weather conditions to optimize irrigation, reducing water use and ensuring better crops.
Cost reduction: Through monitoring and predictive maintenance, companies can detect and solve problems before they become costly failures. This is especially relevant in the industry, where machinery failure can have high costs.
Improvement in decision-making: With the vast amount of data that IoT devices can collect, businesses and individuals have more information to make decisions based on real and current data.
Integration and communication between devices: IoT devices not only collect data but can also communicate with each other to perform coordinated actions. For example, in a smart home, if a smoke detector is activated, it can communicate with other devices to turn on lights, open windows, and send alerts to the owner.
Innovation and new business opportunities: With the growth of IoT, new opportunities arise to innovate in products and services, creating new markets and business possibilities.

It is important to mention that, although the benefits of IoT are numerous, it is also essential to address the challenges it presents, especially in terms of security, privacy, and standardization. Responsible and strategic adoption of IoT is key to making the most of its benefits. However, with great opportunities also come great challenges. Security and privacy are primary concerns in the world of IoT. With so many connected devices, there is a need to ensure that these devices are protected against external threats and that the data they transmit is handled responsibly and with protection.

In the business realm, the role of the AI-Manager is fundamental to navigate this constantly evolving technological landscape. The implementation of IoT-based solutions requires a deep understanding of the underlying technology, as well as a strategic vision to integrate it effectively into operations and business objectives. With the right combination of knowledge and strategy, IoT has the potential to transform not only businesses but also our daily lives.

How to define IoT?
The Internet of Things is a network of physical devices that…
- … communicate with each other (receive/send commands).
- … generate, exchange, and process data (transactional data).

The term "Internet" has a dual interpretation:
- Internet as representation (network).
- Internet as a communication channel (connection).

IoT rapidly generates large volumes of varied data (-> Big Data), including structured and unstructured data, from text and numerical values to images, video, audio, etc., which can be leveraged for advanced analysis and to gain insights that facilitate decision-making in various areas.

8.1. Components of IoT: The Idea of the "Digital Twin"

The concept behind "IoT components" refers to the fundamental components or elements that make up the IoT Internet. One of the central ideas highlighted is the creation of a "digital twin" (Digital Twin) of the physical device. But what does this really mean?

The "digital twin" is a real-time digital representation of a physical object or system. Imagine having a machine in a factory: as this machine operates, all its movements, temperatures, speeds, and other metrics are recorded and represented in a virtual model in cyberspace. This virtual model, or digital twin, exactly reflects the state and behavior of the machine in the real world.

The idea behind this is that, by having a digital twin, simulations, analysis, and tests can be done without having to interfere with the actual physical object. For example, if we want to know how the machine would react to certain extreme conditions, we don't need to subject the real machine to those conditions; we simply do the simulation on its digital twin.

Additionally, the digital twin serves as an interface between the physical world and data analysis systems. By collecting and analyzing information from the physical device in real time, valuable insights can be obtained, failures predicted before they occur, and the performance of the equipment optimized.

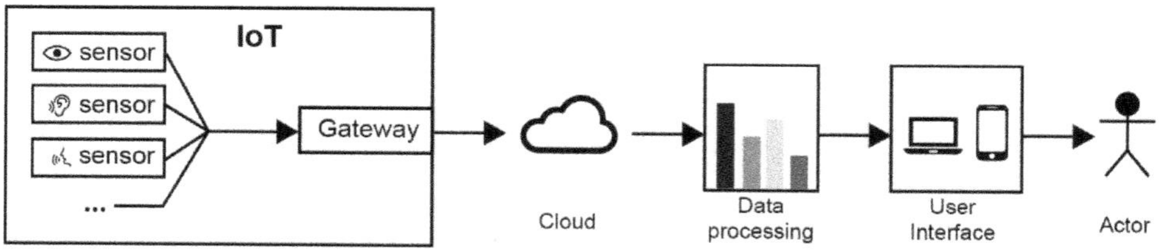

In the context of IoT, this idea is revolutionary. Connected devices not only transmit data, but can also have their own digital twins, allowing for a much more advanced level of analysis, simulation, and response. With thousands or even millions of interconnected devices, having an exact digital representation of each one can transform the way we interact with and understand our environment.

8.2. IoT in Everyday Life

We live in an era where the connection between devices and interaction with technology has transcended beyond simple computers or mobile phones. IoT has become a revolution redefining how we interact with the world around us. From smart watches monitoring our health and physical activity to entire cities adapting and responding to the needs of their inhabitants, IoT is present in almost every aspect of our daily lives.

The basic concept behind IoT is simple: connect physical devices to the network so they can collect, share, and respond to information. However, the implications and applications of this idea are vast and transformative. Devices previously considered "mute," like home appliances or even vehicles, now have the ability to communicate, learn, and make decisions based on the data they collect.

Whether adjusting your home's temperature from your workplace, monitoring your heart rate during a run, or even improving the efficiency of large warehouses and traffic systems, IoT promises not only to enhance our comfort and convenience but also to drive innovation and efficiency in industries and entire cities.

As we continue to advance into the 21st century, the role of IoT in our daily life will become even more prominent, opening doors to possibilities once considered science fiction. However, as we have already discussed, with these opportunities also come challenges, especially in terms of security and privacy. Navigating this new connected world will require a balance between leveraging the advantages of IoT and ensuring that our information and privacy are protected. I emphasize security because, as an AI Manager, you must ensure the security of the company and the data used for AI creation in your projects. For this and other reasons, you must always keep the word security very present in your daily life and not take this point lightly.

8.3. Examples of IoT

Smart Watch:
The smart watch is a clear example of how IoT has been integrated into our daily lives. These devices are not just for telling time; they are true hubs of information and connectivity. Let's delve a little deeper to understand how it works.

- **Sensor:** Smart watches are equipped with multiple sensors. For example, they have an accelerometer that measures changes in speed and direction. They also have GPS to determine the user's location in real-time.
- **Gateway:** This is the phase where data from different sensors are combined or "joined." For example, data from the accelerometer and GPS can be merged to get a more complete picture of the user's movement and location.
- **Cloud:** The collected data is uploaded to the cloud for storage and analysis. This allows the information to be stored not only locally on the watch but also available on other devices and platforms.
- **Data Processing:** Once in the cloud, the data is processed to extract useful information. For example, accelerometer data can be used to calculate the number of steps the user has taken, while GPS can determine the distance traveled.
- **User Interface (UI):** Finally, all this information is presented to the user in an easily understandable way. Smart watches usually have applications that display statistics like steps, distance, heart rate, and other relevant data in graphs and numbers.

Smart Home:
Smart homes represent a revolution in how we interact with our living spaces. In a smart home, technical devices and home appliances can be remotely controlled, whether through a smartphone, tablet, or voice command. This ranges from adjusting lighting and temperature to monitoring the house with connected security cameras.

Smart Warehouses:
In the logistics and storage sector, IoT has enabled the creation of smart warehouses. These warehouses use sensors, cameras, and automated systems to track, organize, and distribute products more efficiently.

Self-Driving Cars:
Autonomous cars, which are vehicles that can operate without human intervention, are made possible by IoT. These vehicles use a combination of cameras, sensors, and advanced algorithms to navigate roads and make real-time decisions.

Smart Cities:
Smart cities leverage the power of IoT to improve the quality of life of their inhabitants. This can include everything from intelligent traffic systems that reduce congestion to energy-saving public lighting systems or sensor networks that monitor air quality in real time.

The Internet of Things is rapidly reshaping the world around us, making everyday objects more interconnected and "smart." These are just some examples of how IoT has infiltrated different aspects of our daily lives. With technological advancements, we are likely to see even more integrations and innovative applications in the future that, despite all their applications today, we may not yet be able to imagine.

8.4. Challenges of IoT

IoT promises to revolutionize the way we live and work, but it also presents a series of challenges that must be addressed to ensure its safe and efficient adoption. Below are some of the main challenges:

Privacy and data protection

- **Cloud connection:** Many IoT devices require a constant connection to the cloud to function properly. While this allows remote access and control, it also raises concerns about the privacy and security of the data that is transmitted and stored in the cloud.
- **Large volumes of data:** The nature of IoT implies the generation of large quantities of data. This abundance can lead to a loss of overview and make it difficult to determine which data are relevant and which are not.
- **Greater number of devices:** The more devices that are connected, the greater the attack surface for cybercriminals. Each device represents a potential entry point for threats.
- **Digital profiling:** With the constant collection of data, there is a risk that companies will create detailed digital profiles of users, which can lead to privacy breaches and commercial exploitation of personal information without the user's knowledge or consent.

Loss of control
- Control without a user interface: A valid concern is whether IoT devices can be controlled (or stopped) without a user interface (UI). If a device starts to function erratically or undesirably, there must be a simple and direct way to intervene.

High costs and administrative effort
- Return on investment: Implementing IoT solutions may require a significant initial investment. In some cases, the return on this investment, in terms of efficiency and savings, may not be immediate and take time to materialize.
- Expert development: The creation and management of IoT infrastructures require the intervention of subject matter experts. These professionals must develop "Pipelines & Interfaces" to ensure the correct communication and functioning of the devices.
- Integration of new devices: As the technological landscape evolves, incorporating new devices into existing IoT systems can present challenges, requiring adaptations and modifications to ensure compatibility. IoT has the potential to drastically change many aspects of our society, but it is essential to address these and other challenges to ensure that its adoption is safe, efficient, and beneficial for everyone. As with any technological advance, it is crucial to balance opportunities with inherent responsibilities.

8.5. Integration of Artificial Intelligence into IoT

IoT refers to a vast network of interconnected devices, from home appliances to vehicles and beyond. These devices continuously collect and transmit data. But, how can we make this data truly useful? This is where Artificial Intelligence, and more specifically, Machine Learning, comes into play.

Main idea: The proposal is to use ML to simplify and enrich the user experience with IoT devices. Instead of just collecting data, devices can learn from it and act accordingly.

Pattern recognition in historical data
ML is excellent at identifying patterns in large data sets. For example, if we consider a wearable device, like a smartwatch:
- Activity on specific days: The device might notice that the user tends to walk or run more on certain days of the week. Does the user regularly exercise on Tuesdays and Thursdays, for example?
- Frequent routes: The device might identify that the user frequently travels certain routes or journeys. Does he have a favorite route for running or walking?

Interpretation of historical data
Beyond simply recognizing patterns, ML can help explain why certain patterns exist.
- Less activity on Sundays: From the data, the device might deduce that the user is less active on Sundays. Is this a rest day for the user? Or are there other factors at play?
- Speed on specific routes: If the device detects that the user runs faster on certain paths, it might try to deduce why. Is that path flatter or has less traffic?

Prediction of future actions
With enough data and identified patterns, ML can begin to make predictions.
- **Health risk:** If the device detects that the user has significantly decreased their physical activity, it could predict and alert possible health risks, such as an increased risk of heart disease.

Recommendations based on learning
One of the most tangible benefits of ML is its ability to offer personalized recommendations.
- **Activity stimulation:** If the device notices that the user is less active on certain days, it might suggest: "How about increasing your activity on Sunday? It could be a good opportunity for an outdoor walk."

The integration of Artificial Intelligence and Machine Learning into IoT not only makes devices "smart," but also turns them into proactive, adaptive, and personalized assistants to enhance the user experience and quality of life. These systems not only understand the habits and needs of the user, but can also anticipate and act accordingly, creating a more intuitive and tailored environment.

8.6. IoT and its intersections with AI

The Internet of Things has emerged as one of the most transformative technological trends of the last decade. It refers to the network of physical devices, from simple household appliances to complex industrial systems, all interconnected and sharing data via the internet. But, what happens when we combine the omnipresence of IoT with the power and processing capacity of Artificial Intelligence? The answer is simple: we enter a new era of possibilities and advancements that redefines how we interact with the world around us. To conclude this topic on IoT, we will summarize it in five points.

Advanced analytics and decision-making
With AI, IoT devices are not limited to simply collecting data; they can interpret it, learn from it, and act based on that learning. For example, a smart thermostat can not only measure the temperature of a room but can also learn the user's preferences and adjust heating or cooling accordingly, optimizing energy consumption and improving comfort.

Enhanced automation and control
AI can take automation to an entirely new level. Imagine an agricultural system that, based on historical data and learned patterns, can predict the best time to plant or harvest and automatically adjust irrigation and fertilization.

Predictive maintenance
In the industrial sector, the combination of IoT and AI can be a real game changer. Sensors can continuously monitor machinery and, using AI algorithms, predict when a part is likely to break or need maintenance, thus reducing downtime and costs.

Personalized experiences
From retail to healthcare, the combination of IoT and AI allows for highly personalized experiences. A retailer could, for example, offer personalized promotions to a customer in real-time based on their previous shopping habits, while a medical wearable could constantly monitor a patient's health and alert doctors to any anomalies.

Smart and sustainable cities
The cities of the future will not only be "smart" in terms of efficiency but also in adaptability and sustainability. Traffic systems that adapt in real-time to road conditions, waste management systems that optimize collection and recycling, or sensor networks that monitor air quality and automatically adjust industrial emissions are just some of the possibilities.

The convergence of IoT and AI represents one of the most exciting and promising mergers in the world of technology. While IoT provides the infrastructure and the ability to collect data from the physical world, AI brings the intelligence and processing power to transform that data into meaningful and valuable actions. Together, these technologies have the potential to reshape entire industries, improve the quality of life, and take innovation to heights we could previously only imagine. However, with these opportunities also come challenges, especially in terms of security, privacy, and ethics. Navigating this new connected and "smart" world will require a combination of technological innovation, responsibility, and forward-thinking.

9. Methods of Artificial Intelligence

In our constant search for technologies that mimic and, on occasions, surpass the capacity of the human brain, we have developed systems and algorithms that take direct inspiration from biology. These systems, known as artificial neural networks, not only replicate the basic structure of our brain but also attempt to emulate its ability to learn and adapt. In this topic, we will explore in detail how Artificial Intelligence, especially through Machine Learning and advanced techniques like Deep Learning and NLP, has been inspired by the complex network of neurons that constitutes our brain, leading to the creation of machines that "think" and "learn" in ways that were previously unthinkable.

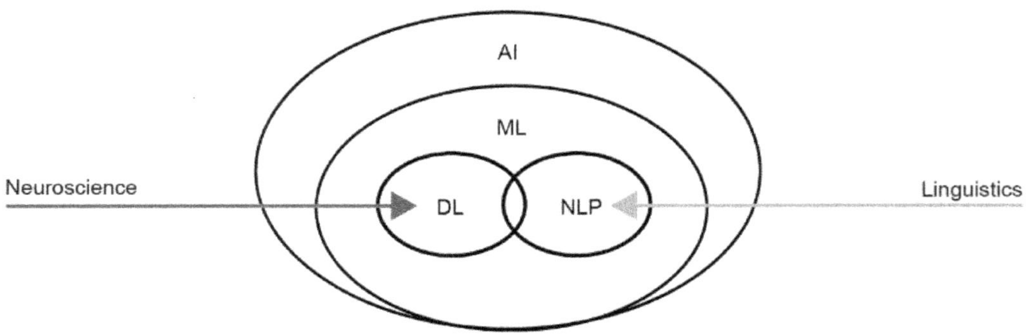

9.1. Artificial Intelligence Methods and their Relation to Neurons

At the beginning of the book, we already discussed intelligence and defined its context in reference to Artificial Intelligence, as well as looking at several examples of its definition and experiments. Now, having reached this point, we will delve deeper into the human brain, in order to understand the functioning of neural networks and how artificial neural networks (Artificial Neuronal Networks (ANN)) resemble our brain.

Excursus: Neurons
Neurons, or nerve cells, are the fundamental units of the nervous system, including the brain. Their main function is to transmit information in the form of electrical impulses.

Function of the neuron: Neurons receive stimuli or information from other cells through structures called dendrites. Once the information is processed, the neuron sends a signal or impulse through a structure called an axon, which in turn connects with other neurons, muscles, or tissues.

Processing in the brain: When these impulses reach the brain, they are processed, and as a result, a response or reaction is generated. For example, if we touch something hot, the neurons transmit this information to the brain, which quickly processes the stimulus and makes us withdraw the hand.

Implicit learning: Through repeated experiences and constant transmission of impulses between neurons, humans learn behaviors and responses. For example, a child can learn not to touch a hot object after having been burned once.

Neural network: In the human brain, a neural network is an interconnected set of neurons that work together to process information and generate responses. These networks are essential for all our cognitive and motor functions.

Artificial Neural Networks
Artificial Neuronal Networks (ANN) are inspired by the functioning of neural networks in the human brain. They are algorithms that attempt to recognize underlying patterns in data sets through a process that mimics how the human brain functions.

Artificial neurons: Like a biological neuron, an artificial neuron receives information, processes it, and passes on a signal. However, instead of electrical impulses, artificial neurons work with weights, activation functions, and thresholds.

Deep Learning: As we already know, DL is a subcategory of Machine Learning that uses networks with many levels (deep layers) to analyze various data factors. Deep neural networks can process information at increasingly complex levels, allowing the identification and classification of intricate patterns.

Natural Language Processing: As we already know, it is a branch of AI that focuses on the interaction between computers and human language. NLP heavily utilizes DL and neural networks for translation, text generation, and semantic analysis.

Artificial neural networks, inspired by the functioning of the human brain, represent one of the most significant advancements in the field of Artificial Intelligence. These networks, especially when used in Deep Learning and NLP applications, have the potential to revolutionize areas such as computer vision, voice recognition, automatic translation, and many others. By understanding and emulating how we process information at the neural level, we are opening doors to machines that can "think" and "learn" in ways previously considered exclusively human.

9.2. Artificial Neural Network (ANN): Imitating the Complexity of the Human Brain

Artificial neural networks are one of the fundamental pillars in the field of Machine Learning and Artificial Intelligence. Inspired by the structure and function of the human brain, ANNs attempt to emulate the way biological neurons process and transmit information. Let's see it in the following image:

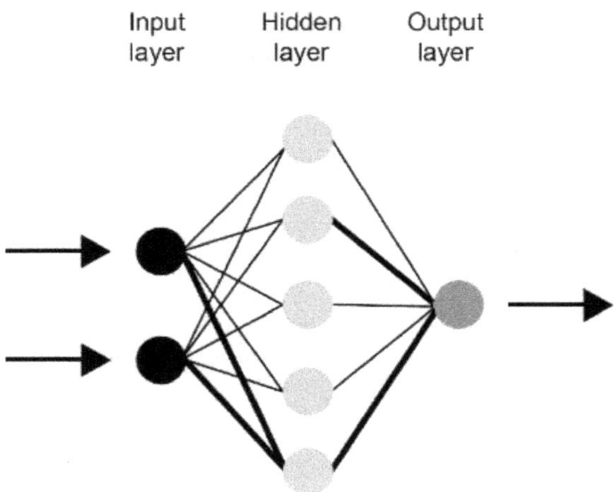

Central idea: The premise behind ANNs is to mimic human brain behavior, particularly in how it processes, learns, and recognizes patterns in data. Just like the brain uses interconnected networks of neurons to interpret stimuli and generate responses, ANNs use artificial "neurons" to process and classify information.

1. Input Layer
- **Data entry:** This is the first layer of the network and receives raw, unprocessed data. It can be any type of data, from image pixels to numerical values of a dataset.
- **Minimal preprocessing:** Unlike other machine learning methods, ANNs can work with data that has had little or no preprocessing, although in practice, they often benefit from some normalization or standardization.

2. Hidden Layers
- **Implicit rules and weights:** These layers contain neurons that establish implicit rules for processing information. Each connection between neurons has a "weight," which is adjusted during training to improve the network's accuracy.
- **Non-human interpretability:** A feature of ANNs is that the rules and patterns they identify are not easily interpretable by humans. That is, we cannot "look inside" an ANN and understand exactly how it is making decisions.
- **Activation function:** Each neuron in these layers has an activation function that determines whether a signal should be transmitted and with what intensity. This function can be as simple as a binary output (0 or 1) or more complex, like the Sigmoid or ReLU function. We have already seen this procedure in previous topics, such as sentiment analysis and image recognition.
- **Multiple hidden layers:** It is common in deep neural networks (a subcategory of ANN) to have multiple hidden layers (Multilayer Perception (MLP)), which allows for identifying more complex patterns.

3. Output Layer
- **Network results:** This layer provides the network's "decision" or outcome. Depending on the task, this output can be a classification, for example, identifying whether an image is a cat or a dog (image recognition) or a regression, such as predicting the price of a house (linear regression).
- **Multiple Outputs:** ANNs can have multiple neurons in the output layer, especially useful when there are multiple classes or categories in classification tasks.

Artificial neural networks represent a bold attempt to emulate the incredible processing capacity of the human brain. Through a structure of interconnected layers and the continuous adjustment of weights during training, ANNs can identify complex patterns and relationships in large datasets, making them a powerful tool in the arsenal of Artificial Intelligence. As we continue to advance in the field of Deep Learning and Machine Learning, we are likely to see even more innovations and applications based on this fascinating structure.

9.3. Deep Neural Networks (DNN) and their specific Typologies

Deep Neural Networks, or "Deep Neural Networks" (DNN), are an extension of basic neural networks that incorporate multiple hidden layers to process information in a more complex and detailed way. Look at the following image.

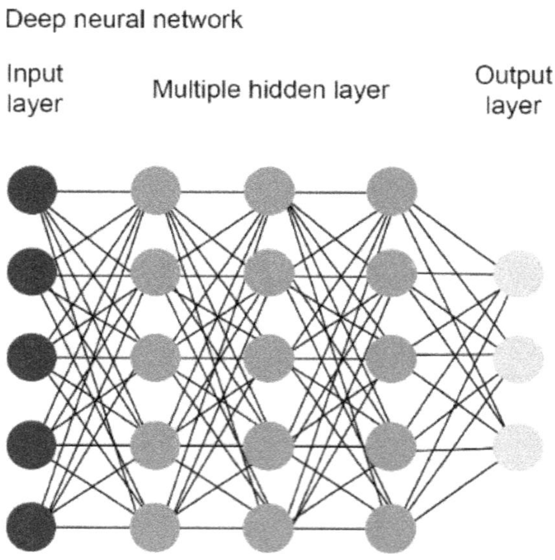

What does "Deep" mean?
The word "Deep" in "Deep Learning" refers to the presence of multiple hidden layers in the network. These additional layers allow the network to learn and model more complex relationships and patterns in the data.

Convolutional Neural Network (CNN)
Main Application: CNNs are ideal for image recognition tasks due to their ability to process visual data hierarchically.
Convolution: The key operation in a CNN is convolution, which involves analyzing an image using small "filters" to break it down into essential features or "Merkmale," such as edges, textures, and patterns.

Classification: Once the image has been broken down into its essential features through convolutions, the network uses these features to classify the image into a specific category, such as identifying whether it is an image of a cat or a dog.

Recurrent Neural Networks (RNN)
Main application: RNNs are ideal for processing sequential data or data with a temporal structure, such as time series or word sequences.
Recurrence: Unlike traditional neural networks, in an RNN, the neurons in the hidden layers have connections that "fire" backwards, allowing the network to have a "memory" of the previous data in the sequence.
Speech Recognition: RNNs are also widely used in speech recognition tasks due to their ability to process data sequences, such as a series of words or sounds.

Transformer Model
Main application: Transformer models are especially useful for tasks of understanding and generating natural language (NLU & NLG, respectively).
Base of popular models: Transformers are the underlying architecture of popular models like GPT (Generative Pre-trained Transformer), which has revolutionized natural language processing tasks.
Central idea: What distinguishes Transformers is their ability to process words or substrings of a text in parallel, assigning different "weights" or "Gewichtung" to different parts of the text according to their relative importance in the context.

Deep neural networks represent the cutting edge of Machine Learning and Artificial Intelligence. Whether processing images, interpreting voice sequences, or understanding and generating language, these networks, in their various forms and architectures, are redefining what is possible in the field of AI. As we continue to delve deeper into their potential, we are likely to see even more innovations and advances driven by these powerful tools.

MODULE 3

Diagrams

Module 3 - Diagrams in Machine Learning

10. Introduction to Visualization in Machine Learning

Data visualization is a powerful tool that plays a crucial role in the field of Machine Learning. Before delving into the various types of diagrams and how they relate to specific algorithms, it is essential to understand why visualization is so vital and how it can influence the decision-making process and the understanding of algorithms and data. As an AI-Manager, it is very important that you have a broad knowledge of this field, as you, as a Project Manager, must be able to read and interpret data, to ultimately make the correct decision and above all be able to advise and guide companies on the path of adaptation. Remember that the company trusts you with much more than a budget, the company trusts you absolutely everything when it decides to take the step of implementing Artificial Intelligence, and, although it may be a small project today, tomorrow it will be a larger and more important one. Therefore, with every step that the company takes to implement Artificial Intelligence, it is putting everything at stake following your advice and guidance. If you do not do a good job, whether due to lack of professionalism, motivation, or lack of training and/or preparation, it is your fault, not the company's. It is your duty to be professional, well-trained, and well-prepared. There is a saying that goes, "don't sell chocolate if you can't compete with the Swiss." Well, it doesn't exist, I just made it up, but it still fits perfectly in this case. The important thing is that you understand the importance of this point, that you understand that this is your main task and that the success of your projects, as well as the success of the companies you work for, depend on your knowledge and skills in this field. Reading data, interpreting it, making predictions from it, and decision-making is your day-to-day. Now it only depends on you, on how well you prepare to be an AI-Manager. I must tell you that in this aspect is where many of those who call themselves "AI-Managers" fall short. Now, let's get back to what's important.

* ***Note:*** *all the notebooks of the diagrams I'm going to show you next can be downloaded for free from my website for your training. THEY ARE NOT FOR COMMERCIAL USE.*

10.1. Importance of Visualization in Machine Learning

Understanding data: Before applying any Machine Learning algorithm, it is vital to explore and understand the data we are working with. Visualization allows us to identify patterns, trends, and possible anomalies that might not be evident at first glance or through basic statistical analysis.

Interpretation of results: Once a model has been trained, it is vital to be able to interpret its results. Through graphs and visualizations, we can better understand the model's behavior, identify areas where it performs well, and others where it may need improvement.

Communication: Not everyone involved in a Machine Learning project will be an expert in the field. Visualizations allow for effective and efficient communication of findings, results, and decisions to different stakeholders, such as executives, other departments, or clients.

Problem diagnosis: With the help of appropriate visualizations, we can diagnose problems in the model, such as overfitting or underfitting, and make informed decisions on how to improve the model.

10.2. Benefits of Using Diagrams to Understand and Communicate

Clarity and speed: A good diagram can convey an idea or concept quickly, avoiding misunderstandings that could arise from verbal or written descriptions.

Facilitating decision-making: In the business world, where time is crucial, clear and concise visualizations can help decision-makers quickly understand a problem or situation and act accordingly.

Engagement and retention: Visualizations are engaging and can help keep the audience's attention. In addition, people are more likely to remember information presented visually compared to information conveyed verbally. It is well known that when learning, it is easier to learn with images than with numbers or words. So when you present a visualization, for example, of clustering using k-Means, it will be much easier for people to understand what is happening in the process. This, thanks to my years of experience as a professional trainer, I can assure you will save you many questions in a meeting.

Highlighting valuable insights: Through effective visualization, important insights or discoveries in the data that might have gone unnoticed otherwise can be highlighted.

Visualization in Machine Learning is not just a tool to make data and models "pretty." It is an essential tool that facilitates understanding, analysis, and effective communication in the field of machine learning. As we have progressed through the book's topics, we have seen how different types of diagrams fit different situations and algorithms, and how they can be used to maximize the impact and understanding of our models and data. Now let's dissect the different groups of algorithms that exist so that you better understand everything learned so far.

11. Scatter Plots

Scatter plots, also known as Scatter Plots, are one of the most fundamental and versatile tools in data visualization. These graphs show individual points distributed along Cartesian axes, generally representing two variables. Each point on the graph represents an observation, and its position is determined by the value of the two variables being compared.

11.1. Concept and Utility

Two-dimensional representation: Scatter plots allow visualizing the relationship between two quantitative variables. If more variables are available, multiple graphs can be created, or dimensionality reduction techniques can be used to represent them in two dimensions.
Pattern identification: One of the main utilities of these graphs is to identify patterns in the data. If the points tend to cluster in a certain way or form some structure, that may indicate a relationship between the variables.
Outlier detection: Points that deviate significantly from the general pattern are easily visible in a scatter plot, allowing for the identification of atypical values or anomalies in the data.
Verification of assumptions: In many algorithms and statistical techniques, a linear relationship between variables is assumed. Scatter plots are ideal for visually verifying these assumptions.

11.2. Related Algorithms

11.2.1. k-Means and other clustering algorithms: These algorithms seek to group data into clusters or groups based on similarity. In a scatter plot, it is possible to visualize how these clusters have formed and whether the algorithm has successfully separated the data. For example, after applying k-Means, you can color the points in the scatter plot according to the cluster they belong to visualize the separation.

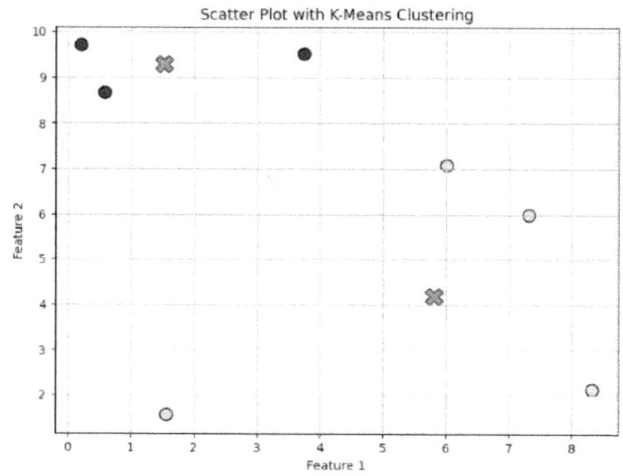

11.2.2. Linear and Polynomial Regression: These algorithms seek to find a linear or polynomial relationship between two or more variables. By visualizing the data in a scatter plot and drawing the regression line or curve, you can visually assess how well the model fits the data. If the regression line closely follows the trend of the points, the model is probably adequate. If not, it may be necessary to consider more complex models or check the assumptions.

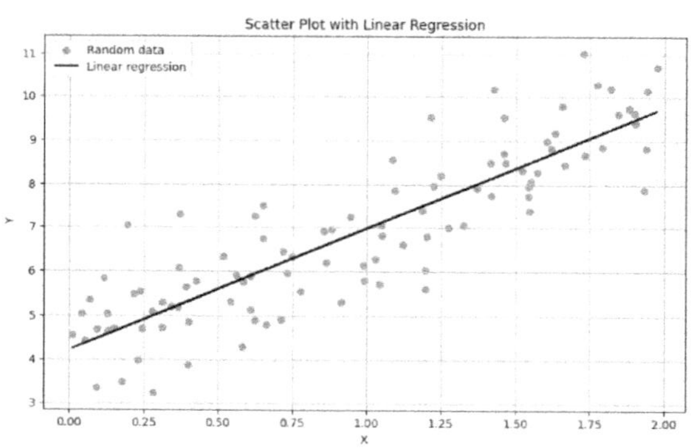

11.3. Practical Example

Let's assume you have a dataset with housing prices and their size in square meters. When using a scatter plot to visualize these data, the X-axis could represent the size of the house and the Y-axis the price. By observing the chart, you could identify if there is a trend (for example, as the size of the house increases, so does the price). If you decide to apply a linear regression, the resulting line would show the estimated relationship between size and price. Let's see it with an image.

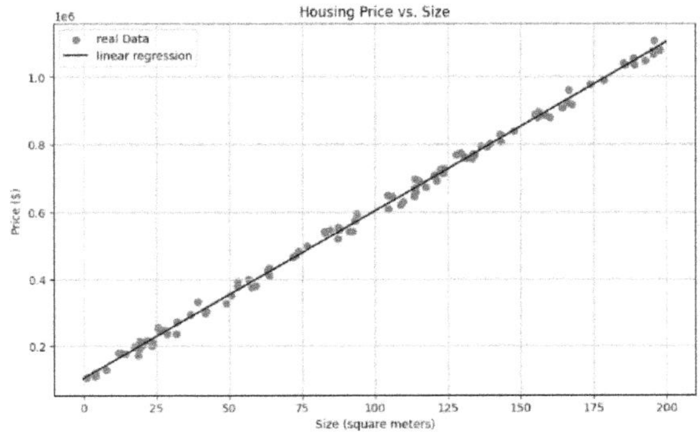

Scatter plots are an essential tool in the arsenal of any data scientist or Machine Learning professional, and for you, as an AI-Manager, they are essential. They are simple yet powerful, and their ability to reveal patterns and relationships in data makes them invaluable for exploration and initial analysis.

12. Histograms and Bar Charts

Histograms and bar charts are essential tools for visualizing and understanding the distribution and frequency of data. Although often confused due to their similar appearance, they have distinct uses and meanings. If you have already worked with other programs, even at a basic level like Excel, this visualization might be more familiar to you. Let's break down these concepts and understand how they relate to Machine Learning.

12.1. Histograms

A histogram is a graphical representation of the distribution of a set of data. It is primarily used to represent continuous data, divided into intervals or "bins," and to show the frequency with which data occur in each interval.

Characteristics and Utility:
Data Distribution: Histograms are essential for understanding how data are distributed. They allow quick identification of whether the data follow a normal distribution, are skewed to the left or right, or show multiple peaks.
Identification of Outliers: If there are intervals with unusually high or low frequencies, this may indicate the presence of atypical values.
Interval Selection: The choice of the number of intervals can influence the interpretation of the histogram. Too many intervals can show unnecessary variability, while too few can hide important details.

let's take a look at the diagram on the next page.

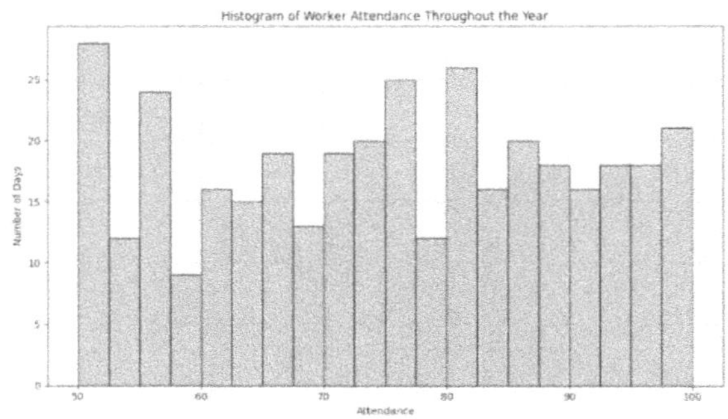

12.2. Bar Charts

A bar chart represents categorical data using rectangular bars with lengths proportional to the values they represent. Unlike a histogram, it deals not with intervals, but with specific categories.

Characteristics and usefulness:
Comparison between categories: Bar charts are ideal for comparing different categories or groups. For example, you could use a bar chart to show the sales quantity of different products.
Clear visual representation: Since each bar represents a category, it's easy to quickly identify and compare the differences between them.
Ordering: The bars can be arranged in descending or ascending order to facilitate interpretation and highlight the most relevant categories.

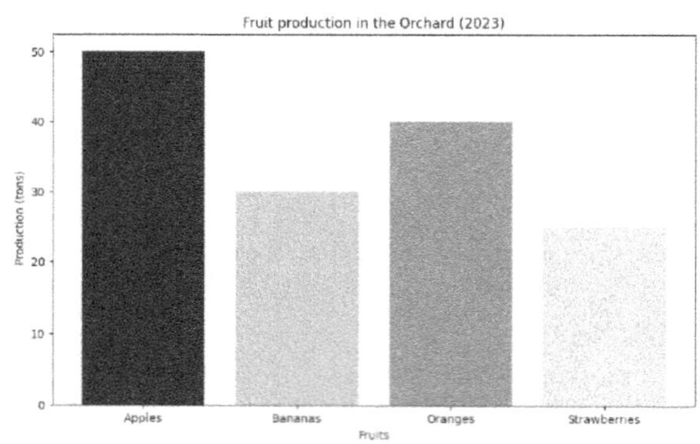

12.3. Related Algorithms

12.3.1. Kernel Density Estimation (KDE): Although not a histogram itself, KDE can be considered a smoothed version of a histogram. It is used to estimate the probability density function of a continuous random variable. This technique can be useful for visualizing data distribution in classification and regression problems.

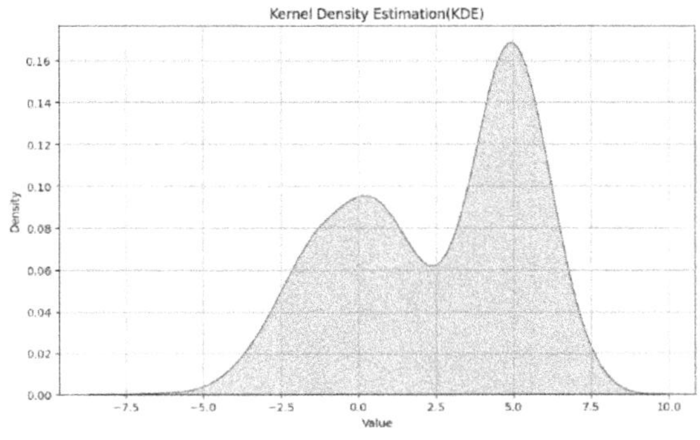

12.3.2. Naive Bayes: It is a classification algorithm that works well when features are categorical. A bar chart can be useful to visualize the frequency of different categories in the dataset and understand how Naive Bayes uses them to make predictions. Next, I will graphically represent a simplified scenario of Naive Bayes for the classification of emails. In this example, I will assume that we have a set of emails with the presence or absence of the words "offer" and "discount". The emails will be classified as "spam" or "not spam" based on these words. I will use a scatter plot to visualize the presence/absence of these words in emails and how they are classified into "spam" or "not spam".

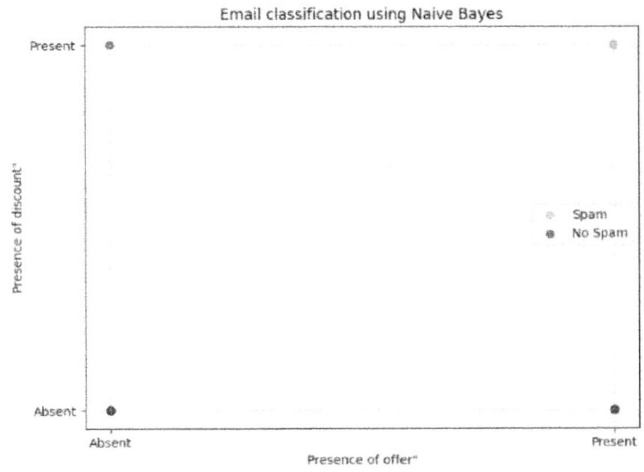

12.3.4. Practical Example

Imagine you are analyzing the results of a survey on media consumption habits in different age groups. A histogram could show the age distribution of the respondents, allowing identification of whether there are age groups more represented than others. On the other hand, a bar chart could be used to represent the number of people in each age group who prefer a specific type of medium, for example, television, radio, digital media.

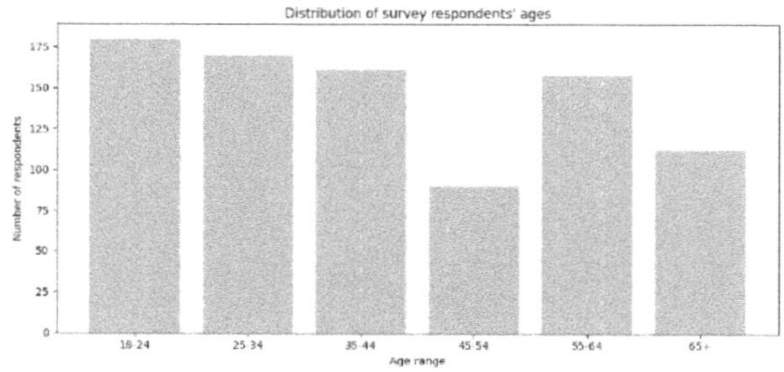

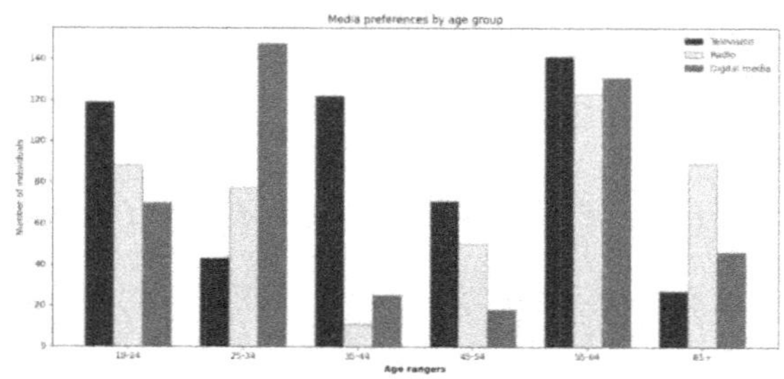

Both histograms and bar charts are fundamental tools in data visualization. They help to understand the structure and characteristics of data, facilitating decision-making in the process of modeling and Machine Learning analysis.

13. Box-Plots

Box plots, commonly known as Box-Plots, are a standardized graphical tool that offers a schematic view of the distribution of a data set based on a summary of five numbers. These five numbers are the minimum, the first quartile (Q1), the median, the third quartile (Q3), and the maximum. Box-Plots provide a visual representation of the dispersion and centrality of data and are particularly useful for identifying outliers and understanding data variability.

13.1. Concept and Utility in Outlier Detection

Distribution and Dispersion: The Box-Plot gives us a quick overview of data dispersion and its central tendency. The central "box" of the chart represents the interquartile range (IQR), which is the difference between Q3 and Q1, and offers a view of where most data are located.

Identification of Outliers: One of the most significant benefits of Box-Plots is their ability to highlight outliers. These are typically represented as individual points outside the "whiskers" of the chart. The whiskers are usually defined as 1.5 times the IQR above Q3 and below Q1, and any data outside these limits is considered an outlier.

Comparison between Groups: Box-Plots are exceptional for comparing data distribution among different groups or categories. By placing multiple Box-Plots side by side, we can quickly compare median, dispersion, and outliers between groups.

13.2. Related Algorithms

Anomaly detection-based algorithms: Identifying outliers is crucial in anomaly detection. Algorithms like the nearest neighbor-based anomaly scoring method or the matrix factorization method can benefit from an initial exploration with Box-Plots to understand where these potential anomalies are located.

13.3. Practical Example

Suppose you are analyzing employee salaries in a company and want to understand salary disparity among different departments. Using Box-Plots, you could represent the salary distribution of each department in a single graph. This would allow you to quickly compare median salaries, identify if there are departments with greater variability in salaries, and detect if there are atypical or extreme salaries in any of the departments.

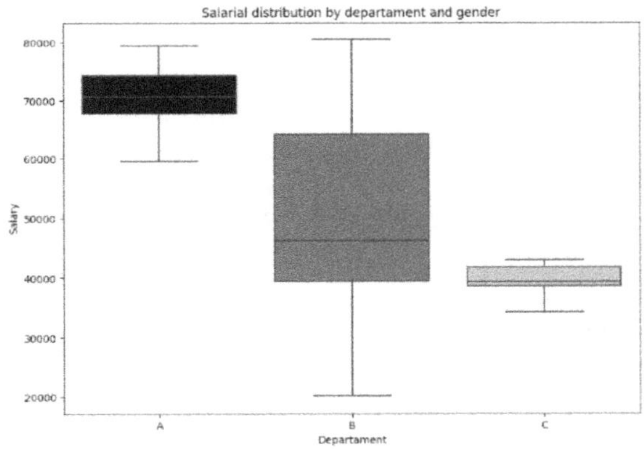

Additionally, if you suspect gender-based wage discrimination, you could divide each box plot by gender, allowing you to compare the wage distribution between men and women within each department.

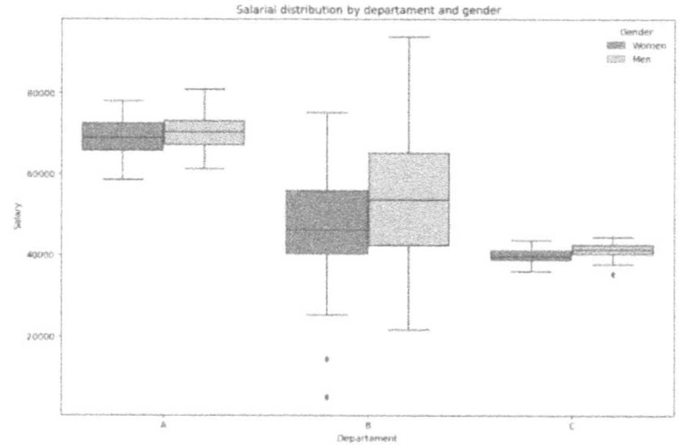

Box plots are a powerful and versatile tool in data visualization. They offer a compact and efficient way to represent and compare distributions, being especially useful for identifying outliers and understanding data dispersion. Their ability to compare multiple groups makes Box-Plots an essential tool in any analysis project or Machine Learning.

14. Receiver Operating Characteristic (ROC)

ROC curve diagrams are an essential tool for evaluating and comparing the performance of classification models, especially in contexts where classes are imbalanced or when choosing a decision threshold is critical. The ROC curve is a graph that shows the performance of a classification model at all possible classification thresholds.

Here is a ROC curve for a decision tree trained with simulated data. The orange line represents the ROC curve of the decision tree, and the diagonal blue line represents a random classifier.

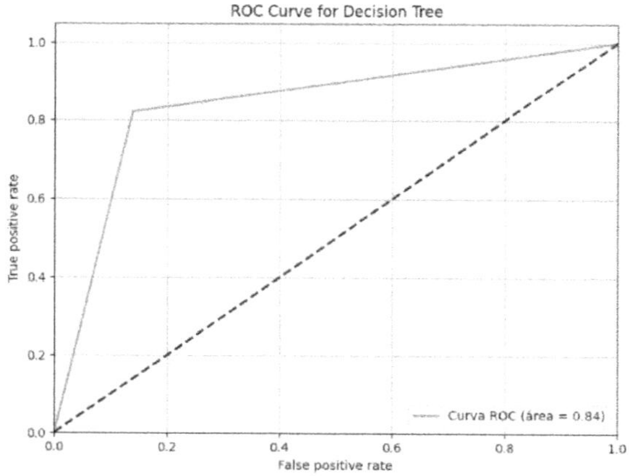

The area under the curve (AUC) for the decision tree is 0.61, indicating that the performance of the decision tree is better than a random classifier.

Keep in mind that these results are specific to this simulated data set and may vary with different data sets or decision tree settings.

14.1. Concept and utility in classification

Sensitivity vs. specificity: The ROC curve plots the true positive rate (sensitivity) as a function of the false positive rate (1 - specificity) for different cutoff points. A perfect classification tool would result in a curve that passes through the upper left corner of the graph, meaning a true positive rate of 1 and a false positive rate of 0.

Area under the curve (AUC): A commonly used metric along with the ROC curve is the AUC, which represents the area under the ROC curve. A perfect model has an AUC of 1, while a random model has an AUC of 0.5. The higher the AUC, the better the overall model.

Model evaluation: The ROC curve is useful not only for evaluating the performance of a single model but also for comparing multiple models. By plotting several ROC curves on the same graph, we can visually compare and contrast the performance of different models.

Threshold selection: In many practical problems, adjusting the decision threshold can be essential to achieving a balance between sensitivity and specificity. The ROC curve helps visualize this balance and choose an appropriate threshold according to the needs of the problem.

14.2. Related Algorithms

All classification algorithms: Any classification algorithm that produces probabilities or scores, such as logistic regression, support vector machines (SVM), neural networks, decision trees, among others, can be evaluated with an ROC curve. It is especially useful in contexts where the costs of false positives and false negatives are different.

14.3. Practical Example

Imagine you are developing a model to detect a rare disease in patients based on certain medical characteristics. Since the disease is rare, most patients do not have it, leading to an unbalanced data set.

After training your model, you want to evaluate its performance. If you simply use accuracy as a metric, the model might appear very accurate by just predicting that no one has the disease. But this would be a grave mistake, as it would not detect sick patients.

By plotting your model's ROC curve, you can visualize how it behaves at different thresholds. If the AUC is significantly greater than 0.5, it indicates that the model has discriminative power. From the curve, you can also choose a threshold that maximizes the true positive rate while keeping the false positive rate at an acceptable level.

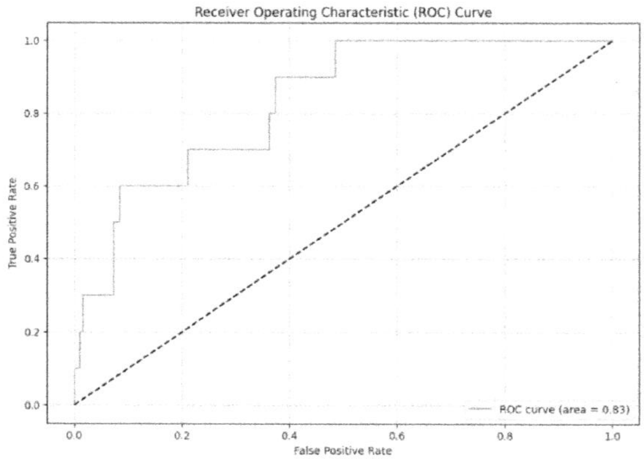

As you can observe, the curve is above the diagonal line, indicating that the model has discriminative power. The area under the curve (AUC) is 0.83, suggesting that the model performs well in discriminating between patients with and without the disease.

From this curve, you could choose a threshold that maximizes the true positive rate (sensitivity) while keeping the false positive rate at an acceptable level. For example, if it is crucial to identify most patients with the disease (even at the expense of some false positives), you could select a threshold that gives a high true positive rate. On the other hand, if minimizing false positives is essential, you could opt for a more conservative threshold.

Remember that the choice of threshold depends on the clinical context and the consequences associated with false positives and false negatives.

As you will have understood, ROC curve diagrams and the AUC are indispensable tools in the toolbox of any data scientist or Machine Learning professional working with classification, and now also for you as an AI-Manager. They provide a more complete and nuanced view of model performance than traditional metrics and are essential for making informed decisions in practical problems.

15. Correlation Matrix and Heatmaps

When working with datasets with multiple features, it is essential to understand how these features relate to each other. The correlation matrix and heatmaps are powerful tools for visualizing and understanding these relationships, allowing us to identify patterns, redundancies, and potential problems in our data.

15.1. Correlation Matrix

A correlation matrix is a table that shows the correlation coefficients between variables. Each cell of the matrix shows the correlation between two features, and each feature is compared with itself and all other features of the dataset.

Features and utility:
Values between -1 and 1: The correlation coefficient ranges from -1 to 1. A value close to 1 implies a strong positive correlation: as one feature increases, the other does too. A value close to

-1 implies a strong negative correlation: as one feature increases, the other decreases. A value close to 0 implies a lack of correlation.

Identification of linear relationships: It is important to understand that correlation, especially Pearson correlation (the most common), measures linear relationships. If the features have a non-linear relationship, the coefficient could be misleadingly low.

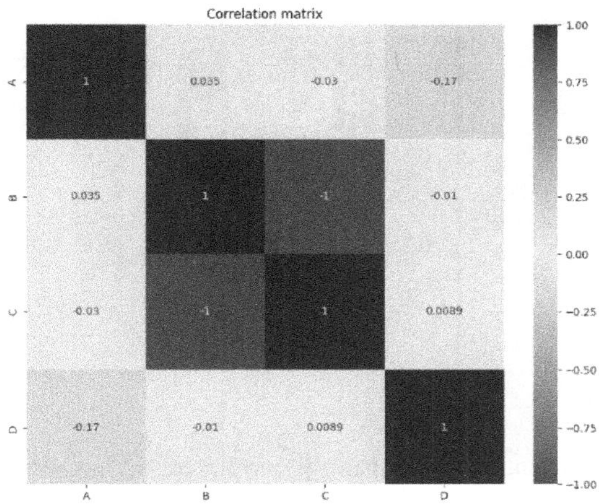

15.2. Heatmaps

A heat map is a graphical representation of data where individual values contained in a matrix are represented as colors. They are perfect for visualizing correlation matrices because they allow you to quickly see which variables are strongly correlated.

Features and utility:
Intuitive visualization: The colors (often on a cold to warm scale) provide a quick and easy way to identify which features are strongly correlated and which are not.

Easy comparison: When looking at a Heatmap, you can quickly identify which features have similar correlation patterns and which differ.

let's take a look at the diagram on the next page.

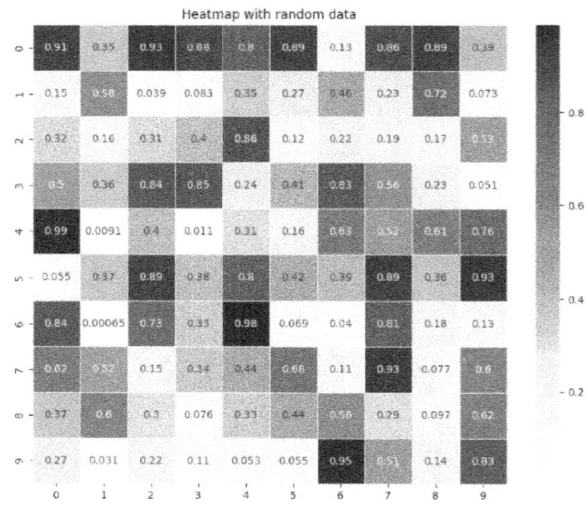

15.3. Related Algorithms

Feature Selection: If two features are strongly correlated, adding both to the model might be redundant. Correlation matrices can help to identify and eliminate redundant features, which can improve the efficiency and accuracy of the model.

Multiple Linear Regression: In linear regression, multicollinearity (when two or more features are strongly correlated) can be a problem. Identifying and addressing these correlations is crucial for obtaining an accurate and stable model.

15.4. Practical example

Suppose you are working on a project to predict housing prices based on different features like size, number of rooms, age of the house, and distance to the city center. Before building your model, you decide to create a correlation matrix to understand how these features relate to each other.

After visualizing the correlation matrix with a heatmap, you observe that the size of the house and the number of rooms have a strong positive correlation. This makes sense, as larger houses tend to have more rooms. Since these features provide similar information, you might consider using only one of them in your model to avoid redundancies.

let's take a look at the diagram on the next page.

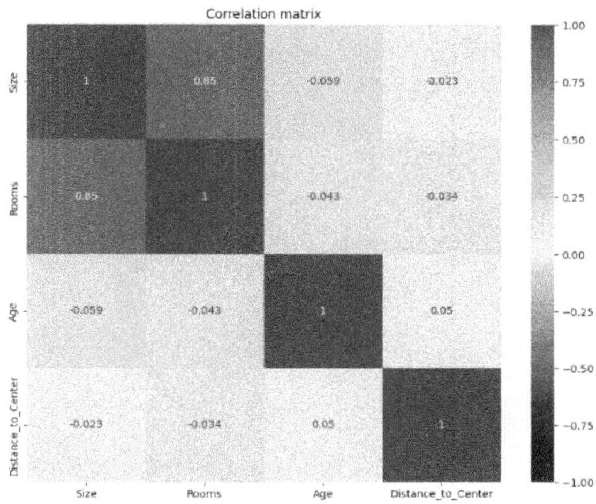

Correlation matrices and heat maps provide a clear and quick view of the relationships between features, aiding in feature selection, problem identification, and overall model improvement. For these reasons, just like other diagrams and types of visualization, correlation matrices and heat maps are also essential tools. As you can see, data analysis, knowing how to read them, interpret them, as well as having a good understanding of them, is a very important task for an AI-Manager, since as you have seen, and from the beginning of the book, data accompany us at every step, in every topic, and at every point. Having great skill in the field of data will open many doors for you, and not only that, but it really qualifies you as a true AI-Manager and this will always put you in a better position compared to other AI-Managers.

16. Tree Diagrams

Tree-based algorithms are an essential family within Machine Learning. These algorithms divide the feature space into regions, making decisions based on questions about the data's features. Tree diagrams allow visualizing these divisions and decisions, facilitating the interpretation and understanding of how the model reaches its conclusions.

16.1. Concept and Utility

Hierarchical Structure: A tree is composed of nodes and branches. Each node represents a question or decision based on a feature, and the branches represent the possible answers to that question.

Terminal Nodes or Leaves: These are the final nodes of the tree where there are no more questions and a final decision is made. In the case of a classification Decision Tree, the decision will be a class label. In the case of regression, it will be a value.

Remember that:

- Supervised Learning:
  - Classification = Labels
  - Regression = Values (Numbers)

Intuitive Visualization: One of the major attractions of Decision Trees is their interpretability. Through a tree diagram, even someone without deep technical knowledge can follow the model's decisions and understand how a conclusion is reached.

16.2. Related Algorithms

Decision Trees: This is the base and simplest algorithm of this family. It makes decisions by dividing the feature space based on questions about these features.

Random Forest: This technique uses multiple decision trees, each trained with a random sample of the dataset. Although visualizing an entire forest can be overwhelming, it is often helpful to visualize some individual trees to understand the decisions being made.

Tree Boosting: Techniques like XGBoost or LightGBM use a series of trees, where each tree attempts to correct the errors of the previous one. As with random forests, although it is complicated to visualize the entire model, a visual idea can be obtained by visualizing some of the individual trees.

16.3. Practical example

Imagine you are building a model to predict whether a customer will buy a product based on features like age, income, and number of previous purchases. You decide to use a decision tree and, after training your model, you want to understand how it makes decisions.

When visualizing the tree diagram, you can see that the first node (or root node) divides customers based on the number of previous purchases. Those with more than 5 previous purchases go towards one branch, while those with 5 or less go towards another. As you descend through the tree, you see more divisions based on age and income.

This tree allows you to understand, for example, that younger customers with higher incomes and a history of frequent purchases have a high probability of buying the product, while older customers with lower incomes and few previous purchases have a low probability.

Let's look at the example with the three related algorithms I mentioned earlier: Decision Tree, Random Forest, and Tree Boosting using XGBoost.

Example with Decision Tree:

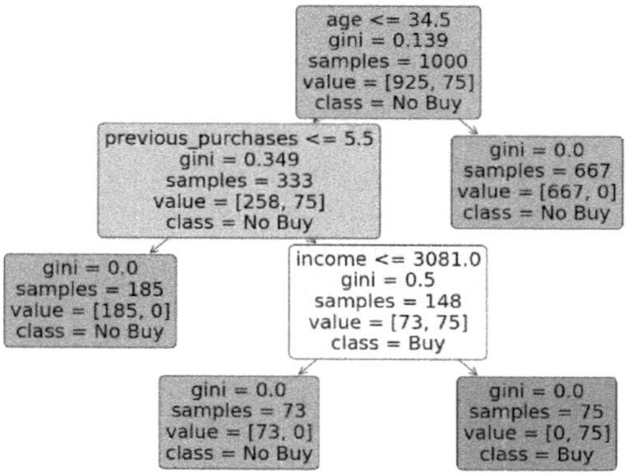

Example with Random Forest:

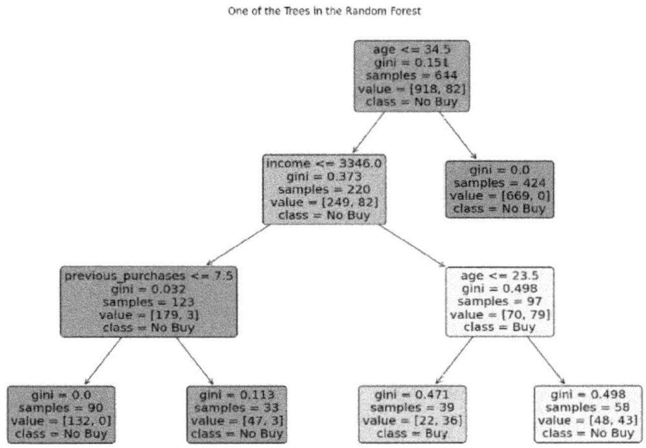

Example of Boosting using XGBoost:

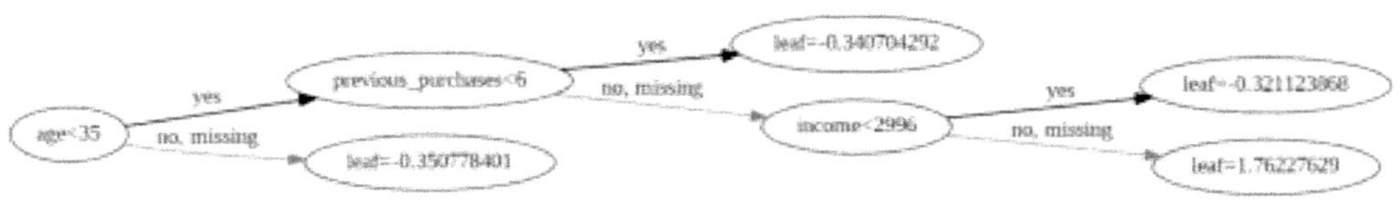

Tree diagrams provide a visual and intuitive window into the internal logic of tree-based algorithms. They are often used. They allow professionals, and also non-technical stakeholders, such as your colleagues or clients, who often do not know what you are talking about, to understand and trust the model, facilitating interpretation, validation, and communication of results.

17. Dimensionality Reduction and Visualization

As we advance in the data era, it is common to encounter high-dimensional data sets, I mean huge data tables. These data can be difficult to analyze and visualize due to the "curse of dimensionality." Dimensionality reduction techniques seek to transform these high-dimensional data into a lower-dimensional representation, preserving, as much as possible, the inherent structures and relationships between the data. Basically said, they reduce the table to a smaller size while preserving the most important data, so these reduced representations are more manageable and can be visualized effectively.

17.1. Introduction to Techniques like PCA and t-SNE

PCA (Principal Component Analysis):
PCA is a linear technique that seeks to find the directions (or components) in the data that maximize variance. It transforms the data by projecting them onto these principal components.

Utility: In addition to dimensionality reduction, PCA is used for data visualization, noise removal, and uncovering important structures in the data.
Visualization: By reducing the data to two or three principal components, they can be visualized in a 2D or 3D scatter plot.

t-SNE (t-Distributed Stochastic Neighbor Embedding):
Concept: Unlike PCA, t-SNE is a nonlinear technique that preserves local relationships between data. It seeks to ensure that points close in high-dimensional space are also close in reduced space.
Utility: It is especially useful for visualizing clusters or groups in high-dimensional data.
Visualization: As with PCA, after reducing the data to two dimensions using t-SNE, they can be visualized in a 2D scatter plot.

17.2. Related Algorithms

PCA: It is often used before applying supervised or unsupervised learning algorithms to reduce dimensionality and speed up training. In addition, by removing components with low variances, it can help reduce noise. This is a task that I advise you to perform without hesitation when working with very large data.

t-SNE: Commonly used in exploratory data analysis to visualize clusters or groups in complex data sets, such as genetic or image data.

17.3. Practical example

Suppose you are working with a data set that contains gene expression measurements for thousands of genes in different tissue samples. You want to visualize if the samples cluster according to tissue type (e.g., healthy tissue vs. cancerous tissue). Since you have thousands of genes, visualizing all this data in a chart would be impossible.

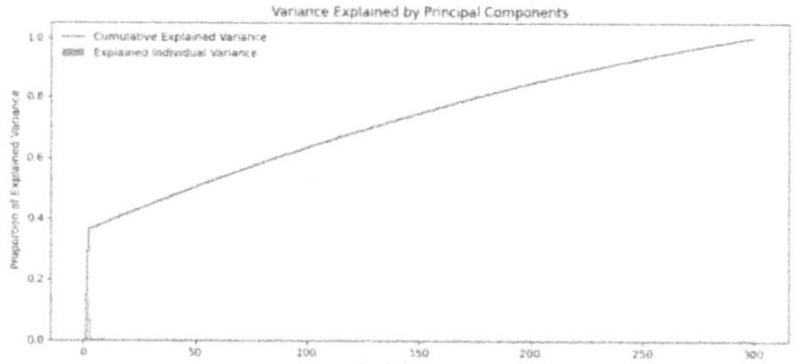

First, you could apply PCA to reduce the dimensionality of the data. By examining the variance explained by each principal component, you decide that the first two principal components capture a significant amount of the total variance. When visualizing the samples on a 2D scatter plot using these two components, you observe a separation between samples of healthy and cancerous tissue.

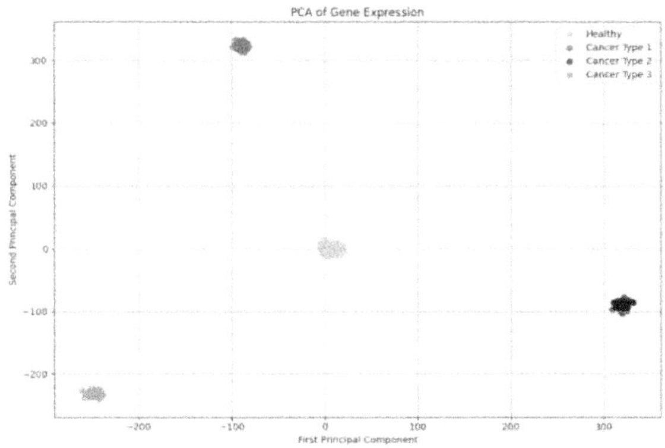

Additionally, you decide to apply t-SNE to see if you can identify more detailed subgroups within these main categories. After reducing the data to two dimensions with t-SNE and visualizing them, you identify several clusters that could correspond to cancer subtypes.

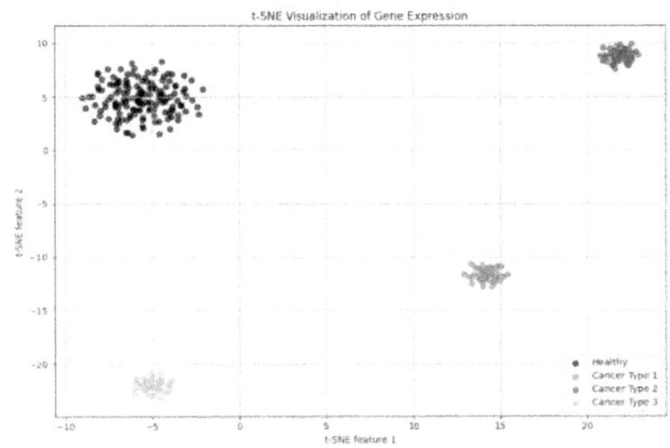

Dimensionality reduction techniques are an incredible weapon in the analysis and visualization of high-dimensional data. They provide effective ways to discover patterns, structures, and relationships in the data, facilitating understanding and decision-making in Machine Learning projects. This is of great help to both professionals and beginners.

18. Flowcharts for Machine Learning Processes

A flowchart is a graphical representation of a process or system, using symbols to represent operations, flows, and sequences. In Machine Learning, these diagrams are very important for visualizing and understanding the steps and decisions involved in the construction, training, and deployment of models.

18.1. Concept and Utility

Process Visualization: Flowcharts provide a high-level view of the steps involved in a Machine Learning project, from data acquisition and cleaning to training, validation, and model deployment.

Communication and Collaboration: They are excellent tools for communication between teams and stakeholders, allowing all involved to understand the process and collaborate effectively.

Documentation: They serve as visual documentation of the Machine Learning process, facilitating review, iteration, and scaling of projects in the future.

18.2. Common Components in ML

Data Acquisition: Represents the obtaining of data from various sources, whether databases, files, APIs, or any other means.

Preprocessing: Reflects the operations of cleaning, transforming, and preparing data for use in Machine Learning models.

Data Splitting: Symbolizes the division of data into training, validation, and test sets.

Model Selection: Represents the choice of appropriate algorithms and techniques for the problem at hand.

Training and Validation: Denotes the process of training the model with data and validating its performance.

Optimization and Tuning: Symbolizes the fine-tuning and optimization of the model's parameters.

Evaluation: Represents the final evaluation of the model on a test set to determine its performance.

Deployment: Denotes the implementation of the model in a production environment.

18.3. Practical example

Suppose you are developing a recommendation system for an online store. The goal is to recommend products to users based on their purchase history and behavior on the site.

The flowchart might start with data acquisition, where purchase records and browsing behaviors are extracted from the database. Next, preprocessing, where the data are cleaned and transformed, followed by a split into training and test sets.

Then, a model is selected, such as a collaborative filtering system. Training and validation are carried out iteratively, adjusting and optimizing the model until satisfactory performance is achieved. Once the model is ready, it is evaluated with the test set to ensure that it functions as expected.

Finally, the model is deployed on the website, where it begins to recommend products to users in real-time.

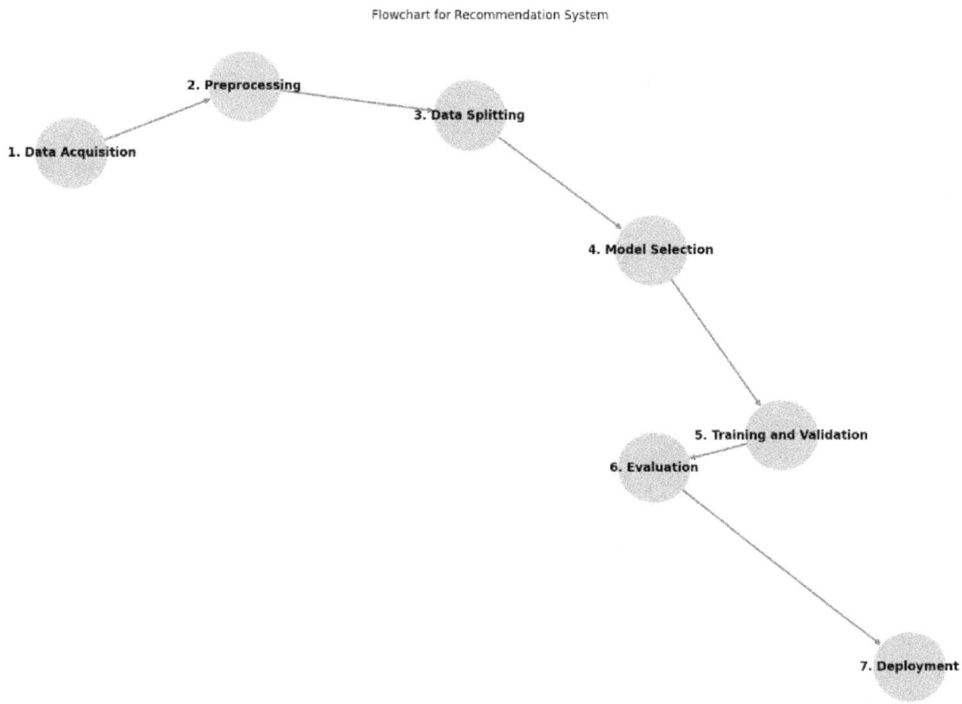

This flowchart would serve as a visual guide for the team, helping to understand each step of the process and ensuring that everyone is aligned in their efforts.

Flowcharts, in addition to visualizing and documenting Machine Learning processes, facilitate communication, collaboration, and understanding, and are crucial for ensuring the success and scalability of projects.

19. Neural Network Architectures Diagrams

Neural networks are a subfield of machine learning inspired by the structure and function of biological neural networks. They are especially popular in tasks of image processing, natural language, and more. As these networks become more complex, visualizing their architecture becomes an essential task both for design and interpretation.

19.1. Concept and utility

Layer Visualization: A neural network is composed of layers of neurons. The diagrams help visualize how these layers connect to each other, how many neurons are in each layer, and what type of operations are performed.

Deep Understanding: By visualizing the architecture, it's easier to understand and communicate how the network works, what type of information it processes, and how it makes decisions.

Documentation: Like other diagrams, these serve as visual documentation that can be essential for review, iteration, and replication of models.

19.2. Common components in neural network diagrams

Neurons: Usually represented as circles or nodes, they symbolize the basic processing units in the network.

Connections: The lines that connect the neurons represent the weights or connections between these processing units.

Layers: Can be visualized by grouping neurons. Networks typically have an input layer, several hidden layers, and an output layer.

Operations: In more complex networks, like Convolutional Neural Networks (CNN) or Recurrent Neural Networks (RNN), specific operations such as convolutions, Pooling, or loops can be represented.

19.3. Related algorithms and architectures

Feedforward Neural Networks (FNN): These are traditional neural networks, where information flows in one direction: from input to output.

Convolutional Neural Network (CNN): Specially designed for processing data with a grid structure, like images. They have convolutional layers that process information in small blocks or "windows".

Recurrent Neural Network (RNN): Networks designed to process data sequences, like time series or text. They have feedback connections to maintain information over time.

Transformers: A more recent architecture designed to process sequences, but without recurrent connections. They are popular in natural language processing tasks.

19.4. Practical example

Imagine you are designing a CNN to classify chest X-ray images in search of signs of lung diseases. Your network might start with several convolutional layers to detect edges, shapes, and patterns in the images. These layers could be followed by Pooling layers to reduce the dimensionality of the information. After several of these convolutional and Pooling layers, you could have some densely connected (Feedforward) layers that take all the detected features and make a decision about the presence or absence of disease.

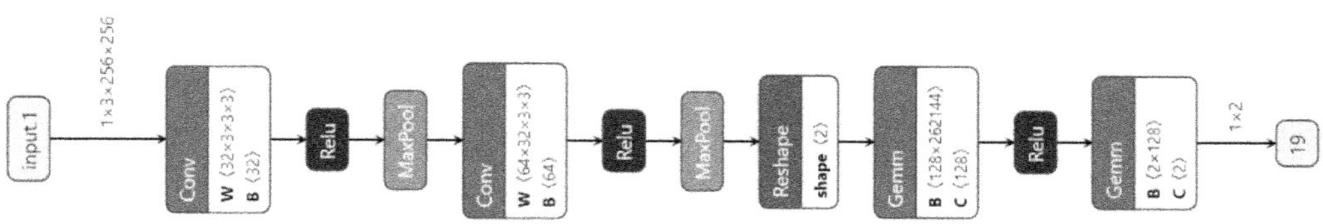

When viewing this architecture, you can clearly see how the network processes information, from detecting basic features to making decisions. This visualization helps you communicate how the network works to other interested parties, ensure that the architecture makes sense for the problem you are trying to solve, and document your work for future references.

To work with these complex techniques, you will need diagrams of neural network architectures, because they provide clarity, facilitate communication, and are crucial for the design, interpretation, and documentation of deep learning models.

20. General Review

Throughout this study plan, we have explored the diversity and importance of diagrams in the field of machine learning. From simple charts like histograms and scatter plots, which allow us to get an initial and exploratory view of the data, to more complex and specialized visualizations like the ROC curve and neural network architecture diagrams. These diagrams are not only used to interpret and understand data and models, but also to communicate findings, decisions, and processes to a diverse audience, from technical experts to non-technical stakeholders.

20.1. Importance of Correct Interpretation of Diagrams

Correctly interpreting a diagram is essential for making informed decisions in any Machine Learning project. A misinterpretation can lead to wrong conclusions, suboptimal decisions, and ultimately inefficient or even harmful models. Moreover, in contexts where models impact people's lives, such as in medical diagnosis or recommendation systems, an incorrect interpretation can have real and tangible consequences.

On the other hand, diagrams also play a crucial role in building trust in models. In an era where the "black box" of machine learning is often criticized, being able to visualize and explain how a model makes decisions is vital for its adoption and acceptance.

20.2. Recommendations for Continuing Learning

Constant Practice: As with any skill, the best way to learn to create and interpret diagrams is through regular practice. Take advantage of datasets available online to practice your visualization skills.

Courses and Tutorials: There are many online resources offering tutorials and courses on data visualization and machine learning. Platforms like Coursera, Udemy, and edX offer courses covering both fundamentals and advanced techniques.

Software and Tools: Familiarize yourself with visualization tools like Matplotlib, Seaborn, and Plotly for Python, or ggplot2 for R. For neural network architectures, tools like TensorFlow's TensorBoard or Netron can be very useful.

Participate in the Community: Join forums, groups, and online communities related to Machine Learning and data visualization. Sharing your work and receiving feedback, as well as seeing others' work, will help you improve your skills.

Read and Stay Updated: Don't be lazy! The day has 24 hours. The field of Machine Learning and data visualization is constantly evolving. Stay up to date with the latest research, techniques, and tools by reading blogs, articles, and academic papers. Dozens of news related to Artificial Intelligence and its advancements are published almost daily on the internet.

As you have seen, and after conducting a light analysis of the main types of diagrams and visualizations, diagrams are among the most important tools you have for your day-to-day as an AI Manager. They facilitate understanding, interpretation, and communication of complex data and models. With practice and continuous learning, you can master the art of visualization and use it to improve and communicate your Machine Learning and Artificial Intelligence projects. Thanks to these tools and the development of your skills in this field, you will be able to develop great projects, lead your teams in the best way and, what is also so important, properly advise your company or clients, and let's not forget that thanks to this knowledge you will make better decisions. Do not take it lightly and stop giving importance to this field. Always stay informed and in continuous evolution.

MODULE 4

Software

Module 4 - Software

21. Software

21.1. Notebooks

What are Notebooks?
Notebooks, commonly known as Jupyter Notebooks or IPython Notebooks, are interactive programming tools that allow combining code, text, graphics, and equations in a single document. Originating from the IPython project in 2001, they have become an indispensable tool in Data Science, Data Analysis, and particularly in the field of Artificial Intelligence and Machine Learning. To put it simply, they are somewhat like the text editors in Windows, but for programming.

Importance of Notebooks in ML
Notebooks are essential in machine learning for several reasons:
Interactivity: They allow code execution in blocks or cells, facilitating experimentation and step-by-step analysis.
Integrated Documentation: Being able to combine text and code, they serve not only as an analysis tool but also as a means to document and share findings.
Visualization: With the capability to integrate graphics and visualizations directly into the document, Notebooks facilitate data exploration and understanding.
Reproducibility: Notebooks make the reproducibility of code and analysis easier, which is essential in Data Science and ML to validate results.

The Role of AI-Manager in Using Notebooks
An AI-Manager must be familiar with these tools not only from a theoretical perspective but also practically. Here are some reasons:
Data-based decision making: An AI-Manager must be able to analyze data, interpret results, and make informed decisions. Notebooks facilitate this process by combining analysis and documentation.
Communication with technical teams: Having knowledge about how code is structured and executed in a Notebook, an AI-Manager can communicate more effectively with Data Scientists and Data Engineers.
Validation of results: To ensure the accuracy and reliability of ML models and analyses, an AI-Manager should be able to review and, if necessary, execute Notebooks to validate findings.

Programs and Applications for Working with Notebooks Recommended
Some of the most well-known and recommended programs and applications in the world of Notebooks are:
Jupyter Notebook: The most popular and widely used in the data science community.
Google Colab: A Google service offering a Jupyter Notebook environment in the cloud with free computing resources. I will use Google Colab for the topics we are going to cover in this book, as, due to its simplicity, not only because it does not require local installation, but also because of its easy-to-use user interface, I consider it the best option for anyone who is starting. If, on the

other hand, you already have an advanced level and have Python installed on your computer, you just have to follow the steps using Python.
RStudio (for R): Although it is not a "Notebook" in the traditional sense, RStudio offers a similar environment for users of the R programming language.
Zeppelin: Mainly used with Apache Spark and other big data systems.
Deepnote: A new generation of cloud Notebooks with collaborative features.

Notebooks are an essential tool in the AI and ML ecosystem, and an AI-Manager well-versed in their use will be better prepared to successfully lead AI projects.

21.2. Programs and Applications

There are many programs and tools used in the field of Artificial Intelligence and Machine Learning. These programs facilitate the development, training, and deployment of AI/ML models, as well as data analysis and visualization. Most programs must be installed autonomously, but there are now many online tools that allow you to work with data in the cloud without needing to have the program directly installed locally. Although during a project you may not be responsible for analyzing the data, debugging it, creating the structures needed for training algorithms, or even programming the algorithm yourself, it is your duty and obligation, as the project manager, to have at least medium-level programming skills, as this not only develops your understanding of the data during the project but also strengthens your capacity as a leader in managing the project and directing the team. Imagine that one day the data engineer falls ill, who is responsible for processing and preparing the data. If that day you have a meeting where you must show the data and you don't know with which program you should open them, or how to represent the graphs, then you have a very serious problem. With this, you, your team, and consequently, you put the project at risk, not to mention that in front of the company's management you give a very unprofessional and careless image. Now imagine for a moment that the data engineer or the data scientist takes a leave for one or even two weeks. Then you have a huge problem, not to mention the consequences for the company.

Before we delve into the world of data we need to train the algorithms and perform our analyses, I am going to give you a list of programs that you can use both for programming and for analysis. At this point, I warn you that I am not going to deal with this topic in depth, since just with this topic I could write an entire book. It is your obligation, and by now, to work and train yourself to acquire the necessary knowledge to understand the topics and points that we will discuss next. If you still have no knowledge, then I strongly recommend that you search the different platforms for both videos and courses that help you advance in this aspect of programming. On my website, there are free Cheet-Sheets available that will help you with the basic formulas.
I advise you to focus on Python. As we delve deeper into this topic, you will see that depending on the type of project you are working on, you will need one library or another.

21.2.1. List of Most Used and Valued Programs

Python

Application and Use: Python is one of the most popular programming languages for AI and ML. It has a wide variety of libraries and frameworks that facilitate the implementation and training of models, as well as data analysis and visualization.

Advantages:

- Versatile and easy to learn.
- Large community, meaning abundant documentation and support.
- Wide variety of libraries such as TensorFlow, Keras, PyTorch, scikit-learn, pandas, among others.

R

Application and Use: R is another widely used programming language, especially in statistics and data analysis.

Advantages:

- Specialized in statistical analysis.
- Wide variety of packages for different data analysis and visualization tasks.
- Interface with many other tools and languages.

TensorFlow

Application and Use: It is an open-source framework developed by Google for creating and training AI and ML models.

Advantages:

- Scalable and can be deployed on multiple platforms.
- Support for deep neural networks and other ML algorithms.
- Integration with Keras, a high-level interface for building models.

PyTorch

Application and Use: It is an open-source framework developed by Facebook for the construction and training of ML models.

Advantages:

- More oriented towards research, allowing greater flexibility.
- Supports dynamic operations, unlike TensorFlow which is static.
- Intuitive and easy to use.

scikit-learn

Application and Use: Python library for machine learning. Ideal for traditional ML algorithms.

Advantages:

- Easy to use and widely adopted.
- Wide variety of implemented ML algorithms.
- Excellent documentation.

Jupyter Notebook
Application and Use: It is an interactive development environment that allows the creation and sharing of documents with code, equations, visualizations, and text.
Advantages:
- Interactive and easy to share.
- Supports multiple languages, although it is most commonly used with Python.
- Ideal for exploratory data analysis and prototyping.

SQL and Relational Databases
Application and Use: SQL databases are essential for managing and querying large datasets.
Advantages:
- Standardized and widely adopted.
- Allows complex data query and analysis operations.
- Many options available (MySQL, PostgreSQL, Microsoft SQL Server, among others).

These are just some examples of the many tools available. Other popular programs and tools include Weka, MATLAB, KNIME, RapidMiner, H2O, Google Colab, and more. The choice of the right tool or program will largely depend on the specific problem you are trying to solve, your personal preferences, and the context in which you are working. Personally, if you are starting, I recommend that you use Google Colab, as it is free and very easy to use. You just have to register, create a new Notebook, and start programming, not forgetting that also, of course, you can upload Notebooks, view them, reproduce them, edit them, and generally do everything you would do with Python, scikit-learn, Jupyter Notebook, and the rest of the applications. The only drawback I see to Google Colab, but it's logical, is that, being free to use, when you finish working and come back, the next time you must upload the project data file again, but sincerely, I have used Google Colab and it is not so annoying, just do not forget this point. Otherwise, time will tell with which program you have more affinity and you perform better. Something positive also is that by not being installed locally, you can have your projects always at your disposal and you can connect from any other computer or device.

21.3. Libraries

Libraries are essential in the field of machine learning and data science, as they provide predefined tools that simplify and speed up the development process. They are called "libraries" in the context of programming. To avoid ambiguities, it is more accurate to refer to them as 'Libraries' when talking about sets of functions and methods that offer specific abilities in a programming language. However, colloquially they are always called 'libraries'. Below, I introduce you to some of the most important and popular Libraries in the field of AI and ML, especially in the context of Python:

21.3.1. Some of the most used and valued libraries

pandas
Description: Data manipulation and analysis library.
Main features:
- Provides data structures like Series and DataFrame.
- Integrated tools for reading and writing data between different formats.
- Data manipulation functions such as grouping, merging, and reshaping.

NumPy
Description: Library for numerical computing in Python.
Main features:
- Provides the ndarray object for storage and manipulation of multidimensional arrays.
- Mathematical functions for operations with matrices and linear algebra.
- Integration with other Python Libraries.

TensorFlow and Keras
Description: TensorFlow is an open-source machine learning framework. Keras is a high-level interface for TensorFlow.
Main features:
- Creation and training of deep learning models.
- Ability to run on multiple CPUs and GPUs.
- Keras provides a simplified and modular way to define and train ML models.

PyTorch
Description: Open-source machine learning library.
Main features:
- Designed to be flexible and dynamic, especially useful in research.
- Provides tensors that can perform calculations on GPUs.
- Autograd for automatically calculating gradients.

scikit-learn
Description: Library for machine learning in Python.
Main features:
- Implementation of a wide variety of ML algorithms, including classification, regression, clustering, among others.
- Tools for model selection, evaluation, and preprocessing.

Matplotlib and Seaborn
Description: Data visualization libraries in Python.
Main features:
- Matplotlib is a versatile tool for creating static, animated, and interactive graphics.
- Seaborn is a high-level interface based on Matplotlib designed to make statistical graphics more attractive and easier to create.

NLTK and SpaCy
Description: Libraries for natural language processing (NLP).
Main features:
- NLTK includes tools and corpora in English for working with human language data.
- SpaCy is a modern NLP library that is fast and designed to be used in real-world applications.

OpenCV
Description: Computer vision library.
Main features:
- Functions for image and video processing.
- Tools for feature detection, object recognition, and construction of graphical interfaces.

These are just some of the most popular and widely used Libraries in the field of AI and ML. There are many others specialized in different areas and applications. The choice of the right Library largely depends on the specific problem you are trying to solve and the developer's preferences. In your case, as an AI-Manager, you should be familiar with them and know their possibilities, as sooner or later you will have to work with them.

21.4. Most Prominent Platforms

Machine Learning, as you well know, focuses on the development of systems that can learn from data, identify patterns, and make decisions with minimal human intervention. This ability to learn and adapt is what makes ML so powerful and versatile. Advances in hardware, such as increased processing capacity and access to large amounts of data, have facilitated the rapid evolution of these fields. This is where hardware comes into play.

In the most fundamental part of AI and ML work, the programming and training of algorithms and models, various platforms and tools are used that facilitate this process, providing robust, flexible, and accessible environments for data scientists, engineers, and developers. And most importantly, they offer affordable solutions for those who, for example, do not have the necessary hardware for algorithm training, or even the algorithm itself. These platforms vary in their capabilities, from offering powerful data processing tools to enabling ML model training in the cloud or on edge devices (Edge Computing).

Each platform has its own strengths, focusing on different aspects of the ML and AI development process, such as ease of use, accessibility to computational resources (like GPUs and TPUs), team collaboration, integration with other services and platforms, and specific capabilities for certain types of projects or industries. The choice of the right platform can depend on several factors, including the nature of the project, available resources, and the user's level of expertise. Here you will find a very important ally, as these platforms can help you, not only to increase your knowledge, but also to boost your projects and experiments.

Here I offer you a list of some of the most important ones to me, and the ones you should definitely consider in your journey as an AI-Manager.
I recommend, if you don't use Python, PyCharm, etc., use these platforms, as each one offers different possibilities and all are of great help in your very different AI and ML projects.

Google Colab:
One of my favorites for data analysis and result visualization. It is a cloud-based platform that allows you to write and execute Python code through the browser. It is especially useful for Machine Learning, data analysis, and education.

Advantages: Offers free access to GPUs and TPUs, facilitates real-time collaboration, and requires no setup. Ideal for those looking for a fast and collaborative development environment.

Edge Impulse:
This platform is specifically designed for the development of Artificial Intelligence applications on edge devices (edge computing). With this platform, I began my first image analysis projects. In its free version, it is not suitable for large projects due to its limitations, but in its paid version, I have no doubt that it will be of great help.

Advantages: Allows real-time data processing on the device, reducing the need for constant connectivity and improving energy efficiency. Optimal for IoT and mobile device projects.

Amazon SageMaker:
A fully managed service that allows developers and data scientists to build, train, and deploy Machine Learning models quickly.

Advantages: Integration with AWS, a wide range of tools for experimentation and debugging, and facilities for scaling and deploying models.

IBM Watson Studio:
A platform that offers a set of tools and a collaborative environment for data scientists, developers, and domain experts to work together on data and AI projects.

Advantages: Strong data analysis and visualization capabilities, integration with IBM Cloud and other data sources, and tools for developing Machine Learning and Artificial Intelligence models.

Kaggle:
A popular platform for data science competitions, which also offers a free notebook environment.

Advantages: Large community of data scientists, a wide variety of available data sets, and a competitive environment to test and improve skills.

Microsoft Azure Machine Learning:
A cloud computing service that allows users to build, train, and deploy Machine Learning models using Microsoft Azure tools.

Advantages: Integration with various Microsoft tools, options for automatic model development, and facilities for deployment and large-scale model management.

Each of these platforms has its unique characteristics and adapts to different needs and scenarios in the field of Machine Learning and Artificial Intelligence. Whether you are starting out, a professional in a large company with many resources, or an independent professional like me, these tools will be of great help. Knowing how to handle and combine them for your projects can save you valuable time and help you in your decision-making when facing and tackling a project.

MODULE 5

TinyML

Module 5 – TinyML

22. What is TinyML?

TinyML stands for "Tiny Machine Learning", which refers to the deployment of machine learning models on extremely small and low-power devices. These devices include microcontrollers, embedded systems, and other devices that have memory, processing power, and energy constraints. The main purpose of TinyML is to bring Artificial Intelligence directly to the "edges" or "edge", which means processing the information directly on the device where it is collected, instead of sending it to a server or cloud for analysis.

22.1. Importance and applications of TinyML in the industry and in everyday life

Importance

Energy efficiency: Since TinyML devices are designed to be low-power, they can operate for long periods with a small battery or even with energy collected from the environment.

Reduced latency: By processing data directly on the device, transmission times to remote servers are eliminated, allowing for real-time or near-real-time responses.

Privacy and security: Processing data on the device can help ensure that sensitive data is not transmitted or stored in vulnerable places.

Applications

Smart home appliances: For example, a coffee maker that "learns" how you like your coffee based on your previous interactions.

Health and wellness: Wearable devices that constantly monitor vital signs and detect anomalies, such as an irregular heartbeat.

Precision agriculture: Sensors in the field that detect soil conditions and adjust irrigation or fertilization in real time.

Industry: Machines that can detect wear or imminent failures through constant monitoring and alert for preventive maintenance.

Smart cities: Streetlights that adjust their brightness based on the presence of pedestrians or vehicles, saving energy when it is not necessary to illuminate at full power.

TinyML represents a revolution in how and where AI can be implemented. By bringing ML processing capability to small and ubiquitous devices, endless possibilities are opened up for innovations that can improve efficiency, safety, and quality of life.

23. Difference between traditional ML and TinyML

Traditional Machine Learning and TinyML have the same theoretical foundation, but are applied in very different contexts. Below are the main differences between the two:

23.1. Scalability and hardware limitations

Traditional ML:

High-performance devices: They run on servers, GPUs, or clusters of computers with large amounts of memory and processing capacity.

Ample resources: There are no significant restrictions in terms of memory or processing capacity. This allows for larger and more complex models.

TinyML:

Low-performance devices: They run on microcontrollers or embedded systems with significant limitations in terms of memory and processing capacity.

Limited resources: Memory and processing power constraints must be considered when designing and deploying models. This often requires specific optimizations and simplifications.

23.2. Energy Consumption Requirements

Traditional ML:

High consumption: GPUs and other high-performance devices consume large amounts of energy.

Continuous connection: Generally, these systems are permanently connected to the electrical grid.

TinyML:

Low consumption: Designed to be extremely energy-efficient. They can operate on small batteries for months or even years.

Collected energy: Some devices can operate with energy collected from the environment, such as solar or thermal energy.

23.3. Latency and Response Time

Traditional ML:

Variable latency: There can be latency due to the need to communicate with remote servers, especially in cloud-based applications.

More data: Capable of processing large volumes of data, which can introduce delays depending on the size of the dataset.

TinyML:

Reduced latency: By processing the data locally, transmission times are eliminated, allowing for action in real-time or almost in real-time.

Limited data: Generally process data in small batches or even in real-time as it is collected.

While traditional ML focuses on brute power and the ability to process large data sets, TinyML focuses on efficiency, speed, and the ability to operate in environments with limited resources.

Both have their own strengths and applications, and the choice between one and the other will depend on the specific needs of the project or application.

24. Platforms and Tools for TinyML

Implementing TinyML on low-power devices requires specialized tools and platforms that enable optimizing, converting, and deploying machine learning models on these devices. Before delving into this topic, I want to first make it clear that the information and platforms may not be current at the time you are reading this book. Technologies change, and therefore, it is expected that these platforms will too. These are just a few, and they are the ones I personally recommend.

24.1. TensorFlow Lite for Microcontrollers

TensorFlow Lite for Microcontrollers is an extension of TensorFlow Lite specifically designed for microcontrollers and other low-power hardware devices.

Features:
Optimized for memory: Designed to function on devices with only a few kilobytes of memory.
Reduced operators: Includes a reduced set of operators to keep the model size to a minimum.
Integration with hardware platforms: Compatible with a variety of platforms, including Arduino, ESP32, and ARM Cortex-M based platforms.

24.2. Edge Impulse

Edge Impulse is a development platform that facilitates the creation and deployment of ML models on edge devices, including microcontrollers, general-purpose CPUs, and FPGAs.

Features:
Integrated development environment: Eases data collection, model training, and deployment on devices.
Automatic optimization: The platform automatically performs quantization and optimization of models for specific devices.
Support for diverse sensors: Can work with data from a wide variety of sensors, including accelerometers, cameras, and microphones.

24.3. CMSIS-NN (Neural Network libraries for ARM Cortex-M)

CMSIS-NN is a set of efficient software functions developed to maximize performance and minimize memory consumption on ARM Cortex-M based devices.

Features:
Optimized for ARM: Specifically designed to maximize efficiency on ARM Cortex-M devices.
Low-Level Functions: Provides low-level functions for common operations in neural networks, such as convolutions and activations.
Integrable with other platforms: Can be used in conjunction with tools like TensorFlow Lite for Microcontrollers for a smoother workflow.

These tools and platforms facilitate the development and deployment of TinyML solutions by providing specific optimizations for low-power hardware, as well as streamlined workflows for implementation on real devices. It is essential to familiarize oneself with these tools to effectively carry out TinyML projects.

25. Optimization of Models for TinyML

Given the restricted nature of the hardware on which TinyML models are deployed, it is essential to perform specific optimizations to ensure that the models function efficiently and effectively. Here are some of the most common and relevant techniques:

25.1. Quantization and Pruning

25.1.1. Quantization

Quantization involves reducing the precision of the numbers used in a model, for example, moving from floating-point numbers to 8-bit integers.

Benefits: This can significantly reduce the model size and speed up inferences, with minimal impact on model accuracy.

Types of quantization:
Post-training Quantization: Applied to an already trained model.
Quantization during training: Integrates quantization as part of the training process, often resulting in greater accuracy.

25.1.2. Pruning

Pruning involves removing certain weights or neurons from the model that have little impact on the output.

Benefits: Can significantly reduce the model size and the number of calculations needed for inference without greatly affecting accuracy.

Common techniques:
Magnitude-based Pruning: Removing weights based on their magnitude.
Structured Pruning: Removing entire structures, such as channels or layers.

25.2. Transfer Learning

Transfer learning involves taking a pre-trained model on a large dataset and adapting it to a specific task with a smaller dataset.

Benefits: Allows leveraging large and powerful models, but adapted to work on devices with memory and processing constraints.
Common use: Especially useful when limited data is available for a specific task.

25.3. Dimensionality Reduction and Simplification of Architectures

Techniques like PCA or Autoencoders: These techniques can be used to reduce the dimensionality of input data, which can speed up the inference process.

Lightweight architectures: Use neural network architectures specifically designed to be small and fast, such as MobileNet or TinyDarknet.

Optimizing models for TinyML is a crucial step that can make the difference between a model that works in real-time on a low-power device and one that does not. It is essential to consider these techniques and take them into account based on the specific needs of the project and the limitations of the target hardware.

26. Hardware Development for TinyML

To effectively implement TinyML, having suitable hardware is essential. Devices intended for TinyML are designed to be energy-efficient, fast, and capable of running machine learning models in real-time or near real-time, all within memory and processing power limitations. Before delving into this topic, as I mentioned in point number 26, I want first to make it clear that the information and hardware might not be current at the time you are reading this book. Technologies change, and therefore it is expected that the hardware will change too. The following information should only be treated as a reference or guide for finding the necessary hardware adapted to each project.

26.1. Popular Microcontrollers for TinyML

ARM Cortex-M: A family of 32-bit RISC microcontrollers widely used in industrial, automotive, and consumer applications. Several members of this family, such as the Cortex-M4 and

Cortex-M7, are popular for TinyML applications due to their balance between processing power and energy efficiency.

ESP32: A low-cost microcontroller with support for Wi-Fi and Bluetooth, popular in IoT projects. It has enough power to handle basic TinyML tasks.

RISC-V: An open instruction set architecture (ISA) that has gained popularity in embedded applications. Some RISC-V-based microcontrollers are being adapted for TinyML applications.

26.2. Sensors and Actuators

Sensors: TinyML devices are usually equipped with various sensors to collect environmental data. These can include motion sensors (such as accelerometers and gyroscopes), environmental sensors (such as thermometers and humidity sensors), cameras, microphones, among others.

Actuators: Once the information has been processed, TinyML devices can take action using actuators. These can include motors, LEDs, speakers, and other means to interact with the environment or with the user.

26.3. Power Consumption and Battery Management

Consumption Optimization: It's essential that TinyML devices are extremely efficient in terms of power consumption. This can be achieved through techniques like deep sleep mode, where the device "sleeps" when not active, and "wakes up" quickly when needed to process information.

Alternative Power Sources: Some TinyML devices can operate on energy collected from the environment, such as solar, thermal, or kinetic energy. This allows them to function for extended periods without needing to change or recharge batteries.

Battery Management: Devices must be able to monitor their battery charge level and adapt their behavior accordingly, possibly reducing sampling frequency or disabling certain functions to conserve energy.

The right hardware is essential for the success of any TinyML project. When selecting and designing hardware for TinyML, it's crucial to consider the specific needs of the application and carefully balance processing power, energy consumption, and other key factors.

27. Implementation of Models in Devices

Once a model has been optimized for TinyML, the next step is to implement it in a specific device. This process involves a series of steps and considerations to ensure that the model works correctly on the target hardware.

27.1. Process for Deploying a Model on a Microcontroller

1. Model Conversion: Depending on the tool or platform used, you may need to convert the model to a specific format. For example, TensorFlow Lite for Microcontrollers requires models to be in `.tflite` format.

2. Integration with the Development Environment: Import the converted model into your development environment, which could be a specific IDE for microcontrollers like PlatformIO, Keil, or Arduino IDE.

3. Development of Inference Code: Write the code that will manage the inference on the device, including feeding data to the model, executing the inference, and interpreting the results.

4. Code Optimization: Depending on the device, further optimizations in the code may be necessary to ensure that the inference is performed in real-time.

5. Testing on the Device: Before final implementation, it is crucial to test the model on the device to identify and correct any potential performance or accuracy issues.

6. Final Deployment: Once everything works as expected, the code and model are deployed on the device for use in a real environment.

27.2. Integration with Other Systems and IoT Devices

Communication: In many cases, TinyML devices will need to communicate with other devices or systems. This can be done through common protocols such as MQTT, CoAP, or directly via Wi-Fi or Bluetooth.

Synchronization with the Cloud: Although the purpose of TinyML is to process data locally, sometimes it is useful to synchronize or send data to the cloud for additional analysis, long-term storage, or to receive model updates.

User Interaction: Depending on the application, you may want to provide an interface for users to interact with the device, whether through a mobile app, a web interface, or directly on the device.

Effective implementation of models on devices is a critical step in any TinyML project. It requires a combination of skills in machine learning, embedded development, and communication systems to ensure that the device operates reliably and efficiently in the real world.

28. Use Cases and Real Applications

TinyML has found applications in a wide variety of sectors, from industry to everyday consumption. These use cases leverage the ability to process data directly on the device, offering quick responses and improving privacy and efficiency. Some of the most notable use cases include:

28.1. Voice Recognition in Low-Power Devices

Allow devices with limited resources, such as toys, home appliances, or wearables, to recognize voice commands without having to connect to the cloud.
Benefits: Improves privacy by processing audio locally, reduces latency by not depending on network connections, and allows interactivity in devices that do not have traditional screens or keyboards.

28.2. Anomaly Detection in Industrial Machinery

Sensors placed on industrial machinery can constantly monitor vibrations, temperatures, and other parameters to detect anomalous behaviors that may indicate an imminent failure.
Benefits: Reduces downtime and maintenance costs by allowing proactive interventions before severe failures occur. Also, by processing data locally, the volume of data transmitted is minimized, which can be essential in industrial environments where connectivity can be expensive or limited.

28.3. Monitoring of Personal Health and Well-Being

Wearable devices, like smart watches or fitness bands, can use TinyML to process biometric data in real time, detecting events like falls, abnormal heart rhythms, or irregular sleep patterns.
Benefits: Provides immediate feedback to the user and can alert in emergency situations. By processing data locally, privacy is improved and dependence on a cloud connection is reduced.

28.4. Precision Agriculture

Sensors deployed in agricultural fields can use TinyML to analyze soil conditions, moisture, and other factors, automatically adjusting irrigation or fertilizer administration.
Benefits: Maximizes efficiency in the use of resources such as water and fertilizers, which can result in more abundant and sustainable crops.

28.5. Security and Surveillance

Cameras equipped with TinyML capabilities can detect movements, recognize faces, or identify objects without needing to send images to a central server.
Benefits: Improves privacy by not transmitting video continuously, and can alert in real time about suspicious situations.

These use cases illustrate the potential and versatility of TinyML in practical applications. By bringing ML processing capability directly to devices at the "edge," opportunities are opened for innovations that improve efficiency, privacy, and functionality across a wide range of sectors.

29. Challenges and Limitations of TinyML

Despite the transformative potential of TinyML, it also faces challenges and limitations inherent to its nature and the hardware on which it operates. These challenges must be understood and addressed to achieve successful implementations.

29.1. Memory and Processing Capacity Constraints

Devices intended for TinyML, such as microcontrollers, have significant limitations in terms of RAM and storage capacity. In addition, their processing power is limited compared to servers or GPUs.
Implications: These constraints force the use of smaller and simplified models, and may limit the complexity of tasks these devices can handle.

29.2. Durability and Lifecycle of Devices

Devices operating in difficult or remote environments must be robust and durable. In addition, once deployed, they may not be easily accessible for updates or maintenance.
Implications: This can make it difficult to update models or correct problems once the device is operational. The need for durability can also influence the choice of components and materials.

29.3. Security and Privacy in Edge Devices

Although local processing can improve privacy by reducing data transmission, edge devices can be vulnerable to physical attacks or tampering.
Implications: It is essential to implement robust security measures, both at the hardware and software level, to protect data and ensure the integrity of the device and inferences.

29.4. Integration with existing Systems

In many cases, TinyML devices must integrate with existing systems or infrastructures, which can present challenges of compatibility or interoperability.
Implications: It may be necessary to develop adapters, interfaces, or middleware to ensure that TinyML devices communicate and function correctly with larger or older systems.

29.5. Evaluation and Validation in the Real World

Since TinyML operates at the "edge," real-world conditions can vary widely and present scenarios not anticipated during the training or validation of the model.
Implications: It is crucial to perform thorough testing and possibly adopt approaches of continuous or adaptive learning to ensure that models behave correctly in all possible situations.

While TinyML offers exciting opportunities to bring AI to new places and applications, it is crucial to be aware of these challenges and address them proactively. This will ensure that TinyML-based solutions are robust, secure, and effective in their intended applications.

30. Future Trends and Advances in TinyML

The field of TinyML is dynamic and constantly evolving. As technology advances and new applications are identified, trends and advances emerge that shape the future of this sector. Some of the most promising trends and advances include:

30.1. Innovations in Specialized Hardware for TinyML

As the demand for TinyML grows, so does the interest in developing hardware specifically designed for these applications.

Examples:
NPU (Neural Processing Units): Chips specifically designed to accelerate neural network operations on low-power devices.
Low-power FPGAs: These programmable devices allow hardware configurations tailored to specific ML tasks, optimizing performance and energy efficiency.

30.2. Advances in Optimization Algorithms for Low-Power Models

As TinyML becomes popular, research in algorithms and optimization techniques adapted to low-power devices also intensifies.

Examples:
Federated learning models: Techniques that allow models to be trained on the device using local data, and then combine these models globally to improve accuracy without compromising privacy.
Sparse neural networks: Networks designed with minimal connections and neurons from the outset, rather than being pruned later.

30.3. Integration with next-generation Networks and their Impact on IoT

The combination of TinyML with high-speed, low-latency networks can enable new applications and enhance existing ones in the realm of the Internet of Things (IoT).
Implications:
Real-time transmission: With faster networks, it is possible to transmit inferences or raw data in real-time to servers or other devices.
Improved interoperability: Enhanced connectivity can facilitate the integration of TinyML devices into broader systems or networks of devices.

30.4. Continuous and Adaptive Learning at the Edge

Instead of relying solely on pre-trained models, devices can adapt and fine-tune their models in real-time based on recent data or changing environmental conditions.
Benefits:
Adaptability: Devices can respond to changes in the environment or data patterns.
Improved Accuracy: As more data are collected, models can improve their performance.

These trends and advances reflect the rapid evolution and untapped potential of TinyML. As technology and research in this field advance, new opportunities and applications are likely to emerge that will further revolutionize how Artificial Intelligence is implemented and used in devices of all sizes.

31. Ethical and Privacy Aspects in TinyML

The implementation of TinyML in a variety of devices and applications carries important ethical and privacy considerations. These considerations focus on how data are processed, stored, and used, as well as on the potential implications of an increasingly automated world.

31.1. Data Processing at the Edge versus in the Cloud

At the Edge:
Advantages: By processing data directly on the device, the chances of exposure of personal or sensitive data during transmission are reduced. Additionally, if the data never leave the device, there is less risk of them being stored on vulnerable servers.
Challenges: Devices may not be as protected as data center servers, making them more susceptible to physical attacks or manipulations.

In the Cloud:
Advantages: Data center servers usually have more robust security measures and are regularly updated.
Challenges: Data transmission to the cloud can be intercepted, and data centers can be targets of large-scale attacks. Additionally, storing personal data in the cloud can raise privacy concerns.

31.2. Privacy Implications of bringing Data Processing closer to the User

Benefits:
Local control: Users have more control over their data when processing is done locally. They can be assured that their data are not being transmitted or shared without their consent.
Less data transmitted: By processing the data and acting on it locally, the amount of data transmitted is reduced, minimizing opportunities for interception or misuse.

Challenges:
Updates and patches: If privacy or security issues arise, it may be more difficult to update or correct individual devices compared to updating a centralized system in the cloud.
Less centralized oversight: Without the oversight of a central system, there could be variations in how different devices handle and protect data.

31.3. Ethical Considerations in the Implementation of AI in Everyday Devices

Transparency and consent: It is essential that users are informed about what data are being collected, how they are being processed, and for what purpose they are used. They should have the option to give or withhold their consent.

Excessive automation: As everyday devices become "smart", there is a risk of becoming too dependent on automation, which could reduce human decision-making and autonomy in certain areas of life.

Social implications: The widespread use of smart devices could widen the digital divide, leaving behind those who do not have access to the latest technology or the knowledge to use it.

Bias and equity: As with any AI application, there is a risk that models in TinyML devices reflect or amplify biases present in the training data. It is crucial to address and correct these biases to ensure that devices act fairly and non-discriminatorily.

Addressing these ethical and privacy aspects is essential to ensure that TinyML is used responsibly and beneficially. Companies and developers must be aware of these concerns and work proactively to address them in their implementations.

MODULE 6

Use Cases

Module 6 – Use Cases

32. The Revolution of AI and ML in the Business World

These technologies (AI and ML), once the domain of science fiction and advanced research laboratories, are now at the heart of many companies' operations, driving innovation and opening new frontiers of possibilities. As you have seen, and from the beginning of the book, Artificial Intelligence has virtually infinite applications. It is, and although we sometimes don't think about it, everywhere. From your Smart watch, your mobile phone, in your robot vacuum cleaner, in your home's smoke detector, in your office's smart thermostat, the surveillance cameras of your usual bank, and even in your sports t-shirt. Generally, when people think of Artificial Intelligence, we do so at a user level, and basically think of a program that thinks and responds to us like any other person, (well, quite nicer than some, to be honest) and that does our tasks for us. And although this reality, which sounds so much like science fiction, is still far from us, the truth is that, as of today, in 2023, we are living the change that will lead to that reality. Artificial Intelligence is here to stay, and whether we like it or not, it is the future today.
For all these reasons, companies around the world are joining the race to implement Machine Learning and Artificial Intelligence in their processes, whether in production for machine maintenance, in marketing to write texts for social networks, in human resources for candidate documentation management, or in finance for the automation of the invoice control process. And the fact is that there is a big difference between the vision of Artificial Intelligence at a user level, and a company's vision of what Artificial Intelligence and its applications are. For companies, Artificial Intelligence are extremely powerful tools that provide them with the ability to be competent in a constantly changing market. Unfortunately, most medium and small companies are not yet aware of the possibilities offered by AI and ML.

Since its inception, Artificial Intelligence has promised to transform our relationship with machines, allowing them to emulate and sometimes surpass human capabilities in specific tasks. Accompanied by Machine Learning, the branch of AI that focuses on the development of algorithms that allow machines to learn for themselves from data, we have witnessed a tectonic shift in how organizations and businesses process information, make decisions, and adapt to a constantly changing environment. The irruption of Big Data has been a crucial catalyst for this revolution. We live in a world where every click, every transaction, and every interaction generates data. These data, in their raw form, may seem overwhelming and disordered. However, with the right tools, as we have seen earlier and throughout the book, they represent a gold mine of information that, if leveraged properly, can offer unparalleled competitive advantages. This is where AI and ML come into play, providing the necessary tools and techniques to distill, analyze, and act on these vast data sets.

But what does all this really mean for the business world? Is AI simply a passing fad or does it represent a true metamorphosis in the way we do business? Am I going to lose my job because of AI? In the following topic, we will embark on a journey to answer these questions, exploring various use cases of Artificial Intelligence and Machine Learning in businesses. From process automation to customer experience personalization, from supply chain optimization to fraud prevention, we will discover how these technologies are shaping the present and future of organizations around the world.

We are on the brink of a new era, where machines not only assist in our daily tasks, but also learn, adapt, and, in many cases, anticipate our needs. The use of AI and its implementation in companies still generates much debate, especially in the aspect of the labor market, since its implementation, in many cases, involves the dismissal of workers. It is logical to think that if a company needs ten people to do a job, but with only three people and an AI it saves 85% just in one department, then it wants to optimize processes and therefore layoffs occur along the way. However, you should not think that it is an AI that is going to take your job. AI is just a tool, but the job will be taken away by someone who is able to work with AI and who is able to recognize and offer the company many more improvements with this AI. Therefore, it is in your hands to adapt, learn, and be competitive. For example, the finance manager of a company will always have much more affinity with those who, at least, know how to read and understand data using Excel. Because this means that the worker has a better understanding of what these data mean and their importance for the company. You have a greater affinity towards people who share your hobbies or who think like you. Well, with AI it's the same. It is your duty as an AI-Manager to make workers aware, show them the potential of AI and ML, and help them in the adaptation process, as well as train them to work with it, and to develop their understanding of it.

For this topic, I have made a list of a total of twenty departments within a company to see the use cases considering the most important topics within each of these departments. On the other hand, and as I have mentioned before, I have developed a unique book for each department, which includes ten projects per department. This means that you have at your disposal a total of two hundred projects. These books can be acquired separately and serve both as a complement to this book in your learning, and to implement these ideas in your company. They are a complete guide, which step by step, indicate the path to follow and the processes to perform in each project, the people involved and the tasks to be performed by each, among other topics that are dealt with.

Now we are going to delve into the different departments within a company, and analyze them to discover what are the possibilities of using Artificial Intelligence in each of them, which will help you to develop your understanding of Use Cases and everything learned so far. Before starting, and as I have also mentioned at the beginning of the book, this is one of those topics that I have to summarize, since by itself, one can talk long and hard about each department and its use cases, and the content of this topic gives me enough to make a new book. So here I have to summarize again.

33. Production Department

At the heart of every company, especially those dedicated to manufacturing and production, lies the production department. This is where ideas become tangible products, where raw materials are transformed into goods that satisfy consumer needs. With the emergence of AI and ML, the production landscape is undergoing an unprecedented transformation, driving efficiencies and opening new possibilities. Everything is possible, from intelligent automation to predictive maintenance, supply chain optimization, improved quality control, rapid design and prototyping, and even customization at scale.

Let's look at the most important topics to consider within the production department.

Planning and Production Control

Meticulous planning is essential for efficient production. With AI, companies can predict future demands based on historical patterns and current trends, allowing for better resource allocation. Production control, on the other hand, can be monitored in real time with AI systems that detect deviations and automatically adjust operations to maintain efficiency.

Automation and Technology

Automation has been taken to the next level with AI. Intelligent robots can learn and adapt to new tasks, improving their efficiency over time. Adaptive production, where machines automatically adjust their operations based on real-time data, is now a reality thanks to ML, bringing flexibility and precision to unprecedented heights.

Quality Management

Ensuring product quality is paramount. With AI-driven computer vision, detailed inspections can be performed in real time, detecting defects imperceptible to the human eye. In addition, ML algorithms can predict failure points based on historical data, allowing proactive corrections and consistently improving quality.

Maintenance

Predictive maintenance, powered by ML, has revolutionized how machinery is cared for. Instead of relying on fixed schedules, sensors and algorithms work together to predict when equipment is likely to fail or require attention, minimizing downtime and maximizing equipment life.

Supply Chain Optimization

AI offers a panoramic and detailed view of the entire supply chain. Advanced algorithms can predict bottlenecks, optimize logistical routes, and ensure that inventories are kept at optimal levels, all based on real-time data analysis and accurate predictions.

Inventory Management

With the help of ML, future demands can be predicted with astonishing accuracy, automatically adjusting inventory levels. This not only reduces costs by avoiding excess stock but also ensures that a product is never missing when needed.

Cost Control

AI systems can monitor and analyze costs in real time, identifying opportunities for efficiencies and reductions. By predicting fluctuations in raw material or energy prices, for example, companies can adapt their production strategies to maximize profitability.

Health and Safety at Work
AI plays a crucial role in ensuring a safe work environment. Intelligent systems can monitor conditions in real time, detect potential hazards, and alert workers and supervisors. In addition, safety training can be personalized and improved with AI-based simulations.

Sustainability and Green Production
In the pursuit of greener production, AI and ML are valuable tools. They can optimize resource use, reduce waste, and aid in the design of more sustainable and efficient products. In addition, by analyzing large data sets, AI can identify opportunities to reduce emissions and consumption, aligning production with ecological goals.

Artificial Intelligence and Machine Learning are not mere additions to production; they are redefining its essence. They offer tools to make production more efficient, adaptive, safe, and sustainable. These technologies ensure that production operations not only stay up-to-date but lead the way into the future. The Production Department is at the forefront of the AI revolution. These technologies are enabling companies to produce faster, more efficiently, and with superior quality. In a world where the demand for customization and efficiency has never been greater, AI and ML are proving to be indispensable allies in any modern company's production journey.

34. Research and Development Department (R&D)

At the epicenter of innovation and technological advancement of any company, we find the Research and Development (R&D) department. This is the space where the most revolutionary ideas are conceived, where there is a constant pursuit to improve and push the limits of what is possible. With the entry of AI into the scene, R&D is witnessing a golden era of expanded possibilities, where the speed of innovation, precision in research, and the ability to predict market trends and needs are reaching levels never seen before. From advanced simulation to material improvement, to identifying new market opportunities and creating prototypes in record time, everything is being redefined by AI and ML.

Let's look at the most important topics to consider within the Research and Development department.

Development of New Materials
With the help of AI, the creation and improvement of materials have accelerated. Algorithms can predict properties of materials not yet created, allowing scientists to focus on those with the greatest potential, reducing time and costs.

Rapid Prototyping
The development of prototypes, indispensable for testing and refining ideas, has greatly benefited from ML. Algorithms can suggest improvements, identify potential failures, and optimize design, speeding up the process of turning an idea from paper to reality.

Simulations and Modeling
Before the creation of a new product or solution, simulations play a crucial role. Using AI, these simulations become more precise and versatile, allowing researchers to accurately predict how a product will behave under various circumstances or how a material will react under certain conditions.

Enhanced Collaboration
AI facilitates collaboration among multidisciplinary teams, recommending experts based on skills, experience, and previous projects, and providing tools for more efficient communication.

Automation of Research Tasks
Many repetitive tasks in R&D, such as data analysis or laboratory tests, can be automated with AI, allowing researchers to focus on more complex and creative tasks.

Identification and Risk Assessment
In any research, identifying and mitigating risks is essential. AI can predict potential challenges or problems in development, allowing companies to make informed decisions and reduce the risk of unprofitable investments.

Optimization of Research Processes
ML can analyze past and current research processes to identify areas for improvement, optimize resources, and accelerate innovation.

Integration with Other Departments
AI allows for smoother integration of R&D with other departments, such as production or marketing, ensuring that innovations align with production capabilities and market demands.

Sustainability and Ecological Research
R&D plays a crucial role in the search for more sustainable and ecological solutions. With AI, it is possible to quickly identify solutions that reduce environmental impact and improve energy efficiency.

Artificial Intelligence and Machine Learning are driving the Research and Development Department towards unimagined horizons. These technologies not only accelerate innovation but also make it more precise, relevant, and adapted to the changing needs of the world. In an environment where innovation is key to maintaining competitiveness, AI and ML are becoming essential tools for any forward-looking company. R&D, with the integration of these technologies, is redefining the boundaries of what is possible and laying the groundwork for the progress and growth of organizations in the 21st century.

35. Sales Department

The sales department is the engine that drives many companies to success. It's the bridge between an organization's products or services and its customers, where relationships are built and nurtured, and where vital revenue is generated. Thanks to AI and ML, the world of sales is being redefined. Tools powered by these technologies are expanding the capabilities of sales teams, from predicting buying behaviors to automating routine tasks, personalizing offers, and optimizing sales strategies.

Let's look at the most important topics to consider within the sales department.

Prediction and Lead Generation
Acquiring new customers begins with identifying leads or prospects. AI and ML can analyze vast datasets to identify potential customers based on behaviors, interests, and demographics. These systems can predict which leads are most likely to become customers, allowing sales teams to focus on high-value prospects.

Automation of Customer Relationship Management (CRM)
AI-driven CRM systems can automate routine tasks, such as data entry, tracking interactions, and scheduling meetings. Additionally, they can provide insights about individual customers, suggesting actions or strategies based on customer history and behavior.

Personalization of Offers
Through the analysis of purchase data and behavior, ML systems can suggest specific products or services for each customer, increasing the likelihood of a successful sale. This personalization improves customer experience and increases loyalty.

Price Optimization
Through analysis of market data, competition, demand, and other factors, AI can suggest dynamic pricing strategies, maximizing revenue and ensuring competitiveness, as well as adapting them in real-time, always offering the best prices, the most adapted offers, and maintaining a competitive activity in sales.

Sentiment Analysis and Feedback
AI can analyze customer comments and reviews to determine the overall sentiment towards products or services. This provides valuable feedback and allows companies to adapt their strategies and products according to customer needs and opinions.

Chatbots and Virtual Assistants
These tools can handle frequent inquiries, assist in the purchasing process, and provide real-time information, freeing up sales staff to focus on more complex and strategic tasks. In these types of examples, it is clear that AI and ML should be seen as potential tools and not as enemies.

Training and Development
AI systems can personalize training programs for salespeople based on their strengths and identified areas for improvement. Additionally, they can simulate sales situations to train and improve skills. They can generate both scripts for learning and simulate telephone conversations. This makes it an extremely powerful tool for training qualified personnel, improving the department, the service, and therefore also customer relations.

Sales Prediction
With the ability to analyze historical patterns and current trends, AI can accurately predict future sales, allowing for better planning and resource allocation.

Integration and Analysis of Multichannel Data
In a world where sales are made through multiple channels (online, physical stores, social networks, etc.), AI can integrate and analyze data from all these touchpoints to provide a unified view of the customer and optimize sales strategies.

Improving Customer Retention
By predicting which customers are at risk of leaving or reducing their consumption, ML systems allow companies to act proactively, offering incentives or solving problems before they become crises.

Artificial Intelligence is capable of taking the sales department to levels never before imagined, providing tools that not only optimize operations but also improve relationships with customers. In a business environment where competition is fierce and customer expectations are constantly evolving, AI and ML are becoming essential allies for any sales team aspiring to excellence and sustained success. These technologies ensure that sales strategies are smarter, more proactive, and customer-focused, paving the way for a future where sales are based on data, personalization, and adaptability.

36. Marketing Department

The marketing department is the center of creation and communication of value for a company to its customers and consumers. It is in this department where market trends are deciphered, strategies are designed, and messages are delivered that resonate with the target audience. With the inclusion of AI and ML, marketing has undergone a revolution, offering precision in segmentation, real-time personalization, and a deep understanding of consumer behavior. From predictive analysis to the automation of campaigns, content optimization, and social media engagement, AI and ML are reshaping the landscape of modern marketing.

Let's look at the most important topics to consider within the marketing department.

Segmentation and Personalization
AI and ML allow for more precise audience segmentation, identifying specific niches based on behaviors and preferences. Additionally, real-time personalization, from ads to web content, is now possible thanks to algorithms that adapt content based on user profile and behavior, increasing engagement and conversion.

Predictive Analysis
ML can anticipate future consumer trends and behaviors based on historical data. This allows companies to get ahead and adapt their marketing strategies before the competition.

Campaign Automation
AI-driven marketing platforms can manage and optimize campaigns across multiple channels, automatically adjusting parameters to maximize ROI and ensure that the right message reaches the right audience at the perfect time.

Content Optimization
AI tools can analyze vast amounts of content and interaction data to determine which topics, formats, or styles resonate most with the audience, allowing for the creation of more effective content.

Sentiment Analysis and Social Media Monitoring
Through natural language processing, AI can analyze comments, reviews, and discussions on social networks to determine perception and sentiment towards a brand or product, allowing for quick and strategic interventions.

Programmatic Advertising
Ad purchasing through AI allows companies to automate the acquisition of advertising space, ensuring that ads are shown to the most relevant audience and in the right context.

User Experience (UX) Optimization
ML can analyze navigation and interaction patterns on websites and applications to offer design and structure recommendations that improve the user experience.

Customer Retention and Loyalty
Advanced algorithms can identify early signs of declining engagement or customer dissatisfaction, allowing proactive interventions to retain and build consumer loyalty.

Measurement and Analysis of Results
AI offers advanced tools for analyzing metrics and KPIs, providing deeper insights into campaign performance and offering recommendations for future strategies.

The marketing department, armed with Artificial Intelligence and Machine Learning tools, is positioning itself as an innovative force at the forefront of the relationship between brands and consumers. These technologies not only optimize operations but also create more personalized and meaningful experiences for consumers. In a world saturated with messages and stimuli, AI and ML offer the precision and relevance necessary to stand out and connect genuinely. The future of marketing is undoubtedly one driven by data and technology, and companies that embrace and adapt to these tools will be better positioned to succeed in today's market. For a reason, it is said that "knowledge is power."

37. Human Resources Department (HR)

This department is fundamental in any organization. The Human Resources (HR) department is the core that manages the most valuable asset of a company: its staff (although many still do not believe it, it is so!). This is also where the question arises: am I going to lose my job to AI? It is in HR where labor relations are cultivated, developed, and managed, where crucial decisions about hiring, training, performance evaluations, and workplace wellbeing are made. The introduction of AI in this department is redefining human talent management, optimizing processes, improving decision-making, and personalizing the work experience. These technologies are enabling more efficient staff selection, training tailored to employee needs, more objective evaluation, and anticipation of labor needs and conflicts.

Let's look at the most important issues to consider within the Human Resources department.

Recruitment and selection
The recruitment process is fundamental to attract and select the right talent. AI and ML are revolutionizing this area by automating CV selection and filtering, identifying the most suitable candidates based on predefined criteria. In addition, AI-assisted virtual interviews can analyze responses and behaviors, providing additional insights to recruiters.

Training and development
Training staff is essential to maintain a competent and motivated workforce. AI systems can personalize training programs according to the needs and preferences of each employee. Additionally, ML can identify skill gaps in the organization and propose specific trainings. If you think about it, you can understand that AI is a very powerful tool that can help you not only optimize your company and improve processes, but it helps and encourages your workers to improve, learn, adapt, which ultimately leads them to be motivated, and this is what truly leads a company towards success.

Performance evaluation
AI offers tools for a more objective and data-based evaluation. By analyzing employee performance and behavior in real time, areas for improvement can be identified and achievements highlighted. These analyses can be used for constructive feedback and professional development.

Workplace wellbeing and health
Monitoring employee wellbeing is crucial to maintaining a healthy work environment. Intelligent systems can detect signs of stress or dissatisfaction, allowing early interventions and personalized support strategies. In aspects like this, you should pay very sensitive attention, as you will understand, not all employees will like to be monitored. It is a very sensitive and controversial issue.

Retention and engagement
Anticipating staff turnover is essential to reduce costs and maintain continuity. ML algorithms can analyze behavioral patterns and feedback, which can be combined with an analysis of the current situation of the company, to predict possible exits and allow preventive actions.

Talent management
Identifying and nurturing talent within an organization is essential. With the help of AI, it is possible to detect employees with leadership potential or specific skills, and develop personalized career plans.

Workforce planning
AI can predict future staff needs based on market trends, company growth, and historical patterns, ensuring there is always enough and adequately trained staff.

Compensations and benefits
Intelligent systems can analyze labor market data and internal feedback to propose competitive salary structures and benefits packages tailored to employee needs. Aspects like this can be analyzed in conjunction with others such as the financial situation of the company and sales department forecasts. This allows for better short and long-term measures.

Conflict resolution
By analyzing communications and feedback, AI can identify potential labor conflicts or tensions before they escalate, allowing early interventions and effective mediations. It is possible that one day we will see workers being dismissed using Artificial Intelligence, but isn't it the same when a boss fires a worker by Twitter (X)? Or even by letter?!

Predictive analysis
Beyond daily management, ML can provide predictive analyses on labor trends, future training needs, labor market evolution, and other valuable insights for long-term strategy. With supervised learning, you can prevent through anticipation using classification algorithms like k-NN and linear regression to make future forecasts.

The introduction of Artificial Intelligence and Machine Learning in the Human Resources department is not simply an improvement in processes; it is a revolution in human talent management, in the management of the most precious value of a company, its employees. These technologies offer tools to make people management more efficient, objective, and personalized. In a world where talent is key to business success, AI and ML are becoming essential allies to attract, develop, and retain the best. The Human Resources Department, traditionally focused on human relations, now finds in these technologies the perfect support to take its mission to the next level.

38. Finance Department

In any company, and as the backbone of its operations, we find the finance department. This department is responsible for managing financial resources, ensuring profitability, controlling expenses, and guaranteeing long-term financial sustainability. With the implementation of AI and ML, the financial landscape is undergoing a radical metamorphosis. These technologies are facilitating everything from the automation of accounting tasks to the prediction of cash flows, risk analysis, fraud detection, and more efficient capital management.

Let's look at the most important issues to consider within the finance department.

Predictive Analysis of Cash Flows
Cash flow is vital for the survival and growth of any company. AI and ML allow companies to accurately predict incoming and outgoing flows based on historical data, market trends, and other

external factors. This forecast allows for better financial planning and more informed decision-making.

Detection and Prevention of Fraud
Financial systems are often the target of fraudulent activities. Advanced ML algorithms can analyze transactions in real time, identifying anomalous and potentially fraudulent patterns. These systems not only detect fraud but also constantly learn to improve their accuracy.

Automation of Accounting and Reconciliation
AI is revolutionizing accounting by automating repetitive tasks such as account reconciliation, expense classification, and transaction recording. This not only saves time but also reduces the margin of human error.

Risk Management and Analysis
Assessing and mitigating risks is essential in the financial world. ML-based systems can analyze vast amounts of data to identify risk patterns and trends, allowing companies to make safer and more strategic financial decisions.

Investment Optimization
AI tools can assist in the management of investment portfolios by analyzing market trends, assessing risks, and maximizing returns. These systems can adapt and learn from market changes, providing real-time recommendations.

Accounts Receivable and Payable Management
AI can automate the process of tracking and collecting outstanding accounts, as well as optimize the timing and method of payment to suppliers, improving working capital efficiency.

Credit Analysis and Assessment
When evaluating the solvency and credit risk of clients or partners, ML algorithms can analyze a large number of variables and historical data to provide a more accurate and rapid assessment.

Financial Planning and Budgeting
With the ability to analyze trends and predict future economic scenarios, AI can assist in the development of more realistic budgets and long-term financial strategies.

Reporting and Financial Analysis
AI systems can generate detailed and customized financial reports in real time. In addition, they can offer valuable analysis and insights on financial health and areas for improvement.

Compliance and Regulation
Given the constantly changing regulatory environment, AI can help companies keep up with regulations and ensure compliance, reducing risks and potential penalties. A task that consumes a lot of time and therefore very valuable capital for companies.

Artificial Intelligence and Machine Learning are rewriting processes in the finance department, making it a more agile, accurate, and proactive nexus within organizations. Remember, a company with 30 employees is not the same as one with 200, or a consortium with close to 3000 employees, etc. In a world where financial accuracy and operational efficiency are crucial, AI and ML emerge as high-value business tools for any modern financial strategy. These technologies are enabling companies to anticipate challenges, optimize resources, and lead confidently in a dynamic economic environment. In short, the Finance Department, traditionally seen as a conservative area, is at the forefront of the technological revolution, demonstrating once again its central role in business strategy and success.

39. Logistics Department

The logistics department is also a very important structure within companies, being responsible for the planning, execution, and efficient management of the flow of products, from the acquisition of raw materials to the final delivery to the customer. In a globalized world, where supply chains extend across the planet, effective logistics management is crucial to ensure competitiveness and customer satisfaction. The incorporation of AI and ML in this field is radically transforming logistics, making possible greater optimization, prediction, and real-time adaptability.

Let's look at the most crucial topics in the field of logistics.

Planning and Forecasting
AI can analyze large sets of historical and current data to forecast product demand, optimizing production and distribution. With the use of ML algorithms, companies can anticipate peaks and falls in demand, adapting more agilely to market fluctuations. For example, applied to the purchasing department, in the purchasing department of an industrial company that produces metal products, AI can monitor current prices and, by analyzing historical data, can supply the company with metal, obtaining the best price, preventing stock shortages and high price increases due to market inflations, always conducting real-time analysis. Meanwhile, the department's employees can take care of other tasks such as improving relations with suppliers, organizing more personalized meetings for new projects.

Inventory Management
Intelligent systems allow precise control of stock levels, minimizing excesses and avoiding shortages. Through patterns and predictive analysis, it is possible to have a "just in time" inventory, reducing costs and improving product turnover.

Route Optimization
AI algorithms can calculate optimized transport routes, taking into account variables such as traffic, weather conditions, and fuel costs. This not only speeds up deliveries but also reduces the carbon footprint and associated costs. Aspects like this truly give companies the right to earn the distinction of sustainable companies. Something that in recent decades has been highly valued by society.

Environmental Impact Analysis
ML can assess the environmental impact of logistics operations, proposing measures to reduce the carbon footprint and comply with ecological regulations.

Warehouse Automation
AI-guided robots can manage storage and retrieval tasks, increasing efficiency and reducing human errors. These systems can adapt to changes in demand and autonomously reorganize the storage of products.

Supplier Management
Through data analysis, it is possible to evaluate the performance of suppliers, anticipate delays in the supply chain, and make decisions based on the quality and efficiency of the same. Some companies perform an analysis of their suppliers only once a year, this is due to the complexity of the task, the time that must be invested, and the people involved in it. This system generally, especially in small companies of fewer than 500 employees, is a task that is not usually liked much when it has to be done, so optimization through AI is an incredible advantage for any company due to its effectiveness.

Real-Time Monitoring
AI allows real-time tracking of products and workflows, providing instant information on the status and location of shipments, improving transparency and communication with customers.

Predictive Failure Analysis
Through ML, it is possible to predict failures in machinery or transport vehicles, allowing preventive maintenance and reducing downtime. This, as we have already seen previously in other departments, frees up personnel and grants very valuable time, minimizing costs and therefore freeing up capital to invest in other aspects.

Returns Management
AI can automate and optimize the return process, analyzing the causes and proposing corrective measures, thus improving customer satisfaction. This can not only review returned products but also find the causes of their defects, proposing improvements for the solution of these problems.

Integration with Other Departments
AI-based systems, as we have already seen previously, allow seamless integration with other departments. Integration with departments such as sales, production, and finance creates an interconnected, agile, and effective business ecosystem.

The implementation of Artificial Intelligence and Machine Learning in the logistics department is not just a technological update, it is a metamorphosis in how companies manage and optimize their workflows. In a scenario where speed, efficiency, and sustainability are imperatives, AI and ML emerge as first-impact tools to maintain and improve competitive position in the market. The logistics department, traditionally rooted in established procedures, now benefits from these technologies to innovate, adapt, and lead in an ever-changing business world.

40. Warehouse Department

The warehouse department plays a critical role in the operations of any organization. It is in this core where inventory is managed, logistics organized, and products made available for distribution or sale. Through proper storage and distribution, products are ensured to reach the right place, at the right time, in optimal conditions. The advent of Artificial Intelligence and Machine Learning in warehousing is leading to unprecedented optimization, from inventory management to demand prediction, including process automation and anomaly detection.

Let's explore the most relevant topics in the realm of the warehouse department.

Inventory Management
AI and ML are facilitating the optimization of inventories, allowing for more precise stock management. Through algorithms, future demands can be predicted and inventory levels proactively adjusted. This minimizes storage costs and reduces losses due to obsolescence or expiry.

Logistics and Distribution
Intelligent systems are revolutionizing logistics. Through predictive analysis, it is possible to anticipate bottlenecks, optimize distribution routes, and efficiently allocate resources. Automation, thanks to AI, enables vehicles and drones to make deliveries without human intervention, reducing costs and delivery times.

Process Automation
Robots equipped with AI are performing storage and retrieval tasks, improving efficiency and reducing human errors. These robots can work continuously, further optimizing warehouse operations, not to mention improving the health and quality of life of warehouse employees.

Anomaly Detection
ML-based systems can monitor inventory status in real-time, identifying discrepancies, damages, or losses. This continuous surveillance ensures high quality standards are maintained and losses reduced.

Storage Space Optimization
AI can design and reorganize storage space optimally, considering variables such as product turnover, accessibility, and efficiency in item retrieval.

Security and Surveillance
AI can also be used in surveillance systems, detecting intrusions or suspicious activities in real time, thus ensuring the security of inventory and workers.

The implementation of Artificial Intelligence and Machine Learning in the Warehouse Department is a transformation that goes beyond simple automation; it is the redefinition of how to manage, store, and distribute products efficiently. The Warehouse Department, traditionally seen as a passive storage space, is now perceived as a dynamic center of innovation and efficiency, where technology and logistics merge to create cutting-edge solutions.

41. Customer Service Department

The customer service department is the foundation for customer satisfaction and retention, playing a crucial role in the overall perception of the brand. It is here where relationships with consumers are established and maintained, where doubts are resolved, complaints managed, and technical support provided. The integration of Artificial Intelligence and Machine Learning in this department is transforming the way companies interact with and understand their customers, enabling faster, more personalized, and effective care. Thanks to these technologies, companies now have the ability to anticipate customer needs, offering proactive solutions and improving consumer experience. The advantages offered by AI in this field are extremely necessary for companies, and without a doubt, it is one of the first departments any company should automate.

Below, we analyze the most relevant topics in the customer service department.

Chatbots and Virtual Assistants
AI-powered chatbots are revolutionizing customer service, providing immediate responses to common queries, freeing up human staff for more complex issues. These assistants can learn from previous interactions and offer increasingly accurate and personalized responses. Think of ChatGPT as a heavily trained chatbot, an evolution of what was once a chatbot.

Customer Segmentation
As you have already learned at the beginning of the book, ML allows analyzing large volumes of data. This can be used to segment customers based on their behaviors, preferences, and needs, according to the objectives, you could use a classification through Labels or make groups through Clustering, allowing for more personalized and appropriate attention for each segment.

Process Automation
AI enables the automation of repetitive tasks, such as ticket management or query classification, improving efficiency and allowing agents to focus on higher-value tasks.

Customer Needs Prediction
Through data analysis and behavior patterns, ML can anticipate customer needs or problems before they express them, offering proactive solutions.

Sentiment Analysis
AI tools can analyze customer feedback, whether through comments, emails, or social media, to identify the general sentiment towards the brand or product. This allows companies to adjust their strategies and improve customer satisfaction. As you can see, some possibilities are "repeated" from one department to another, but this is where the true strength of Artificial Intelligence and Machine Learning lies, as it can adapt to any situation, specialize in a specific topic, and exploit all possibilities. Therefore, never underestimate the power of Artificial Intelligence; as an IA-Manager, you must have a very broad and deep understanding of the use cases.

Advanced Technical Support
AI can guide customers through technical solutions more efficiently, quickly identifying the root of the problem and offering step-by-step solutions. This, for example, can save a lot of time for workers when a customer calls for technical assistance. Daily, there are many cases where customer service does not know how to answer customer questions or solve the problem, so the call must be diverted to an expert in the department in charge. This person must again listen to the customer's problem and try to guide them, which along the way generates much confusion, uncertainty, and many questions. In this situation, experts lose a lot of valuable time, often the customer calls back, and the story repeats throughout the day with the same customer and other customers. This translates as costs for the company. With the help of Artificial Intelligence, this would be a thing of the past.

Personalized Communication
Based on customer history and preferences, AI can personalize communication, from special offers to specific solutions for each individual.

Continuous Improvement
ML systems can continuously learn from interactions with customers, identifying areas for improvement and adapting their responses to provide better future care.

Reduced Waiting Times
The automation and efficiency provided by AI significantly reduce waiting times, resulting in a better experience for the customer.

Predictive Analysis
Like in HR and other departments, ML can provide predictive analysis on consumption trends, peaks in demand for attention, and other valuable insights to prepare the customer service team for future challenges.

The incorporation of Artificial Intelligence and Machine Learning into the customer service department is not just a modernization of processes or a simple improvement in service quality; it is a complete transformation in the way of connecting and understanding customers. These technologies offer tools that significantly improve efficiency, speed, and personalization of care. In a world where customer experience is fundamental to the success and differentiation of a company, AI and ML stand as strategic allies, taking customer care to a higher level and ensuring a closer and more satisfactory relationship with the consumer. This ultimately translates into sales volume for the company.

42. Department of Information Technology (IT)

The Department of Information Technology (IT) is a fundamental part of the backbone of any modern organization. It acts as the central nervous system, ensuring that all components and departments of the company communicate and function smoothly. From keeping the company's critical data safe to ensuring that tools and applications are available and functioning properly, IT plays a crucial role in day-to-day operations. With the advent of AI and ML, the responsibilities and capabilities of this department are constantly evolving, allowing companies to operate more efficiently, securely, and scalably. This department plays a crucial piece in your role as an AI Manager.

I have tried to gather the most important topics to consider within the IT department, something that due to its importance and complexity is not easy.

Infrastructure Management and Monitoring
AI enables proactive monitoring of IT infrastructure, identifying potential problems before they become critical failures. ML systems can predict when hardware is about to fail or when a resource is about to be depleted, allowing for preventive actions.

Cybersecurity and Defense
Through the use of advanced algorithms, AI can detect anomalous patterns in network traffic, identifying potential threats and taking automatic actions to counteract them. This improves the security posture and reduces the risk of data breaches.

Process Automation
By applying RPA (Robotic Process Automation) powered by AI, routine and repetitive tasks can be automated, freeing up IT staff to focus on more strategic and valued tasks. As you can see, this point occurs in almost all departments.

Data Management and Analysis
AI and ML enable companies to analyze large amounts of data at incredible speeds, offering insights that were previously difficult or impossible to obtain. This is essential for real-time data-driven decision-making.

Software Development and Maintenance
Intelligent systems can assist in software development, identifying errors in code, suggesting improvements, and speeding up the testing and deployment process.

Technical Support and User Service
Chatbots and virtual assistants, powered by AI, can resolve frequent user queries, these being, for example, the employees of the company, reducing the load on support staff and improving user satisfaction.

Network and Communications Optimization
Through ML, networks can self-optimize, managing traffic efficiently and adapting to changing demands without human intervention.

System Integration and Compatibility
Intelligent systems facilitate the integration of different platforms and applications, ensuring that all systems work in harmony and reducing compatibility issues. When you implement Artificial

Intelligence in the purchasing department, you will inevitably have to implement it with the company's ERP (Enterprise Resource Planning) system.

Planning and Strategy, Innovation and Technological Adoption
AI allows for the forecasting of technological trends, future infrastructure needs, and resource demand. AI and ML, being constantly evolving, offer opportunities for the IT department to explore new solutions and technologies, keeping the company at the forefront of digital transformation, ensuring that the IT department is always one step ahead.

The assimilation of Artificial Intelligence by the Information Technology department is a revolutionary cry in the way companies operate and grow. These technologies offer the opportunity not only to do more with less but also to explore new frontiers and provide solutions that were previously unthinkable. In a world where, as we have seen throughout the book, technology is a key differentiator, AI and ML are redefining the rules of the avant-garde, and the IT department is at the forefront of this transformation.

43. Purchasing Department

At the heart of many business operations is the purchasing department. This department, often underestimated, plays a crucial role in ensuring that the organization runs smoothly, providing the necessary resources and services, from raw materials to essential services. In addition, it ensures that the company gets the best value for its money, while maintaining quality and efficiency. With the introduction of AI and ML in the field of purchasing, we are witnessing a revolution in the way companies acquire goods and services, optimize costs, and manage their relationships with suppliers.

Let's take a look at the most relevant topics in the purchasing department.

Supplier Selection
We have already discussed this aspect in previous cases, but we will not give it less importance, as the success of the company depends on the right choice of suppliers. The right choice of suppliers is essential for any business. With AI and ML, it is possible to automatically analyze large databases of suppliers, evaluating their history, quality, prices, and reliability. This allows companies to identify and collaborate with the most suitable suppliers for their specific needs, opening up great and important future opportunities.

Negotiation and Pricing Strategy
AI can analyze historical price patterns, market fluctuations, and trends to advise on negotiation. These analyses can be essential to obtain the best deals and optimize the budget.

Inventory Management
ML can predict future demand for products or raw materials based on historical data and current trends. This allows companies to maintain an optimal inventory, reducing storage costs and

avoiding shortages, as well as automatically synchronizing information between different departments such as warehouse, production, sales, etc

Purchasing Process Automation
With the help of AI, routine and repetitive tasks, such as generating purchase orders or verifying invoices, can be automated, freeing up time and resources for more strategic tasks. Previously I gave the example that employees can dedicate themselves, for example, to improving relationships with suppliers. A topic that is also very important and underestimated, unfortunately.

Supplier Risk Assessment
Through data analysis and pattern recognition, AI can predict potential supply chain disruptions or problems with specific suppliers, allowing companies to anticipate and plan contingencies, as well as, if necessary, adapt the procurement system.

Supplier Relationship Management
AI-based systems can help monitor and manage relationships with suppliers, identifying opportunities for collaboration, optimization, or renegotiation.

Supplier Integration
Intelligent systems allow seamless communication with suppliers, anticipating replenishment needs, negotiating prices based on predicted demands, and optimizing the supply chain. This is basically the day-to-day of the purchasing department. If this is optimized, the advantages and benefits for the company are unimaginable.

Expense Analysis and Cost Optimization
Through the analysis of spending data, AI can identify areas for savings, inefficiencies, or unnecessary spending patterns, proposing strategies to optimize the budget.

Integration with Other Departments
Like previous points, the AI systems of the purchasing department can be integrated with other departments, such as sales or production, to ensure smooth communication and efficient coordination in the supply chain. From my point of view and experience, the purchasing department is the central structure of a company. Therefore, I consider, and I repeat, from my experience, that automating these tasks between departments is vital for a company today.

Predictive Analysis
Again, ML can provide insights into market trends, price evolution, or changes in demand, allowing companies to adapt their purchasing strategies proactively, also finding potential suppliers.

The way companies acquire and manage resources is the central piece of any company. This depends on all the actions taken in the company, from logistics, warehouse, production, the quality department, the measures taken by the human resources department, to the decisions made by the finance departments and the management of the company. The implementation of Artificial Intelligence and Machine Learning in the purchasing department is a transformation in the way companies acquire and manage resources. AI allows for more strategic, efficient, and adaptive management of purchases, which translates into significant savings and greater competitiveness in the market. In a world where every penny counts and where operational agility is essential, AI and ML are positioning themselves as fundamental tools for any purchasing department that seeks excellence and optimization.

44. Quality Department

The quality department is the immune system of any company, ensuring that products and services meet established standards and expectations, guaranteeing customer satisfaction and operational efficiency. This department is responsible for establishing, monitoring, and continuously improving internal processes to ensure optimal performance at all levels. The incorporation of Artificial Intelligence and Machine Learning in this department is transforming how companies approach quality, allowing for greater accuracy, predictability, and adaptability in their quality control and improvement efforts.

Let's explore the most crucial aspects in the realm of the quality department.

Automated Quality Control
With the help of AI, companies can automate visual inspections, tests, and other quality control procedures. Smart cameras and sensors can detect defects or inconsistencies in real time, reducing human error and increasing efficiency. If you've paid attention to the earlier topics in the book, you can imagine a system of sensors that, coordinated and with the necessary algorithm, analyze images, videos, audio, and other data, providing invaluable information that otherwise would have been unattainable or translated into high costs.

Prediction and Fault Detection
Here we have another example of departmental coordination, as ML algorithms can analyze large amounts of historical data to predict potential failures in machinery or processes before they occur. As we have seen, this allows companies to take preventive measures and reduce downtime. Developing the quality department as soon as possible is important for any start-up company, and on the other hand, it is a key piece for large companies.

Customer Feedback Management
As we know, AI can analyze customer comments and reviews received through other departments to identify areas for improvement or recurring problems in products or services. For example, as in complaints or returns. Through the use of NLP, this allows companies to quickly adapt to customer needs.

Compliance with Regulations and Standards
Intelligent systems can monitor and ensure that products and processes comply with industrial or governmental regulations and standards, reducing the risk of penalties or recalls. Basically, this is fundamental in this department and represents the day-to-day, as well as the basis of the decisions made here.

Continuous Improvement
With the ability to analyze patterns and trends in real time, companies can implement continuous improvement strategies, adjusting and improving processes based on objective data.

Quality Staff Training and Development
AI can identify areas where staff needs additional training, and customize training programs based on individual and collective needs, which for the human resources department translates as "gold information."

Root Cause Analysis
When facing a quality issue, AI can quickly analyze large amounts of data to identify the root cause, allowing for a faster and more efficient solution.

Predictive Analysis
Similar to other departments, ML in the quality department can offer predictive insights on quality trends, product lifespan, and other valuable data for long-term planning and strategy.

The implementation of Artificial Intelligence in the quality department revolutionizes both processes, and how companies ensure and improve the quality of their products and services. AI provides the necessary tools for companies to be more proactive, precise, and adaptable in their quality efforts. In a market where customer satisfaction and operational efficiency are essential for success, AI and ML are becoming indispensable tools for any quality department seeking excellence in its field.

45. Legal Department

The legal department is the guardian of integrity, compliance, and protection of a company in a complex and constantly evolving legal landscape. This department ensures that the operations of a company are carried out within the legal framework, minimizing risks and defending its interests. The integration of Artificial Intelligence and Machine Learning in the legal department is transforming the way legal challenges are approached, streamlining processes, improving accuracy and efficiency, and providing proactive solutions to potential legal problems.
Although it is not my field, I guide myself by my experience and knowledge as an expert in companies, AI, and the industrial sector to analyze the most relevant issues to consider within the legal department.

Document Review and Analysis
AI is revolutionizing legal review by automating the identification and classification of relevant information in large volumes of documents through NLP. ML algorithms can quickly analyze contracts, agreements, and other documents to identify risky clauses or those incompatible with company policies, and even translate them from other languages, which favors business expansion and opens the doors to possible partnerships.

Legal Investigations and Due Diligence
AI can quickly explore vast databases of jurisprudence and legislation to identify relevant precedents and laws, saving countless hours of manual work and improving the accuracy of investigations.

Litigation Prediction
Through the analysis of historical data and patterns, ML can predict the likelihood of success in future litigation, allowing companies to make informed decisions about whether to proceed with legal actions or seek settlements.

Contract Automation
AI systems can automatically generate contracts and other legal documents based on predefined parameters, ensuring consistency and compliance.

Regulatory Compliance
With the constant evolution of regulations and laws, AI can monitor and alert about relevant changes, ensuring that the company is always up-to-date and avoiding possible sanctions.

Virtual Legal Advice
Legal chatbots and virtual assistants can provide immediate responses to basic legal queries, easing the workload of lawyers and providing quick information to other departments.

Intellectual Property Management
AI can monitor and detect possible intellectual property infringements, from patents to copyrights, allowing quick actions to protect the company's assets.

Legal Strategy and Planning
By analyzing legal trends and industry data, AI can help formulate proactive legal strategies that anticipate and address potential future challenges.

Dispute Resolution
ML can analyze past and present cases to identify effective resolution strategies, optimizing the process and improving success rates.

Predictive Analysis
Once again, ML can offer insights on legal trends, emerging risks, and opportunities, allowing for better planning and preparation.

The incorporation of Artificial Intelligence and Machine Learning in the Legal Department presents a new way for companies to approach and manage their legal challenges. These technologies provide tools that not only optimize processes but also improve accuracy, reduce risks, and provide proactive solutions to complex problems. In a world where legal risk can have significant implications, AI and ML are essential to ensure that companies are always one step ahead, protecting their interests and confidently navigating the complex legal world. The Legal Department, traditionally based on human expertise and judgment, now greatly benefits from these technologies, elevating its service and defense capabilities to unprecedented levels.

46. Documentation Department

The documentation department maintains and manages information and knowledge within any company. It is in this department where information is collected, organized, classified, and distributed, ensuring that the organization operates with precision and efficiency. The adoption of Artificial Intelligence and Machine Learning is transforming document management, optimizing processes, improving information retrieval, and ensuring data integrity. These technologies are enabling more efficient document organization, faster classification, and information retrieval based on user patterns and needs.

Some of the most relevant applications of AI and ML in the documentation department could be the following.

Automatic Organization and Classification
Using ML algorithms, it is possible to automatically organize and classify large volumes of information, identifying patterns and categories in the documents. This reduces processing time and ensures greater accuracy in classification. From product model blueprints to quality certificates of materials that suppliers send to the purchasing department.

Information Retrieval
AI-based systems can provide customized search results and recommendations, analyzing user behavior and preferences to offer the most relevant information in real time.

Document Validation and Verification
AI can identify and alert about duplicated, outdated, or irrelevant documents, ensuring the integrity and timeliness of the database. For example, when a quality certificate arrives at the purchasing department, it can be analyzed by AI, and if it is not properly filled out, it can be claimed immediately. Otherwise, it might take a long time until employees notice the error in a failed first review, which could affect the production chain. Some companies cannot start production until they receive the corresponding quality certificate properly filled out and sealed, which in some cases could mean very high capital and time expenses.

Automatic Summary Generation
Using natural language processing techniques, it is possible to generate automatic summaries and abstracts of extensive documents, facilitating understanding and quick access to key information.

Translation and Transcription
With AI support, documents can be translated into multiple languages or automatically transcribed from audio to text, expanding accessibility and information distribution. This basically facilitates the understanding of documentation for all employees who must work with this information.

Access Control and Security
AI can monitor and control access to sensitive documents, detecting anomalous behaviors and ensuring the confidentiality of information. Remember that data security is a very important point in your role as an AI-Manager and that you will have it very present in your day-to-day life. Clearly speaking, this topic will always be on the table.

Predictive Analysis of Needs
ML can analyze user behavior patterns and preferences to predict future information needs, optimizing the acquisition and generation of new documents. This can help improve documentation systems and free up staff from certain tasks.

Optimization of Storage Spaces
With AI, it is possible to analyze and optimize document storage, identifying those that can be archived, compressed, or moved to cloud storage systems.

Conversion and Adaptation of Formats
Intelligent systems can convert documents to different formats or adapt them for display on various devices, ensuring their readability and accessibility.

Integration with Other Departments
Departments such as purchasing, sales, IT, production, quality, and warehousing rely heavily on working together with the documentation department. AI and ML can facilitate the integration of document management with other departments by providing relevant information in real time and improving decision-making.

With AI and ML, the documentation department receives a well-deserved "update," an evolution in knowledge and information management, ensuring that the right information is available at the right time, optimizing processes, and guaranteeing precision. In a world where, as we have already demonstrated, information is power, AI and ML become very powerful, albeit sadly underestimated, tools for managing, protecting, and distributing knowledge. The documentation department, traditionally in charge of the custody and distribution of information, finds in these technologies the perfect ally to elevate its mission to new heights.

47. Health and Safety Department

The health and safety department ensures that employees work in optimal and safe conditions, reducing risks and promoting a healthy work environment. With the implementation of Artificial Intelligence and Machine Learning, the management of occupational health and safety is being profoundly transformed, allowing more effective prevention of accidents, a faster response to emergencies, and adaptation to the specific needs of each employee. Companies like Philips are developing augmented reality systems in glasses included in first aid kits to guide people in the process of resuscitating a person. This, for example in factories, is a very valuable asset.

How can we improve this field with the use of AI and ML?

Risk Detection and Prevention
Using sensors and AI systems, it is possible to identify high-risk areas in real time and detect patterns that indicate a possible threat. This allows for preventive measures to be taken before an accident occurs.

Monitoring of Working Conditions
Intelligent systems can monitor variables such as air quality, noise levels, or exposure to toxic substances in real time, and alert when these conditions exceed safe limits.

Employee Health Assessment
With wearable devices and AI systems, it is possible to track the health of employees, detecting signs of fatigue, stress, or any other health problem that may affect their performance or safety.

Safety Training
AI can customize safety training programs based on the profile of each employee, their position, and their specific needs, as well as raise awareness of the importance of complying with these norms in other departments. Additionally, through assisted simulations, employees can be trained on how to react in risky situations.

Emergency Response
In the event of accidents or emergencies, intelligent systems can guide employees on how to act, indicating evacuation routes, offering virtual first aid, and automatically alerting emergency services.

Incident Analysis
After any incident, AI and ML can analyze the causes, identify patterns, and propose measures to prevent it from happening again.

Mental Health and Well-being
AI can detect signs of mental health problems, such as stress or anxiety, based on employee behavior and communication patterns. This allows for personalized support and resources to improve mental and emotional well-being.

Regulatory Compliance
Intelligent systems can ensure that the organization complies with all health and safety regulations and norms, alerting about potential deviations or non-compliance.

Integration with Other Departments
AI can integrate data from the Health and Safety Department with other departments, such as HR or Production, to offer a more complete and holistic view of the organization.

The adoption of Artificial Intelligence in the Health Department ensures the safety and well-being of employees. This allows for proactive, personalized, and data-driven management, ensuring that employees are not only safe but also feel safe. In a constantly evolving work world, where risks and challenges change constantly, AI and ML are becoming essential tools to guarantee a healthy and safe work environment. As you can see, data serve to guarantee both your health and your safety.

48. Maintenance Department

The maintenance department, often underestimated, is essential to ensure the continuity and operational efficiency of any organization. It is this department that is responsible for keeping the physical and technical assets of a company in optimal condition, ensuring that operations are carried out without interruptions or setbacks. With the incorporation of Artificial Intelligence (AI) and Machine Learning (ML), maintenance is transforming from being reactive to proactive, anticipating problems before they occur and ensuring maximum efficiency.

Let's analyze the main applications of AI and ML in the maintenance department.

Predictive maintenance
The use of AI and ML allows for the analysis of machine and equipment data in real time to predict when they are likely to fail. This means that repairs and maintenance can be scheduled before a failure occurs, reducing downtime and maximizing efficiency.

Resource optimization
Through data analysis, it is possible to determine when and where maintenance will be needed, allowing for more efficient resource allocation and cost reduction.

Anomaly detection
ML algorithms can identify patterns and detect anomalies in the behavior of machines and systems, allowing for early interventions before they become major problems.

Inventory control
AI can predict when spare parts will be needed and automatically place orders, ensuring that there are always enough supplies in stock for maintenance.

Training and capacity building
With the help of augmented reality and AI, personalized training can be offered to technicians, teaching them to deal with specific problems and continuously improve their skills.

Energy management
Intelligent systems can monitor and analyze energy consumption, proposing solutions to optimize energy efficiency and reduce costs.

Process automation
Using robots and autonomous systems, maintenance tasks can be performed in hard-to-reach areas or under dangerous conditions, ensuring staff safety.

Documentation and reporting
AI can automatically generate detailed reports on maintenance tasks performed, problems encountered, and solutions applied, creating a historical record and facilitating decision-making.

Integration with other departments
By connecting the maintenance system with other departments, such as Production or Sales, a more global view of the organization can be obtained and processes can be jointly optimized.

Predictive analysis
ML can provide predictive analysis on the lifespan of equipment, future spare parts needs, and trends in operational efficiency.

The integration of Artificial Intelligence in the maintenance department is a change in how companies approach the care and management of their physical assets. It is an opportunity to maximize efficiency, reduce costs, and ensure that operations are carried out without interruptions. Operational continuity is essential to maintain competitiveness, and here AI and ML have become indispensable tools for any modern maintenance department. Without a doubt, this is a weapon to convince companies and demonstrate once again the possibilities offered by AI.

49. Administration Department

The administration department is the operational and financial center of every company. It is here that paths for efficient management are drawn, finances are monitored and controlled, and vital strategic decisions are made for the success and sustainability of the company. Thanks to Artificial Intelligence and Machine Learning in this department, traditional forms of administration are being transformed, allowing for sharper, proactive, and adaptive management to the volatility of today's business world.

These are some of the most relevant areas in the administration department where you, as an AI-Manager, can make a difference with AI and ML.

Financial planning
AI allows for more accurate financial planning by analyzing past trends, current conditions, and future projections. ML algorithms can identify patterns in revenue and expenses, aiding in the creation of more realistic budgets and in predicting cash flows.

Optimization of administrative processes
Automation, assisted by AI, is reducing the burden of repetitive tasks, from invoicing to supplier management, allowing teams to focus on higher value-added tasks.

Risk management
Through the analysis of large data sets, AI can identify potential financial, operational, or market threats, allowing companies to anticipate and take preventive measures.

Sales forecasting
ML models can predict future sales based on sales department forecasts, historical data, market trends, and external factors, allowing companies to adapt their production, inventory, and marketing strategies.

Investment analysis
AI can quickly analyze multiple variables to determine the viability and profitability of an investment, from acquiring a new company to expanding into a new market.

Audit and compliance
AI systems can automatically review large volumes of transactions and detect anomalies or deviations, facilitating audits and ensuring regulatory compliance.

Customer relationship management
AI and ML allow for detailed analysis of customer behavior, anticipating their needs and personalizing the offer, resulting in a better customer experience and increased loyalty.

Market analysis
Through data and trend analysis, companies can identify market opportunities, unattended niches, or areas where competition is less intense.

Pricing strategies
Based on historical data, competition, and demand, ML algorithms can suggest dynamic pricing strategies, thus maximizing revenue and profitability.

Strategic decision making
With the ability to process and analyze vast amounts of information, AI provides valuable insights that can guide strategic decision-making, from expansions to restructurings.

Artificial Intelligence is enabling companies to be more agile, adaptive, and resilient. The administration department, traditionally focused on numbers and processes, now benefits from these tools to provide a deeper and more strategic vision, being the fundamental pillar in decision-making and in directing the future of the company.

50. Department of Communication and Public Relations

The image and perception of a company to the public, clients, and other stakeholders are vital for its success and longevity. The Department of Communication and Public Relations (Com&RP) is responsible for shaping, consolidating, and protecting this image, being the bridge between the company and the outside world. The arrival of Artificial Intelligence and Machine Learning in this department is reconfiguring the way companies communicate and relate to their environment, making strategies more precise, personalized, and efficient.

We have already seen how the implementation of AI is improving other departments. In this one, and very similarly, they are also having a very important influence, and although the tasks sound repetitive, we must not underestimate the strength and importance of these. Remember that each department has a mission, and therefore the purpose of task automation is always different, although it always sounds the same to you.

Sentiment and Reputation Analysis
AI can analyze large volumes of data from social networks, forums, blogs, and media to determine the general sentiment toward a brand or company. This allows companies to adapt their communication and respond quickly to any negative perceptions.

Audience Segmentation
ML can identify and segment audiences based on their behaviors, interests, and demographics, allowing for more targeted and personalized communication campaigns.

Communication Automation
Chatbots and virtual assistants, powered by AI, can manage frequent queries, reservations, or any type of interaction with stakeholders, providing immediate and consistent responses.

Real-time Monitoring
AI tools can track real-time brand mentions, relevant news, or emerging trends, allowing companies to be proactive in their communication.

Content Creation
ML algorithms can help in creating personalized content for different platforms and audiences, from writing articles to designing images and videos.

Crisis Prediction
AI can identify patterns or early signals of a possible public relations crisis, allowing companies to prepare and handle it effectively.

Media Optimization
ML can analyze the effectiveness of different communication channels and recommend where to invest efforts and resources to maximize impact.

Relations with Influencers
Identifying the right influencers and measuring their actual impact on the brand is essential. AI can analyze metrics and behaviors to find ideal collaborators.

Campaign Evaluation
AI can measure the real-time success of a communication campaign, providing insights into what works and what doesn't, and allowing for agile adjustments.

In this department, a profound transformation is managed in how companies present themselves and relate to the world. The new tools allow for more agile, personalized, and data-based communication, ensuring that company messages reach the right people, at the right time, and in the right way. In an environment where image and perception can make or break brands, AI and ML become essential tools for any communication strategist and public relations professional looking to be at the forefront.

51. Reception Department

The first impression is essential in any interaction, and the reception department is the gateway, the face that the company presents to the world. This is where the first interaction with clients, suppliers, visitors, and even employees is managed. Efficiency, speed, and cordiality are fundamental in this department, and that is why the implementation of Artificial Intelligence can make a substantial difference.

AI and ML are entering the reception scene with the goal of improving the visitor experience, accelerating processes, and offering a more personalized service. From the automation of tasks to security management, these technologies are reinventing the world of reception in a very positive way.

Let's look at some of the most relevant points in the implementation of AI and ML in the reception department.

Automated Check-in
With the help of intelligent systems, the registration process can be quick and frictionless. These systems can recognize visitors, provide access, and even guide them if necessary, all autonomously.

Facial Recognition
AI allows identifying visitors through their facial features, speeding up the entry process and increasing security by allowing or denying access based on pre-established lists.

Virtual Assistants
Chatbots and virtual assistants can answer frequently asked questions, help orient visitors, and provide real-time information, reducing the workload of reception staff.

Appointment Management
Through ML, it is possible to predict and manage waiting times, optimize visitor flow, and schedule appointments efficiently, adapting to the needs of visitors and the organization.

Security and Surveillance
Intelligent surveillance systems can detect suspicious or unauthorized behavior, alerting security staff and taking proactive measures.

Personalization of the Experience
Based on historical data and known preferences, AI can offer a personalized experience to visitors, from personalized greetings to tailored recommendations.

Feedback Analysis
ML can analyze comments and feedback from visitors to identify areas for improvement and adjust the services offered accordingly.

Space Optimization
By analyzing movement and occupancy patterns, it is possible to reorganize and adapt the reception space to maximize efficiency and comfort.

Emergency Management
In critical situations, intelligent systems can guide people to emergency exits, provide real-time information, and alert emergency services.

Integration with Other Departments
AI can collaborate with other departments, such as security or logistics, to ensure a smooth and safe experience for visitors, from their arrival to their departure.

AI not only offers greater efficiency but also elevates the level of service and security. In the world we live in, the first impression can be decisive. AI and ML are proving to be powerful tools to ensure that this impression is always positive. The reception department, traditionally based on human interaction, now benefits from the precision, speed, and personalization that these technologies can offer. An aspect that also favors companies, demonstrating their adaptability, predisposition to change, and proving their market leadership capability.

52. Department of Management

The department of management is the epicenter of strategic decision-making in any organization. The core, where the paths and goals to follow are defined, where the future of the company is designed, and where guidelines for the rest of the departments are established. The absorption of Artificial Intelligence in this area is transforming the way leaders make decisions, providing tools that allow a clearer vision of the market, an anticipation of possible risks, and more effective management of available resources.

I have left this department for last intentionally. First, as the brain of any organization or company, the management department benefits from having a complete vision of how AI is transforming every corner of the company. By addressing this department after analyzing all the others, we can ensure that leaders are equipped with a holistic understanding of AI's capabilities and possibilities, allowing them to make informed and strategic decisions.

Furthermore, the process of implementing AI is a journey of transformation. By starting with other departments, it allows the organization to gradually acclimate to new technologies and processes. When the time comes to incorporate AI into management, the company already has fertile ground, with familiar employees and already optimized systems, ensuring that integration at the highest level is as smooth and effective as possible.

Lastly, management, being at the pinnacle of decision-making, must be an example of adaptability and forward-thinking. By presenting the implementation of AI in this department as the culmination of our journey, we are underlining the importance and value that technology brings to the strategic core of the company. It is a strong message that the organization not only embraces innovation but is ready to lead in the AI era. Of course, this in practice is not possible, as processes must adapt according to the needs of each company and therefore each project you lead. Always keep this in mind, you must advise companies in the best way for them and according to their needs. Remember that we cannot always have what we want, but what we need is more effective.

Let's now look at the key areas in which AI and ML are making a difference in the management department.

Strategic Decision Making
AI and ML facilitate decision-making by providing predictive analytics based on large amounts of data. These analyses allow anticipation of market trends, assessment of risks and opportunities, and informed decisions that maximize benefits and minimize risks.

Risk Management
We have already seen in other departments that with the help of advanced algorithms, it is possible to identify patterns that indicate potential financial, operational, or market threats. This anticipation allows management to implement preventive and contingency strategies.

Planning and Forecasting
ML provides tools for making accurate forecasts about sales, product demand, investment needs, and business growth, based on historical data and current trends.

Resource Optimization
AI systems can analyze the efficiency of used resources (both human and material), identify areas for improvement, and propose solutions to maximize productivity and reduce costs.

Stakeholder Relationship Management
AI can help better understand the expectations and needs of shareholders, customers, suppliers, and other stakeholders, allowing more effective communication and decisions that benefit all parties.

Innovation and Product Development
ML algorithms can identify emerging market trends and consumer preferences, guiding management in developing new products or improving existing ones and making better decisions.

Competition Monitoring

AI enables real-time analysis of competitors' actions and strategies, providing valuable insights that can influence a company's strategic decisions.

Organizational Culture and Vision

With the help of AI, it is possible to measure and analyze employees' perception and satisfaction with the company's culture, allowing management to adjust and reinforce the organization's vision and values. Although, especially in large companies, consortia, or groups of companies, this may be the responsibility of the human resources department.

Interdepartmental Integration

AI can facilitate communication and collaboration between departments, identifying areas of synergy and optimizing processes for a more cohesive functioning of the organization.

Global Market Analysis

With ML, it is possible to analyze and foresee trends in international markets, identify expansion opportunities, and adapt strategies to the particularities of each region.

AI offers a data-driven perspective and precise analysis, allowing for more proactive, strategic, and market-adapting management. Adaptability and anticipation are key; AI and ML present themselves as tools for leading with vision, precision, and efficiency. It is an era where management not only leads but also relies on technology to navigate with certainty towards the future.

To conclude the topic of use cases

Throughout this topic, during our journey through the insides of the company, we have seen how Artificial Intelligence and Machine Learning can be implemented in virtually every task, in every system, in every machine, not only to economize but to improve, to free employees from tedious and repetitive tasks, thus improving, for example, health and increasing motivation, saving time, materials, eliminating costs, and optimizing processes and therefore improving the quality of products and services. The world we know in the business realm is changing. You, today and now, have not only the possibility but the responsibility to give your best in each project, to be well-prepared and trained, to have a clear vision about Artificial Intelligence and to use this great power responsibly. You can use Artificial Intelligence to create virtually anything you can imagine. In each project, in each implementation, with each algorithm and model, you are changing the world in which you live. Even if you don't believe it yet, what you are doing today is marking our future and changing our world and consequently our lives.
The implementation of AI in companies implies changes in the lives of their workers and also their customers, partners, and suppliers. These changes go beyond mere process automation; it is a true transformation that affects all levels of the organization. By integrating Artificial Intelligence into their operations, companies not only become more efficient and competitive but can also offer more personalized and satisfying experiences to their customers. In addition, employees benefit by being able to focus on more creative and strategic tasks, leaving routine activities to machines.

This new business paradigm requires a change in mindset at all levels of the company. Leaders must be open to new ways of working and willing to invest in training and developing their staff so they can adapt and thrive in this constantly changing environment. The collaboration between humans and machines opens a world of possibilities, but it also poses ethical and practical challenges that must be addressed with care and responsibility.

Artificial Intelligence is not just a tool for improving efficiency and reducing costs; it is a catalyst for innovation and transformation in all aspects of business. As professionals, we have the opportunity and the duty to lead this change, ensuring that technology is used in a way that benefits society as a whole, always respecting ethical principles and human values. The way we approach this technological revolution today will determine the world we will live in tomorrow.

MODULE 7

Projectmanagement

Module 7 – Project Management

53. Introduction to Project Management in Artificial Intelligence Projects

Project management has long been a cornerstone in the business world, guiding projects from their inception to successful completion. However, with the growing adoption of emerging technologies like Artificial Intelligence, it becomes evident that traditional project management does not always perfectly fit this new reality. AI projects, with their highly technical, experimental, and constantly evolving nature, require a different approach to ensure their success. Being a true AI expert is necessary to carry out a successful project. Moreover, and from my most sincere recommendation and opinion, the more knowledge you have of a company, its departments, and its processes, the more and better equipped you will be to direct and manage AI projects. Keep in mind that anyone can take a two or three-month AI-Manager course and obtain a certificate that qualifies them as such, but, what knowledge and skills does this AI-Manager have compared to an AI-Manager who has obtained their degree by completing the nine-month AI-Manager Master's program at the European University of Madrid? Frankly, practically none in comparison. Since the AI-Manager who has obtained their degree by completing the Master will be much better prepared and will truly be an expert, thus being much more capable of advising companies. Also, keep in mind that not everyone has the same knowledge of a company, nor of its processes, so when advising a company the difference is very broad. My only intention with this book is to convey my knowledge, my experience, and as far as possible, to offer you new points of perspective so that you yourself can value the possibilities that open up before you. It's in your hands to qualify yourself as a genuine AI-Manager. And now I tell you, it doesn't matter if you have the university Master's degree or a course, if you prepare well as an AI-Manager, you can face any project you set your mind to.

If you have no experience in project management, probably everything we are going to see next will sound literally foreign to you, but if you already have experience, then you might miss some things. Again, I have to summarize, since project management is a trade in itself, so then this book would be eternal, and I would not fulfill my main objective, which is to write a clear, concise book focused on the management of Artificial Intelligence projects. For this reason, it is impossible for me to write about many more topics in more detail and deepen them much more. I really want to achieve a "manual", a pocket book, and not a book of laws.

When managing Artificial Intelligence projects, many questions arise, which of course, vary from one project to another.

53.1. What makes an AI project unique?

To begin with, AI projects focus on creating systems that can perform tasks that normally require human intelligence, such as pattern recognition, decision-making, and natural language processing. Unlike traditional software projects, where outcomes are predictable and specifications are clearly delineated from the start, AI projects are inherently uncertain. It is not always known in advance which model or approach will work best, and it is common to need multiple iterations and experiments before arriving at a viable solution.

53.2. How important is Data?

The fuel that powers any AI project is data. Here lies one of the first and greatest challenges: the acquisition, cleaning, and preparation of high-quality data. A project can stall or fail if the data are not adequate, whether because they do not correctly reflect the reality that is desired to be modeled, or because they are biased, incomplete, or simply erroneous. Moreover, data management involves important ethical and legal considerations that we have already talked about along the way, especially in terms of privacy and security.

53.3. Who should be part of the project team?

Interdisciplinarity, the confluence of experts, is a distinctive aspect of AI projects is the need for collaboration among various experts. From data scientists and Machine Learning engineers to domain experts, software engineers, and ethics specialists, the confluence of these disciplines is crucial. Effective management of interdisciplinary teams is essential, as each member brings a unique and essential perspective to the success of the project.

53.4. How to address and care for the ethical aspect of an AI project?

AI is not just a technical tool; it has profound ethical and social implications as we have already seen. AI models can perpetuate or even amplify existing biases, which can result in unfair or discriminatory decisions. Therefore, it is essential to consider and address these issues from the outset, establishing ethical frameworks and audit practices to ensure that systems are fair and transparent.

Project management in the field of AI is a fascinating and challenging journey. It requires a combination of technical skills, adaptability, and a deep understanding of the human and ethical complexities involved, as well as extensive knowledge of the field to which Artificial Intelligence is to be applied. As AI continues to integrate into all aspects of society and the economy, the need for well-informed and AI-focused project management will become increasingly critical. It is an exciting territory, full of possibilities and challenges, and is waiting for those who are willing to navigate it with curiosity, integrity, and vision.

54. Aspects to consider in an AI Project

Here I present a list of aspects to consider in a project focused on Artificial Intelligence. Although depending on the type of project these points may vary, I offer you this list based on my experience and knowledge.

1. Clear definition of the problem: It is crucial to define precisely the problem that is to be solved with AI. This definition must be specific enough to guide development, but flexible enough to adapt to findings during the research and development phase. At the base of any successful project lies a clear and concrete definition of the problem to be solved. When facing an AI project, this definition becomes even more essential. The field of AI is vast, and the possible solutions can be countless. Precisely determining what is expected to be achieved not only provides a clear direction but also sets boundaries that prevent the project from deviating or becoming too broad. While it is important to be specific, it is also crucial to maintain some flexibility. AI, with its experimental nature, can present unexpected findings that might require adjustments to the initial direction of the project.

2. Managing expectations: AI is often perceived as a magic solution to all problems. It is vital to set realistic expectations with stakeholders and communicate the inherent limitations of AI systems. The AI revolution has led many companies to perceive it as a panacea. However, it is essential to keep expectations anchored in reality. Not all problems are suitable for AI-based solutions, and not all AI solutions will be transformative. Communicating this to stakeholders from the beginning avoids future disappointments and ensures that everyone is aligned with what can be achieved and in what timeframes.

3. Understanding the data: AI projects heavily depend on data. It is essential to understand the quality, quantity, and availability of the data needed for the project. In addition, aspects related to privacy and ethics of the data should be considered. Always keep in mind that the quality of any AI solution is intrinsically linked to the quality of the data that feed the model. As I have been telling you since the beginning of the book, it is vital to understand where these data come from, what they represent, how they have been collected, and above all, that you can read them for yourself. Inadequate or biased data can lead to erroneous or unfair solutions. Additionally, in the digital age, privacy and data ethics have become central concerns. An AI project must consider these aspects, ensuring that data are used responsibly and ethically.

4. Iteration and experimentation: Unlike traditional software projects, AI projects are often more experimental. It should be taken into account that there will be iterations and adjustments as the models are trained and validated. Unlike traditional software, where a set of specifications clearly defines what is to be built, AI projects are a journey of discovery. Multiple attempts, tests, and adjustments are likely needed before arriving at a model that works adequately. This iterative nature should be planned and budgeted from the beginning.

5. Interdisciplinarity: An AI project usually requires collaboration between data experts, software engineers, domain experts, and other roles. Effective management of an interdisciplinary team is crucial. For this reason, you must be qualified to manage the team and I give you as an example soccer (as it is the most known team sport in the world). Although personally, I don't like soccer, the team management system has the same bases. Imagine Real Madrid with eleven Cristiano Ronaldos, or Barcelona with eleven Messis. It would be something impossible to manage, since all are and want to be the best on their team. You have a team with eleven players who play in the same position and perform the same task. It cannot be. A team is made up of professionals in different fields, each has a role and each brings value to the project, so you must understand the field of each one and properly manage the stability of the team to thus ensure success at the end of the season.

6. Evaluation and validation: It is essential to establish clear metrics to evaluate the performance and effectiveness of AI models. These metrics must be relevant to the business problem being addressed. Once a model has been developed, it is essential to measure its performance. This goes beyond technical metrics. While it is important for a model to have high accuracy or a low error rate, it is even more crucial that those metrics translate into tangible business outcomes. Validation must be performed under conditions that resemble operational reality as closely as possible to ensure that the model not only works in theory but also in practice.

7. Implementation and Scaling: Once the model is developed, it is crucial to consider how it will be implemented and scaled in a production environment. This may include considerations about hardware, integrations with other systems, and ongoing maintenance. An AI model that is not properly implemented may not provide any value. The transition from an experimental model to a production solution is a critical step that can present challenges, from the need for specialized hardware to integration with other business systems. Additionally, once in production, it is vital to ensure that the model can scale to handle the actual operational load.

8. Ethical Aspects: AI can have ethical implications, such as bias in models or concerns about privacy. It is essential to address these issues from the beginning and have a plan to mitigate potential risks. In the modern era, decisions made by AI models can have a profound impact on people's lives. Whether in medical decision-making, loan approvals, or candidate selection for a job, AI models can introduce biases or make decisions that negatively affect individuals or groups. It is imperative to address these ethical issues from the start, ensuring that the systems are fair and transparent.

9. Training and Continuous Updating: AI models can degrade over time or with changes in data. It is important to have strategies for retraining and updating the models as needed. The world changes, and with it, the data that feed our models. A model that works today may not work tomorrow. Establishing mechanisms for retraining and updating models is essential to ensure their relevance and effectiveness over time.

10. Communication and Documentation: Since AI can be a technical and complex discipline, it is essential to effectively communicate both the technical details and the business results to different stakeholders. AI is a field still very complex and technical. However, its results and decisions affect the entire organization. It is essential that the technical details and business results are communicated effectively to all stakeholders.
Additionally, proper documentation can help ensure reproducibility, project maintenance, and that models can be improved over time.

These are just some of the key aspects to consider in AI project management. As I am sure you are already clear, each project will have its own particularities and challenges, but keeping these points in mind can help you navigate successfully in the complex world of AI. Each AI project is a challenge, but also an opportunity. With a clear understanding of these key aspects, organizations can make the most of AI's potential, creating solutions that are not only technically advanced but also ethical, relevant, and valuable to the business. You, as a conductor, must have them very clear to thus transmit both the correct information, as well as doing it in the right way.

55. Frameworks (Techniques for project management)

Frameworks in project management are basic conceptual and methodological structures used to organize knowledge and guide project management within an organization. These frameworks provide a set of tools, processes, techniques, and best practices that are designed to help project managers initiate, plan, execute, control, and close projects more effectively.
The frameworks vary in complexity and can be generic or industry-specific, but they generally include elements such as:

Project Phases: Clearly defined stages through which a project must pass, such as initiation, planning, execution, monitoring and control, and closure.
Documentation: Standard forms, templates, and documents that help maintain consistent and complete documentation throughout the project's life.
Methodologies: Prescribed approaches to managing and carrying out project work, which may include Agile, Waterfall, PRINCE2, etc.
Tools and Techniques: Resources such as project management software, estimation techniques, prioritization methods, and risk assessment tools.
Management Principles: Underlying principles that guide the behavior of the project manager and the project team, such as communication, leadership, and professional ethics.
Best Practices: Recommended practices that have been identified through experience and research that contribute to the success of the project.

The use of frameworks in project management helps to standardize practices and increase efficiency, providing a common base from which all project managers can work. This is especially useful in large organizations or complex projects, where consistency and predictability are critical to success. In your role, not only as an AI expert but also as a project manager, you must be very clear about these techniques, know them well, and know how to apply them according to the caliber of the project, since your own organization, as well as your ability to organize, depends on the course of the project and the flow and transfer of information, as well as a positive development of the same. Let's look at 3 examples of the most used and well-known techniques for project management.

55.1. Waterfall

It is a sequential and linear approach to project management and software development, where the process flows downward (like a waterfall) through several established phases. You can find this technique with five, six, and seven steps, however, I present it to you with eight steps, which I consider are truly important when applying this technique.

1. Conception: Define the initial requirements and the scope of the project.
2. Initiation: Analysis of the requirements and more detailed planning.
3. Analysis: Create business models, specifications, and feasibility studies.
4. Design: Establish the architecture and design of the system or product.
5. Construction: The actual development and coding phase of the product.
6. Testing: Test the system for errors and quality issues.
7. Implementation: Launch the product or system into the production environment.
8. Maintenance: Perform continuous improvements and correct problems as necessary.

Advantages:
Simple and easy to understand structure: The waterfall model is linear and sequential, which makes it easy to understand and manage, especially for those new to project management.
Detailed documentation: As each phase has specific deliverables, the waterfall model often results in exhaustive project documentation.
Complete planning at the beginning: A detailed plan is established from the start, which can facilitate coordination with other stakeholders and departments.
Ease of management: Clearly defined phases and linear processes allow for simpler management and time planning.

Disadvantages:
Rigidity: The waterfall model is very rigid and does not handle changes well once a project has started.
Delay in delivery: Complete products or systems are only tested at the end, which can delay the detection of problems or errors.
Little adaptability to change: If customer requirements change, the waterfall model does not adapt well to these changes.
Risk of not satisfying the end user: Since the final product is only revealed at the end, there is a risk that it does not meet the current expectations or needs of the user.

Most Known Tools
Microsoft Project: A project management software that allows planning projects, assigning resources, tracking progress, managing budgets, and analyzing workloads, all with a structure that adapts well to the linear and sequential approach of the waterfall model.
GanttProject: A free tool for creating Gantt charts, which are fundamental in the planning and tracking of waterfall projects, as they visualize the sequence of activities and their chronology.
In the waterfall model, each phase must be completed before the next begins. There is no overlap or iteration between phases. This approach fits well with projects with very well-understood requirements and little expected change during development. However, it has limitations, especially in projects where the requirements are uncertain or very prone to changes, which has led to the development of more flexible and iterative methodologies like Agile and Scrum.

55.2. Agile Framework

It is not a technique in itself, but rather a set of principles and practices for project management and development that emphasizes flexibility, collaboration, quick response to changes, and incremental delivery of products.

Agile development emerged as a response to traditional project management methods, such as the waterfall approach (Wasserfall), which is linear and sequential. In contrast, Agile is iterative, which means that work is divided into small sections called iterations or sprints, which usually last a few weeks.

Key Features of Agile
Iterative and incremental: Agile allows for the iterative and incremental development of products. Work is divided into short cycles that provide regular opportunities to reevaluate project directions.
Collaborative: Encourages active collaboration among all team members, as well as with clients or end users.
Adaptable: Designed to accept and expect changes in requirements, even in late stages of the project, based on feedback and continuous learning.
Focus on customer value: Puts significant emphasis on delivering value to the customer and on the ability to respond to their changing needs.
Continuous communication and feedback: Constant communication and feedback are promoted through regular meetings such as planning sessions, sprint reviews, and retrospectives.
Simplicity and efficiency: The search for the simplest and most efficient way to perform a task is encouraged.

Advantages:
Flexibility: Agile allows for greater adaptation to changes in customer requirements, even in late stages of the project.
Incremental delivery: Work is divided into short cycles, allowing for frequent reviews and adjustments, and incremental deliveries of the product.
Customer collaboration: The customer is involved throughout the process, increasing satisfaction and relevance of the final product.
Early identification of problems: Problems and defects are detected and resolved more quickly due to frequent testing and continuous reviews.

Disadvantages:
Less predictable planning: The iterative nature can lead to less clear and predictable long-term planning.
Lighter documentation: There is often less emphasis on documentation, which can be problematic for knowledge transfer and compliance with regulations.
Time management: It can be more difficult to estimate the time needed to complete the project due to the changing nature of the requirements.
Team dependency: Agile requires highly collaborative and self-organized teams and may not work as well with teams that do not have these characteristics.

Most Known Tools
Jira: Designed specifically for software teams working with agile methodologies, Jira allows tracking iterations, backlogs, and task management in real-time.
Trello: Based on the Kanban system, it is useful for managing agile projects by allowing visualization of tasks, their progress, and changing their status as they move through the workflow.

Scrum is a subset of Agile and is one of the most popular approaches to implementing Agile. It uses a specific set of roles, responsibilities, and meetings that are not prescribed in the more general Agile framework. Therefore, while all projects using Scrum are agile, not all agile projects use Scrum. Again, you must know how to decide which technique to employ and develop based on the needs of the project and the team.

55.3. Scrum

As we already know, it is a technique within the agile framework for managing and developing projects. Scrum is iterative and incremental, which facilitates flexibility and adaptation to changes.

Key features of Scrum
Sprints: Scrum divides the project into work cycles called Sprints, which usually last between one and four weeks. Each Sprint is a unit of time during which a set of features is developed until it reaches a potentially deliverable state.
Scrum Roles: There are three main roles: the Product Owner (responsible for maximizing the value of the product and working with the development team to meet the requirements), the Scrum Master (facilitates and ensures that the team follows Scrum practices) and the Development Team (professionals who do the work of delivering the product increment at the end of each Sprint).
Scrum Ceremonies: These are held in four different events and include:
- Sprint planning (defining what will be done in the next Sprint),
- the daily Scrum (a brief meeting to update progress and plan the day),
- the Sprint review (demonstrating the work done),
- the Sprint retrospective (an analysis to improve).

Scrum Artifacts: These include:
- the Product Backlog (an ordered list of everything the product might need),
- the Sprint Backlog (a set of Product Backlog items selected for the Sprint, plus a plan to deliver the product increment and achieve the Sprint goal),
- the increment (the sum of all Product Backlog items completed during a Sprint and all previous Sprints).

Advantages:
Adaptability: Scrum allows for quick adaptation to changes in requirements and priorities, making it ideal for projects in volatile environments.
Continuous value delivery: With regular sprints and iteration reviews, constant delivery of value to the customer is ensured.

Transparency: The regularity of Scrum meetings promotes transparency and continuous tracking of progress.
Emphasis on feedback: Scrum encourages frequent feedback from stakeholders, which can improve the final product.

Disadvantages:
Requires experience: Implementing Scrum correctly can be challenging without prior experience or adequate training.
Meeting overload: The multitude of Scrum meetings (daily stand-ups, sprint reviews, retrospectives) can be perceived as an overload and reduce effective working time.
Less predictability: Although sprints are of fixed duration, the work that can be completed in each sprint may vary, making it difficult to accurately predict the completion of the project.
Team commitment dependency: The success of Scrum depends largely on the commitment and cooperation of the team and stakeholders.

Most known tools
Scrumwise: A tool dedicated to Scrum management, facilitating sprint planning, backlog tracking, and burndown chart visualization for sprint progress tracking.
Asana: Although flexible and adaptable to various frameworks, Asana is particularly useful for Scrum teams by allowing task and responsibility management, as well as sprint planning and tracking.

Scrum focuses on collaboration, team self-organization, the ability to adapt to emerging problems, and the delivery of high-value products in short periods of time. This is basically a daily task and your own human ability to develop and adapt.

56. Resource Management

Good resource management and handling in project management ensures that all necessary resources are available at the right time and are used efficiently. This includes human, financial, technological, and information resources. Let's see what they are and how to deal with them.

Resource Identification:
- **Human:** Data engineers, data scientists, AI developers, business analysts, and support staff.
- **Technological:** Specialized hardware such as GPUs, TPUs, servers and software such as development platforms and data analysis tools.
- **Financial:** Budget for research, development, tools, platforms, and personnel.
- **Information:** Structured and unstructured data, databases, training data sets, etc.

Allocation Planning:
- **Task allocation:** Ensuring that the right staff are working on the right tasks according to their skills and experience.
- **Hardware and software scheduling:** Scheduling the use of technological resources to avoid bottlenecks.

- **Budget:** Ensuring that funds are available and properly allocated for each phase of the project.

Optimization:
- **Cost efficiency:** Looking for ways to reduce costs without sacrificing quality, such as using cloud services when possible.
- **Resource utilization:** Monitoring resource utilization to maximize their use and avoid idleness or overutilization.

Monitoring and adjustment:
- **Progress tracking:** Using metrics and KPIs to assess resource use and project progress.
- **Flexibility:** Being prepared to reallocate resources quickly in response to unforeseen changes or challenges.

Collaboration and communication:
- **Transparency:** Keeping all stakeholders informed about the use and availability of resources.
- **Conflict resolution:** Effectively managing any resource conflicts, ensuring that teams have what they need to move forward.

Compliance and risks:
- **Legal compliance:** Ensuring that all resources used comply with relevant regulations, especially regarding data.
- **Risk management:** Identifying and mitigating risks associated with resource scarcity or misuse.

Training and development:
- **Continuous training:** Offering development opportunities for the team, ensuring that skills are up to date with the latest AI technologies.
- **Learning and improvement:** Fostering a continuous learning environment to constantly improve resource management processes.

Resource management in AI projects is a complex activity that requires careful, meticulous planning and constant monitoring. You as a project manager and leader must be proactive, strategic, and flexible to ensure that resources are used in the best possible way to facilitate project success.

57. Risk Analysis

Risk analysis in the management of Artificial Intelligence projects ensures the identification, evaluation, and mitigation of potential obstacles that could affect the project's success. An AI-Manager must address several key points to perform an effective risk analysis.

1. Risk Identification: List all the possible risks that could impact the project, from technical issues, such as data quality and availability, to changes in AI regulation and ethical standards.

2. Risk Evaluation: Assign a probability and impact to each identified risk. This can be done through qualitative techniques, such as expert judgment, or quantitative ones, like statistical analysis.

3. Risk Prioritization: Order the risks according to their severity to determine which require immediate attention. This helps to allocate resources effectively and focus on the most critical risks.

4. Development of Mitigation Plans: Create strategies to reduce the likelihood of risks occurring or to minimize their impact in case they materialize. This can include diversifying data suppliers or implementing robust security protocols.

5. Assignment of Responsibilities: Designate project team members to oversee the management of specific risks, ensuring there is clear accountability and a quick response in case any issues arise.

6. Monitoring and Review of Risks: Establish a regular review process to assess the status of risks and the effectiveness of mitigation strategies. This should include the disposition to adjust plans according to project progress and the external environment.

7. Communication of Risks: Keep all stakeholders informed about the risks and how they are being managed. Transparent communication can help prevent surprises and ensure everyone is prepared for potential contingencies.

8. Integration with Project Management: Ensure that risk analysis is integrated with other project management areas, such as planning for time, costs, and quality. Risk management is not an isolated process and should align with the project's overall objectives.

In summary, risk analysis in AI projects requires careful consideration of the unique nature of the technology and its application. An AI-Manager must be proactive, methodical, and always attentive to the changing dynamics of the field of Artificial Intelligence.

57.1. SWOT Analysis

The SWOT analysis (Strengths, Weaknesses, Opportunities, Threats) is a strategic tool used to understand the internal and external factors that can influence a project.

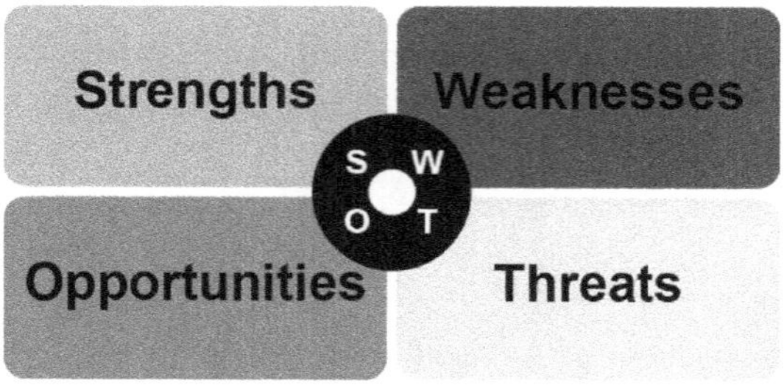

Strengths
Technical expertise: Evaluate the team's level of knowledge and technical skill in AI.
Innovation: Consider the innovative technologies and unique methodologies applied in the project.
Available resources: Identify internal resources, such as high-quality data, infrastructure, and funding.
Distinctive competence: Determine which aspects of the project or team offer a competitive advantage in the market.

Weaknesses
Resource limitations: Acknowledge the lack of resources, such as qualified personnel or adequate technology.
Knowledge gaps: Admit areas where the team needs improvement or additional training.
Time and budget constraints: Identify possible financial or schedule constraints that could limit the scope of the project.
Data security risks: Be aware of vulnerabilities in data management and privacy that could compromise the project.

Opportunities
Technological advances: Stay up-to-date with advances in AI that can be leveraged to improve the project.
Strategic collaborations: Seek potential partnerships or collaborations that could strengthen the project.
New markets: Explore uncharted AI application areas or emerging markets.
Favorable regulations: Utilize any regulatory change or government policies that may benefit the project.

Threats
Competition: Analyze the competition and how their actions could affect the project.
Changes in regulation: Be aware of new laws or regulations that may impose restrictions on the use of AI.
Technological obsolescence: Consider the risk that the technology used becomes rapidly obsolete.
Ethical and privacy issues: Recognize ethical and privacy issues that may arise and how they could affect public perception and the viability of the project.

Advantages
Comprehensive vision: Offers a clear and comprehensive view of all critical aspects - internal and external - that affect a project or business.
Ease of use: It is a simple and easy-to-implement tool that does not require extensive technical or financial resources.
Strategic decision making: Helps decision-makers identify and prioritize actions based on systematically analyzed concrete elements.
Versatility: Can be applied to a wide range of situations, from AI project planning to assessing new market opportunities.

Disadvantages
Subjectivity: Can be highly subjective; personal perceptions can influence how strengths, weaknesses, opportunities, and threats are identified and prioritized.
Lack of prioritization: Does not provide direct guidance on how to prioritize identified elements, which can lead to an overload of information without clear direction.
Not predictive: SWOT analysis takes into account the current situation but does not predict how factors will change over time or how strategies should be adjusted.
Analysis paralysis: There is a risk of remaining in the analysis phase without moving towards action, especially if the team focuses too much on the negative aspects.

An AI-Manager should conduct a SWOT analysis to systematically evaluate these aspects, which will help develop a solid strategy for the AI project. My opinion is that this analysis should be an ongoing process, adapting to new information and the changing context of the project.

57.2. Risk Matrix

The Risk Matrix is a tool used in project management to assess and prioritize risks based on the likelihood of their occurrence and the impact they would have on the project if they materialized. It is particularly useful in the management of Artificial Intelligence projects, where risks can be complex and their impact significant.

5x5 Risk Matrix example

Impact

How severe would the results be if the risk ocurred?

Probability

What is the probability of the risk ocurring?

	1 Insignificant	2 Minor	3 Significant	4 Major	5 Severe
5 Almost certain	Medium 5	High 10	Very high 15	Extreme 20	Extreme 25
4 Likely	Medium 4	Medium 8	High 12	Very high 16	Extreme 20
3 Moderate	Low 3	Medium 6	Medium 9	High 12	Very high 15
2 Unlikely	Very low 2	Low 4	Medium 6	Medium 8	High 10
1 Rare	Very low 1	Very low 2	Low 3	Medium 4	Medium 5

1. Definition of the axes:
Horizontal Axis (Probability): Represents the frequency with which a risk is expected to occur, generally classified as low, medium, or high.
Vertical Axis (Impact): Shows the degree of effect on the project, also classified as low, medium, or high.
2. Risk Identification: Involves the collection and listing of all potential risks that could affect the project.
3. Risk Assessment: Each identified risk is evaluated in terms of its probability and impact.
4. Placement in the matrix: Risks are placed in the matrix at the intersection corresponding to their probability and impact.
5. Interpretation of the matrix:
- Risks in the upper right (high probability and high impact) are the most critical and should be managed as a priority.
- Risks in the lower left (low probability and low impact) are the least critical and may require fewer resources.

6. Development of mitigation strategies: For priority risks, specific action plans should be developed to mitigate or eliminate the risk.
7. Assignment of responsibilities: Responsible parties are assigned for the management of each risk, ensuring necessary attention and resources.
8. Continuous review and update: The matrix should be regularly reviewed and updated to reflect any changes in the project or external environment.
9. Communication: The findings of the matrix should be communicated to all stakeholders to ensure understanding and cooperation in risk management.
10. Integration with SWOT analysis: The risks identified in the Risk Matrix can be fed into SWOT analysis to provide a more complete view of the project's challenges and opportunities.

Advantages
Effective risk prioritization: The Risk Matrix allows for the identification and prioritization of the most critical risks, helping project managers focus their efforts where they are most needed.
Clear visualization: Provides a visual representation that facilitates the understanding of the risk landscape and communication with the team and stakeholders.
Improved decision making: By evaluating risks in a structured manner, managers can make more informed decisions about where to allocate resources and how to prepare for potential problems.
Proactive management: Encourages a proactive attitude towards risk management, allowing for the identification and mitigation of risks before they affect the project.

Disadvantages
Subjectivity in assessment: The evaluation of the probability and impact of risks can be subjective and vary according to the perception of the evaluators, which could lead to inaccurate classification of risks.
False sense of security: The presence of a Risk Matrix could lead to a false sense of control over risks, potentially overlooking unidentified or underestimated risks.
Need for constant updating: Risks change as the project progresses and the matrix needs to be continuously reviewed and updated, which can be a time-consuming process.
Does not capture risk interdependence: The matrix typically does not reflect how risks can interact with each other, which could lead to an incomplete understanding of the cumulative effect of multiple risks.

An AI-Manager must be methodical in applying the risk matrix, bearing in mind that it is a dynamic tool that helps visualize and manage risks throughout the AI project life cycle. The key is not only to identify and assess risks but also to act on them proactively.

57.3. Monte Carlo Simulation

Monte Carlo simulation is a mathematical technique that allows understanding the impact of uncertainty and variability in complex prediction models, such as those used in Artificial Intelligence projects. This technique uses randomness to simulate outcomes of a process or system that may not be easily predictable due to the intervention of random variables. Here are the most fundamental aspects to consider when applying Monte Carlo simulation in AI project management:

1. **Base Model:** Defines the model or process to be simulated, including all relevant variables.
2. **Probability Distributions:** Determines which probability distributions (normal, log-normal, uniform, etc.) best apply to the uncertain variables of the model.
3. **Randomness Generation:** Uses algorithms to generate random values according to the established probability distributions for the variables.
4. **Multiple Simulations:** Runs the model many times (thousands or even millions) with different sets of random values for the variables.
5. **Results Analysis:** Collects and analyzes the results of the simulations to obtain a range of possible outcomes and the likelihood of their occurrence.
6. **Risk Evaluation:** Identifies potential risks and adverse outcomes through the variability in the simulation results.
7. **Data-Based Decision Making:** Uses the collected data to make informed decisions about the project, considering the most likely outcomes and their potential impacts.
8. **Critical Variables Identification:** Determines which variables have the greatest impact on the outcomes to focus mitigation and control efforts.

9. Planning and Optimization: Applies the acquired knowledge to improve project planning and optimize resources.
10. Uncertainty Communication: Explains to stakeholders the nature and impact of uncertainty in the project.
11. Continuous Update: Updates the simulation with new information and data as they become known to refine predictions and improve the accuracy of the model.

Advantages
Uncertainty Management: Allows modeling and better understanding of the effect of uncertainty in complex systems, essential in AI where outcomes can be highly unpredictable.
Decision Optimization: Helps make more informed decisions by providing a probability distribution for different scenarios, facilitating the selection of options with higher success rates.
Flexibility: Applicable to a wide range of problems and can integrate a variety of probability distributions for the involved variables, making it useful in different contexts and with different types of data.
Critical Variables Identification: Reveals the most influential variables in the outcomes of a model, allowing improvement and control efforts to be focused where they will be most effective.

Disadvantages
Computational Complexity: Requires a large number of iterations to produce accurate results, which can result in high computational resource consumption and time.
Data Quality Dependence: The results are as good as the input data. If the data are inaccurate or the probability distributions are not well chosen, the results can be misleading.
Results Interpretation: The produced data can be complex and require careful interpretation; misunderstandings in interpretation can lead to wrong decisions.
Implementation Cost: Can be expensive and requires specialized software and expert knowledge to develop and execute simulations properly, which may not be feasible for all organizations or projects.

In the context of AI, Monte Carlo simulation can be particularly useful for testing machine learning algorithms, optimizing hyperparameters, and predicting the performance of models under different conditions. For an AI-Manager, understanding and correctly applying this technique can be a valuable skill for effective management of uncertainty and risk in AI projects.

58. Management Control

Management control refers to the activities of monitoring, evaluating, and ensuring that the project meets its objectives, budget, and planned schedule.

Definition of metrics and KPIs: Establish specific key performance indicators for AI that reflect the project's objectives. This could include model accuracy, training time, latency in inferences, and operational costs.

Continuous monitoring: Implement tools and processes to track the project's progress in real time. This involves using project tracking dashboards, error logs, and automated reporting tools.

Risk assessment: Identify and analyze potential risks that could affect the project's performance or delivery. This includes technical risks, such as overfitting models, as well as operational and compliance risks.

Quality management: Ensure that the project deliverables, such as AI models and associated applications, meet established quality standards. This may require rigorous validation and verification testing.

Audit and compliance: Verify that the project adheres to external and internal regulations, including data protection laws and ethical standards in AI.

Financial reporting: Monitor and report financial expenditure compared to the project budget. This includes managing costs of resources, computing infrastructure, and software licenses.

Change management: Have established processes to handle changes in the project, whether in scope, schedule, or resources. This helps keep the project aligned with the original objectives despite modifications that may arise.

Effective communication: Maintain clear lines of communication with all project stakeholders, including the project team, executive management, and end-users.

Documentation: Maintaining comprehensive and up-to-date documentation of the project is essential for the control process. This includes code documentation, decision records, and lessons learned.

Post-project review: At the end of the project, conduct a review to assess performance against KPIs, identify lessons learned, and improve practices for future projects.

Implementing an effective control system in an AI project requires a deep understanding of the involved technology, as well as project management skills. It is a balance between technical supervision and the management of operations and human resources. As you can see, from the beginning of the book, I have always emphasized, sometimes subtly and other times not so much, that you must be well prepared to face an AI project. Having a certificate does not qualify you for a position, it only certifies you, on the other hand, it is the experience, knowledge, and comprehensive understanding of a topic that qualifies you to develop the activities.

59. Quality Management

Quality management in projects ensures that the project meets the required standards, both technical and business. Quality management in AI projects involves establishing processes and criteria that ensure excellence in all phases of the project. This discipline focuses on three main aspects: design quality, data quality, and the quality of the AI model.

1. Design Quality: Before starting any AI project, it is essential to define requirements and specifications clearly. This includes understanding the end-user's needs and how the AI solution aligns with business objectives.

2. Data Quality: Data is the heart of any AI project. It is essential to ensure its relevance, accuracy, completeness, and representativeness. Quality management should address data cleaning, preparation, and enrichment to effectively feed AI models.

3. AI Model Quality: Models should be robust, transparent, and explainable. Quality management should include model validation and testing, evaluating their performance and bias. Continuous monitoring is also important to detect and correct model drift or changes in data patterns.

4. Regulatory Compliance: In many sectors, AI projects must comply with specific regulations. Quality management must ensure that legal and ethical guidelines are followed, such as GDPR in Europe or specific industry regulations.

5. Continuous Quality Control: Quality should be monitored throughout the entire project lifecycle. This includes periodic reviews, audits, and the implementation of improvements.

6. Risk Management: Identify, evaluate, and mitigate risks associated with AI quality. This can range from data bias risk to the possibility of failure in production.

7. Feedback and Improvement: The lifecycle of an AI project is iterative. Feedback from users and stakeholders is vital for continuously improving the project's quality.

8. Documentation and Transparency: Maintaining detailed records of all processes and decisions facilitates transparency and is essential for traceability and accountability.

Each of these points must be integrated into the project's quality management plan and regularly reviewed to ensure that the project remains on the right track and meets the high standards required.

59.1. International Organization for Standardization (ISO)

ISO standards are international standards that provide requirements, specifications, guidelines, or characteristics that can be used consistently to ensure that materials, products, processes, and services are fit for their purpose. In the management of Artificial Intelligence projects, there are several relevant ISO standards that stand out for their importance. Below is a list I have compiled of what I consider to be the most important and that you should take into account.

ISO 9001 - Quality Management Systems: This is one of the most recognized and widely implemented standards in the world. It provides a framework for quality management in all areas of an organization, focused on meeting customer needs and improving their satisfaction.

ISO 10006:2017 - Quality Management in Projects: This is a specific standard for quality management in projects. It provides guidelines based on ISO 9001 quality practices, but adapted to the needs of project management. This standard is very useful for AI project managers to ensure that project management processes are aligned with quality principles.

ISO 21500:2012 - Guidelines for Project Management: Provides guidance on project management concepts and processes that are important for, and have an impact on, the performance of projects. This standard can be applied to any type of project, including those involving AI, and is useful for organizations in coordinating their projects and processes with international recognition.

ISO 21503 - Program Management: This standard complements ISO 21500 by providing specific guidelines for program management, which is the coordinated handling of multiple related projects. It is particularly relevant for AI managers working on complex programs that require the coordination of multiple AI projects to achieve strategic objectives.

ISO/IEC 27001 - Information Security Management Systems: Fundamental for any project handling data, this standard helps ensure information security, a crucial aspect when working with sensitive or personal data in AI projects.

ISO/IEC 25000 - Quality Systems and Software: Also known as the SQuaRE (Software Product Quality Requirements and Evaluation) standards family, this series provides guidelines for evaluating the quality of software and information systems, including AI products.

ISO 31000 - Risk Management: Provides guidelines for risk management that organizations can use to identify, analyze, and mitigate risks associated with their activities, including those in AI projects.

ISO/IEC 2382 - Information Technology - Vocabulary: Offers terms and definitions in the IT field, which can be useful for establishing a common understanding in AI projects that often use specialized terminology.

ISO/IEC 15288 - System Life Cycle Engineering: This standard provides a framework for describing the life cycle processes of systems, including AI systems, from conception to retirement.

ISO/IEC 12207 - Software Engineering: Establishes a software life cycle process and is applicable to any type of software, including AI development.

ISO/IEC 38500 - IT Governance for the Organization: Provides guidelines for effective IT governance within organizations, which is applicable to AI project management to ensure that IT supports the organization.

These ISO standards are essential because they provide a set of best practices that can help you ensure that your AI projects are safe, reliable, and of high quality, while also ensuring that they meet regulatory requirements and satisfy the expectations of your company or clients and other stakeholders. Therefore, if you associate with these ISOs and keep them in mind, you will be leading the project on a very good path, ensuring both quality and a promising future for the model and resources.

59.2. Techniques and methods for quality control

Quality management in AI projects involves a variety of tools and methods to ensure that the final product meets the desired requirements and standards. Although throughout the book we have been talking and mentioning both techniques and tools, I offer you here a generalized list, which I have extended as much as possible so that you have where to choose and with which you find adaptable tools for each type of project in terms of quality management.

Quality management plan: Document that defines quality practices, quality objectives, necessary resources, responsibilities, and schedule for quality-related activities in the project.

Requirements analysis: It is important to fully understand what is needed and expected from the AI project. Analysis techniques can include interviews, surveys, workshops, and brainstorming sessions.

Peer review: Consists of critically evaluating a colleague's work to ensure that it meets quality standards before it is considered complete.

Total Quality Management (TQM): It is a comprehensive management approach that focuses on continuous improvement in all aspects of the organization with the goal of meeting or exceeding customer expectations. In AI projects, TQM would imply the incorporation of quality at every stage of the development and operation process.

Software testing and model validation: Includes a series of tests, such as unit tests, integration tests, system tests, and user acceptance tests to verify the functionality and performance of AI software.

Checklists: Tools that ensure that all necessary steps are followed in a process. In AI projects, checklists can be used for code review, model configurations, data preparation, and other critical processes to ensure that all required tasks are systematically completed and quality standards are met.

Statistical process control (SPC): Uses statistical methods to monitor and control a process to ensure that it operates at its maximum potential.

Quality audits: Regular audits help verify that project management processes follow established practices and quality standards.

FMEA (Failure Mode and Effects Analysis): It is a proactive methodology used to identify all possible failures in a design, a manufacturing process, or a product or service, evaluating the severity, likelihood, and detection of failures to prioritize which ones require immediate attention. In AI, it can be used to anticipate potential failure points in algorithms and data systems.

Six Sigma: Method that uses statistical tools to improve quality and reduce variability by identifying and eliminating the causes of defects.

Kaizen (Continuous Improvement): Japanese philosophy focused on the continuous improvement of business processes, operational efficiency, and customer satisfaction.

Ishikawa diagrams (Cause and effect diagrams): Visual tool used to identify all possible causes of a problem to discover its root.

Benchmarking: Comparing processes and performance with industry best practices to identify areas for improvement.

5 Whys: It is a problem analysis technique that involves asking "Why?" repeatedly (usually five times) to get to the root of a problem. It is useful in AI projects to diagnose failures in systems and to understand the fundamental causes of quality problems in data, algorithms, and model performance.

Risk management: Identifying, analyzing, and responding to project risks, which includes quality management as a key component.

Code review and static analysis: For AI software, it is crucial that the code is reviewed by other developers and that tools are used to statically analyze the code, looking for errors or quality issues without running the program.

Data Quality Assurance: Ensuring the accuracy, completeness, and reliability of the data used to train and operate AI models.

Usability testing: Evaluation of how end-users interact with the AI system to ensure that it is intuitive and meets their needs.

Cross-validation: Technique used in modeling to evaluate how the results of a statistical model will generalize to an independent data set.

These tools and methods not only help you maintain the quality of the AI project, but also ensure alignment with business objectives and the satisfaction of the customer or end user. In addition, they promote transparency and improve the reliability and interpretation of AI systems.

60. Phases of a Project

In the creation and development of Artificial Intelligence projects, it is crucial to go through several preliminary stages before reaching a final product. These early stages serve to mitigate risks, validate technical and economic feasibility, and ensure that the final product meets the expectations and needs of the users.
Moreover, there are several crucial preliminary phases before launching a complete product. These phases are essential to validate the viability, functionality, and potential of the project. Below, I offer you a list of what I consider to be the most important phases to take into account, and in the order that I think is most important for you to consider when carrying out your projects.

1. Feasibility Study: Before diving into development, it is essential to evaluate whether the project is technically feasible and economically viable. This involves analyzing data availability, technological capacity, and financial resources.

2. Proof of Concept (POC): A POC helps determine if an idea can be put into practice. In the context of AI, this can mean developing a basic model to demonstrate that the chosen machine learning technique is suitable for the problem at hand.

3. Research and Development (R&D): This phase is crucial for exploring and developing new techniques or algorithms that might be necessary for the project. It is a space for innovation and experimentation.

4. Prototype: A more advanced model than the POC is built, demonstrating more functionalities and how the product could operate in real situations, although it is not yet ready for widespread use.

5. Pilot Project: In this phase, the prototype is tested in a real operational environment, but on a smaller scale. This allows for identifying practical problems and adjusting the system before a broader deployment.

6. Minimum Viable Product (MVP): The MVP is a more developed version that is launched to the market with enough features to attract early users and provide valuable feedback for future improvements.

7. Alpha and Beta Testing: These tests involve deploying the product in real conditions, first internally (Alpha) and then to a limited external group (Beta), to identify and correct faults.

8. Soft Launch: Before the full launch, a soft launch is conducted to assess market reception and make final adjustments based on a broader set of data and user feedback.

As you can see, the list shows a series of stages from the beginning of the project, and each of these stages is fundamental in the development of Artificial Intelligence projects, as they allow for validating ideas, continuously improving the product, and ensuring that the final launch is successful and meets market and user expectations. Since you will not have to go through all these stages in all projects, let's focus on the one you will have to develop in each project, the "POC" (Proof of Concept).

60.1. Proof of Concept (POC)

When tackling the development of a Proof of Concept in the field of Artificial Intelligence, we are embarking on a process that serves as a tangible first step towards realizing an AI-based idea or solution. An effective POC not only demonstrates the technical viability of an idea but also provides a solid foundation for justifying additional investment and ongoing development. Due to its importance and its early appearance among all other processes, I will choose to develop it further, in this way, and if you still have no experience in projects, you will be able to get a broader and more defined idea of what awaits you and how it will develop, preparing you for the moment.

In the process of developing a POC, it is important to follow a structured methodology that ensures that all critical areas are considered and properly evaluated. The steps we are going to follow are essential to ensure that the POC meets its objectives efficiently and effectively.

These steps include:

1. **Define objectives:** Establish clear and specific goals that the POC must achieve.
2. **Select relevant data:** Identify and prepare the necessary data sets for the POC.
3. **Establish resources and tools:** Determine what human, technological, and financial resources are necessary, as well as choose the appropriate tools and platforms.
4. **Set a timeframe:** Define a realistic timeline for the development and evaluation of the POC.
5. **Manage risks:** Identify potential risks and prepare strategies to mitigate them.
6. **Establish success criteria and evaluation methods:** Define how the success of the POC will be measured and what methods will be used to evaluate its performance.

Each of these steps is vital to the success of the POC, allowing not only to validate the central idea but also to provide valuable information for the later phases of the project. Once you have reviewed this introduction, we can proceed with the detailed development of the first point.

60.1.1. Define Objectives

Defining clear and measurable objectives is a fundamental step in developing a Proof of Concept (POC), especially in the field of Artificial Intelligence, a field still unexplored for most companies. The objectives of the POC must align with the global goals of the project and be specific, measurable, achievable, relevant, and time-bound (SMART criteria. We will see this point in more detail later). Next, I describe how to approach this process.

Identification of needs and problems

Needs Analysis: Understand the specific needs of the business or client for which the AI solution is being developed. What problem or challenge is being addressed?

Dialogue with Stakeholders: Involve all interested parties to ensure that their expectations and needs are reflected in the POC objectives.

Setting SMART objectives
Specific: Objectives should be concrete and clear. For example, "Demonstrate the AI model's ability to classify images with 95% accuracy."
Measurable: There should be a clear way to measure success. This could include metrics such as accuracy, response time, cost reduction, etc.
Achievable: Objectives should be realistic given the resources and time available. It is vital to be ambitious but also realistic.
Relevant: Ensure that the objectives align with the broader objectives of the project and the company's strategy.
Time-based: Establish a clear timeframe for achieving the objectives. This could be at the end of the POC period or at specific milestones during its development.

Examples of objectives for an AI POC:
- Evaluate the technical feasibility of applying machine learning to improve efficiency in a specific process.
- Demonstrate the model's ability to process and analyze data in real-time with a certain accuracy.
- Identify the limitations and challenges of integrating the AI solution into the existing infrastructure.

Documentation and communication:
- **Clear Documentation:** All objectives should be clearly documented and distributed among all team members and stakeholders.
- **Feedback and adjustment:** Be open to stakeholder feedback and be willing to adjust the objectives if necessary during the POC development process.

Establishing clear and well-defined objectives is essential to guide the development of the POC, providing a reference framework for making decisions and evaluating progress. Once the objectives are defined, the team can proceed with a clear direction and a defined purpose.

60.1.2. Select Relevant Data

The quality and relevance of data are fundamental to the success of any AI model. This process involves several key stages:

Identification of data sources
Analysis of available sources: Identify all possible data sources that might be useful for the POC. This may include internal company databases, user-generated data, sensor data, public data, among others.
Quality and relevance assessment: Ensure that the data is relevant to the problem being addressed and that it is of high quality in terms of accuracy, completeness, and timeliness.

Data preparation

Cleaning and preprocessing: Involves removing erroneous or irrelevant data, handling missing values, and normalization.

Exploratory Data Analysis (EDA): Perform exploratory analysis to understand the characteristics and trends in the data. This may include data visualization, statistical analysis, and identifying patterns or anomalies.

Ensuring data representativeness

Diversity and coverage: The data must be representative of the environment in which the AI model will be deployed. This is crucial to avoid biases and ensure that the model is generalizable and reliable.

Training and test data sets: Divide the data into training and test sets, ensuring that both reflect the diversity and challenges of the real problem.

Legal and ethical compliance

Privacy and data protection: Ensure that data handling complies with all applicable privacy and data protection regulations, such as GDPR in Europe.

Consent and anonymization: If the data involves personal information, it is crucial to obtain appropriate consent and consider data anonymization.

Data documentation and management

Documenting sources and processes: Maintain a detailed record of data sources, preprocessing methods, and any relevant decisions made during the selection and preparation of the data.

Secure storage and access: Implement solutions for secure data storage and control access to it, especially if it is sensitive or confidential.

The proper selection and preparation of data is a fundamental pillar in the development of any AI solution. Careful attention to these aspects will ensure that the POC is built on a solid foundation, allowing the developed AI model to be as effective and reliable as possible.

60.1.3. Establish Resources and Tools

This point is especially important for you, especially in the field of Artificial Intelligence. It involves defining and securing the necessary human, technological, and financial resources, as well as selecting the appropriate tools and platforms for the development and testing of the POC. You have many tools and platforms that offer solutions that can be of great help, but knowing how to choose them is of vital importance for you, as some solutions, being free, can be very limited, and therefore can jeopardize this stage and consequently the project. Knowing the potential of each tool, its limitations, and the possibilities they offer can save you from many bad and uncomfortable moments.

Human Resources

Project team: Identify and assign team members with the necessary skills, including data experts (Data Scientists), software engineers, AI specialists, and business analysts.

Training and development: Assess whether the team needs additional specific training in tools, programming languages, or methodologies relevant to the project.

Technological Resources
Hardware and software: Determine hardware requirements, such as servers and data processing devices, and software, including operating systems and development tools.
AI platforms and analytical tools: Select the most suitable AI development platforms and tools, considering factors such as scalability, compatibility, and community support. This may include TensorFlow, PyTorch, scikit-learn, among others.

Infrastructure and development environment
Development and testing environment: Set up flexible and replicable development and testing environments, using containers or cloud services if necessary.
Code and version management: Use source code management tools like Git, and collaboration platforms like GitHub or GitLab.

Financial Resources
Budget: Establish a clear budget covering all necessary resources, including personnel, technology, training, and any other operational expense.
Funding and support: Identify potential internal or external funding sources if necessary, and secure support from management or relevant stakeholders.

Project management and collaboration tools
Project management tools: Adopt project management tools like Jira, Trello, or Asana to plan, track, and manage project activities.
Communication and collaboration: Facilitate communication within the team and with other stakeholders using tools like Slack, Microsoft Teams, or Zoom.

Compliance and security
Regulatory compliance: Ensure that all tools and resources used comply with applicable regulations and laws, especially regarding data privacy and security.
Information security: Implement appropriate security measures to protect the data and systems used in the project.

By selecting and securing the right resources and tools, a solid foundation is created for the successful development of the POC. This step is essential to ensure that the team has everything needed to carry out the project efficiently and effectively.

60.1.4. Setting a Time Frame

Point 4, "Setting a Time Frame," is a critical aspect in the planning and execution of a Proof of Concept (POC) in Artificial Intelligence projects. A well-defined time frame helps manage expectations, organize resources efficiently, and provide clear milestones for progress monitoring.

Establishment of the General Timeline
Duration of the POC: Determine the total duration of the POC. This is usually a few weeks to several months, depending on the complexity of the project.
Key Milestones: Identify and plan key milestones within this period. This could include the completion of data collection, initial model development, testing phases, etc.

Detailed Planning
Task Breakdown: Create a detailed breakdown of all tasks necessary to complete the POC. This includes data preparation activities, model development, testing, and revisions.
Time Allocation per Task: Estimate and allocate specific time for each task, taking into account the complexity and resources available.

Flexibility and Continuous Review
Margin for Uncertainty: Include extra time for unforeseen events or unexpected delays, which are common in AI projects due to the exploratory and experimental nature of the field.
Regular Review and Adjustment: Plan regular progress reviews and be willing to adjust the schedule as necessary.

Integration with the Overall Project Schedule
Alignment with the Larger Project: Ensure that the POC schedule is aligned with the overall timelines of the broader project, especially if the POC is part of a larger effort.

Communication of the Time Frame
Clarity with the Team and Stakeholders: Clearly communicate the time frame to all team members and stakeholders, ensuring everyone is aligned and aware of the deadlines.
Planning and Tracking Tools: Use project management tools to visualize and track the schedule, such as Gantt charts or Kanban boards.

Documentation
Planning Record: Maintain detailed documentation of the time planning, decisions made, and any changes made to the schedule.

By establishing a clear and realistic time frame, effective management of the POC is facilitated, ensuring that each phase of the project is completed timely and that the team can quickly adapt to any challenges or changes in circumstances. A well-planned schedule is an essential tool for keeping the project on track and achieving the set goals. To maintain a structure in the project timeline, it is important that you are well organized, or at least that you are good at organization and time control, as otherwise, you will not only go crazy, but you will also jeopardize the project's deadlines, preventing other colleagues and participants from advancing in their tasks, further delaying the project.

60.1.5. Managing Risks

Risk management involves identifying, assessing, and mitigating potential issues that could impact the development and success of the POC. This process is fundamental to ensuring that the project develops smoothly and to minimize any negative impact on the results.

Risk Identification
Technical Assessment: Identify risks related to technology and AI implementation, such as inappropriate algorithm selection, data quality issues, or hardware and software limitations.
Project Risks: Consider risks associated with project management, such as schedule delays, communication problems, or budget deviations.
External Risks: Take into account external factors such as changes in regulations, market issues, or unforeseen situations (like health emergencies or natural disasters).

Risk Evaluation and Prioritization
Impact and Probability Analysis: Assess each risk in terms of its likelihood of occurrence and potential impact on the project. This helps prioritize risks that require more attention.
Risk Matrix: Create a risk matrix to visualize and categorize risks according to their severity and probability.

Mitigation Strategy Development
Contingency Plans: Develop action plans for identified risks, defining how they will be managed or mitigated if they occur.
Reduction and Prevention: Implement measures to reduce the likelihood of risk occurrence or minimize their impact. This can include improving data quality, training staff, or enhancing team communication.

Continuous Monitoring and Review
Regular Tracking: Establish a process for regular risk tracking throughout the project, allowing for a quick response to any changes.
Strategy Review and Adjustment: Be prepared to review and adjust mitigation strategies as necessary, in response to new risks or changes in the project environment.

Documentation and Communication
Risk Record: Maintain a detailed record of all identified risks, their assessments, and associated mitigation plans.
Communication with Stakeholders: Inform stakeholders about significant risks and how they are being managed, ensuring transparency and fostering trust in the project management.

Effective risk management in an AI POC not only helps to prevent problems but also ensures that the team is prepared to handle challenges proactively, keeping the project on track towards success.

60.1.6. Establishing Success Criteria and Evaluation Methods

Well-defined success criteria and clear, objective evaluation methods allow for effective measurement of the POC's performance and efficacy. They ensure that the POC in an Artificial Intelligence project meets its objectives and provides real value.

Definition of Success Criteria
Alignment with POC Objectives: Success criteria should be directly related to the specific objectives set in the objective definition phase. For example, if the goal is to demonstrate the accuracy of an AI model, the success criterion could be achieving a certain percentage of accuracy in data classification.
Quantifiable and Measurable: It is important that these criteria are quantifiable to be objectively evaluated. This can include metrics such as accuracy, response time, reduction in operational costs, etc.

Selection of Evaluation Methods
Quantitative Methods: Use statistical methods and performance metrics like accuracy, sensitivity, specificity, F1 Score, among others, to evaluate the performance of the AI model.
Testing and Validations: Implement validation tests, including A/B tests or user tests, to evaluate the efficacy of the POC under real or simulated conditions.
Comparison with Industry Benchmarking or Standards: Compare the POC results with industry standards or benchmarks to evaluate its competitiveness and relevance.

Review and Feedback Process
Continuous Review: Establish regular reviews during and after the POC to assess progress and compliance with success criteria.
Feedback Collection: Obtain feedback from end-users, stakeholders, and subject matter experts for a qualitative evaluation of the POC.

Documentation and Analysis
Detailed Record: Maintain detailed documentation of evaluation results and how they were measured.
Result Analysis: Conduct an in-depth analysis of the results to understand not only if the success criteria were met, but also why and how these lessons can be applied in future project phases.

Adjustments Based on Evaluation
Iteration and Improvement: Use the evaluation results to make adjustments and improvements in the POC. This is fundamental in an iterative and agile approach, typical in AI projects.

The establishment of clear success criteria and the selection of appropriate evaluation methods are essential for effectively measuring the success of an AI POC. They allow not only to validate the proposed solution but also to provide valuable insights for continuous improvement and informed decision-making for future project phases.

We have reached the end of this topic, and since this point is so important to you as a project manager, we will make a summary as short as possible to have on hand all the most important points.

Main Objectives of the POC
Technical Feasibility Validation: Verify if the proposed AI/ML solution is technically feasible.
Preliminary Results Assessment: Obtain an initial indication of the results that can be expected from the complete project.
Risk and Challenge Identification: Recognize and plan how to address potential obstacles before large-scale implementation.
Value Demonstration: Present to stakeholders how the AI solution can add value to the business or process.

Advantages of the POC
Risk Reduction: Limits risk exposure by testing the idea at an early stage.
Resource Optimization: Allows for efficient resource allocation before committing to a full investment.
Facilitated Decision Making: Provides concrete data to support strategic decisions.
Support and Commitment Generation: Helps gain stakeholder backing by demonstrating practical potential.

Potential Pitfalls in Conducting a POC
Unrealistic Expectations: Setting overly ambitious or unclear goals.
Data Selection Limitations: Using a dataset that does not reflect the reality of the production environment.
Lack of Scalability: Not considering how the project will scale after the POC.
Inadequate Results Evaluation: Not properly analyzing the results or ignoring negative aspects.

Critical Success Factors
Clarity in Objectives: Clearly define what is being tested or demonstrated.
Appropriate Data Selection: Use a representative and quality dataset.
Stakeholder Commitment: Ensure the support and active participation of all relevant parties.
Effective Project Management: Maintain an organized and flexible approach during the POC.

POC Process Structure
Objective and Success Metric Definition: Establish what is to be achieved and how success will be measured.
Tool and Technology Selection: Choose the appropriate platforms and tools for the POC.
Development and Execution: Implement the proposed solution in a controlled environment.
Data Collection and Analysis: Gather data on the performance and effectiveness of the POC.
Documentation and Presentation of Results: Prepare detailed reports for stakeholders.

POC Evaluation
Comparison with Original Objectives: Verify if the POC meets the established objectives.

Performance and Reliability Analysis: Evaluate the accuracy, efficiency, and consistency of the proposed model or solution.
Economic Feasibility: Consider the involved costs and potential return on investment.
Stakeholder Reception: Obtain feedback from users, participants, and decision-makers.

61. Steps to Follow for the Successful Development of a Project.

Now let's delve into project development. For this, I will detail a list of steps to follow for the correct realization of a project. It is important to add that each professional will have a more subjective vision of this list and therefore a different opinion regarding the order and content of the points, so there will probably be those who consider that points are missing, or that some points are not important. I offer you the list considering what is most important for the project and in the order that I consider to be the most logical and optimal. Finally, it will be you who with practice decide how you approach an Artificial Intelligence project and how you execute it. To elaborate the points of development, I will focus mainly on three aspects: the objectives to be achieved in each step, the phases of each step, and the most known methods to carry it out. Each step in the development of a project can vary according to its needs, so it is very possible that throughout the development I take into account extra aspects that perhaps in other points I do not take into account.

1. Initial advisory meeting with the company:
- Identification of the company's needs and objectives.
- Preliminary analysis of the project's feasibility.
- Presentation of possible AI-based solutions.

2. Definition of project scope and objectives:
- Establish clear goals and objectives.
- Definition of technical and functional specifications.
- Identification of potential limitations and restrictions.

3. Construction of the project team:
- Selection of AI experts, developers, Data Scientists, and other relevant roles.
- Definition of roles and responsibilities.

4. Data collection and analysis:
- Identification of data sources.
- Data cleaning and preprocessing.
- Exploratory data analysis.

5. Design of the AI model:
- Choice of appropriate algorithms and techniques.
- Design of the model architecture.
- Establishment of evaluation metrics.

6. Training and validation of the model:
- Splitting data into training, validation, and test sets.
- Training the model.
- Evaluation and adjustment of the model.

7. Implementation and deployment:
- Integration of the model into the company's infrastructure.
- Deployment in a production environment.
- Establishment of monitoring and maintenance protocols.

8. Monitoring and optimization of the model:
- Monitoring the model's performance in real time.
- Retraining and adjustment based on fresh data and feedback.

9. Documentation and knowledge transfer:
- Development of technical and user documentation.
- Training and capacity building for company users and teams.

10. Final presentation of the project to the company:
- Demonstration of the model's functionality and results.
- Analysis of ROI (return on investment) and benefits obtained.
- Collection of feedback and suggestions for future improvements.

11. Project closure and review:
- Evaluation of the project's success in relation to the established objectives.
- Identification of lessons learned.
- Planning of possible future phases or related projects.

Now let's 'dissect' the processes one by one and make a detailed list of each process. Keep in mind that this list, like the previous one, can be relative as well as subjective. Take it as guidance and adapt it to your needs as necessary. The important thing here is that you use it as a Checklist so you don't forget any points along the way.

61.1. Initial advisory meeting with the company

Point 1, "Initial advisory meeting with the company", is critical as it lays the foundation for mutual understanding and the success of the Artificial Intelligence project. This step is detailed as follows:

Objectives to be achieved with this step
Understanding the business: Deeply comprehend the nature of the client's business, its industry, its key processes, and the challenges it faces.
Definition of needs: Identify and document the specific needs that AI should address, which may include process automation, data analysis, decision improvement, etc.

Establishment of expectations: Clarify what is and what is not possible with AI, and establish realistic expectations regarding results, timing, and costs.
Building relationships: Build trust and a working relationship with the client, ensuring that all involved parties are aligned and committed.
Preliminary evaluation: Conduct a preliminary evaluation of the available data, the client's technological infrastructure, and resources, to determine the project's feasibility.

The phases of this step:

1. Preparation:
- Gathering prior information about the company.
- Defining key participants for the meeting.
- Developing a detailed agenda for the meeting.

2. Execution:
- Presentation of participants and explanation of their roles.
- Guided discussion to understand the business objectives and its challenges.
- Exploration of AI use cases relevant to the business.
- Initial collection of information about existing data and systems.

3. Evaluation:
- Analysis of information gathered during the meeting.
- Identification of potential AI solutions and estimation of their impact.
- Determination of the technical and economic feasibility of the proposed solutions.

4. Follow-up:
- Documentation and summary of key points discussed.
- Communication of next steps and assignment of tasks.
- Establishment of a schedule for the next phase of the project.

Known methods for doing it
Face-to-face meetings: In-person sessions that allow direct communication and building a stronger relationship with the client.
Group dynamics: Workshops or workshops that involve interactive activities to explore the client's needs and generate ideas.
Structured interviews: Use of questionnaires and interviews with predefined questions to obtain detailed information from stakeholders.
SWOT Analysis (Strengths, Weaknesses, Opportunities, Threats): Strategic tool to understand the business position and the potential impact of AI solutions.
Business Model Canvas Method: To visualize the key components of the business and how AI could influence each of them.
Prototypes and demonstrations: Presentation of AI prototypes or demos to illustrate possible solutions and their operation in a real context.

Each of these methods can help ensure that the initial meeting is productive and that the proper groundwork is laid for the AI project. A tip that could be very helpful to you would be to prepare a Briefing adapted to you, whether you are a Freelancer or directly hired, the Briefing can be of great help for all types of projects, and getting used to its use can save you both time and disappointment.

61.2. Definition of Scope and Objectives of the Project

Point 2, "Definition of scope and objectives of the project" sets the expectations and limits within which all future work will be developed. Although this point could and should be done together with point 1 during the meeting, I detail it separately for you to understand its importance.

Objectives to be achieved with this step
Clarity in the desired outcomes:
- Clearly define what the project must achieve.
- Ensure that all stakeholders have the same understanding and expectations.

Feasibility and scope:
- Determine what is and is not part of the project.
- Identify limitations such as time, budget, and resources.

Prioritization:
- Establish the priority of the project objectives and features.
- Align the objectives with the strategic objectives of the company.

Measurability:
- Create measurable objectives to be able to track the progress and success of the project.

Foundation for planning:
- Provide a basis for detailed project planning, including time, budget, and resource allocation.

Phases of this step:
1. Requirement Gathering:
- Collection of detailed information from all stakeholders.
- Interviews, surveys, focus groups, and brainstorming sessions.

2. Requirement Analysis:
- Analysis and classification of the collected requirements.
- Differentiation between necessary and desirable requirements.

3. Scope Definition:
- Creation of a project scope statement.
- Delimitation of the project boundaries.

4. Objective Establishment:
- Definition of SMART objectives (Specific, Measurable, Achievable, Relevant, Time-Bound).
- Alignment with the interests of the company and stakeholders.

5. Validation:
- Review of the scope statement and objectives with all stakeholders.
- Adjustments based on feedback received.

6. Documentation:
- Document everything in a project plan or a project scope document.

Known methods for doing it
Stakeholder Analysis: Identifying all interested parties and understanding their needs and expectations.
Nominal Group Technique: Technique to reach group consensus and prioritize requirements or features.
Problem Statement Technique: Describing a problem and its effects clearly and concisely to understand the central problem and find the most suitable solution.
Delphi Method: Iterative collection of expert opinions to reach a common understanding.
GAP Analysis: Evaluation of the difference between the current situation and the desired future state.
Scope-Definition: Establish the limits and deliverables of the project. Define what will be included in the project and what will be out of scope, helping to avoid uncontrolled project expansion, known as 'scope creep'.
Brainstorming: Creative sessions to generate ideas and solutions.
Affinity Diagrams: Organization of ideas and requirements into groups based on their relationship or affinity.
User Stories and Epics in Agile Methodologies:
- Description of the features from the end user's perspective.
- Used in agile methodologies like Scrum or Kanban.

MoSCoW Method: Prioritizing requirements as: Must have, Should have, Could have, and Won't have (this time).
SMART: Establish objectives that are Specific, Measurable, Achievable, Relevant, and Time-Bound. This technique helps ensure that project objectives are clear and achievable within a specific time.
Impact Analysis: Study of how changes in requirements can affect the project.
Prototyping: Creation of initial versions of the product to obtain early feedback and validate requirements and assumptions.
Cost-Benefit Analysis: Evaluation of the relationship between the expected benefits and the costs associated with the project.

By following these steps and using these methods, you can ensure that the AI project is well defined and aligned with the needs and capabilities of the organization. This will help mitigate risks, avoid misunderstandings, and provide a clear roadmap for the execution of the project that will be both of great value and of great help for the development of the project.

61.2.1. Orchestrating Success

When addressing project management in the field of Artificial Intelligence, clarity in defining the scope and objectives is fundamental to success. This is where specialized techniques become important, providing a solid structure to guide teams through the inherent complexity of these innovative projects.

We will begin by exploring the "Problem-Statement-Technique," a methodology that helps us precisely articulate the problem to be solved. This technique ensures that all involved have a unified understanding of the challenge to develop effective AI solutions.

Next, we will delve into "Scope-Definition". This phase is vital to outline the project's boundaries, establishing what is included and what is not. In the dynamic field of AI, having a well-defined scope allows for efficient resource management and avoids the risk of deviating towards secondary objectives that could dilute the project's focus.

Finally, we will look at the "SMART" technique, a strategy to set concrete, measurable, achievable, relevant, and time-bound goals. By applying this framework, you as an AI-Manager can set clear goals that are not only ambitious but also realistic, ensuring that the team remains motivated and on the right track.

Together, these techniques form the backbone of an efficient AI project management process, ensuring that every step, from conception to execution, is well-founded and aligned with a strategic vision.

61.2.1.1. Problem Statement Technique

The problem statement technique in the field of AI project management is a structured method that helps to clearly define a problem before seeking solutions. It is divided into three essential steps:

1) Current State: In this step, the current situation is described in detail, identifying and documenting the specific problem that needs solving. In an AI project, this could involve recognizing limitations in the accuracy of a predictive model, performance issues in existing algorithms, or the lack of integration of AI systems with other technologies in use. It is important to be as concrete and objective as possible, using specific data and examples to illustrate the problem.

2) Desired State: Here, the ideal state or outcome to be achieved with the problem's solution is defined. In terms of AI, this might mean setting a precision goal for the predictive model, improving the performance of algorithms to process data in real-time, or achieving complete and seamless integration with other technological platforms. The desired state should be clear, achievable, and preferably measurable.

3) Obstacles: The last step involves identifying the obstacles that prevent moving from the current state to the desired state. This can include technological limitations, lack of specialized skills in the team, budget constraints, or scalability issues. Recognizing these obstacles is crucial to planning how to overcome them and achieve the project's goals.

The problem statement is a very effective technique because it forces the team to focus on the root of the problem before starting to generate possible solutions, ensuring that all aspects of the problem are fully understood before proceeding.

61.2.1.2. Scope-Definition

The "Scope-Definition" technique clearly defines what will be included in the project (In-Scope) and what will be left out (Out-of-Scope), thus establishing precise boundaries and avoiding misunderstandings or changes in scope that could affect resources, timelines, and the success of the project.

In-Scope: Here, the functions, tasks, deliverables, and processes that the AI project commits to perform and develop are detailed. For example, if the project is about developing a recommendation algorithm, the types of data to be used, the success metrics, and the specific functionalities that the algorithm will be able to perform will be specified.

Out-of-Scope: It is equally important to define what is outside the project's scope to manage expectations and focus efforts on what will actually be delivered. For example, it may be decided that integration with certain external systems will not be covered in the current project or that certain types of data analysis are outside the scope.

Boundary Criteria: These are the rules or parameters used to determine if something is in or out of scope. These criteria help make decisions when there are doubts about whether a specific task or functionality should be part of the project. They include the justification for the scope, documentation of constraints, and criteria for accepting or rejecting additional requests.

When defining the scope with the "Scope-Definition" technique, all technical and functional aspects of the project, as well as time and budget limitations, should be considered. It is also crucial to involve all stakeholders in this process to ensure a common understanding and alignment with business objectives.

61.2.1.3. SMART

We have previously talked about the SMART technique, but as you can see, it reappears and is always present in your day-to-day project management. This technique is a method for setting goals and objectives effectively and clearly, ensuring that they are achievable and measurable. SMART is an acronym that summarizes the key criteria for defining successful project goals, and this is why you should always have the word SMART present.

Specific: The objectives must be clear and precise. Instead of having a broad goal, exactly what is expected to be achieved should be detailed. This involves answering the questions: What? Who? Where? When?
Example: Implement a customer service chatbot system on the company website before the end of the fourth quarter.

Measurable: Parameters must be established to measure progress towards each goal. This allows close monitoring of the project's development and knowing when the goal has been reached. The key questions are: How much? How many? How will I know when the goal has been achieved?
Example: Increase the chatbot's first-instance query resolution rate to 75% in six months.

Achievable: The objectives must be realistic and within the available capabilities and resources. It is important to maintain a balance between a challenging goal and one that is practically impossible. Ask yourself: Is this goal possible? How can I achieve it?
Example: Train the AI team in the use of natural language processing tools within the next three months.

Relevant: The objectives must matter to the business or organization and align with other relevant goals. They should be timely and pertinent in the broader context. Pertinent questions include: Why? Is this the right time? Is it in tune with other needs?
Example: Develop a recommendation algorithm to personalize product suggestions, increasing cross-sales by 20% for next year.

Time-Bound: Each objective needs a deadline or a specific time frame for its realization. This creates urgency and commitment. The questions to consider are: When? What can I do today? What can I do in six weeks?
Example: Complete the pilot testing phase of the voice recognition project for the call center before the end of the second quarter.

By applying these criteria, an AI-Manager can define more clearly and precisely what is to be achieved in an AI project, establishing a structure that facilitates effective planning, execution, and monitoring of the project. When you get used to working with these techniques, everything will be easier for you. Create a routine in your day-to-day to get used to having these terms always close to you. Always keep these definitions very present and this will speed up your performance and effectiveness. Once these techniques are implemented in your professional habits, everything will flow much better and you will notice a great improvement in your day-to-day as well as an increase in your motivation in yourself, as you will notice how your abilities to manage, not only AI projects but any project you set out to do, will increase considerably.

61.3. Project Team Building

Building a team for an Artificial Intelligence project is a critical step that can determine the success of the project. It's important to remember that the project team will undoubtedly vary depending on the type of project and its scale. For example, if you're doing a project for the medical sector, like an Artificial Intelligence capable of recognizing in lung X-ray photographs whether the lungs are infected with pneumonia or tuberculosis, then you will undoubtedly need a radiology expert as well. Another example, if you work for an industrial sector company that manufactures engines, and you must develop an Artificial Intelligence that can recognize with great detail errors in the manufacturing of engine crankcases, then you will undoubtedly need to include an expert engineer in crankcases on the team.

Goals to achieve with this step

Form a competent and multifunctional team: The team must have the skills and experience necessary to cover all aspects of the development and implementation of the AI solution.

Ensure alignment of objectives: All team members must understand and commit to the project's objectives to work efficiently towards a common goal.

Promote effective collaboration: Foster a work environment where communication and cooperation among team members are facilitated.

Maximize the use of resources: Efficiently allocate available human resources to optimize the project's progress and productivity.

People needed, positions, and tasks

AI-Manager (Project Manager): Coordinates the project, manages resources, and is the link between the team and stakeholders.

Data Scientist: Analyzes and models large data sets. In charge of creating Machine Learning algorithms.

Machine Learning Engineer: Implements models developed by data scientists in scalable and efficient solutions.

Data Engineer: Prepares the data "pipeline" and ensures that data is ready to be processed and analyzed.

AI Developer: Codes the AI software base, working closely with Machine Learning engineers and Data Scientists.

DevOps Specialist: Ensures continuous integration and deployment (CI/CD) of AI applications.

UX/UI Expert: Designs the user experience and interface to ensure that the application is user-friendly and meets the end-user's needs.

Business Analyst: Assesses business requirements and ensures that the AI solution aligns with business needs and expectations.

AI Ethics Specialist: Ensures that the AI solution complies with ethical and legal standards.

Phases of this step:

1. **Planning:** Define the necessary skills and roles based on the project's objectives.
2. **Recruitment:** Search for and select candidates that meet the defined criteria.
3. **Evaluation:** Interview candidates to assess technical skills and teamwork.
4. **Selection:** Choose the most suitable candidates for each position.
5. **Integration:** Onboarding and training to ensure all team members are aware of the policies, tools, and project processes.
6. **Team Development:** Team-building activities to foster cohesion and establish good communication.

Known methods for doing this

Tuckman's Team Formation Model: This model describes the phases of forming, conflict, normalizing, and performance for team development.

Agile Methodologies: Promote collaboration among multidisciplinary teams and adaptability throughout the project.

Competency-based recruitment: Focuses on specific skills and experience relevant to the AI project.

Belbin Role Analysis: A method for assessing and balancing personality types and work roles within a team.

By following these steps and methods, you can build an effective and well-prepared team to face the unique challenges of an Artificial Intelligence project.

61.3.1. The Tuckman Model for Team Formation

Let's look at the Tuckman Model for Team Formation in more detail. This model is one of the most used models when managing teams. Like other points we have already covered throughout the book, the Tuckman model is also somewhat subjective. It depends on each one's interpretation, and also relative because it depends on the needs of the project plan. You can find this model ranging from four to seven points and possibly eight points. Here, I explain the most important ones that you should always keep in mind when forming work teams.

The Tuckman Team Formation Model is a theory developed by Bruce Tuckman in 1965, explaining that teams go through different phases during their development. Tuckman originally identified four stages of group development: Forming, Storming (Conflict), Norming, and Performing. Later, in 1977, he added a fifth stage called Adjourning (Dissolution).

Below, I detail a five-stage summary.

1. Forming

Characteristics: Team members get to know each other and seek to understand group boundaries. There is dependence on leadership figures for guidance and direction. There is little agreement on goals beyond those provided by the leader. Processes are simple and unclear.

Behaviors: Members may be anxious, curious, and polite. First impressions are formed, and the basis for future group dynamics.

Leader's tasks: Provide direction and establish clear goals, help team members to get to know each other.

2. Storming

Characteristics: Team members tackle more difficult tasks and begin to express stronger opinions. Conflicts and polarization arise around interpersonal issues and tasks. There is resistance to group supervision and feedback on differences.

Behaviors: Members may challenge authority or team goals. Conflicts may arise over leadership, structure, and power.

Leader's tasks: Facilitate and mediate conflicts, encourage participation, and ensure that discussions do not become counterproductive.

3. Norming
Characteristics: Relationships develop and the team shows cohesion. There is a strong sense of team identity and camaraderie. Team roles and operating norms are accepted. Members are willing to change their ideas or agreements for the benefit of the team.
Behaviors: Trust develops among team members, and a clearer structure is established.
Leader's tasks: Facilitate participation and promote teamwork, consolidate team norms and values.

4. Performing
Characteristics: The team works more effectively towards goals. Roles become flexible and functional, and there is no interpersonal friction. The team structure supports the tasks being carried out. There is a focus on goal achievement and task efficiency.
Behaviors: Team members are autonomous and capable of handling decision-making without supervision. Team energy is channeled into the task.
Leader's tasks: Delegate tasks and projects, develop team capabilities, and foster autonomy.

5. Adjourning
Characteristics: The team prepares to dissolve, and attention turns to finishing tasks and reducing dependence. There is a sense of closure and the possibility of mourning the project's completion.
Behaviors: Members may feel uncertainty and sadness about the dissolution of the team. Achievements are celebrated, and everyone's work is acknowledged.
Leader's tasks: Confirm the completion of goals, recognize and celebrate team achievements, and assist members in transitioning to new projects or roles.

This model is widely used in project management and organizational development to help leaders and team members understand their progress and adapt their strategies and behaviors to be more effective.

61.4. Data Collection and Analysis

Developing the data collection and analysis step in an Artificial Intelligence project in this way is crucial for a positive project completion, as the quality and structure of the data will largely determine the performance of the AI model.

Objectives to be achieved with this step:
Ensure data quality: Ensure that the data is accurate, complete, and relevant to the project's objectives.
Understand the data: Get a clear view of the data's characteristics, including distributions, correlations, and potential biases.

Prepare data for modeling: Transform the data into a format suitable for use in machine learning algorithms.
Establish a solid foundation for model development: Ensure that the data is ready to be processed by AI models without problems that could compromise the validity of the results.

Phases of This Step:
1. Data requirements definition:
- Identify the types of data needed.
- Determine the volume of data required for reliable results.

2. Data collection:
- Obtain data from various internal and external sources.
- Ensure that data collection complies with privacy and data protection regulations.

3. Data cleaning:
- Remove or correct erroneous or incomplete records.
- Deal with missing values and outliers.

4. Exploratory Data Analysis (EDA):
- Perform descriptive statistical analysis.
- Visualize the data to detect patterns or anomalies.

5. Data preprocessing:
- Normalize or scale the data.
- Encode categorical variables.
- Generate new features (feature engineering).

6. Data integration:
- Combine data from different sources.
- Resolve redundancy and consistency issues.

7. Dimensionality reduction:
- Apply techniques to reduce the number of input variables without losing important information.

8. Data splitting:
- Divide the data into training, validation, and test sets.

Known methods for doing this:
Data cleaning:
- Use of scripts in languages such as Python or R to automate cleaning.
- Application of ETL (Extract, Transform, Load) tools to prepare the data.

Exploratory Data Analysis (EDA):
- Data visualization techniques such as histograms, box plots, and heat maps.
- Descriptive statistics such as mean, median, mode, interquartile range.

Data preprocessing:
- Transformations such as standardization and normalization.
- One-hot encoding for categorical variables.

Data integration:
- Data integration tools such as Talend, Informatica PowerCenter.
- Databases and data management systems to unify data sources.

Dimensionality reduction:
- Principal Component Analysis (PCA).
- Feature selection using methods like feature importance or model-based methods.

Data splitting:
- Stratified sampling techniques to maintain class distribution in different sets.
- Use of machine learning library tools like scikit-learn in Python to split the data.

The implementation of these phases and methods must be meticulous and adapted to the specifics of the project to ensure that the data will be a true reflection of the reality that the AI model will attempt to learn and on which it will make predictions or take decisions.

61.5. AI Model Design

The design of the AI model is a component in the life cycle of an Artificial Intelligence project. Including the objectives, phases, and known methods for doing it, we will look at the development of this step.

Objectives to be achieved with this step:
Selection of the appropriate architecture: Choose a model structure that is appropriate for the data and the specific problem.
Effectiveness and efficiency: Design a model that is not only accurate but also efficient in terms of computational resources.
Scalability: Ensure that the model can scale appropriately with the increase in data or task complexity.
Interpretability: Make the model transparent enough so that the decisions it makes can be understood and justified, especially in regulated domains.
Generalization: Design a model that works well not only on training data but also on new and unknown data.
Compliance and ethics: Ensure that the model design complies with relevant legal and ethical requirements.

Phases of this step:
1. Literature review and precedents: Investigate existing models and similar use cases to complement and improve the design.

2. Feature selection: Determine which data are relevant to the problem and how they should be processed.
3. Algorithm choice: Decide which algorithms are most suitable for the objectives and available features.
4. Model architecture design: Specify layers, neurons, activation functions, etc., in the case of neural networks; or equivalent structures in other types of models.
5. Performance metric definition: Establish how the model's success will be measured.
6. Prototyping: Create an initial prototype that can be iterated and improved.
7. Preliminary evaluation: Perform an initial evaluation of the model to identify deficiencies and areas for improvement.

Known methods for doing this:
Model benchmarking: Test various base models to establish a performance benchmark.
Cross-validation: Use cross-validation techniques to evaluate the model's generalization.
Hyperparameter optimization: Employ grid search, random search, or Bayesian optimization methods to find the best combination of hyperparameters.
Proof of Concept (PoC): Build minimum viable models to quickly validate the feasibility of a solution.
Automated model design (AutoML): Use AutoML tools to automatically explore various architectures and model configurations.
Design of Experiments (DoE): Apply statistical methods to plan experiments that can effectively test the model's hypotheses.
Regularization and ensemble techniques: Implement regularization techniques to prevent overfitting and use ensemble methods to improve the robustness and performance of the model.

The design of the AI model is an iterative process and often requires returning to previous phases as new information is gathered and adjustments are made. Collaboration between data experts, domain experts, and stakeholders is vital to ensure that the model meets the project's requirements and expectations.

61.6. Model Training and Validation

This is the training and validation step of an Artificial Intelligence model. Here the effectiveness and accuracy of the model in real-world tasks are determined. Again, keep in mind that, depending on the type of project, you will require one methodology or another.

Objectives to achieve with this step:
Optimize model performance: Adjust the model parameters to maximize its ability to make accurate predictions on unseen data.
Prevent overfitting: Ensure that the model generalizes well and does not memorize the training data.
Validate the robustness of the model: Check that the model works consistently across different data sets and under various conditions.

Adjust hyperparameters: Find the best set of hyperparameters that produces the most effective model.
Evaluate performance metrics: Use appropriate metrics to assess the quality of the model, such as accuracy, recall, F1 score, AUC-ROC, among others depending on the type of problem (classification, regression, clustering, etc.).

Phases of this step:
1. Data Division: Split the data set into training, validation, and testing. This is generally done randomly to ensure representativeness.
2. Model Training: Use the training set to teach the model from the data. This is where the model adjusts its internal parameters.
3. Model Validation: Use the validation set to adjust hyperparameters and perform a preliminary evaluation of the model's performance. This allows for adjustments without touching the test set.
4. Model Testing: With the test set, evaluate the final performance of the model. It is crucial that this set has not been used during training or validation.
5. Fine-Tuning: Depending on the test results, it may be necessary to retrain the model with different hyperparameters or even reconsider the model design.
6. Final Evaluation: Once the model has been adjusted, it is evaluated using the test set to obtain a final estimate of how it will perform on new and unseen data.

Known methods to perform it:
Cross-validation: Particularly useful when there is a limited data set. The data set is divided into "k" parts, and the model is trained and validated "k" times, each time using a different part as the validation set and the rest for training.
Holdout method: The data set is divided into two subsets, one for training and one for validation. Not as robust as cross-validation, but simpler and faster.
Bootstrap: A resampling technique with replacement that allows estimating the distribution of a statistic. It is used to estimate the variability of the model.
Bayesian Optimization: Used to select the best set of hyperparameters based on the posterior probability that a set of hyperparameters is the best given the observed data.
Grid Search: Test a range of hyperparameters and select the set that provides the best performance on the validation set.
Random Search: Similar to Grid Search, but hyperparameters are randomly selected. More efficient when dealing with a high-dimensional search space.
Early Stopping: A way to prevent overfitting by stopping training as soon as performance on the validation set begins to worsen.
Regularization (like L1, L2, Dropout): Techniques to reduce overfitting by modifying the cost function or the architecture of the model during training.
Each of these methods and phases has its own subtleties and must be selected and adjusted according to the specific needs of the project and the type of data available.

61.7. Implementation and Deployment

The implementation and deployment of an Artificial Intelligence model is a stage where the model is transferred from a development or testing environment to a production environment, where it will be actively used to perform the tasks for which it was designed. This stage can be complex and requires careful planning to ensure a smooth and efficient transition.

Objectives to achieve with this step:
Effective Integration: The AI model must be seamlessly integrated with existing systems and business operations.
Scalability: The model and surrounding infrastructure must be capable of scaling to handle increasing workloads.
Availability: The model must be available to end-users with as little interruption as possible.
Performance: The model must perform according to the expectations and metrics defined during the training and validation phase.
Security: Implement the model securely to protect data and infrastructure from potential threats.
Monitoring and Maintenance: Establish monitoring and maintenance systems to ensure that the model continues to function correctly over time.

Phases of this step:
1. Preparation for Deployment:
- Review and comply with security and compliance requirements.
- Prepare the production infrastructure, including servers, storage, and network resources.
- Plan the deployment strategy, including version handling and rollback if necessary.

2. Initial Deployment:
- Launch the model in a controlled environment or in test mode for a limited group of users.
- Monitor the performance of the model and infrastructure.
- Correct errors and make adjustments as necessary.

3. Full Deployment:
- Perform a full launch of the model to all end users.
- Monitor system load and model performance to ensure it meets requirements.

4. Post-Deployment:
- Collect user feedback for future improvements.
- Establish a maintenance plan and regular updates.

Known methods to perform it:
Manual Deployment: Perform all steps manually, suitable for smaller or less critical systems.
Automated Deployment: Use CI/CD (Continuous Integration/Continuous Deployment) tools to automate the deployment process. Examples include Jenkins, GitLab CI, and GitHub Actions.
Containers and Orchestration:
- Use containers, like Docker, to package and deploy the model and its dependencies.
- Use orchestration systems, like Kubernetes, to manage and scale containers in production.

Platform as a Service (PaaS): Deploy the model on cloud platforms that automatically handle many aspects of the infrastructure, such as AWS Elastic Beanstalk, Google App Engine, or Heroku.

Function as a Service (FaaS): Implement the model as a serverless function on services like AWS Lambda or Azure Functions, which is ideal for models with variable workloads and can be more cost-effective.
Microservices: Break down the application into smaller microservices and deploy them independently, making management and updates easier.

Each method has its advantages and challenges, and the choice depends on several factors, including the complexity of the model, existing infrastructure, security and compliance requirements, and the skills of the implementation team.

61.8. Monitoring and Optimization of the Model

Monitoring and optimization of the model must ensure that the Artificial Intelligence solution continues to function as expected after its implementation and adapts to changing conditions or new data.

Objectives to be achieved with this step:
Maintain model accuracy: Ensure that the model's performance does not decline over time due to data drift or changes in underlying patterns.
Identify performance issues: Detect and correct any anomalies or performance degradation that may arise due to changes in operational conditions.
Adaptability: Update and adapt the model to remain relevant in the face of changes in data trends and market dynamics.
Continuous improvement: Continuously optimize the model to improve efficiency, reduce costs, and enhance prediction accuracy and speed.

Phases of this step:
1. Continuous monitoring:
- **Data collection:** Obtain real-time performance data.
- **Performance analysis:** Evaluate the model's accuracy and compare it with established benchmarks.
- **Data drift detection:** Monitor data for significant changes that may affect the model (concept drift and data drift).

2. Diagnosis:
- **Problem identification:** Determine the causes of any decrease in performance or accuracy.
- **Impact assessment:** Measure the impact of identified issues on the model's operation.

3. Optimization and tuning:
- **Model tuning:** Modify hyperparameters or make fine adjustments to the model.
- **Retraining:** Update the model with new data to correct data drift or improve performance.
- **A/B testing:** Test changes in the model in a controlled environment to assess their impact before full implementation.

4. Implementation of improvements:
- **Updating the model in production:** Deploy the improved version of the model.
- **Post-implementation monitoring:** Verify that the improvements have the desired effect on model performance.

Known methods for doing this:
Monitoring dashboard: Real-time visualization tools that display KPIs (key performance indicators) and alerts when the model deviates from its expected performance.
Statistical tests: Model stability analysis through tests such as CUSUM and Page-Hinkley, which detect significant changes in data distribution.
Continuous retraining: Machine learning techniques that periodically or trigger-based retrain the model.
A/B testing: Compare two or more model versions in the real environment to evaluate which performs better.
Hyperparameter tuning: Use techniques such as grid search, random search, or evolutionary algorithms to optimize the model's hyperparameters.
Ensemble techniques: Combine multiple models to improve robustness and overall performance.
Lifelong Learning: Implement models that continuously adapt to new data without forgetting previous knowledge.
Sensitivity and attribution analysis: Evaluate which variables have the most impact on the model's predictions and how changes in these can affect performance.

By following these phases and applying these methods, you can ensure that the AI model remains effective and efficient over time, adapting to the changing needs of the business and maintaining its relevance and accuracy.

61.9. Documentation and Knowledge Transfer

You must ensure that the value of the AI project is maintained over time and that the team of the client company or for which you work can operate and maintain the system independently. To do this, you must carry out documentation and knowledge transfer.

Objectives to be achieved with this step:
Clarity and understanding: Ensure that all participants and end users understand the operation and logic of the AI system.
Self-sufficiency: Enable the company's team to use, maintain, and update the system without external assistance.
Scalability and maintenance: Facilitate the expansion and scaling of the system, as well as its continuous maintenance.
Compliance and standards: Ensure that the documentation complies with industry standards and relevant regulations.
Project continuity: Provide all the necessary resources so that future teams can continue developing or modifying the system.

Training and development: Train staff to improve their understanding and skills in using AI technologies.

Phases of this step:
1. Documentation planning:
- Identify the target audience for the documentation.
- Determine the type and scope of the required documentation.

2. Creation of the documentation:
- **Technical documentation:** Includes details of system design, algorithms, architecture, source code, and testing protocols.
- **User documentation:** User guides, operation manuals, and FAQs.
- **Maintenance documentation:** Update procedures, backup and recovery protocols, and troubleshooting guides.

3. Review and improvement:
- Validate the accuracy and clarity of the documentation with stakeholders.
- Make improvements based on feedback.

4. Knowledge transfer:
- Training sessions and workshops.
- Practical demonstrations and hands-on sessions.
- Webinars and online learning materials.

5. Evaluation of knowledge transfer:
- Assessments and tests to ensure understanding.
- Surveys and feedback to improve future training sessions.

6. Maintenance of the documentation:
- Update the documentation to reflect any changes or improvements in the system.

Known methods for doing this:
In-person training: Seminars and workshops that allow direct interaction and real-time problem solving.
Digital training materials: Videos, interactive tutorials, and e-learning that offer flexibility and self-learning.
Interactive documentation: Platforms like Swagger for APIs or Jupyter Notebooks for sharing code and explanations.
Mentoring and coaching: Assign experts or mentors to provide personalized guidance.
Communities of practice: Create groups or forums where users can share experiences and best practices.
Q&A and FAQs: Sections for frequently asked questions to efficiently resolve common queries.
Knowledge Base or Wiki: Online repositories where documentation can be accessed and contributed to collaboratively.

By following these steps and methods, you can ensure an effective knowledge transfer and provide the company's team with the necessary tools to operate the AI system autonomously and efficiently.

61.10. Final Project Presentation to the Company

As a lover of presentations, I consider this point to be fundamental in the management of projects of any kind. Although we could delve into this topic endlessly, I will summarize it, as I could write a book with all that I can tell you about this field. In fact, I am already working on one, which I have put on pause to give priority to this. It is titled "PowerPoint ≠ Presentation", and it deals precisely with what a presentation truly is, how it is executed, what techniques you should use for it, and how you should care for and work on your body language, in addition to never believing that your PowerPoint is the presentation itself, this last would be the biggest mistake you will make in your life as a professional. I advise you to search on YouTube for Steve Jobs' video for the presentation of the first iPhone. It is simply a masterpiece.

Objectives to Achieve with This Step:
Demonstrate the value of the project: Show how the project meets the set objectives and provide tangible evidence of the return on investment (ROI).
Validate the AI solution: Confirm that the AI model or system works as expected in a real production environment.
Transfer knowledge: Ensure that the client company understands how the system works, how it should be used, and how it can be maintained and updated.
Collect feedback: Obtain impressions, suggestions, and constructive criticism from the company for future improvements.
Establish the basis for project closure: Formalize that the project deliverables have been completed and are to the client's satisfaction, preparing the ground for the formal closure of the project.

Phases of This Step:

1. Preparation of the presentation:
- Compilation and synthesis of the obtained results.
- Preparation of visual materials, such as slides, graphs, and demonstrations.

2. Internal review:
- Conduct an internal presentation for the project team.
- Adjust the presentation based on feedback and ensure all key points are covered.

3. Presentation to the company:
- Introduction and recapitulation of the project objectives.
- Demonstration of the AI system's operation.
- Presentation of results, performance metrics, and achievements.

4. Question and answer session:
- Interact with stakeholders to answer questions and clarify doubts.

5. Collection of feedback:
- Use tools or methods to collect impressions from attendees.

6. Agreements and next steps:
- Establish any final agreement or next step for delivery or future phases of the project.

Known Methods for Doing It:
Storytelling: Use a narrative to tell the story of the project, how it has developed, and how the AI solution meets the business needs.
Live demonstrations: Present the AI system in action, showing real use cases and how it solves specific problems.
Data visualizations: Use graphs, dashboards, and visualizations to show system performance and benefits in quantitative terms.
Case studies: Present case studies showing the application of the system and the results obtained.
User testimonials: Include comments or testimonials from users who have interacted with the system during the testing phase.
Surveys and feedback forms: Use digital tools to collect feedback in a structured manner during or after the presentation.
Final documentation and reports: Deliver documents detailing the project's development and results, as well as guides for its operation and maintenance.

The final presentation of the project is an opportunity to not only close the cycle of the current project but also to establish the relationship for future projects and collaborations.

61.11. Project Closure and Review

Although you have most likely had many problems and inconveniences along the way, really, if you have reached this point, it is because you and your team have overcome all obstacles and have been up to par to a greater or lesser extent. Now, before you start making plans for another project, it is time to close the project and conclude this new experience you have added to your career.

Project closure and review are phases in project management that ensure all objectives have been met and provide an opportunity to learn from the experience and improve in future projects.

Objectives to Achieve with Project Closure and Review

Confirm the completion of all deliverables: Ensure that all project components have been successfully completed.
Evaluate the fulfillment of project objectives: Compare the project's results and deliverables with the initial objectives to determine if they have been met.

Document lessons learned: Record both positive and negative experiences to improve future project management.
Make an adequate transition: Facilitate the transfer of knowledge and resources from the project to the normal operation of the company or to other projects.
Release resources: Demobilize and reassign human and material resources used during the project.
Conduct a post-project review: Evaluate the management of the project, including the process, communication, collaboration, and quality of deliverables.
Provide closure to participants: Recognize the team's work and effort and provide a sense of closure that allows the team to move on to new initiatives.

Phases of Project Closure and Review:
1. Closure administration:
- Verification that all tasks are complete.
- Confirmation that project milestones have been reached.
- Ensuring that all deliverables have been approved by the client or stakeholders.

2. Project performance evaluation:
- Comparison of project performance with the original plan.
- Analysis of budget, schedule, and quality management.
- Collection of performance metrics and test results.

3. Post-mortem review or lessons learned:
- Organizing meetings with the project team to discuss what went well and what can be improved.
- Documentation of issues, solutions, and recommendations.

4. Financial closure:
- Ensuring that all payments and invoices have been processed.
- Conducting the final accounting of the project.

5. Contractual and legal closure:
- Completion of all contracts with suppliers and partners.
- Resolution of any pending legal matters.

6. Archiving of project documentation:
- Ensuring that all project documents are complete and stored correctly.

7. Communication of closure:
- Informing all stakeholders about the completion of the project.
- Publishing a final project report.

Known Methods for Conducting Project Closure and Review:
Post-Project Review (PPR): A PPR is an evaluation conducted after project delivery to examine successes and failures, aiming to improve performance in future projects.

Lessons Learned Meeting: A formal meeting with the project team to discuss and document what worked well and what did not.
Surveys and interviews: Use structured questionnaires and interviews with team members and stakeholders to gain a deeper insight into project performance.
Variance analysis: Compare planned goals with actual results to understand deviations in cost and time.
Project audit: An independent review of project procedures and results to ensure compliance with company policies and procedures.
Final project report: A document summarizing the project's performance, including cost analysis, schedule, quality of deliverables, and client or your company's satisfaction.

Each of these methods provides different perspectives and levels of detail and can be used together to provide a comprehensive understanding of project performance and areas for improvement.

The journey through the management and execution of an Artificial Intelligence project is both challenging and deeply rewarding. With each step, from the initial advisory meeting to the final project presentation, you, as an AI professional, have the unique opportunity not only to shape the technological future but also to influence the strategic direction of the organizations you work with.
Each project is a story of innovation and overcoming, where creativity meets logic, and where bold ideas are tested by the rigor of data and science. It is in the meticulous preparation of data, the careful design of the model, and persistence in training and optimization where the true craftsmanship of the AI expert is revealed. Remember that every model you build, every analysis you perform, and every strategy you implement has the potential to transform industries, revitalize operations, and improve lives. It is a considerable responsibility, but also a source of great power and possibilities. Therefore, I invite you to take every aspect of your work seriously, but also to embrace the possibility of making mistakes and learning from them. Be open to change and adaptive; AI is a rapidly evolving field that requires an equally agile mind.
Aspire to excellence, but never at the expense of your ethics and values. In your quest for smarter and more efficient solutions, never forget the human impact of your work. Artificial Intelligence is not just a business tool, but an extension of our own collective intelligence, and should be used for the common good. You must make people aware of this. So, as you close one project and prepare for the next, take a moment to reflect on the achievements made and the lessons learned. Celebrate your successes, learn from challenges, and keep moving forward with curiosity and determination. The future is bright for those who have the courage to shape it. Go forward with boldness and vision!

62. Employee Acceptance of Artificial Intelligence

As we have seen throughout this book, the era of digital transformation we live in, the adoption of advanced technologies such as Artificial Intelligence and Machine Learning, are not only redefining the business landscape, but also our society and with this, our life. We have seen, discussed, summarized, and deepened. We are living a historic change for all humanity. These technologies not only promise operational efficiencies and competitive advantages, but they also pose unique challenges, especially in terms of acceptance by employees. Employee acceptance becomes a fundamental pillar for the success of any AI and ML project. Without the support and active participation of those who are part of the organization, even the most innovative technological solutions can fail to reach their full potential.

The shift towards AI-driven systems is not just a technological transition; it is an organizational transformation that affects all layers of a company. Employees often may feel intimidated or concerned about the integration of these new technologies into their work environment. Concerns such as job security, privacy invasion, understanding and control over new tools, and fear of skill obsolescence, are common. Therefore, effectively managing employee acceptance is as critical as the technical implementation of the project.

To successfully navigate this transition, organizations must adopt a multifaceted approach. This approach begins with clear and transparent communication that not only informs but also educates employees about what AI and ML are, how they work, and what they imply for the future of the company and for their personal and professional development. Training and skill development play a crucial role in this process, equipping employees with the knowledge and tools necessary to interact effectively with new technologies.

Furthermore, change management becomes a key strategy. Addressing resistance to change, offering continuous support, and fostering a culture of innovation and experimentation are fundamental aspects to build an atmosphere of trust and collaboration. Active employee participation in the development process and decision-making not only increases their sense of control and belonging but also enriches the project with their valuable perspective and experience.

Lastly, but not least, is the ethical and transparency aspect. In an era where data privacy is a growing concern, assuring employees that their data will be handled ethically and securely is vital to gain their trust. Later on, we will delve a little deeper into the ethical and legal aspect.

The successful integration of AI and ML in the workplace depends as much on the technical robustness of the solution as on the acceptance and commitment of the employees. By addressing these challenges in an integrated manner, organizations will not only improve the efficiency and effectiveness of their AI initiatives but will also cultivate a more dynamic, inclusive, and future-ready work environment.

62.1. Clear and Transparent Communication

Clear and transparent communication is the cornerstone for fostering employee acceptance in Artificial Intelligence and Machine Learning projects. This aspect is vital not only to ensure understanding and support from the staff but also to align expectations and demystify any concerns related to these technologies. Let's develop in detail the two main components of this communication:

Informing about objectives and benefits
The implementation of AI and ML in the business environment aims to improve processes and increase efficiency, but its impact goes much further. It is essential to clearly communicate how these technologies can add value not only at the organizational level but also to the individual work of employees. This includes:

- **Improving operational efficiency:** Explain how AI and ML can automate repetitive tasks, thus freeing employees from monotonous workloads and allowing them to focus on more strategic and creative tasks.
- **Data-driven decision making:** Highlight how these technologies can provide deep insights and predictive analysis, improving decision-making at all levels of the organization.
- **Personalization and improvement of customer service:** Demonstrate how AI can help personalize the customer experience, which in turn can translate into greater customer satisfaction and better business outcomes.
- **Professional development and growth opportunities:** Emphasize the opportunities that arise for employees to learn and work with advanced technologies, thus increasing their employability and professional progression.

Demystifying AI
AI and ML are often perceived as complex and mysterious fields, surrounded by myths and misunderstandings. Effective communication must focus on clearing these fears and providing a realistic understanding of what these technologies can and cannot do:

- **Clarifying concepts and workings:** Offer a basic explanation of what AI and ML are, how they work in general terms, and what can be expected from them in a practical context.
- **Dispelling fears about job replacement:** Address the common concern that AI will replace human jobs, emphasizing how technology is designed to complement and enrich human work, not to replace it.
- **Highlighting limitations and challenges:** It is crucial to be honest about the limitations and challenges of AI and ML, such as the need for large volumes of quality data, potential biases in algorithms, and the importance of human supervision and intervention.
- **Practical examples and use cases:** Presenting real use cases and examples where AI and ML have had a positive impact will help employees visualize their application and benefits concretely.

Effective communication in AI and ML projects must be continuous, bidirectional, and tailored to the audience. By informing about the objectives and benefits, and at the same time demystifying these technologies, organizations can foster an environment of understanding, trust, and enthusiasm towards the integration of AI and ML in their work processes.

62.2. Employee Involvement

The success of Artificial Intelligence and Machine Learning projects depends not only on technical robustness or innovation but also on the extent to which employees feel involved and integrated into the development and implementation process. Let's see how this effective involvement can be fostered:

Participation in the development process

Involving employees from the early stages of design and implementation is essential to ensure that they feel an integral part of the change that AI and ML bring with them. This can be achieved through:

- **Work groups and workshops:** Create work teams or workshops where employees can contribute ideas and feedback on how they see the integration of AI and ML in their work areas.
- **Technology ambassador roles:** Appoint employees as 'AI ambassadors' within their departments, to act as liaisons between the project team and their colleagues, promoting communication and the exchange of ideas.
- **Pilot tests and prototypes:** Involving employees in pilot tests or in the evaluation of prototypes allows them to directly experience the new technologies and contribute with their perceptions and suggestions for improvements.
- **Co-creation and collaboration:** Encourage employees to participate in the co-creation of solutions, which can improve the relevance and adaptability of the technology to the specific needs of the organization.

Collecting continuous feedback

Establishing effective communication channels for employees to express their opinions and concerns is crucial for a successful implementation process. This includes:

- **Surveys and feedback forums:** Conduct regular surveys and maintain open forums where employees can share their thoughts and concerns about AI and ML.
- **Regular meetings and Q&A sessions:** Organize regular meetings or question-and-answer sessions with project teams so that employees can get updates, ask questions, and provide feedback in real-time.
- **Anonymous suggestion systems:** Implement systems where employees can leave anonymous comments or suggestions, which can be particularly useful for collecting honest opinions on sensitive topics.
- **Continuous employee sentiment evaluation:** Use sentiment analysis tools or conduct periodic assessments to understand how employees feel about the integration of AI and ML into the company.

By actively involving employees in the development process and continuously collecting their feedback, organizations not only increase the likelihood of successful implementation but also foster a sense of ownership and commitment among the staff. This participatory approach leads to AI and ML solutions that are more tailored, accepted, and effective, creating a collaborative and proactive work environment towards innovation.

62.3. Training and Capacity Building in AI Projects

A crucial element for the successful integration of Artificial Intelligence and Machine Learning in organizations and companies is the training and capacity building of employees. This not only increases competence and confidence in using new technologies, but also facilitates greater acceptance and appreciation of their benefits. Let's examine how these training aspects can be addressed:

Technical Training
Technical training focuses on teaching employees how to use new AI/ML tools and systems. It is essential to ensure they can effectively handle these technologies in their daily tasks. Key components of this training include:

- **Practical sessions:** Organize hands-on workshops where employees can directly interact with the new tools and systems. These sessions should be guided by experts who can provide immediate assistance and resolve doubts.
- **Personalized learning materials:** Provide learning material that adapts to different levels of skill and knowledge, from basic for beginners to more advanced content for more experienced users.
- **Continuous training:** Ensure that training is an ongoing process to adapt to updates and improvements in AI and ML tools.
- **Online support and resources:** Offer online resources, such as tutorials, discussion forums, and helplines, so employees can access support outside of scheduled sessions.

Education on AI and ML
Beyond technical training, it is important to provide general education on the basic principles and potential of AI and ML. This helps employees understand the broader context and strategic value of these technologies. Aspects to consider are:

- **Courses and workshops:** Offer courses or workshops covering the fundamentals of AI and ML, including how they work, where they are applied, and their ethical and social implications.
- **Information sessions and lectures:** Invite AI and ML experts to give talks or lectures, providing a broader and up-to-date perspective on trends and developments in the field.
- **Accessible educational material:** Create or curate easily accessible educational content, such as articles, videos, and podcasts, that employees can explore at their own pace.
- **Case studies and real-life examples:** Use case studies to show real and successful applications of AI and ML in the industry, which can inspire and motivate employees by seeing the tangible impact of these technologies.

Combining practical technical training and general education on AI and ML is essential to empower employees, not only to feel comfortable using these technologies but also to understand and appreciate their value and potential. By investing in the skill and knowledge development of their workforce, organizations not only facilitate a smoother transition to AI-driven systems but also foster an innovative and future-oriented work environment.

62.4. Change Management

Addressing resistance to change and providing ongoing support are fundamental aspects of facilitating a smooth transition and ensuring effective adoption of these new technologies. Let's develop these points in more detail:

Addressing Resistance to Change
Resistance to change is a natural phenomenon in any transformation process. It is vital to proactively identify and address resistances related to the implementation of AI and ML:

- **Understanding the causes of resistance:** Conduct surveys, interviews, or focus groups to understand why employees may feel reluctant or concerned about AI and ML. This may include fears of job obsolescence, lack of confidence in new technologies, or simply discomfort with the unknown.
- **Effective communication:** Address fears and concerns through open and honest communication. It is crucial to clear up misunderstandings and provide clear information on how AI and ML will affect the work and opportunities of employees.
- **Involving leaders and supervisors:** Train leaders and supervisors to act as change agents, offering support and guidance to their teams. They can play a key role in motivating and reducing resistance to change.
- **Celebrating early successes:** Demonstrating and celebrating the early successes of AI and ML implementation can help build trust and show the practical value of these technologies.

Ongoing Support
Providing continuous support to employees during the transition process is essential to maintain morale and productivity:

- **Support resources and assistance:** Establish a support system where employees can get help and resolve doubts related to new technologies. This may include helplines, technical support, and access to AI and ML experts.
- **Training and professional retraining:** Offer ongoing opportunities for training and professional development so that employees can improve their skills and adapt to new job requirements.
- **Monitoring and feedback:** Implement a monitoring process to assess how the workforce is adapting to AI and ML, and collect regular feedback to continuously improve the implementation process.
- **Fostering a culture of learning and adaptability:** Promote a work environment that values continuous learning, experimentation, and adaptability, which can help employees feel more comfortable and engaged with constant changes.

Change management in the context of AI and ML projects involves not only the implementation of new technologies but also managing the people affected by these changes. By proactively addressing resistance to change and providing ongoing support, organizations can ensure a more harmonious transition to technology-enhanced work environments, while maintaining the motivation and commitment of their employees.

62.5. Demonstrating Early Success

An effective strategy to boost adoption and support for Artificial Intelligence and Machine Learning projects is to demonstrate early success. Showcasing tangible success cases and sharing achievements and improvements can build confidence and enthusiasm around these technologies. Let's examine how these successes can be achieved and communicated:

Pilot Projects or Success Stories
Pilot projects are an excellent way to demonstrate the potential and benefits of AI and ML in a controlled and small-scale environment:

- **Strategic selection of pilot projects:** Choose pilot projects that have a high potential for success and that are visible and relevant to the organization. This could include applications where AI and ML can generate significant improvements in efficiency, accuracy, or customer experience.
- **Careful monitoring and evaluation:** Ensure close monitoring of these pilot projects and evaluate their results objectively. This includes collecting data before and after implementation to compare performance.
- **Success stories:** Document and share success stories, highlighting how AI and ML have contributed to solving specific problems, improving processes, or increasing efficiency.

Visibility of Positive Results
Making positive results visible and understandable to the entire organization is crucial to foster a positive attitude towards AI and ML:

- **Active internal communication:** Use internal communication channels, such as newsletters, intranet, meetings, and company events, to share the successes and achievements of AI and ML projects.
- **Presentations and demonstrations:** Organize presentations or demonstrations where teams can show how they have used AI and ML to improve their processes or outcomes.
- **Testimonials and real cases:** Include testimonials from employees who have directly interacted with these technologies, highlighting their experience and perceived benefits.
- **Clear success indicators:** Present clear and quantifiable success indicators that demonstrate the impact of AI and ML. This can include metrics such as cost reduction, productivity increase, improvement in customer satisfaction, among others.

Demonstrating early success not only validates the investment in AI and ML but also acts as a powerful catalyst for positive change, generating a multiplier effect throughout the organization. Seeing tangible results and clear benefits, employees are more likely to embrace these technologies and be open to future innovations and changes.

62.6. Ethics and Transparency

In implementing AI and ML projects, ethics and transparency are fundamental aspects that must be carefully considered and managed. These principles are not only key to building and maintaining the trust of employees and stakeholders but are also essential to ensure that technologies are developed and used responsibly. Let's see how to address these issues:

Ethical Considerations
Ethics in AI and ML encompass a variety of important considerations, from how data is used to how decisions are made based on algorithms:

- **Transparency in data use:** Be clear about what data is being collected, how it is being used, and for what purpose. This involves informing employees and stakeholders about data collection practices and project objectives.
- **Explainability of algorithms:** Make algorithms as explainable as possible, which means that decisions made by AI systems should be understandable to end users. This is crucial to avoid the "black box" in AI, where decisions cannot be traced or understood.
- **Mitigation of biases:** Recognize and address potential biases in AI and ML algorithms. This includes implementing strategies to identify and reduce biases in data sets and modeling processes.
- **Participation in decision-making:** Involve employees in discussions about how AI and ML should be used, especially in contexts where algorithmic decisions can significantly affect individuals or work processes.

Privacy and Security

Protecting data privacy and security is another critical aspect in the ethical management of AI and ML projects:

- **Compliance with privacy regulations:** Ensure that all projects comply with relevant data privacy laws and regulations, such as GDPR in Europe. This includes obtaining necessary consents and handling data in a way that respects individuals' privacy rights.
- **Robust security measures:** Implement robust security measures to protect data against unauthorized access, leaks, or any other security vulnerabilities.
- **Data risk assessments:** Conduct regular risk assessments to identify and mitigate potential vulnerabilities in data security.
- **Data security training:** Provide training to employees on best practices in data security, including how to handle sensitive data and how to identify and report potential security breaches.

Addressing ethical considerations and ensuring data privacy and security are fundamental aspects for the sustainable success of any AI and ML project. By being transparent about how data is used and how decisions are made based on algorithms, and by ensuring the privacy and security of that data, organizations can build a solid foundation of trust and accountability, essential for the ethical development and implementation of advanced technologies.

62.7. Creating a Culture of Innovation

Creating and fostering a culture of innovation is essential for the long-term success of AI and ML projects. A culture that values and promotes innovation not only improves the adoption of new technologies but also drives continuous growth and evolution of the organization. Let's explore how to encourage experimentation and recognize and reward innovation:

Encouraging Experimentation

Encouraging employees to explore and experiment with new technologies is fundamental to a vibrant innovation culture:

- **Testing spaces and innovation labs:** Create safe spaces where employees can try out new ideas and experiment with AI and ML technologies without fear of failure. This could include innovation labs, hackathons, or assigned times for personal projects.
- **Providing resources and tools:** Ensure that employees have access to the necessary resources and tools to experiment. This could range from specific software and hardware to access to courses or workshops on the latest technologies and trends.
- **Encouraging creative thinking and problem-solving:** Encourage employees to think creatively and use AI and ML to solve problems in novel ways. This can be incentivized through brainstorming sessions, design thinking workshops, and interdepartmental collaborations.

Recognizing and rewarding innovation
Establishing a system of recognition and rewards is crucial to motivate employees to actively adopt and promote AI and ML technologies:

- **Recognition systems:** Implement recognition programs that highlight and celebrate employees who contribute significantly to innovation projects. This could be through awards, mentions in internal communications, or even featured presentations at company meetings.
- **Incentives and rewards:** Offer tangible incentives, such as bonuses, promotions, or additional benefits, for those who demonstrate exceptional commitment to innovation and the adoption of new technologies.
- **Professional development opportunities:** Provide professional development opportunities, such as attending conferences, participating in advanced courses, or leading new projects, as a reward for innovative initiatives.
- **Sharing success:** Spread the success stories and innovations achieved by employees through internal and external channels, which not only recognizes the employee's work but also inspires others to follow their example.

Fostering a culture of innovation where experimentation is encouraged and innovation is recognized and rewarded creates an environment where employees feel empowered to explore new ideas and actively contribute to the growth and success of the organization. This culture not only facilitates the adoption of AI and ML but also positions the company as a leader in innovation and technological progress.

63. Roll-Out

The term "Roll-Out" in project management refers to the phase where a solution, product, system, or service is implemented and made available to end-users or launched to the market. In the context of technology projects, such as those involving Artificial Intelligence and Machine Learning, Roll-Out is the step that follows the development and testing of the project. This is where the developed solution is deployed in a real production environment.

Key aspects of Roll-Out in project management include:

1. **Careful planning:** This involves defining the Roll-Out strategy, including the timeline, necessary resources, and protocols for the transition.
2. **Communication with stakeholders:** Keep all involved parties, including internal teams, clients, and end-users, informed about when and how the Roll-Out will take place.

3. Training and support: Ensure that end-users receive the necessary training to use the new system or product and that there is adequate support during and after the Roll-Out.
4. Gradual or phased implementation: In many cases, Roll-Out is carried out gradually or in phases, especially in large or complex projects, to minimize risk and allow adjustments based on initial feedback.
5. Monitoring and troubleshooting: Closely monitor the performance of the product or system during the Roll-Out to quickly identify and resolve any issues that arise.
6. Feedback collection and adjustments: Collect feedback from users and make necessary adjustments to improve the system or product's experience and performance.
7. Success evaluation of the Roll-Out: Measure the success of the Roll-Out based on predefined criteria, such as user adoption, system performance, and customer satisfaction.

63.1. Challenges and Solutions

In the implementation of AI and ML projects, there are several challenges that must be carefully managed. Although, from my point of view, there is always a group of standard challenges that you will have to consider in each project, be very aware that each project will offer its own challenges and you will have to find solutions to all those challenges to ensure the success of your project.

Here I present some of these challenges, along with their possible solutions:

1. Security and privacy concerns
Challenge: Implementing AI and ML often involves handling large volumes of data, some of which may be sensitive or personal, raising concerns about security and privacy.
Solution: Establish robust data security policies and practices, comply with data privacy regulations like GDPR, and conduct regular security audits and testing.

2. Risk management and contingency planning
Challenge: AI and ML projects may face technical, operational, and market risks.
Solution: Conduct detailed risk analyses and develop contingency plans for identified scenarios. Implementing an agile development approach can help adapt quickly to changes and challenges.

3. Budgetary and time limitations
Challenge: Projects often have time and budget constraints that can limit their scope or quality.
Solution: Set clear priorities, manage expectations realistically, and apply project management methodologies that optimize resources and time, such as agile or Lean methods.

4. Stakeholder management
Challenge: Different stakeholders may have divergent expectations and objectives, leading to conflicts or misunderstandings.
Solution: Maintain constant and transparent communication with all stakeholders, and ensure that their expectations and needs are understood and considered in the decision-making process.

5. Scalability and maintenance
Challenge: Ensure that AI and ML systems are scalable and maintainable in the long term.

Solution: Design systems with scalability in mind from the start, using modular architectures and scalable technologies. Additionally, plan for ongoing maintenance and system updates.

6. Evaluation and feedback
Challenge: Effectively evaluate the performance of AI and ML systems and collect useful feedback for future improvements.
Solution: Establish clear performance metrics from the start and use data analysis tools to evaluate system performance. Additionally, regularly collect and analyze user feedback to identify areas for improvement.

Each of these challenges requires a strategic and considered approach to ensure the success of AI and ML projects. By proactively addressing these issues and developing robust solutions, organizations can maximize potential and achieve their objectives effectively.

MODULE 8

Bias

Module 8 - Bias in Artificial Intelligence

64. Introduction to Bias

This is one of the most crucial and transcendental sections you have to face, which is why I've left it as the last module. Throughout the book, we have seen and learned everything related to Artificial Intelligence, Machine Learning, algorithms, methods, and we have been analyzing situations in very different types of applications where to implement Artificial Intelligence and ML algorithms. In our profession as IA-Managers, it is imperative that we understand and address the ethical, social, and legal implications that arise with its implementation, especially in the business sphere. Therefore, and after all this information, I consider that now is the best time to chat and examine the issue of Bias. Because this way, and now, we can better judge the importance of these in society and their relationship with Artificial Intelligence.

Let's first analyze the meaning of the word “Bias”. Bias refers to an inclination or prejudice towards or against an individual, group, or concept. In the context of AI, these biases translate into unfair or inaccurate decisions or predictions that a system can make due to the information with which it was trained. While these biases can arise inadvertently, their consequences can be profoundly harmful, reinforcing stereotypes, perpetuating inequalities, and, in general, making decisions that do not reflect a fair and equitable interpretation of reality.

64.1. Where do these biases come from?

Mainly, the Bias in AI comes from the data with which the models are trained. If the training data reflect, even unintentionally, existing biases or stereotypes, the model will also reflect them. For example, if an AI system is trained with images of business leaders and the majority of these images are of men, the system may erroneously infer that business leaders are usually men.

64.2. Implications and repercussions

The consequences of Bias in AI go beyond simple errors. They can have significant impacts on people's lives. Imagine an AI system in charge of personnel selection that, due to biases in its training data, favors candidates of a certain gender, race, or socioeconomic background. These decisions can affect diversity in the workplace, perpetuate inequalities, and limit opportunities.

64.3. The role of the IA-Manager

As IA-Managers, our role will not only be to implement and manage AI projects but also to ensure that these systems are developed and used ethically and fairly. This involves being aware of potential Bias, implementing practices to detect and correct these biases, and promoting a culture of accountability and transparency around the use of AI. While we celebrate the achievements and possibilities that AI offers us, it is essential that we also address its challenges with the seriousness they deserve. Bias in AI is not just a technical problem, but also a social, ethical, and legal one. By facing these challenges head-on, we not only create more accurate and effective AI systems but also ensure that they reflect and respect the values and principles we all share.

65. Bias and AI: a more detailed journey

65.1. Definition and types of Bias

When addressing the vast topic of Bias, it is fundamental to start by defining what we understand by "Bias". Essentially, a bias is an inclination or prejudice, either for or against, towards a particular group, individual, or concept. In the context of AI, this prejudice can infiltrate our models and algorithms, leading them to make decisions that are not entirely fair or accurate. It is vital to understand that bias can arise at any stage, from data collection to the interpretation of results. Additionally, it is essential to classify biases, such as selection bias, confirmation bias, cultural bias, among others, to understand their diverse manifestations and origins.

65.2. History and examples

Throughout recent history, we have seen several cases where biases in AI have led to unfavorable decisions and outcomes. These real-life examples, ranging from facial recognition systems that do not adequately detect certain skin tones to hiring algorithms that favor one gender over another, serve as stark reminders of the tangible repercussions of Bias. Analyzing these cases in detail not only provides us with a clear understanding of the problems but also motivates us to address and prevent such incidents in the future.

65.3. Identification of Bias

Once we understand the nature and manifestations of biases, the next step is to learn to identify them. This involves a careful review of data sets and the evaluation of AI models to detect problematic patterns and trends. Analytical tools and statistical techniques, such as fairness tests and validation, can be essential in this phase. In addition, it is crucial to instill a sense of curiosity and healthy skepticism, encouraging professionals to continuously question and scrutinize data and results.

65.4. Mitigation of Bias

Identifying a problem is only half the solution. Once biases are detected, it is imperative to take steps to mitigate them. This could include techniques such as rebalancing data sets, where data proportions are adjusted to better represent the entire population, or implementing unbiased learning techniques that adjust algorithms to reduce bias. Mitigation is an ongoing process and requires a constant commitment to ensure that our AI solutions are fair and equitable.

65.5. Ethical and Social Aspects

Beyond technology and techniques, it is essential to reflect on the broader implications of Bias in AI. How do these biases affect marginalized communities? What does it say about our society when we allow technology to perpetuate stereotypes and prejudices? These ethical and social reflections are crucial to understanding the full scope of the problem and to fostering an AI development culture that prioritizes justice and equality.

65.6. Regulations and legislation

Given the growing concern about Bias in AI, several countries and organizations are taking steps to address the problem legally. Familiarizing oneself with these laws and regulations is essential for any AI professional, and in this case, for you, as an IA-Manager and expert in Artificial Intelligence. The law not only ensures compliance but also provides a framework and guidelines on how to address and prevent Bias.

65.7. Responsibility and transparency

At the heart of the fight against Bias in AI is the principle of accountability. It is essential that developers, data scientists, and industry leaders take responsibility for their systems and decisions. Additionally, transparency in how models work, how decisions are made, and how these processes can be audited and questioned is fundamental to building AI systems that society can trust.

65.8. Evaluation and feedback

Education is a two-way process. While knowledge about Bias and how to address them is imparted, it is crucial to obtain feedback from students and professionals. Periodic evaluations, both formal and informal, can help identify areas for improvement and adjust the pedagogical approach as needed. This, for example, applies to customer service chatbots. With customer feedback, you can take steps to improve the model and avoid these problems. With these solutions, you can avoid losing customers, maintaining and even increasing trust, and always showing due interest in these aspects.

65.9. Practical project

Theory is essential, but practice consolidates learning. A good idea would be to assign practical projects where students and company learners work with real data and AI models, identifying and mitigating Bias, offering them invaluable experience and helping the company in the future to develop and maintain this mindset among employees. This practical experience not only reinforces the understanding of the topic but also prepares participants of these projects to face similar challenges both during work and in the real world.

65.10. Final reflection and conclusion

To conclude the topic, it is essential to take a moment to reflect on what has been learned. Highlight the importance of always being alert to Bias, being proactive in their identification and mitigation, and being advocates for justice and equity in the field of AI. This final reflection serves as a call to action for all future professionals in the field.

MODULE 9

Ethics and Rights

Module 9 – Ethics and Law in the Field of Artificial Intelligence

66. Ethics and its Relationship with Artificial Intelligence

This topic, just like the one on biases, is so sensitive and important that it requires a whole module to itself. Ethics in relation to Artificial Intelligence, especially for an AI-Manager, who needs not only to understand the technical and administrative aspects of AI projects but also their ethical implications, becomes a cornerstone of their training and professional practice. A competent AI-Manager must be able to address not only the fundamental principles of ethics in AI, such as transparency, equity, responsibility, and respect for privacy, but also how these principles translate into daily decisions in the development and management of AI projects. Therefore, it is important to analyze real cases and discuss hypothetical scenarios to prepare you for the ethical challenges you will inevitably face. It is important that you can develop in this field, as you will have to equip the different members of your team and external parties of your projects with a deep understanding and sensitivity towards ethical issues, not only to improve the quality and sustainability of your AI projects but also because this contributes to the development of a fairer and more humane technology.

With the powerful potential of Machine Learning, we receive a great responsibility: to ensure that AI is developed and applied ethically and responsibly. This is a primary task for you, who will not only lead AI projects but also shape the future of its implementation in society.
Ethics in AI is not just a complement to its technical functionality; it is the pillar that supports the integrity and sustainability of its application. In a world where machines can make decisions that affect human lives, ethics guides the development of AI so that these decisions are fair, transparent, and beneficial for everyone. Ethics in AI addresses fundamental questions: How can we ensure that AI systems act in the best interest of humanity? How do we prevent AI from perpetuating or even intensifying social inequalities? How do we protect privacy and individual rights in an era dominated by algorithms processing personal data?

For an AI-Manager, understanding these ethical challenges is crucial. It's not just about leading projects that meet technical and business requirements, but also about ensuring that these projects respect and promote fundamental ethical principles. This involves a deep understanding of how AI technology interacts with human values, social norms, and legal implications. AI experts must be equipped to navigate this complex landscape, balancing technological innovation with ethical, moral, and legislative considerations.

Furthermore, ethics in AI is not static; it evolves with society, technology, and philosophical understandings. This means that AI-Managers must be in a constant process of learning and adaptation, staying abreast of the latest developments, debates, and regulations in this dynamic field. They must be leaders not only in the implementation of projects but also in promoting an ethical approach throughout the AI industry. Ethics in Artificial Intelligence refers to the principles and values that guide the development and use of AI technology. It is fundamental because AI has the power to significantly influence society, the economy, and personal life.

Ethical Principles in AI

Transparency: AI systems must be transparent in their operations and decisions. This means that users should be able to understand how and why an AI reaches certain conclusions or decisions.

Justice and Equity: AI must be designed and operated fairly. This involves avoiding discriminatory biases and ensuring that technology is accessible and inclusive for all society's groups.

Responsibility and Accountability: There must be clarity about who is responsible for the decisions made by AI systems. This includes mechanisms for accountability in cases of errors or harm caused by AI.
Respect for Privacy and Autonomy: AI must respect individuals' privacy and not infringe on their rights to personal autonomy. This involves careful handling of personal data and informed consent in its use.
Safety and Reliability: AI systems must be safe and reliable. They must operate predictably and without causing unintentional harm to users or society.

Ethical Foundations
Humanism: AI must be developed and used with the aim of improving human well-being and never to its detriment.
Human Rights: AI must align with the universal principles of human rights, ensuring that its implementation does not violate these rights.
Sustainability: AI must contribute to sustainable development, considering its long-term environmental and social impact.

Practical Considerations in Managing AI Projects
Ethical Impact Analysis: Conduct an ethical impact analysis in the early stages of an AI project, evaluating how the technology will affect users and society.
Inclusion of Ethics Experts: Involve ethics experts in the project team to guide the development and implementation of AI.
Continuous Training: Maintain continuous training in ethics for AI developers and project managers to stay abreast of new ethical issues that arise with technological advancement.

Let's analyze some examples.

Bias in Hiring Algorithms: AI systems used in recruitment and selection processes can perpetuate unconscious biases, leading to discrimination in hiring based on gender, age, ethnicity, or other factors.

Discrimination in Law Enforcement: Addresses the problem of discrimination in law enforcement. This is a critical area where AI systems, such as crime prediction algorithms, can perpetuate or amplify existing biases, leading to injustices in law enforcement.

Influence in the Educational System: AI applied in education, like adaptive learning systems, could lead to standardized education that does not consider the individual needs of students or perpetuates outdated educational methods.

Privacy Violations (Cambridge Analytica Case): Refers to privacy violations, illustrated by the Cambridge Analytica case. This case highlights how the collection and misuse of personal data by AI systems can have serious consequences for individuals' privacy and autonomy.

Autonomous Weapons Systems: Focuses on autonomous weapons systems. This is a highly controversial topic, as it involves the use of AI in military contexts, raising questions about the morality and ethical limits in warfare.

Mass Surveillance and Control: The use of AI systems for monitoring and mass surveillance raises serious ethical issues related to privacy invasion and social control.

Unjust and Discriminatory Decisions in the Financial Sector: Examines unjust and discriminatory decisions in the financial sector. AI systems, without proper ethical consideration, can lead to biased decisions in areas like credit and insurance, disproportionately affecting certain groups.

Environmental Impact of AI: The extensive use of computational resources to train advanced AI models has a significant environmental impact, especially in terms of energy consumption and carbon footprint, which sooner or later, will have a massive impact on society that could radically change the world as we know it.

Facial Recognition and Deepfakes: Discusses the ethical issues related to facial recognition and deepfakes. These technologies pose serious challenges in terms of privacy, consent, and the spread of false information.

Bias in Medical and Health Services: AI systems in healthcare can reflect or exacerbate existing biases in diagnosis or treatment, affecting the quality of care for certain patient groups.

Labor Displacement: Addresses labor displacement caused by AI. Automation and AI are replacing some jobs, raising questions about the impact on employment and the economy.

Automation and Economic Inequality: AI-driven automation can increase economic inequality by concentrating wealth and power in the hands of those who control these technologies.

Manipulation and Abuse: Refers to manipulation and abuse through AI. This includes how AI can be used to unduly influence people, whether through targeted advertising, fake news, or opinion manipulation.

Ethics in Targeted Advertising: The use of AI to create highly targeted advertising can lead to consumer behavior manipulation and privacy invasion.

These examples highlight the need for deep ethical reflection and the implementation of safeguards to mitigate these risks. It is essential for AI professionals, especially AI-Managers, to be aware of these challenges and proactively address them in the design and management of AI systems.

Ethics in AI is not just a theoretical issue but an essential and practical aspect in the management of AI projects. An AI-Manager must be equipped to address these issues, ensuring that technology is developed and used in a way that benefits society while respecting fundamental ethical principles. When you find yourself working on an AI project, there will always be someone who has an opinion very far from what ethics dictates, and if that someone holds a high position, it can cause you many headaches. Similarly, it is your duty to educate people, and I believe not only those involved in your projects, to understand the need to respect and tolerate these moral and legal guidelines, not only for the good of the project but because it also directly influences the entire society. This is a point where we must stand united, be tolerant, and respect the opinions of others, as well as their wishes, for example, for privacy.

Let's now look at the legal framework field.

67. The Law and its Relationship with Artificial Intelligence

The topic of the legal framework in relation to Artificial Intelligence covers several key legal aspects that are fundamental for the development and implementation of AI systems. These aspects focus on ensuring that AI is used in a safe, fair, and responsible manner. As AI integrates more deeply into our lives, its interaction with the legal framework becomes increasingly important and complex. The need for a robust and adaptable legal framework for AI is crucial, not only to foster innovation and technological development but also to protect individual rights and maintain social security and well-being.

The legal framework of AI encompasses a variety of aspects, each presenting its own challenges and opportunities. These aspects include the protection of personal data, where laws like the General Data Protection Regulation (GDPR) of the European Union set strict guidelines for the handling of personal data. The issue of copyright in the era of AI is also a complex topic, raising questions about originality and authorship in works generated by AI systems. Additionally, legal liability in situations where AI systems cause harm or errors is an area of great interest, especially in applications such as autonomous vehicles.

Cybersecurity and the fight against discrimination are also essential components of the AI legal framework. It is critical that AI systems are secure and do not perpetuate discriminatory biases, ensuring fair and equitable use. Concurrently, the implementation of technical standards and certification processes is necessary to ensure the quality and reliability of these systems.

Finally, aspects such as export controls and the regulation of specific AI applications highlight the need to consider the potential use of these technologies in sensitive contexts and their appropriate regulation in specific fields such as health or transportation.

The AI legal framework requires a careful balance between fostering technological innovation and protecting society and individual rights. Let's look at the most important points to keep in mind.

Data Protection: In countries like Germany, the protection of personal data is a critical legal aspect in the handling of AI. The need for transparency in data collection and use is emphasized, ensuring informed consent from individuals and protecting their privacy. Legislation, such as the General Data Protection Regulation (GDPR) of the European Union, sets strict guidelines for the handling of personal data, including its processing, storage, and transfer.

Copyright: This aspect addresses the protection of original creations in the context of AI. There are legal complexities regarding who owns the copyright of works generated by AI, as well as the use of copyright-protected material in data sets used to train AI systems. This raises questions about originality and authorship in the era of AI.

Liability: Legal liability in the context of AI is a critical topic, especially in autonomous systems like self-driving vehicles. The discussion centers on who is responsible in cases of errors or damage caused by AI systems: the developer, the operator, the user, or the AI system itself? Laws must adapt to address these new forms of interaction and responsibility.

Cybersecurity, Anti-Discrimination: The security of AI systems is of utmost importance, and cybersecurity laws apply to these systems. Additionally, anti-discrimination laws are fundamental to prevent AI systems from perpetuating or intensifying discriminatory biases, ensuring their fair and equitable use.

Technical Standards and Certification: The implementation of technical standards and certification processes may be necessary to ensure the quality, safety, and reliability of AI systems. This includes compliance with national and international regulations, ensuring that AI systems are robust and reliable.

Export Controls, Regulation of Specific Applications: Some AI technologies may be subject to export controls due to their potential use in sensitive applications, like defense or national security. Additionally, certain AI applications, such as in healthcare or transportation, may require specific regulations to ensure their safe and effective use.

Let's also analyze some examples.

Data Privacy Violation: Refers to concerns about how AI might infringe data protection laws by collecting, storing, and processing personal information without proper consent.

Manipulation through AI in Advertising and Media: The use of AI to create hyper-personalized advertising or fake news, raising questions about the manipulation of public opinion and the integrity of information.

Automation and Legal Responsibility: The question of who is responsible when an AI system makes a mistake or causes harm. For example, in accidents involving autonomous vehicles, who is legally responsible, the vehicle manufacturer, the AI software developer, or the vehicle user?

Copyright Violations: This involves using copyright-protected works (such as texts, images, and music) in training AI systems without proper authorization, posing significant legal issues.

Bias and Discrimination in Decision Making: How biases in training data can lead to AI making discriminatory decisions, for example, in hiring processes or credit granting, potentially violating anti-discrimination laws.

Right to be Forgotten in the Use of Data for AI Training: This concerns the tension between individuals' right to have their personal data deleted and the need to use these data to train AI systems.

Use of AI in Surveillance and Social Control: The legal and ethical challenges associated with using AI technologies for mass surveillance, which may infringe on rights to privacy and individual freedom, especially in authoritarian regimes.

The legal framework around AI is a constantly evolving field that seeks to balance innovation and technological development with the protection of individual rights, security, and social well-being. For us, AI experts, it is crucial to be aware of these legal issues and ensure that our projects comply with all relevant laws and regulations.

★★★★★

I truly hope you enjoyed the book. If so, if you liked it, or maybe it helped you understand Artificial Intelligence better, or perhaps even sparked your curiosity to learn more about AI, then I kindly ask you to write a review.

Did you know that, according to statistics, 67% of customers write a review after a positive experience, while 40% do so after a negative one? However, based on my own research, this is completely wrong and actually the opposite is true. Satisfied customers rarely write reviews, while dissatisfied ones tend to write them almost immediately. At the same time, 93% of consumers read online reviews before making a purchase decision. One study shows that 55% of the reviews on the internet are fake, but according to many investigative reports, the percentage of fake reviews is actually much higher. Still, 94% of consumers avoid a product or company due to negative feedback.

Your review is very valuable and can help me tremendously to keep writing.

★★★★★

Acknowledgements

Dear readers,

as this book comes to a close, I want to take a moment to express my deepest gratitude for accompanying me on this journey through the pages of "AI-Manager - The AI-Manager´s handbook".

Your interest and dedication to exploring the world of Artificial Intelligence and the management of AI projects not only reflect a quest for knowledge but also a commitment to a future where technology and humanity coexist in harmony.

I sincerely hope that this book has not only enriched your understanding of Artificial Intelligence and Machine Learning, but has also provided you with a new perspective on the vital role that an AI-Manager plays in this exciting, and nowadays so important, field. Our responsibility goes beyond algorithms and data; it extends to ethical considerations, respect for the law, and above all, to the impact that our decisions have on the world.

As an AI-Manager and AI expert, my goal has been to share with you not only technical knowledge, but also the experiences and reflections accumulated throughout my career. If this book has contributed to your professional or personal development, I consider my mission accomplished.

I thank each of my readers for their valuable time and for allowing me to be a part of their journey in learning and applying Artificial Intelligence. I hope you continue exploring, learning, and leading in this fascinating field, always with curiosity and responsibility.

With gratitude and best wishes,

Juan García
CEO, AI-Expert, AI-Manager and IBM Advanced Machine Learning Specialist
SMART &PRO AI
DEEP ATHENA

TEST YOUR KNOWLEDGE

Test your knowledge

Questions

1. Which of the following options best describes "Machine Learning" (ML)?
a) A subfield of Artificial Intelligence that focuses on the development of systems capable of automatically learning from data.
b) A programming approach based solely on fixed rules and logic.
c) A branch of data science that focuses on advanced statistics.
d) A set of specific algorithms for processing images and videos.

2. What does the term "Unstructured Data" represent in the context of AI?
a) Data that is organized in a tabular or database format.
b) Information presented in a non-standard format, such as free text, images, or videos.
c) Data collected from IoT sensors in real-time.
d) Data sets that mainly contain numbers and dates.

3. In the context of Deep Learning, what is a Convolutional Neural Network (CNN)?
a) A type of neural network designed to process data in the form of graphs.
b) An artificial neural network specialized in the processing and analysis of sequential data.
c) A type of neural network mainly used for classification and detection tasks in images and videos.
d) A neural network used for processing text and natural language data.

4. What is "Reinforcement Learning"?
a) A type of machine learning where models are trained to make sequential decisions.
b) A supervised learning technique that uses labels to train models.
c) A method focused on grouping unlabeled data into distinct categories.
d) A process involving deep neural networks for text analysis.

5. What is an example of an "Internet of Things" (IoT) application?
a) Recommendation systems on video streaming platforms.
b) Voice recognition in virtual assistants.
c) Algorithms for classifying emails as spam.
d) Stock price prediction models.

6. What visualization technique is commonly used to understand the correlation between features in Machine Learning?
a) Scatter Plots.
b) Histograms.
c) Heatmaps.
d) Flowcharts.

7. In the context of AI projects, what does "SWOT Analysis" represent?
a) A method to assess data security and privacy.
b) A technique for identifying the strengths, weaknesses, opportunities, and threats of a project.
c) An approach to determining the ROI (Return on Investment) of an AI project.
d) A methodology for human resource management in AI projects.

8. What does the module on "Bias in Artificial Intelligence" address in the book?
a) Strategies to increase the efficiency of AI algorithms.
b) Methods for integrating AI into software applications.
c) The identification, mitigation, and understanding of biases in AI systems.
d) Advanced programming techniques in Python for AI.

9. What is "TinyML"?
a) A library for developing Machine Learning models on high-performance servers.
b) The field of applying machine learning models to devices with limited resources.
c) A subfield of ML dedicated exclusively to the analysis of small texts.
d) An optimization technique for large AI models.

10. What is the purpose of "Project Management" in AI projects?
a) To provide coding and software development tools.
b) To manage, plan, and oversee the effective development of AI projects.
c) To teach the fundamentals of AI programming.
d) To implement cybersecurity solutions in AI projects.

11. What is a "Data Warehouse" in the context of Big Data?
a) A distributed database that stores large amounts of real-time data.
b) A storage system that organizes and stores historical data for analysis and querying.
c) A tool for real-time data visualization and analysis.
d) A method for transferring data between different platforms and systems.

12. In Machine Learning, what best describes a "Decision Tree"?
a) A neural network model used for time series analysis.
b) A data structure that represents decisions and their possible consequences.
c) An optimization algorithm for selecting features.
d) A data encryption method.

13. What is an example of "Supervised Learning"?
a) Classifying emails as spam or not spam.
b) Grouping customers into segments based on purchase patterns.
c) Identifying patterns in unlabeled data.
d) Creating predictive models without prior training data.

14. What does "k-Nearest-Neighbors Algorithm" (k-NN) represent in Machine Learning?
a) A method for reducing data dimension.
b) A classification and regression algorithm based on the proximity of sample data.
c) A technique for time series analysis.
d) An approach for natural language processing.

15. What is "Business Intelligence" (BI)?
a) The use of software to automate routine business tasks.
b) The analysis and presentation of data to assist in business decision-making.
c) An operating system used in businesses.
d) A Machine Learning technique applied to business.

16. In the context of AI, what is "Natural Language Processing" (NLP)?
a) The automation of business processes through AI algorithms.
b) The simulation of human interaction by computers.
c) The ability of a computer to understand, interpret, and generate human language.
d) A type of supervised learning algorithm.

17. What best describes "Quantization" in the context of TinyML?
a) The conversion of a Machine Learning model into a smaller and more efficient version.
b) The segmentation of a market into different consumer groups.
c) A method to increase the accuracy of AI models.
d) The creation of a data set to train AI models.

18. What is a common challenge in developing AI projects?
a) Finding a suitable location for data servers.
b) Managing data ethics and privacy.
c) Choosing the color and design of the user interface.
d) Determining the price of AI products.

19. What technique is used in "Text Mining" to divide text into meaningful words or phrases?
a) Data normalization.
b) Sentence segmentation and word tokenization.
c) Regression analysis.
d) Clustering algorithms.

20. What is an "Artificial Neural Network" (ANN)?
a) A type of specialized hardware for AI processing.
b) A computational model based on the structure and functions of the human brain.
c) A storage system for large amounts of data.
d) A software tool for developing mobile applications.

21. What is TensorFlow Lite in the context of TinyML?
a) A programming language for mobile application development.
b) A reduced version of TensorFlow designed for devices with limited resources.
c) A data analysis software for large companies.
d) A tool for visualizing Machine Learning models.

22. What is the main purpose of a "Digital Twin" in IoT?
a) Digitally duplicating a physical device to improve its security.
b) Creating a digital backup of the information on an IoT device.
c) Simulating and analyzing the behavior of a physical device in a virtual environment.
d) Developing a more attractive user interface for IoT devices.

23. What best describes "Image Segmentation" in image processing?
a) Converting images into text using OCR.
b) Classifying images into different categories.
c) Dividing an image into meaningful parts or regions.
d) Enhancing the resolution and quality of a digital image.

24. What is an example of "Artificial Intelligence" application in the Human Resources Department?
a) Designing the company's website.
b) Analyzing and predicting market trends.
c) Automating the selection and recruitment process.
d) Managing the company's social media.

25. What does "Real-world Evaluation and Validation" consist of in the context of AI projects?
a) Developing a marketing strategy for AI products.
b) Testing and adjusting AI models in real environments and situations.
c) Conducting a financial analysis of the AI project.
d) Designing the user interface for AI applications.

26. What role does "Sentiment Analysis" play in Natural Language Processing?
a) Improving the security and privacy of communications.
b) Identifying and classifying emotions expressed in a text.
c) Increasing text processing speed.
d) Automatically translating between different languages.

27. What is a "Data Lake" in the context of Big Data?
a) A method for encrypting large volumes of data.
b) A centralized system for managing company operations.
c) A storage that allows saving large amounts of data in its native form.
d) A real-time data visualization tool.

28. How does "Dimensionality Reduction" contribute in the data analysis of Machine Learning?
a) Increasing data security.
b) Improving data interpretation and visualization.
c) Increasing the amount of data available for analysis.
d) Creating data backups.

29. What is "Edge Computing" in the context of IoT?
a) A communication protocol for IoT devices.
b) Processing data close to the data source, as in IoT devices.
c) A cloud data storage technology.
d) A programming language for developing IoT applications.

30. What best describes "Natural Language Generation" (NLG) in NLP?
a) Translating text between different languages.
b) The ability of a computer to generate humanoid text.
c) An algorithm to classify texts into categories.
d) A technique to protect text privacy.

31. What is a common challenge in implementing AI models in TinyML?
a) The need for constant high-speed internet connection.
b) Memory and processing capacity limitations of devices.
c) Finding enough data to train models.
d) Choosing the color and design of the graphical interface.

32. In the context of AI, what is a "transfer learning model"?
a) A model that is trained from scratch for each new task.
b) A pre-trained model adapted to a new task or dataset.
c) A model that exclusively uses supervised learning.
d) A model designed for natural language processing tasks.

33. What main benefit does "Edge Data Processing" offer in IoT?
a) Increases internet speed on IoT devices.
b) Reduces latency and bandwidth needed by processing data locally.
c) Increases the resolution and quality of images captured by IoT devices.
d) Improves the user interface of IoT devices.

34. What best describes "Linear Regression" in the context of Machine Learning?
a) An algorithm to create artificial neural networks.
b) A method for classifying data into discrete categories.
c) A technique for predicting a continuous numerical value based on one or more independent variables.
d) An approach to segment digital images.

35. In the field of AI, what is "CMSIS-NN"?
a) A framework for developing AI applications on mobile devices.
b) A neural network library for ARM Cortex-M microcontrollers.
c) An operating system specifically designed for AI.
d) A data visualization tool for AI projects.

36. What characterizes an "Agile AI Project" under the Scrum framework?
a) The need for detailed planning and exhaustive design before starting the project.
b) The implementation of traditional software development practices.
c) Iterative development and focus on adaptability to changes.
d) The exclusive use of unsupervised learning.

37. What is the purpose of "Data Normalization" in the preprocessing of Machine Learning?
a) Ensure that all data is in the same language.
b) Convert all data types into text formats.
c) Scale data so that it is within a specific range and comparable.
d) Create data backups.

38. What is a "Cluster" in the context of Machine Learning?
a) A group of computers used to train AI models.
b) A collection of data with similar characteristics grouped together.
c) A specific type of artificial neural network.
d) A technique to accelerate data processing.

39. What is a "Random Forest"?
a) An algorithm that generates random decisions to predict outcomes.
b) A model based on combining multiple decision trees to improve accuracy.
c) A 3D data visualization technique.
d) A method for automatically segmenting a database.

40. What best describes "Principal Component Analysis" (PCA) in dimensionality reduction?
a) An algorithm to increase the number of features in a dataset.
b) A technique to identify and remove irrelevant features from data.
c) A method for transforming data features into lower-dimensional principal components.
d) A tool for real-time data visualization.

41. What best describes "Scatter Plots" in the context of visualization in Machine Learning?
a) Charts that show the relationship between two numerical variables using points on a plane.
b) Diagrams that represent the frequencies of data categories.
c) Charts that illustrate the hierarchy between different data classes.
d) Diagrams used to represent neural networks and their connections.

42. What is the main function of "Google Colab" in the development of AI projects?
a) Providing a cloud storage platform for large data sets.
b) Offering a cloud-based integrated development environment (IDE) for Python.
c) Serving as a specialized operating system for AI applications.
d) Acting as an online database for machine learning algorithms.

43. What is a "Recurrent Neural Network" (RNN)?
a) A type of neural network specialized in processing sequential data.
b) A neural network that is trained exclusively with unstructured data.
c) A neural network structure used for image analysis.
d) An algorithm to optimize energy efficiency in neural networks.

44. What is the purpose of "Word Tokenization" in Natural Language Processing?
a) To translate words from one language to another.
b) To break text into smaller, more manageable words or phrases for analysis.
c) To correct spelling and grammar in texts.
d) To increase text processing speed.

45. What does the concept of "Continuous and Adaptive Learning at the Edge" in TinyML imply?
a) The ability of AI models to learn and adapt in real time on edge devices.
b) The process of continuously updating AI models in the cloud.
c) The need for constant training for TinyML developers.
d) The use of AI algorithms that adapt to different types of hardware.

46. What best describes "SWOT Analysis" in AI project management?
a) A technique for measuring the return on investment (ROI) of a project.
b) A methodology for strategic planning that evaluates strengths, weaknesses, opportunities, and threats.
c) A system for quality management in AI projects.
d) A tool for resource allocation in AI projects.

47. What is the "Waterfall" method in AI project management?
a) An iterative and flexible approach to project development.
b) A sequential process where each phase depends on the delivery of the previous phase.
c) A method that emphasizes adaptability and continuous feedback.
d) A technique based on the use of AI for decision making in projects.

48. What is a "Correlation Matrix" in data analysis?
a) A tool to identify relationships between categorical variables.
b) A diagram that shows the relationship between the costs and benefits of a project.
c) A table that measures the linear relationship between two or more numerical variables.
d) A graph that represents the efficiency of different AI algorithms.

49. What is the function of "Pandas" in data processing for AI?
a) A Python library used for data analysis and manipulation.
b) A programming language specialized in statistics and data analysis.
c) A 3D data visualization software.
d) A tool for creating artificial neural networks.

50. What does Project Management focus on in Artificial Intelligence projects?
a) Exclusively on the development of AI software and algorithms.
b) On the comprehensive management of the project, including planning, execution, and review.
c) Only on the implementation and deployment phase of AI models.
d) Only on evaluating the ethical impact of AI projects.

51. What role do "Convolutional Neural Networks" (CNN) play in image processing?
a) Optimize internet speed for sending images.
b) Reduce the file size of images for storage.
c) Classify, identify, and process images for pattern recognition.
d) Translate text contained in images into different languages.

52. What is an "Agile Framework" in the context of AI project management?
a) A set of practices for detailed long-term project planning.
b) A methodology that emphasizes adaptability, teamwork, and continuous delivery.
c) A system for the complete automation of AI projects.
d) A specific programming tool for AI development.

53. How does "Text PreProcessing" contribute in Natural Language Processing?
a) Improving the security of text data.
b) Automatically translating texts between different languages.
c) Preparing and cleaning text to improve analysis efficiency.
d) Connecting different IoT devices through text.

54. What is "Scrum" in the context of project management?
a) A data analysis technique in AI projects.
b) An agile framework for project management that promotes rapid iteration, adaptability, and feedback.
c) A software specialized in the automation of management tasks.
d) A neural network model used in AI projects.

55. What best describes "Pruning" in the context of Machine Learning model optimization?
a) Adding more layers and neurons to a neural network.
b) The process of removing unnecessary parts of a model to improve its efficiency.
c) Increasing the amount of data used to train a model.
d) The technique of dividing a dataset into smaller subsets.

56. What is the function of an AI-powered "Chatbot"?
a) To facilitate the analysis of large volumes of data.
b) To provide automated and real-time interaction with users through natural language processing.
c) To improve connectivity between different IoT devices.
d) To visualize data interactively.

57. What does "Regression Analysis" imply in Machine Learning?
a) A method to classify data into different categories.
b) A technique to predict the value of a dependent variable based on one or more independent variables.
c) The process of segmenting a dataset into various groups.
d) A strategy to increase the speed of calculations in AI models.

58. In terms of "Big Data," what is "Data Mining"?
a) The process of storing large amounts of data in the cloud.
b) The practice of extracting significant patterns and insights from large datasets.
c) The technique of encrypting data for security.
d) The task of converting raw data into graphs and visualizations.

59. What is an "Evaluation Metric"?
a) An algorithm used to train AI models.
b) A measure to evaluate the performance and accuracy of an AI model.
c) A tool for AI project management.
d) A type of software used for developing AI applications.

60. What best describes "Deep Learning"?
a) A technique for processing large amounts of data quickly.
b) The use of deep neural networks to model and solve complex problems.
c) A strategy to improve the security of AI systems.
d) A method for advanced data visualization.

61. What is an "API"?
a) A set of rules to increase the efficiency of AI algorithms.
b) A tool for advanced visualization of AI data.
c) An Application Programming Interface that allows interaction between different software programs.
d) A software that protects data used in AI applications.

62. What does "Data Visualization" entail in Machine Learning analysis?
a) Process and transform data into AI models.
b) Represent data through graphs and diagrams to facilitate understanding.
c) Convert text data into voice.
d) Compress data to optimize storage.

63. What is "Semi-Supervised Learning"?
a) A method that uses only labeled data.
b) An approach that combines a small amount of labeled data with a large amount of unlabeled data.
c) A type of learning that does not require any labeled data.
d) The use of algorithms to teach models to learn by themselves without human intervention.

64. What is the main goal of "Image Processing" in AI?
a) To improve the visual quality of digital images.
b) To store and organize large quantities of images.
c) To analyze and extract useful information from digital images.
d) To transfer digital images across different devices.

65. What best describes "XGBoost"?
a) A technique for natural language processing.
b) An optimized "Gradient Boosting" algorithm for performance and efficiency.
c) A method for interactive data visualization.
d) A framework for AI application development.

66. How is "Augmented Reality" used in AI projects?
a) To create more intuitive user interfaces for AI applications.
b) As a method to increase the speed of AI algorithms.
c) To combine virtual elements with the real world, enhancing interactions and AI applications.
d) To store and analyze data generated by AI applications.

67. What does the concept of "Explainable AI" (XAI) imply?
a) The ability of an AI system to function without internet.
b) The ability of an AI system to explain its processes and decisions in a way that is comprehensible to humans.
c) An AI system that can program itself.
d) The use of AI to explain natural phenomena.

68. What is a "Rule-Based System" in AI?
a) An AI approach that uses deep neural networks.
b) An AI system that makes decisions based on a predefined set of rules.
c) A method to increase security in AI applications.
d) An AI algorithm used for financial planning.

69. What does "Hyperparameter Optimization" consist of in Machine Learning?
a) Adjusting an algorithm's parameters to improve its performance and accuracy.
b) Reducing the number of variables in an AI model.
c) Increasing the processing speed of an AI model.
d) Changing the type of data used in an AI model.

70. What is "Natural Language Generation" (NLG)?
a) A method for automatic translation between different languages.
b) The automatic creation of understandable and coherent text by a computer.
c) A technique to improve the understanding of human language by computers.
d) An algorithm to detect and correct grammatical errors in texts.

71. What is "Overfitting"?
a) A model that is too simple to capture the complexity of the data.
b) A model that has been excessively fitted to training data and does not generalize well to new data.
c) The ability of a model to process large amounts of data quickly.
d) A method to increase the training speed of an AI model.

72. What does the "Clustering" technique entail?
a) Dividing a dataset into subsets based on similarities.
b) Predicting future values from historical data.
c) Classifying data into predefined categories.
d) Reducing the number of features in a dataset.

73. What is "Model Quantization" in TinyML?
a) Converting an AI model into a mobile application.
b) Reducing the size and complexity of an AI model for use on devices with limited resources.
c) Increasing the accuracy of AI models.
d) Compressing training data for AI models.

74. What is the main function of "Data Visualization Libraries" in Python, such as Matplotlib or Seaborn?
a) Process and analyze large volumes of data.
b) Create graphical representations of data for analysis and interpretation.
c) Develop AI applications.
d) Store and organize large datasets.

75. What is a "Conversational Chatbot"?
a) A system that analyzes large volumes of online conversations.
b) A program that uses AI to realistically imitate human conversations.
c) A tool for automatically translating conversations between different languages.
d) A device that records and transcribes conversations.

76. What does the term "Big Data" imply?
a) The use of AI to solve complex problems.
b) Extremely large data sets that require advanced analysis techniques.
c) Data that are too large to be processed by traditional computers.
d) The process of converting large volumes of data into useful information.

77. How is "Logistic Regression" applied?
a) To make predictions of continuous values.
b) As a classification method to predict the probability of a binary category.
c) To cluster data based on similarities.
d) As a technique for dimensionality reduction.

78. What is "Transfer Learning"?
a) Moving data from one server to another.
b) Using a model trained on one task to perform another related task.
c) Changing the focus of an AI project to another field.
d) Automatically translating the programming language of an AI model.

79. What role does "Reinforcement Learning" play in the development of AI systems?
a) Program AI systems to function without human supervision.
b) Train AI models through rewards and penalties to learn specific behaviors.
c) Improve the security of AI systems.
d) Accelerate the training process of AI models.

80. What does "Text Mining" involve in Natural Language Processing?
a) Automatically translate texts from one language to another.
b) Extract useful information and patterns from large volumes of text.
c) Correct grammatical and spelling errors in texts.
d) Convert voice to text in AI applications.

81. What is understood by "Bias" in Machine Learning?
a) A technique to increase the speed of AI algorithms.
b) A systematic error that makes a model unfair or biased.
c) The ability of a model to process different types of data.
d) A method to improve the security of AI models.

82. What does "Principal Component Analysis" (PCA) involve in dimensionality reduction?
a) Increase the number of variables in a model to improve its accuracy.
b) Reduce the number of features in a dataset while retaining as much information as possible.
c) Divide a dataset into different categories based on its characteristics.
d) Improve data visualization through advanced graphics.

83. What best describes a "Genetic Algorithm"?
a) A method based on biological evolution to solve optimization problems.
b) An algorithm used for genetic analysis in medicine.
c) A supervised learning technique in Machine Learning.
d) A system for automatically generating programming code.

84. What is the purpose of "Customer Segmentation" in data analysis?
a) Reduce the number of customers to focus on a target group.
b) Classify customers into groups based on similar characteristics for better marketing targeting.
c) Increase the customer base by identifying new markets.
d) Evaluate customer satisfaction through surveys.

85. How is "Anomaly Detection" applied in Machine Learning?
a) To identify common patterns in a dataset.
b) To find irregularities or unusual patterns in the data that may indicate problems.
c) To classify data into predefined categories.
d) To predict future trends based on historical data.

86. What is "K-Means Clustering" in Machine Learning?
a) A regression algorithm to predict numerical values.
b) A supervised learning method for classification.
c) A clustering algorithm that divides a dataset into K distinct groups.
d) A technique to increase the efficiency of AI models.

87. What does "Data Mining" involve?
a) Extracting large amounts of data from the internet.
b) Converting raw data into more manageable formats.
c) The practice of discovering patterns and insights in large datasets.
d) Securely storing large volumes of data.

88. What is an "Ensemble Model"?
a) A single model used for different types of AI tasks.
b) A method for combining multiple models to improve the accuracy of predictions.
c) A model that specializes in a single task.
d) A type of neural network used in deep learning.

89. What best describes "Tokenization" in Natural Language Processing?
a) Automatically translate text between different languages.
b) Convert voice to text.
c) Divide text into smaller units, such as words or sentences, for analysis.
d) Automatically correct grammar in texts.

90. What is the main function of "TensorFlow" in AI application development?
a) Serve as a database for machine learning algorithms.
b) Provide an environment for advanced statistical analysis.
c) Offer a platform for the development and training of Machine Learning models.
d) Act as an operating system for AI devices.

91. What is "Explainable Artificial Intelligence" (Explainable AI or XAI)?
a) An AI system that can automatically increase its intelligence.
b) AI designed to explain its decisions and processes in a way that humans can understand.
c) A type of AI that focuses exclusively on solving complex problems.
d) An AI that can self-repair in the event of errors or failures.

92. What does "Deep Learning" involve?
a) Using large amounts of data to improve the performance of algorithms.
b) Employing neural networks with many layers to model complex problems.
c) Developing algorithms that learn quickly with minimal human intervention.
d) Creating AI models that can teach other models.

93. What is a "Recommendation System" in Machine Learning?
a) An algorithm to improve the accuracy of other AI models.
b) A system that provides personalized suggestions to users based on their preferences and historical data.
c) A tool to recommend the best AI algorithms for different types of data.
d) A device that recommends the best configuration for AI systems.

94. What role do "Evaluation Metrics" play?
a) Determine the amount of data needed to train a model.
b) Measure and evaluate the performance and accuracy of a model.
c) Increase the speed at which an AI model learns from data.
d) Reduce the size of AI models to make them more efficient.

95. What does "Bayesian Inference" involve?
a) Calculating probabilities of future events based on past events.
b) Creating predictive models based exclusively on historical data.
c) Using theorems to solve complex AI problems.
d) Predicting outcomes using decision theory.

96. What is "PyTorch"?
a) A specialized database for AI projects.
b) An Integrated Development Environment (IDE) for AI programming.
c) A software library for developing Machine Learning and Deep Learning applications.
d) A communication protocol for AI systems.

97. How is "Semantic Segmentation" used in image processing?
a) To compress images and reduce their file size.
b) To divide an image into regions representing different semantic categories.
c) To improve the resolution and quality of digital images.
d) To translate text contained in images into different languages.

98. What is a "Regression Model"?
a) An algorithm used to classify data into categories.
b) A model that predicts the relationship between independent variables and a dependent variable.
c) A system for automatic anomaly detection in data.
d) A technique for 3D data visualization.

99. What does "Supervised Machine Learning" involve?
a) Training models using only unlabeled data.
b) Using algorithms that can learn and improve without human intervention.
c) Training models with labeled data to predict outcomes.
d) Developing AI systems that do not require data to learn.

100. What is a "Recurrent Neural Network" (RNN)?
a) A network designed for processing time series data.
b) A type of neural network used exclusively for image processing.
c) A neural network that trains itself without input data.
d) An AI model used for financial decision-making.

101. What is a "Support Vector Machine" (SVM)?
a) An algorithm for automatic anomaly detection.
b) An AI model that specializes in language translation.
c) A classification and regression algorithm that seeks the optimal hyperplane to separate different classes.
d) A tool for visualizing large datasets in multiple dimensions.

102. What does "Natural Language Processing" (NLP) involve?
a) Creating systems that can understand and interpret human language.
b) Automatically translating text between different languages.
c) Statistical analysis of large volumes of text.
d) Automatically generating voice from text.

103. What does the term "Unsupervised Learning" imply?
a) Training models using only labeled data.
b) The ability of a model to learn without human intervention.
c) The use of algorithms that learn from unlabeled data to find patterns or structures.
d) A method for programming AI algorithms to perform specific tasks.

104. What is "Moore's Law" in the context of technology and AI?
a) A rule that predicts the doubling of the processing capacity of chips every two years.
b) A law that regulates the ethical use of AI.
c) A theory that describes the exponential increase in data volume.
d) A principle that establishes limitations in the development of Artificial Intelligence.

105. What best describes "Hybrid AI Models"?
a) Systems that combine AI and manual processing.
b) Models that use both supervised and unsupervised learning.
c) The integration of different types of models and AI techniques into a single system.
d) AI models that can operate on both hardware and software.

106. What is "Parameter Optimization" in Machine Learning model training?
a) Selecting the best algorithm for a specific AI problem.
b) Adjusting the parameters of a model to maximize its performance.
c) Reducing the number of variables used in an AI model.
d) Increasing the processing speed of an AI model.

107. What is "Transfer Learning" in AI?
a) The ability of a model to adapt to different types of AI tasks.
b) Transferring data from one model to another to improve its performance.
c) Using knowledge gained in one task to solve problems in another related area.
d) Changing the focus of an AI project to another field.

108. What role does "Dimensionality Reduction" play in data analysis?
a) Increasing the number of features in a dataset.
b) Decreasing the number of variables in a dataset to simplify AI models.
c) Dividing a dataset into smaller subsets.
d) Improving the accuracy of AI models.

109. What is an "Activation Function" in a neural network?
a) An algorithm that decides which neurons will be activated in the next layer of the network.
b) A technique to speed up the training of neural networks.
c) A method for connecting different neural networks.
d) A mathematical operation that determines the output of a neuron.

110. What is "Federated Learning" in Machine Learning?
a) A learning method where several models are trained independently.
b) A learning approach where multiple devices collaborate in training a model without sharing data.
c) Combining data from different sources to train an AI model.
d) An AI system that self-trains with data from multiple sources in real time.

ANSWERS

Answers

1. Correct answer: a) A subfield of Artificial Intelligence that focuses on the development of systems capable of learning automatically from data.
Explanation: Machine Learning is a subfield of AI that allows systems to learn and improve from experience without being explicitly programmed.

2. Correct answer: b) Information that is presented in a non-standard format, such as free text, images, or videos.
Explanation: Unstructured data are those that do not have a fixed or structured format, such as texts, images, and videos.

3. Correct answer: c) A type of neural network that is mainly used for classification and detection tasks in images and videos.
Explanation: CNNs are neural networks specialized in processing visual data, commonly used in image classification and detection.

4. Correct answer: a) A type of machine learning where models are trained to make sequential decisions.
Explanation: Reinforcement Learning focuses on how agents should make decisions to maximize some notion of cumulative reward.

5. Correct answer: b) Voice recognition in virtual assistants.
Explanation: IoT involves connecting everyday devices to the Internet, and voice recognition in virtual assistants is a common example of this.

6. Correct answer: c) Heatmaps.
Explanation: Heatmaps are useful for visualizing the correlation between multiple variables, often used in Machine Learning data analysis.

7. Correct answer: b) A technique for identifying the strengths, weaknesses, opportunities, and threats of a project.
Explanation: SWOT Analysis is a strategic tool used to evaluate these four critical aspects of a project.

8. Correct answer: c) The identification, mitigation, and understanding of biases in AI systems.
Explanation: The module on biases in AI focuses on how to identify and reduce prejudices and biases in AI algorithms and systems.

9. Correct answer: b) The field of applying machine learning models on devices with limited resources.
Explanation: TinyML refers to the deployment of efficient Machine Learning models on low-power and resource-constrained devices.

10. Correct answer: b) Managing, planning, and overseeing the effective development of AI projects.
Explanation: Project Management in AI involves the comprehensive management of the development process, from planning to execution and review of AI projects.

11. Correct answer: b) A storage system that organizes and stores historical data for analysis and querying.
Explanation: A Data Warehouse is a data storage platform designed to analyze and query large amounts of historical data.

12. Correct answer: b) A data structure that represents decisions and their possible consequences.
Explanation: A Decision Tree is an ML model that graphically represents decisions and their possible outcomes or consequences.

13. Correct answer: a) Classification of emails as spam or not spam.
Explanation: Supervised learning involves training a model with labeled data, such as classifying emails into predefined categories.

14. Correct answer: b) A classification and regression algorithm based on the proximity of sample data.
Explanation: k-NN is a simple and effective algorithm that classifies or predicts based on proximity or similarity to the nearest sample data.

15. Correct answer: b) The analysis and presentation of data to assist in business decision-making.
Explanation: Business Intelligence refers to technologies and strategies used for business data analysis, aiding in decision-making.

16. Correct answer: c) The ability of a computer to understand, interpret, and generate human language.
Explanation: NLP allows computers to process and interact with human language, including text comprehension and generation.

17. Correct answer: a) The conversion of a Machine Learning model into a smaller and more efficient version.
Explanation: Quantization in TinyML involves reducing the size and complexity of the model to adapt to resource-constrained devices.

18. Correct answer: b) Managing data ethics and privacy.
Explanation: One of the key challenges in AI projects is ensuring ethics and protecting the privacy of the used and generated data.

19. Correct answer: b) Sentence segmentation and word tokenization.
Explanation: In text mining, this technique divides text into smaller units, such as words or phrases, for analysis.

20. Correct answer: b) A computational model based on the structure and functions of the human brain.
Explanation: ANNs are computational systems that mimic how human brains process information, used in a variety of AI applications.

21. Correct answer: b) A reduced version of TensorFlow designed for devices with limited resources.
Explanation: TensorFlow Lite is a lightweight version of TensorFlow, optimized to run Machine Learning models on resource-constrained devices, such as mobiles and IoT devices.

22. Correct answer: c) Simulate and analyze the behavior of a physical device in a virtual environment.
Explanation: A "Digital Twin" in IoT is a digital replica of a physical device or system that allows for simulation, analysis, and remote control.

23. Correct answer: c) The division of an image into parts or meaningful regions.
Explanation: Image segmentation is an image processing process that divides an image into multiple segments or regions to facilitate its analysis.

24. Correct answer: c) Automate the recruitment and selection process.
Explanation: In the HR Department, AI can automate and optimize the recruitment and selection process, improving efficiency.

25. Correct answer: b) Test and adjust AI models in real-world environments and situations.
Explanation: Real-world evaluation and validation involve testing AI models in real conditions to ensure their effectiveness and accuracy.

26. Correct answer: b) Identify and classify the emotions expressed in a text.
Explanation: Sentiment analysis in NLP focuses on identifying and classifying opinions or emotions expressed in texts to better understand reactions and attitudes.

27. Correct answer: c) A storage that allows saving large amounts of data in its native form.
Explanation: A Data Lake is a massive storage system that allows storing large volumes of data in their original format for future analysis.

28. Correct answer: b) Improving the interpretation and visualization of data.
Explanation: Dimensionality reduction in Machine Learning helps to simplify data, facilitating its interpretation and visualization, without losing relevant information.

29. Correct answer: b) Processing data near the data source, such as in IoT devices.
Explanation: Edge Computing refers to the processing of data close to where it is generated (for example, in IoT devices), reducing latency and bandwidth usage.

30. Correct answer: b) The ability of a computer to generate humanoid text.
Explanation: Natural Language Generation is a subfield of NLP that focuses on the ability of machines to create text that appears to have been written by humans.

31. Correct answer: b) The memory and processing capacity limitations of devices.
Explanation: In TinyML, a key challenge is adapting AI models to devices with limited resources such as memory and processing capacity.

32. Correct answer: b) A pretrained model adapted to a new task or dataset.
Explanation: Transfer learning involves taking an already trained model and adapting it to a new related task, leveraging previous knowledge.

33. Correct answer: b) Reduces latency and bandwidth needed by processing data locally.
Explanation: Edge Processing in IoT involves analyzing data at the place where it is generated, reducing latency and bandwidth usage.

34. Correct answer: c) A technique to predict a continuous numerical value based on one or more independent variables.
Explanation: Linear regression is a statistical method for predicting a continuous numerical value from one or more independent variables.

35. Correct answer: b) A neural network library for ARM Cortex-M microcontrollers.
Explanation: CMSIS-NN is a neural network library optimized for ARM Cortex-M microcontrollers, used in TinyML applications.

36. Correct answer: c) Iterative development and focus on adaptability to changes.
Explanation: In an agile AI project under Scrum, iterative development is emphasized, allowing adaptability and flexibility in the face of changes during the project.

37. Correct answer: c) Scale the data to be within a specific range and comparable.
Explanation: Data normalization in Machine Learning involves adjusting the scale of the data so that all features contribute equally to the model.

38. Correct answer: b) A collection of data with similar characteristics grouped together.
Explanation: In Machine Learning, a cluster refers to a group of data that are similar to each other and different from data in other groups.

39. Correct answer: b) A model based on the combination of multiple decision trees to improve accuracy.
Explanation: The Random Forest method combines multiple decision trees to form a more robust and accurate model.

40. Correct answer: c) A method for transforming data features into lower-dimensional principal components.
Explanation: Principal Component Analysis (PCA) reduces the dimensionality of data by transforming it into a new set of variables (principal components) that are a linear combination of the originals.

41. Correct answer: a) Graphs that show the relationship between two numerical variables using points on a plane.
Explanation: Scatter Plots or scatter diagrams are used to visualize the relationship or correlation between two numerical variables.

42. Correct answer: b) Offering a cloud-based integrated development environment (IDE) for Python.
Explanation: Google Colab provides a Python coding environment in the cloud, especially useful for development and experimentation in AI projects.

43. Correct answer: a) A type of neural network specialized in processing sequential data.
Explanation: Recurrent Neural Networks (RNNs) are suitable for tasks related to sequential data, such as spoken or written language.

44. Correct answer: b) Dividing text into smaller, more manageable words or phrases for analysis.
Explanation: Tokenization in NLP involves breaking text into smaller units, like words or phrases, to facilitate its processing and analysis.

45. Correct answer: a) The ability of AI models to learn and adapt in real-time on edge devices.
Explanation: Continuous and adaptive learning in TinyML refers to the ability of AI models to learn and adapt in real-time on edge devices.

46. Correct answer: b) A methodology for strategic planning that assesses strengths, weaknesses, opportunities, and threats.
Explanation: SWOT analysis is a strategic planning tool used to assess Strengths, Weaknesses, Opportunities, and Threats in projects, including AI ones.

47. Correct answer: b) A sequential process where each phase depends on the delivery of the previous phase.
Explanation: The Waterfall method is a project management approach that follows a sequential and linear process, where each phase begins only after completing the previous one.

48. Correct answer: c) A table that measures the linear relationship between two or more numerical variables.
Explanation: A correlation matrix is a tool that shows how different numerical variables are linearly related to each other.

49. Correct answer: a) A Python library used for data analysis and manipulation.
Explanation: Pandas is a Python library widely used in data analysis, offering data structures and tools for manipulating and analyzing large datasets.

50. Correct answer: b) In the comprehensive management of the project, including planning, execution, and review.
Explanation: Project management in AI focuses on the total management of the project, covering from planning and execution to monitoring and reviewing the project.

51. Correct answer: c) Classify, identify, and process images for pattern recognition.
Explanation: CNNs are a type of deep neural network specialized in image processing and analysis, widely used in pattern recognition tasks.

52. Correct answer: b) A methodology that emphasizes adaptability, teamwork, and continuous delivery.
Explanation: Agile frameworks in AI project management promote flexibility, collaboration, and the continuous delivery of value.

53. Correct answer: c) Preparing and cleaning text to improve the efficiency of analysis.
Explanation: Text preprocessing in NLP involves cleaning and preparing text (such as removing noise or normalizing words) to improve subsequent processing and analysis.

54. Correct answer: b) An agile framework for project management that promotes rapid iteration, adaptability, and feedback.
Explanation: Scrum is an agile framework that focuses on iterative and adaptable project management, with a strong emphasis on regular feedback.

55. Correct answer: b) The process of removing unnecessary parts of a model to improve its efficiency.
Explanation: Pruning in Machine Learning refers to the removal of non-essential components of a model, such as neurons or layers, to improve its efficiency and performance.

56. Correct answer: b) Providing automated and real-time interaction with users through natural language processing.
Explanation: AI-driven chatbots use natural language processing to interact automatically and in real time with users, offering responses and assistance.

57. Correct answer: b) A technique to predict the value of a dependent variable based on one or more independent variables.
Explanation: Regression analysis in Machine Learning is a statistical method used to predict the value of a dependent variable from independent variables.

58. Correct answer: b) The practice of extracting meaningful patterns and insights from large datasets.
Explanation: Data Mining involves analyzing large volumes of data to discover significant patterns, trends, and relationships.

59. Correct answer: b) A measure to evaluate the performance and accuracy of an AI model.
Explanation: Evaluation metrics in Machine Learning are tools used to measure and evaluate the performance of a model, such as its accuracy, sensitivity, and specificity.

60. Correct answer: b) The use of deep neural networks to model and solve complex problems.
Explanation: Deep Learning, a subfield of Machine Learning, involves the use of multi-layer (deep) neural networks to model and solve complex problems, especially those related to large amounts of data.

61. Correct answer: c) An Application Programming Interface that allows interaction between different software programs.
Explanation: An API in software development facilitates interaction between different programs, allowing systems and applications to communicate and share functions or data.

62. Correct answer: b) Representing data through graphs and diagrams to facilitate understanding.
Explanation: Data visualization in Machine Learning involves using graphs and diagrams to represent data in a way that is easier to understand and analyze.

63. Correct answer: b) An approach that combines a small amount of labeled data with a large amount of unlabeled data.
Explanation: Semi-supervised learning uses both labeled (in smaller quantity) and unlabeled data, taking advantage of both approaches.

64. Correct answer: c) Analyzing and extracting useful information from digital images.
Explanation: Image processing in AI focuses on analyzing images to extract relevant information, such as in recognition or classification tasks.

65. Correct answer: b) A "Gradient Boosting" algorithm optimized for performance and efficiency.
Explanation: XGBoost is a Machine Learning algorithm that uses Gradient Boosting techniques, known for its efficiency, performance, and ability to handle large datasets.

66. Correct answer: c) To combine virtual elements with the real world, enhancing interactions and AI applications.
Explanation: Augmented reality in AI projects is used to overlay information or virtual elements on the real world, enriching the user experience.

67. Correct answer: b) The ability of an AI system to explain its processes and decisions in a way that is understandable to humans.
Explanation: Explainable AI refers to AI systems designed to provide clear and understandable explanations about how and why they make certain decisions or actions.

68. Correct answer: b) An AI system that makes decisions based on a predefined set of rules.
Explanation: A rule-based system in AI uses a specific set of logical rules to make decisions or perform analysis, based on defined inputs.

69. Correct answer: a) Adjusting the parameters of an algorithm to improve its performance and accuracy.
Explanation: Hyperparameter optimization in Machine Learning involves adjusting key parameters of a model (such as learning rate) to improve its effectiveness and efficiency.

70. Correct answer: b) The automatic creation of understandable and coherent text by a computer.
Explanation: Natural Language Generation (NLG) is a process in which computers automatically generate natural and comprehensible text, often used in automatic response systems or report generation.

71. Correct answer: b) A model that has been excessively adjusted to training data and does not generalize well to new data.
Explanation: Overfitting occurs when a Machine Learning model learns the details and noise of the training data to the point that it negatively affects its performance on new data.

72. Correct answer: a) Dividing a dataset into subsets based on similarities.
Explanation: Clustering in Machine Learning is an unsupervised learning method that groups data into sets or clusters based on their similarity or proximity.

73. Correct answer: b) Reducing the size and complexity of an AI model for use on devices with limited resources.
Explanation: Model quantization in TinyML involves reducing the size and complexity of the model so that it can run on devices with limited resources, such as microcontrollers.

74. Correct answer: b) Creating graphical representations of data for analysis and interpretation.
Explanation: Data visualization libraries in Python, such as Matplotlib and Seaborn, are used to create graphs and diagrams that facilitate data analysis and interpretation.

75. Correct answer: b) A program that uses AI to realistically mimic human conversations.
Explanation: Conversational chatbots are AI-driven programs designed to simulate the way humans converse, responding realistically to user inputs.

76. Correct answer: b) Extremely large datasets that require advanced analysis techniques.
Explanation: Big Data refers to datasets that are so large or complex that traditional data processing techniques are inadequate to handle them efficiently.

77. Correct answer: b) As a classification method to predict the probability of a binary category.
Explanation: Logistic regression is a statistical technique in Machine Learning used for binary classification, i.e., predicting the probability that an observation belongs to one of two categories.

78. Correct answer: b) Using a model trained on one task to perform a related task.
Explanation: Transfer Learning in AI involves taking a model developed for a specific task and reusing it on a second related task, adjusting it as necessary.

79. Correct answer: b) Training AI models through rewards and penalties to learn specific behaviors.
Explanation: Reinforcement learning is based on the use of rewards and penalties to guide AI models to learn specific behaviors through trial and error.

80. Correct answer: b) Extracting useful information and patterns from large volumes of text.
Explanation: Text mining in Natural Language Processing focuses on extracting relevant information, patterns, and insights from large amounts of text.

81. Correct answer: b) A systematic error that causes a model to be unfair or biased.
Explanation: "Bias" in Machine Learning refers to a systematic bias in the data or algorithm that can lead to partial or unfair outcomes.

82. Correct answer: b) Reducing the number of features of a dataset while retaining as much information as possible.
Explanation: Principal Component Analysis (PCA) is a dimensionality reduction technique that transforms the original features of a dataset into new features (principal components) that retain the most information.

83. Correct answer: a) A method based on biological evolution to solve optimization problems.
Explanation: Genetic algorithms are optimization and search techniques based on the principles of genetics and natural selection.

84. Correct answer: b) Classifying customers into groups based on similar characteristics for better marketing targeting.
Explanation: Customer segmentation in data analysis involves grouping customers into categories based on common characteristics to more effectively direct marketing efforts.

85. Correct answer: b) To find irregularities or unusual patterns in data that may indicate problems.
Explanation: Anomaly detection in Machine Learning is used to identify data points, events, or observations that significantly deviate from the majority of the data, which may indicate a problem.

86. Correct answer: c) A clustering algorithm that divides a dataset into "k" distinct groups.
Explanation: k-Means is a popular unsupervised clustering algorithm that groups data into a predefined number of clusters (k) based on their characteristics.

87. Correct answer: c) In the practice of discovering patterns and insights in large datasets.
Explanation: Data Mining involves analyzing large datasets to discover hidden patterns, correlations, and other useful insights.

88. Correct answer: b) A method for combining multiple models to improve prediction accuracy.
Explanation: Ensemble models in Machine Learning combine the predictions of several base models to improve the robustness and accuracy of the final model.

89. Correct answer: c) Splitting text into smaller units, such as words or phrases, for analysis.
Explanation: Tokenization in natural language processing is the process of splitting text into smaller pieces (tokens), such as words or phrases, to facilitate further analysis.

90. Correct answer: c) Providing a platform for the development and training of Machine Learning models.
Explanation: TensorFlow is an open-source software library developed by Google for the development and training of Machine Learning and Deep Learning models.

91. Correct answer: b) AI designed to explain its decisions and processes in a way that humans can understand.
Explanation: Explainable Artificial Intelligence (XAI) refers to AI systems designed to make their decision-making processes transparent and understandable to humans.

92. Correct answer: b) In the use of neural networks with many layers to model complex problems.
Explanation: Deep Learning uses deep neural networks, with multiple hidden layers, to model and solve complex problems, especially in the field of perception and recognition.

93. Correct answer: b) A system that provides personalized suggestions to users based on their preferences and historical data.
Explanation: Recommendation systems in Machine Learning analyze user data and preferences to provide personalized suggestions, such as products, services, or content.

94. Correct answer: b) Measure and evaluate the performance and accuracy of a model.
Explanation: Evaluation metrics in Machine Learning are tools used to measure and evaluate the performance of a model, such as its accuracy, sensitivity, and specificity.

95. Correct answer: a) In the calculation of probabilities of future events based on past events.
Explanation: Bayesian inference in statistics and Machine Learning uses Bayes' theorem to update the probability of a hypothesis as more evidence or information becomes available.

96. Correct answer: c) A software library for developing Machine Learning and Deep Learning applications.
Explanation: PyTorch is a popular open-source software library used for developing Machine Learning and Deep Learning applications, known for its flexibility and ease of use.

97. Correct answer: b) To divide an image into regions representing different semantic categories.
Explanation: Semantic segmentation in image processing is used to divide an image into parts or regions, each corresponding to a distinct semantic category.

98. Correct answer: b) A model that predicts the relationship between independent variables and a dependent variable.
Explanation: Regression models in Machine Learning are used to predict the value of a dependent variable based on one or more independent variables.

99. Correct answer: c) In training models with labeled data to predict outcomes.
Explanation: Supervised machine learning involves training models using labeled datasets, where each training example includes an input and the corresponding output.

100. Correct answer: a) A network designed for processing time series data.
Explanation: Recurrent Neural Networks (RNN) are suitable for working with sequential or time series data, such as spoken or written language, as they can process sequences of information while maintaining an internal state.

101. Correct answer: c) A classification and regression algorithm that seeks the optimal hyperplane to separate different classes.
Explanation: Support Vector Machines (SVM) are Machine Learning algorithms used for classification and regression that seek to find the optimal hyperplane to separate classes in a feature space.

102. Correct answer: a) In the creation of systems that can understand and interpret human language.
Explanation: Natural Language Processing (NLP) refers to the ability of machines to understand and process human language, including tasks such as text analysis and natural language generation.

103. Correct answer: c) The use of algorithms that learn from unlabeled data to find patterns or structures.
Explanation: Unsupervised Learning involves using algorithms to learn from unlabeled data and discover patterns or structures in the data by themselves, without explicit supervision.

104. Correct answer: a) A rule that predicts the doubling of chip processing capacity every two years.
Explanation: Moore's Law predicts that the processing capacity of chips will approximately double every two years, which has been a trend in the technology industry.

105. Correct answer: c) The integration of different types of AI models and techniques into a single system.
Explanation: Hybrid AI Models refer to the combination of different approaches and techniques of Artificial Intelligence into a single system to improve its performance and capability.

106. Correct answer: b) Adjusting the parameters of a model to maximize its performance.
Explanation: Parameter Optimization involves adjusting the values of the parameters of a Machine Learning model to improve its performance and accuracy in the specific task.

107. Correct answer: c) Using knowledge acquired in one task to solve problems in another related area.
Explanation: Transfer Learning involves using knowledge or models trained in one task to help solve problems in another related task, which can accelerate training and improve performance.

108. Correct answer: b) Decreasing the number of variables in a dataset to simplify AI models.
Explanation: Dimensionality Reduction involves reducing the number of variables or features in a dataset to simplify AI models and improve their efficiency without losing critical information.

109. Correct answer: d) A mathematical operation that determines the output of a neuron.
Explanation: An Activation Function in a neural network is a mathematical function that determines the output of a neuron based on its weighted inputs, introducing non-linearity into the network and allowing it to learn more complex relationships.

110. Correct answer: b) A learning approach where multiple devices collaborate in training a model without sharing data.
Explanation: Federated Learning is an approach in which multiple devices collaborate in training an AI model without sharing their raw data, preserving data privacy while improving the model.

GLOSSARY

Glossary

Creating a glossary of everything related to Machine Learning and Artificial Intelligence is a mammoth task. To give you an idea, imagine the Pacific Ocean. Imagine the most remote corner of the ocean. It's a cloudy day and there's a storm. Imagine floating in the middle of the choppy waters. Suddenly a wave submerges you, and submerged, suspended in the dark and cold waters of the ocean, you observe as a megalodon approaches you. That's how I feel now that I have to tackle the task of creating a glossary. The AI and ML glossary is immense. It's a monster you can't control. If you face it head-on, you can only lose. For this reason, and considering that I suppose many of the terms I have previously mentioned in the book are already clear to you, I will focus first on the most important ones and second on those that we have not touched upon, due to not being able to delve into other aspects of AI and ML, but which, without a doubt, and if you become a good AI-Manager, you will sooner or later have to face.

A

A/B Testing: A/B Testing is a method for comparing two versions of a webpage, application, or product to determine which one performs better.

Accuracy: Accuracy is a measure that evaluates how close the predictions of a machine learning model are to the actual values.

Activation Function: Activation Function is a mathematical function applied to the output of a neuron in an artificial neural network to determine its activation or response.

Adaptive Learning: Adaptive Learning refers to Artificial Intelligence systems that automatically adjust to personalize learning based on the user's responses and individual needs.

Adversarial Attack: Adversarial Attack is a technique used to deceive machine learning models by introducing small but intentional alterations in the input data.

Adversarial Learning: Adversarial Learning is an approach in machine learning where generative models are used to create training examples that can improve the robustness of the models.

Agent-Based Modeling: Agent-Based Modeling is a class of computational modeling that simulates the interactions of autonomous agents (individuals or entities) to assess their effects on the system as a whole.

Agile Methodology: Agile Methodology is an approach to project management, especially in software development, that emphasizes flexibility, ongoing collaboration, and adaptability to changes.

AI Deployment: AI Deployment is the process of operationalizing an Artificial Intelligence system in a real environment.

AI Documentation: AI Documentation refers to the creation and maintenance of records and documentation related to the development and use of Artificial Intelligence systems.

AI Ethics Evaluation: AI Ethics Evaluation involves assessing whether an Artificial Intelligence system complies with established ethical and moral standards.

AI Ethics: AI Ethics is the study and promotion of ethical practices in the field of Artificial Intelligence, including considerations of issues like privacy, fairness, and transparency.

AI Frameworks: AI Frameworks are sets of tools and libraries that facilitate the development of Artificial Intelligence applications.

AI Manager: An AI Manager is a person or role responsible for overseeing, directing, and coordinating AI projects. This role involves a combination of technical skills in AI and management abilities, and typically includes responsibilities such as defining AI strategies, managing teams of data scientists and engineers, ensuring AI projects align with the organization's objectives, and overseeing the implementation and performance of AI-based solutions.

AI Monitoring: AI Monitoring is the continuous supervision of an Artificial Intelligence system to ensure its performance and accuracy.

AI Project: AI Project is an organized effort to develop systems or applications based on Artificial Intelligence to achieve specific objectives.

AI Quality Control: AI Quality Control is the process of ensuring that Artificial Intelligence systems function accurately and reliably.

AI Regulations: AI Regulations refer to government laws and regulations governing the development and use of Artificial Intelligence technologies.

AI Risk Analysis: AI Risk Analysis is the assessment of potential risks and challenges associated with the development and use of Artificial Intelligence technologies.

AI Team: AI Team is the group of professionals who collaborate on the development and implementation of Artificial Intelligence solutions in a project.

Algorithm: An algorithm is a set of defined and unambiguous sequentially ordered rules or instructions executed to perform a task or solve a problem.

Algorithmic Bias: Algorithmic Bias is the tendency of an Artificial Intelligence system to produce biased results due to erroneous assumptions in the machine learning process or in the data used for training.

Algorithmic Efficiency: Algorithmic Efficiency refers to the evaluation of speed and resource utilization in the execution of an algorithm.

Alpha Testing: Alpha Testing is a software testing phase where an early version of the product is evaluated by a limited group, usually within the organization that develops it.

Ambient Intelligence: Ambient Intelligence is an environment where technological devices work together to assist people in an intuitive and non-intrusive manner.

Analytics: Analytics refers to the process of exploring and analyzing large data sets to discover patterns, trends, and gain valuable insights.

Anchor Node: Anchor Node is a fixed reference point used in various network algorithms to assist in the location and mapping of networks.

Annotated Data: Annotated Data are those that have been labeled with additional information, such as tags or comments, to facilitate their analysis or processing in machine learning tasks.

Anomaly Detection System: Anomaly Detection System is a system designed to identify atypical patterns or elements in a data set that do not conform to the expected normal behavior.

Anomaly Detection: Anomaly Detection is the process of identifying unusual data or patterns that do not conform to expected behavior in a data set.

API (Application Programming Interface): API (Application Programming Interface) is a set of protocols and tools for building software and applications, allowing communication between different software systems.

API Gateway: API Gateway is a management point that sits between a set of APIs and their users, facilitating functions such as security, monitoring, and traffic control.

Apprenticeship Learning: Apprenticeship Learning is a method where an Artificial Intelligence system learns by observing and emulating the actions of a human expert or an expert system.

Architectural Pattern: Architectural Pattern refers to a set of software design practices that solve common architectural problems in software development.

ARIMA Model (Autoregressive Integrated Moving Average): ARIMA Model is a statistical model used to analyze and predict time series data, integrating autoregressive and moving average components.

Artificial Creativity: Artificial Creativity refers to the ability of an Artificial Intelligence system to generate novel and innovative ideas, solutions, or artistic works.

Artificial General Intelligence (AGI): Artificial General Intelligence is a type of Artificial Intelligence that has the ability to understand, learn, and apply its intelligence to a wide range of tasks, at the level of human intelligence.

Artificial Intelligence (AI): Artificial Intelligence (AI) is the field of computer science focused on developing systems and computer programs capable of performing tasks that normally require human intelligence, such as learning, decision making, and natural language processing.

Artificial Neural Network (ANN): Artificial Neural Network is a computational model based on the structure and functions of the human brain, used to simulate the way humans learn and process information.

Aspect-Oriented Programming: Aspect-Oriented Programming is a programming paradigm that allows separating cross-cutting concerns in a program structure, thereby improving modularity.

Association Rules: Association Rules are data mining techniques to discover how items in a data set are associated with each other.

Asymmetric Data: Asymmetric Data are those where there is a significant imbalance in the amount of data available for different categories or classes.

Asynchronous Learning: Asynchronous Learning refers to an education format where students are not required to be online at the same time and can access learning material at any time.

Attribute Selection: Attribute Selection is the process of identifying and selecting those features or attributes that are most relevant or useful for a predictive model in machine learning.

Attribute: Attribute is a property or characteristic of an object used in data analysis and modeling.

Augmented Data: Augmented Data are data that have been modified or expanded, typically using Artificial Intelligence techniques, to enhance the training processes of machine learning models.

Augmented Reality (AR): Augmented Reality is a technology that overlays digital information on the user's physical environment, thereby enhancing their perception of reality.

Autoencoder: Autoencoder is a type of artificial neural network used to learn efficient representations (encodings) of unlabeled data.

AutoML (Automated Machine Learning): AutoML (Automated Machine Learning) is an approach that uses software and algorithms to automate tasks of building, training, and selecting machine learning models.

Autonomous Systems: Autonomous Systems are systems capable of performing tasks and making decisions without human intervention, often based on Artificial Intelligence technologies.

AWS Machine Learning: AWS Machine Learning refers to the machine learning services and tools offered by Amazon Web Services, which enable the development and deployment of machine learning models in the cloud.

Azure Machine Learning: Azure Machine Learning is a cloud service from Microsoft that provides tools for developing, training, and deploying machine learning models.

B

Backdoor in AI: A backdoor in Artificial Intelligence refers to a hidden mechanism in a system or software that allows a user to gain unauthorized access or clandestinely control the system.

Backpropagation: Backpropagation is an algorithm used in the training of neural networks to adjust the weights of the connections based on the error in the output.

Bag of Words (BoW): Bag of Words is a natural language processing technique that represents a text as a set of words without considering their order or grammatical structure.

Bagging (Bootstrap Aggregating): Bagging is an ensemble technique that combines multiple machine learning models trained on different subsets of data to improve accuracy and reduce variance.

Balanced Dataset: A Balanced Dataset refers to a dataset in which classes or categories are represented uniformly or proportionally, avoiding biases in model training.

Bandit Algorithms: Bandit Algorithms are used in machine learning for sequential decision problems, where balancing the exploration of new options and the exploitation of known ones is necessary.

Baseline Model: A Baseline Model is a simple model often used as a reference point to compare the performance of more advanced machine learning models.

Batch Learning: Batch Learning is a method of training machine learning models where the system learns from the entire dataset available in a single iteration.

Batch Normalization: Batch Normalization is a technique used in training neural networks that standardizes inputs to a layer for each mini-batch, helping to improve training speed, performance, and stability.

Batch Size: Batch Size refers to the number of training examples used in each iteration of a neural network's training process.

Bayesian Inference: Bayesian Inference is a method of statistical inference in which the probability of a hypothesis is updated as more evidence or information becomes available.

Bayesian Network: A Bayesian Network is a probabilistic graphical model that represents dependency relationships among variables using a directed acyclic graph.

Bayesian Optimization: Bayesian Optimization is a strategy for optimizing costly functions that uses Bayes' theorem to guide the search to find the minimum or maximum of a function.

Beam Search: Beam Search is a heuristic algorithm that explores a graph by expanding the most promising nodes, limiting the number of nodes considered and maintaining a balance between performance and solution quality.

Behavioral Cloning: Behavioral Cloning refers to a technique in Artificial Intelligence where a model learns to imitate or replicate the behavior of an agent, usually through supervised learning.

Belief Network: A Belief Network is another name for Bayesian networks, which are graphical models that represent probabilistic dependency relationships among a set of variables.

Benchmarking in AI: Benchmarking in Artificial Intelligence involves evaluating and comparing the performance of different algorithms, models, or systems using a standard set of tasks or data.

Best-first Search: Best-first Search is a search algorithm that explores a graph by selecting the most promising node according to a specific rule or heuristic function.

Bias: Refers to the tendency of an algorithm to favor certain outcomes over others. In machine learning, a bias can lead to models that ignore important aspects of the data.

Bias Correction: Bias Correction is the process of adjusting estimation methods in statistics and machine learning to reduce biases in the results.

Bias-Variance Trade-off: The Bias-Variance Trade-off refers to the necessary balance between reducing a model's bias (so it fits well to the data) and reducing its variance (so it is robust to new data).

Biclustering: Biclustering is a data mining technique that allows for simultaneously grouping rows and columns of a matrix, useful for finding correlated patterns in high-dimensional data.

Bidirectional Encoder Representations from Transformers (BERT): Bidirectional Encoder Representations from Transformers is a natural language processing model based on transformers, known for its ability to capture bidirectional contexts in texts.

Bidirectional LSTM (BiLSTM): Bidirectional LSTM is a variant of LSTM neural networks that processes information in both directions (forward and backward), better capturing dependencies in data sequences.

Big Data: A large amount of data that exceeds the handling capacity of traditional database tools. It is characterized by its volume, velocity, variety, and veracity.

Binary Classification: A type of classification where there are only two possible outcomes. Commonly used for problems where the response is yes/no or true/false.

Binary Cross-Entropy: Binary Cross-Entropy is a loss function used in binary classification problems in machine learning, measuring the difference between the true and predicted probability distributions.

Binary Decision Diagram (BDD): A Binary Decision Diagram is a data structure used to represent Boolean functions, allowing efficient manipulation of complex logical functions.

Binary Encoding: Binary Encoding is a way of representing data by categorizing each element into two distinct states, usually 0 and 1, for use in computational models.

Binary Search Tree (BST): A Binary Search Tree is a data structure that organizes elements in a way that facilitates fast search, insertion, and deletion of elements.

Binning: Binning or discretization is the process of converting continuous variables into discrete categories, commonly used in data preprocessing for analysis.

Bioinformatics in AI: Bioinformatics in Artificial Intelligence refers to the use of AI techniques to analyze and understand biological data, especially in areas like genomics and proteomics.

Bio-inspired Algorithms: Bio-inspired Algorithms are those that mimic biological processes to solve complex problems, such as genetic algorithms or swarm optimization algorithms.

Biometric Authentication: Biometric Authentication in Artificial Intelligence refers to the use of unique physical or behavioral characteristics of individuals (such as fingerprints or facial recognition) to verify their identity.

Bitwise Operations: Bitwise Operations in Artificial Intelligence refer to the use of binary logical operations to manipulate bits or sets of bits, useful in certain low-level operations.

Bivariate Analysis: Bivariate Analysis in statistics and machine learning refers to the analysis of two variables to determine relationships and correlations between them.

Black Box Model: A Black Box Model is a type of model in Artificial Intelligence and machine learning whose internal decision-making or inference processes are not transparent or are difficult to interpret.

Black-box Optimization: Black-box Optimization is an approach in optimizing algorithms where the internal structure of the problem to be optimized is not known or considered during the process.

Bleeding-edge Technology: Technologies that are at the forefront of technological development. They tend to be innovative but potentially less stable or tested.

Blind Source Separation: Blind Source Separation is a technique that attempts to recover independent signals from mixtures of these without information about the mixing process.

Blind Spot: A Blind Spot in Artificial Intelligence refers to situations or aspects that an AI system cannot identify, understand, or process properly, often due to limitations in data or the algorithm.

Blob Detection: Blob Detection is a process in computer vision that identifies regions in an image that differ in properties, such as brightness or color, compared to surrounding areas.

Blockchain in AI: The use of blockchain technology to enhance security, transparency, and decentralization in Artificial Intelligence applications.

Bloom Filter: A Bloom Filter is a probabilistic data structure used to test whether an element is part of a set, being space-efficient but allowing a certain degree of false-positive errors.

Blue Ocean Strategy: Blue Ocean Strategy in Artificial Intelligence refers to creating markets in areas of little or no competition, exploring new AI applications.

Blueprint: A Blueprint in Artificial Intelligence refers to the detailed representation of the design or structure of an AI system, including components, algorithms, and their interaction.

Boltzmann Distribution: The Boltzmann Distribution is a probability distribution used in physics and computer science to describe the probabilities of different states in a system in thermal equilibrium.

Boltzmann Machine: A type of stochastic neural network that can learn a probability distribution over its sets of inputs.

Boolean Logic: Boolean Logic in Artificial Intelligence refers to the use of logic based on binary values (true/false) for decision-making and processing in AI systems.

Boosting: An ensemble technique used to improve the accuracy of machine learning models. It involves combining multiple weak models to form a strong model.

Bootstrap Method: The Bootstrap Method is a statistical resampling technique that allows estimating properties of a sample, such as the mean or variance, by resampling with replacement from the original sample.

Bot: A bot is a computer program that performs automatic tasks and can be enhanced with Artificial Intelligence capabilities for more complex tasks, such as interacting with users or making decisions.

Bottleneck Features: Bottleneck Features are those that represent critical points in a machine learning model, where dimension reduction or information compression occurs.

Bounded Rationality: Bounded Rationality in Artificial Intelligence refers to the idea that in decision-making, the information processing capacity of the AI agent is limited by various factors such as time and computational cost.

Bounding Box: In image processing and computer vision, a bounding box is a rectangle used to delineate the location of an object within an image.

Box Plot: A Box Plot is a graphical method used in statistics to represent the distribution of a dataset through its quartiles, highlighting the median and outlier values.

Brain-Computer Interface (BCI): A Brain-Computer Interface is a system that facilitates direct communication between the brain and an external device, used in fields such as medicine, robotics, and AI research.

Branch and Bound: Branch and Bound is an algorithm used in optimization and decision-making, which divides the problem into smaller subproblems (branches) and solves them efficiently.

Breadth-first Search: A search algorithm for trees and graphs that explores all nodes at a given depth before moving to the next.

Broad Learning System: A Broad Learning System is an approach in machine learning that seeks to integrate and process information from a wide range of sources or features to improve the model's performance.

Broadband Networks: Telecommunications networks that can carry multiple types of signals and data traffic at high speed.

Broker in AI: A system or service that acts as an intermediary in the processing or exchange of information in Artificial Intelligence applications.

Brownian Motion: Brownian motion in Artificial Intelligence refers to a type of random movement, often used in models and simulations that incorporate elements of randomness or uncertainty.

Brute Force Algorithm: Brute force algorithm is a problem-solving method that consists of testing all possible combinations or paths until finding a solution, if

Buffer: A buffer in the context of Artificial Intelligence and machine learning refers to a temporary storage space used to store data that is being processed or transmitted.

Business Intelligence (BI): Business intelligence is a set of technologies and processes that help companies analyze data to make informed decisions.

Byzantine Fault Tolerance: Byzantine fault tolerance in Artificial Intelligence refers to the ability of a system to continue functioning correctly even when some of its components fail or act maliciously.

C

Capacity: Capacity refers to the ability of a machine learning model to capture and represent complexities in the data, which affects its potential to learn patterns.

Capsule Network: A capsule network is a type of artificial neural network where groups of neurons form what is called capsules, and these capsules allow the model to detect hierarchical features in the data.

Categorical Data: Categorical data are variables that contain labels or categories without an inherent order, such as gender, nationality, or colors.

Categorical Encoding: Categorical encoding is the process of converting categorical variables into a format that can be easily interpreted by machine learning algorithms, typically numbers.

Causal Inference: Causal inference is the process of determining the causal relationship between variables, that is, how one variable affects another.

Centroid: Centroid is the central point in a group of points, commonly used in clustering methods such as k-means.

Chatbot: A chatbot is a computer program designed to interact with human users through natural language conversations, usually online.

Checkpointing: Checkpointing is a technique in machine learning model training where intermediate states of the model are saved, allowing training to be resumed or recovered from failures.

Churn Prediction: Churn prediction is the use of machine learning models to identify customers who are likely to stop using a service or product.

Class Imbalance: Class imbalance refers to situations in which the classes in a classification dataset are unevenly distributed.

Classification: Classification is a supervised learning technique where the goal is to predict the category or class to which an entry belongs.

Clean Data: Clean data refers to data that has been processed and refined, removing errors, inconsistencies, and irrelevant data.

Clickstream Analysis: Clickstream analysis is the process of collecting, analyzing, and reporting data about user clicks on a website or application, to understand their behavior.

Closed-Loop System: A closed-loop system is a type of control system in which the system's action is based on feedback from its results.

Cloud AI: AI in the cloud refers to the use of Artificial Intelligence services hosted on cloud computing infrastructures.

Cloud Computing: Cloud computing refers to the use of computing resources, such as servers, storage, and applications, over the Internet, provided by external services.

Cluster Analysis: Cluster analysis is the process of grouping a set of objects in such a way that objects in the same group are more similar to each other than to those in other groups.

Clustering: Clustering is an unsupervised learning technique used to identify patterns and group similar data into categories or clusters.

Code Generation: Code generation is the ability of an Artificial Intelligence system to automatically generate source code based on given specifications or examples.

Cognitive Architecture: Cognitive architecture is a theoretical framework that seeks to explain how the components of Artificial Intelligence and human cognitive systems interact and are organized to produce intelligent behaviors.

Cognitive Computing: Cognitive computing is an approach to Artificial Intelligence that seeks to mimic the functioning of the human brain, integrating machine learning, reasoning, understanding of natural language, human-computer interaction, and more.

Collaborative Filtering: Collaborative filtering is a technique used in recommendation systems to predict a user's preferences based on the preferences of many users.

Collaborative Learning: Collaborative learning in AI is when multiple models or agents learn and improve together, sharing knowledge or experiences.

Collective Intelligence: Collective intelligence refers to the ability of a group of individuals or systems to collaborate and work together to improve decision-making or solve problems.

Collinearity: Collinearity refers to a linear relationship between two or more explanatory variables in a regression model, which can cause problems in estimating the coefficients.

Color Detection: Color detection is the ability of a computer vision system to identify and classify colors in images or videos.

Combinatorial Optimization: Combinatorial optimization is the process of searching for the best solution to a problem where the solution must be selected from a finite set of possible solutions.

Command-and-Control Interface: Command-and-control interface refers to a computer interaction system where the user gives explicit instructions that the system executes.

Commonsense Reasoning: Commonsense reasoning is the ability of an Artificial Intelligence system to make assumptions and conclusions based on general knowledge of the world.

Community Detection: Community detection is a process in social network analysis and graphs that identifies groups of nodes that are more densely connected to each other than to other nodes in the network.

Comparative Analysis: Comparative analysis in AI involves comparing different algorithms, models, or techniques to determine which works best in a specific context.

Competitive Learning: Competitive learning is a type of unsupervised learning where neurons in a network compete against each other to activate in response to a set of inputs.

Complex Event Processing: Complex event processing is the technique of processing and analyzing real-time data streams to identify patterns, correlations, and significant events.

Component Analysis: Component analysis is the process of breaking down a dataset into parts or components to better understand its structure and dynamics.

Computational Creativity: Computational creativity refers to the use of Artificial Intelligence systems to generate ideas, concepts, or artifacts that are novel and valuable.

Computational Linguistics: Computational linguistics is the study of how computers can be used to understand and manipulate human language.

Computational Neuroscience: Computational neuroscience is the study of how the brain processes information through computational models and simulations.

Computer Vision: The field of Artificial Intelligence that trains computers to interpret and understand the visual world. It uses digital images, pattern recognition, and deep learning.

Concept Drift: Concept drift is a phenomenon in machine learning where the relationship between input data and the output variable changes over time, affecting the model's performance.

Conditional Probability: Conditional probability is the probability of an event occurring, given that another event has already occurred.

Conditional Random Field: Conditional random field is a statistical model used in natural language processing and pattern recognition, which models the contextual dependency between sequences of elements.

Confidence Interval: Confidence interval is a range of values, derived from sample data, that likely contains the value of an unknown population parameter.

Confusion Matrix: Confusion matrix is a tool that allows the visualization of the performance of a classification algorithm, showing the number of correct and incorrect predictions divided by class.

Conjoint Analysis: Conjoint analysis is a statistical technique used in market research to determine how people value different features of a product or service.

Connected Car: Connected car refers to vehicles equipped with internet technologies and sensors, which allow communication with other devices, vehicles, and services.

Consensus Algorithms: Consensus algorithms are methods used in distributed systems, like blockchain, to achieve agreement among the nodes in the network.

Constrained Optimization: Constrained optimization is a branch of optimization where solutions are sought within a set defined by constraints or limitations.

Constraint Satisfaction Problem: Constraint satisfaction problem is a problem-solving paradigm where values must be found for variables that satisfy a series of constraints.

Content Curation: Content curation in AI refers to the use of algorithms to select, organize, and present relevant and personalized digital content to users.

Content-Based Filtering: Content-based filtering is a technique used in recommendation systems that suggest items similar to those a user has preferred in the past, based on the characteristics of the items.

Context-Aware Computing: Context-aware computing is the design of systems that can recognize and adapt to their environment or situation.

Contextual Bandits: Contextual bandits is an approach in reinforcement learning where a model learns to choose actions based on the current context and past rewards.

Continuous Data: Continuous data are variables that can take any value within a range, such as age, temperature, or weight.

Continuous Integration: Continuous integration is a software development practice where code changes are frequently integrated into a central repository, followed by automatic testing.

Continuous Learning: Continuous learning refers to machine learning systems that continuously update and learn from new data without forgetting previously learned information.

Control Theory: Control theory is an interdisciplinary field that deals with the behavior of dynamic systems with inputs, and how to modify the system's behavior through feedback.

Convex Optimization: Convex optimization is a subfield of mathematical optimization that studies the problem of minimizing a convex function over a convex set.

Convolution: Convolution is a mathematical operation that combines two functions to produce a third function, representing the way one shape is modified by another. In the context of neural networks, especially in CNNs, it refers to the operation that mixes the input data with a set of weights, or kernel, to produce a feature.

Convolutional Neural Network (CNN): A type of artificial neural network used in image recognition and processing, characterized by its ability to detect patterns and features in images, such as edges, textures, and shapes.

Coreference Resolution: Coreference resolution is a process in natural language processing that identifies when different words or phrases refer to the same object or entity.

Correlation Coefficient: Correlation coefficient is a measure that indicates the degree of linear relationship between two variables.

Cosine Similarity: Cosine similarity is a metric used to measure how similar two documents or vectors are in terms of the angle between them, regardless of their size.

Cost Function: Cost function is a formula used to measure the error or difference between the output predicted by a machine learning model and the actual output.

Counterfactual Thinking: Counterfactual thinking refers to the ability of an Artificial Intelligence system to consider hypothetical alternatives to given events or situations.

Coupled Model: Coupled model refers to an Artificial Intelligence system where multiple models or components work together, interacting and affecting each other's behavior.

Covariate Shift: Covariate shift is a phenomenon in machine learning where the distribution of independent variables changes between training data and test data, but the relationship between inputs and output remains.

Creative AI: Creative AI refers to Artificial Intelligence systems designed to perform tasks that would normally require human creativity, such as creating art, music, or literature.

Credit Scoring: Credit scoring is the use of statistical models to assess the creditworthiness of a credit applicant.

Critical Path Analysis: Critical path analysis is a project management technique that identifies the tasks that are critical to complete the project in the shortest possible time.

Cross-Domain Learning: Cross-domain learning refers to the ability of a machine learning model to apply knowledge learned in one domain or task to a different one.

Cross-Validation: Cross-validation is a technique used to evaluate the performance of a machine learning model by dividing the data into multiple training and testing sets.

Crowdsourcing: Crowdsourcing in AI refers to the use of a large number of people, usually via the Internet, to train, test, or improve Artificial Intelligence models.

Cryptanalysis: Cryptanalysis is the study of how to break cryptographic systems, understanding their weaknesses and exploiting them to decipher messages without knowing the secret key.

Cryptocurrency Mining: Cryptocurrency mining refers to the process of using computational resources to verify and record transactions on a blockchain, earning cryptocurrencies as a reward.

Cubic Spline: Cubic spline is a type of interpolation used in data processing and computer graphics, which uses cubic polynomials to create smooth curves.

CUDA (Compute Unified Device Architecture): CUDA is a parallel computing platform and API developed by Nvidia to enable a significant increase in computational performance using GPUs.

Cultural Algorithm: Cultural algorithm is a type of evolutionary algorithm in Artificial Intelligence that simulates cultural evolution, where individuals learn and adapt their behavior based on a shared set of beliefs and knowledge.

Curriculum Learning: Curriculum learning is a technique in which a machine learning model is gradually trained, starting with easy tasks and increasing in difficulty as its performance improves.

Curse of Dimensionality: The curse of dimensionality refers to the various problems that arise when analyzing and organizing data in high-dimensional spaces.

Custom Model: Custom model is a machine learning model specifically designed for a particular dataset or problem, as opposed to generic or pretrained models.

Customization: Customization in AI refers to the adjustment of systems, applications, or Artificial Intelligence models to meet the specific needs and preferences of users or tasks.

Cyber-Physical System: Cyber-Physical System is a system in which engineering and computational components are interconnected, allowing interaction between the physical world and the computing world.

Cybersecurity: Cybersecurity in AI refers to the use of Artificial Intelligence techniques to protect systems and networks against cyberattacks, detecting, preventing, and responding to threats.

Cyclic Learning Rate: Cyclic learning rate is a technique in the training of neural networks where the learning rate is periodically adjusted in a cycle, which can help improve convergence and avoid getting stuck in local minima.

Cython: Cython is an extension of Python designed to increase the speed of Python code execution, allowing the integration of C and C++ for performance optimization.

D

Data Augmentation: Data augmentation is a technique used to increase the amount of data by generating new samples from existing ones using techniques such as rotation, translation, or noise.

Data Cleansing: Data cleansing is the process of detecting and correcting incorrect, incomplete, or irrelevant records from a data set.

Data Clustering: Data clustering is the process of grouping a set of objects in such a way that objects in the same group (cluster) are more similar to each other than to those in other groups.

Data Federation: Data federation is a data management technique where information from different sources is collected and aggregated to present a unified view of the data.

Data Fusion: Data fusion is the integration of data from multiple sources to produce more consistent, accurate, and useful data.

Data Governance: Data governance refers to the set of processes and policies that ensure the quality, availability, integrity, and security of data in an organization.

Data Imbalance: Data imbalance refers to a situation where the classes in a classification data set are not equally represented, which can bias the model's performance.

Data Integration: Data integration is the process of combining data from different sources to provide a unified view of these data.

Data Labeling: Data labeling is the process of assigning labels or categories to data sets, especially important in supervised learning.

Data Lake: Data lake is a storage system that allows large amounts of data to be stored in its natural format. It is useful for storing unstructured and semi-structured data.

Data Munging: Data munging is an informal term for cleaning and preparing raw data for analysis.

Data Normalization: Data normalization is a technique used to change the values of numeric columns in a data set to use a common scale, without distorting differences in the ranges of values.

Data Partitioning: Data partitioning is the division of a data set into smaller, more manageable parts for processing or analysis.

Data Pipeline: Data pipeline refers to a set of sequentially organized data processing operations, generally automated, involving the extraction, transformation, and loading of data.

Data Profiling: Data profiling is the process of examining the data available in a data source and collecting statistics or summary information about that data.

Data Quality: Data quality refers to the condition of a data set, including factors such as accuracy, completeness, reliability, and relevance.

Data Replication: Data replication is the process of copying data from one location to another to increase availability and redundancy.

Data Science: Data science is an interdisciplinary field that uses scientific methods, processes, algorithms, and systems to extract knowledge and insights from data in various forms.

Data Scrubbing: Advanced data cleansing is a detailed process to correct or remove corrupt or inaccurate data from a database.

Data Segmentation: Data segmentation is the process of dividing a database into smaller, more manageable subsets of data, often based on certain criteria or characteristics.

Data Stream: Data stream refers to a continuously sent sequence of data, generally in real time, as in monitoring or live analysis applications.

Data Streaming: Data streaming refers to the process of sending and receiving data continuously, often used in applications requiring real-time data.

Data Synchronization: Data synchronization is the process of maintaining the coherence and uniformity of data across multiple databases, systems, or devices.

Data Transformation: Data transformation is the process of changing the format, structure, or values of data to suit a specific purpose.

Data Visualization: Data visualization is the graphical representation of information and data. By using visual elements like charts, graphs, and maps, data visualization provides an accessible way to see and understand trends, patterns, and outliers in data.

Data Warehouse: Data warehouse is a data storage system designed to facilitate analysis and reporting.

Data Wrangling: Data wrangling is the process of cleaning, structuring, and enriching raw data into a desired format for easier and more efficient analysis.

Decision Analysis: Decision analysis is the study of how people make decisions, particularly in the context of complex systems and uncertainty.

Decision Analysis: Decision analysis is the discipline concerned with identifying, evaluating, and choosing between alternatives based on their expected values.

Decision Support Systems (DSS): Decision support systems are computer systems that assist in business or management decision-making using data and analytical models.

Deconvolutional Networks: Deconvolutional networks are neural networks used to perform deconvolution tasks, commonly applied in image analysis.

Deep Autoencoder: Deep autoencoder is a type of neural network used for unsupervised learning. It is effective for learning compact and efficient representations of data.

Deep Belief Network (DBN): Deep Belief Network is a type of artificial neural network composed of multiple layers of stochastic units and is used for unsupervised and supervised learning.

Deep Embedding: Deep embedding is a machine learning technique that uses neural networks to transform data into a lower-dimensional space, facilitating tasks such as classification or clustering.

Deep Fakes: Deep fakes are synthetic images, audios, or videos generated using Artificial Intelligence techniques, particularly deep neural networks, to create false but convincing representations of real people.

Deep Feature Synthesis: Deep feature synthesis is an automatic method for constructing new features from related data, commonly used in machine learning to improve model performance.

Deep Neural Network (DNN): Deep Neural Network is a neural network with multiple hidden layers between the input and output, allowing it to model complex relationships in data.

Deep Q-Network (DQN): Deep Q-Learning Network is a deep reinforcement learning algorithm that combines neural networks with a Q-learning algorithm.

Deep Transfer Learning: Deep transfer learning is a technique in which a model developed for one task is reused as a starting point for a model on a second task.

Denoising: Denoising is a technique used in data and signal processing to remove noise and improve the quality of the data.

Density-Based Clustering: Density-based clustering is a type of clustering algorithm that forms clusters based on the density of data points, allowing for the identification of arbitrary shapes and sizes of clusters.

Dependency Injection: Dependency injection is a software design pattern that implements inversion of control to resolve dependencies in a flexible and decoupled way.

Dependency Parsing: Dependency parsing is an approach in natural language processing that seeks to establish grammatical relationships between words in a sentence.

Deployment: Deployment is the process of putting a machine learning model or an application in a production environment, where it can be used by end-users or integrated systems.

Deterministic Model: Deterministic model is a mathematical or computational model in which the same input data will always produce the same output result.

Differential Evolution: Differential evolution is an optimization method that relies on combining existing solutions to create new candidate solutions, especially useful for optimization over continuous search spaces.

Differential Privacy: Differential privacy is an approach to ensuring data privacy that allows researchers to gain useful information from databases containing personal information, without revealing individual data.

Digital Twin: Digital twin is a virtual representation of a physical object or system, used for simulations and analysis.

Dimensional Modeling: Dimensional modeling is a database design technique used in data warehousing that organizes data into dimensions and facts, facilitating analysis and reporting.

Dimensionality Curse: The curse of dimensionality refers to the various problems that arise when working with high-dimensional data, such as difficulty in visualization and increased computational complexity.

Directed Acyclic Graph (DAG): Directed acyclic graph is a data structure used to represent dependencies and hierarchies, where each edge goes from one node to another without forming cycles.

Directed Graph: Directed graph is a set of nodes connected by edges, where each edge has an associated direction, indicating a one-way relationship between two nodes.

Discrete Data: Discrete data are data that have countable values, like the number of objects or events, and cannot be meaningfully subdivided.

Discrete Optimization: Discrete optimization is a branch of optimization involved in finding the best solution to a problem where the decision variables are discrete or categorical.

Discriminant Analysis: Discriminant Analysis is a statistical method used to find a linear combination of features that best separates two or more classes of objects or events.

Discriminant Function Analysis: Discriminant Function Analysis is a statistical technique used to analyze the difference between two or more groups of objects or events.

Discriminative Model: A Discriminative Model is a type of automatic learning model that models the dependence of a target variable on observed characteristics.

Discriminative Training: Discriminative Training is an approach in automatic learning where the focus is on maximizing the distinction between different categories or classes during training.

Distributed Artificial Intelligence (DAI): Distributed Artificial Intelligence is the study of how networks of autonomous agents can work together to perform complex tasks.

Distributed Computing: Distributed Computing is a model in which the components of a software system are located on different computer networks, but communicate and coordinate their actions through message passing.

Distributed Data Processing: Distributed Data Processing refers to data processing across multiple distributed computing nodes, allowing for efficient handling of large volumes of data.

Distributed Database: A Distributed Database is a database that is distributed across multiple computers or locations, either physically or on a network.

Distributed Ledger Technology (DLT): Distributed Ledger Technology is a digital database that is consensually updated and maintained across multiple sites, institutions, or geographies.

Docker Containers: Docker Containers are standard units of software that package code and all its dependencies, allowing the application to run quickly and reliably in different computing environments.

Docker: Docker is a software platform that provides operating system-level virtualization, also known as containerization, facilitating the deployment and management of applications.

Document Classification: Document Classification is the process of assigning a category or label to a document based on its content, commonly used in natural language processing.

Document Embedding: Document Embedding is the representation of documents as vectors in a feature space, facilitating tasks such as similarity comparison and classification.

Domain Adaptation: Domain Adaptation in machine learning is a field where the goal is to adapt a model trained in one domain to another different but related domain.

Domain Adaptation: Domain Adaptation is a technique in machine learning where a model trained in one domain (data set) is adapted to be effective in another related domain.

Domain Knowledge: Domain Knowledge refers to specialized understanding or expertise in a specific area, such as medicine, engineering, or economics, that is applied in solving problems with AI.

Double Deep Q-Network (DDQN): Double Deep Q-Network is an enhancement of the Deep Q-Network algorithm that reduces bias in the estimation of Q-values in reinforcement learning.

Dropout Regularization: Dropout Regularization is a technique to prevent overfitting in neural networks, where neurons are randomly "turned off" during training.

Dropout: Dropout is a regularization technique in neural networks that involves randomly deactivating a subset of neurons during training to prevent overfitting.

Dynamic Learning Rate: Dynamic Learning Rate refers to the adaptation of the learning rate in a machine learning algorithm during training to improve convergence.

Dynamic Neural Network: Dynamic Neural Network is a type of neural network that can change its structure and operation during runtime, allowing it to adapt to different types of data or tasks.

Dynamic Programming: Dynamic Programming is an algorithmic method for solving complex problems by breaking them down into simpler subproblems, often used in optimization and sequential decision problems.

Dynamic Programming: Dynamic Programming is a problem-solving method that decomposes a problem into simpler subproblems, storing the results of the subproblems to avoid repetitive calculations.

Dynamic Time Warping (DTW): Dynamic Time Warping is an algorithm for measuring the similarity between two temporal sequences that may vary in speed.

E

Embedding: Embedding is a representation of data in a lower-dimensional space, typically used to transform categorical or textual data into vectors in a continuous space.

Early Fusion: Early Fusion is a technique in processing multiple types of data where the combination of data occurs before the modeling process.

Early Stopping: Early Stopping is a technique for stopping the training of a machine learning model before it overfits, based on performance on a validation set.

Edge Computing: Edge Computing is a network architecture where data processing is performed as close as possible to the data source, reducing latency and bandwidth usage.

Efficiency: Efficiency in the context of machine learning refers to the ability of an algorithm to minimize computational resources, such as time and memory, while maintaining adequate performance.

Eigendecomposition: Eigendecomposition is a mathematical technique where a matrix is decomposed into its eigenvectors and eigenvalues, used in methods like PCA.

Eigenvalue: Eigenvalue is a concept in linear algebra representing a special value associated with a linear transformation of an eigenvector, important in techniques like PCA.

Eigenvector: Eigenvector in the context of machine learning is a vector that does not change its direction under a linear transformation, used in methods like principal component analysis (PCA).

Elastic Net: Elastic Net is a regularization method in regression models that combines the properties of L1 (lasso) and L2 (ridge) to improve feature selection and model robustness.

Elastic Search: Elastic Search is a search engine based on Lucene that provides a scalable distribution of real-time searches.

Elasticity: Elasticity in cloud computing systems refers to the ability of a system to adapt to workload changes, scaling resources up or down as needed.

Element-wise Operation: Element-wise Operation is an operation that is applied independently to each element of an array or matrix in programming and data processing.

Embedded System: Embedded System is a computational system designed to perform a specific function within a larger system, often with hardware and software constraints.

Embedding Dimension: Embedding Dimension is the size of the feature space in which data is represented, as in an embedding vector.

Embedding Layer: Embedding Layer is a layer in neural networks used to convert categorical data into dense and meaningful vectors, especially in natural language processing.

Embedding Matrix: Embedding Matrix is a matrix in neural networks used to convert token or word identifiers into feature vectors.

Embedding Space: Embedding Space is a representation space where categorical or textual data is represented as vectors in a continuous vector space.

Embedding Vector: Embedding Vector is a low-dimensional vector in which an object or word is represented, capturing semantic and contextual aspects.

Empirical Risk Minimization: Empirical Risk Minimization is a strategy in machine learning that seeks to minimize error over the training set, assuming that this will lead to low error on unseen data.

Encoder-Decoder Model: Encoder-Decoder Model is a neural network structure used in tasks such as automatic translation, where the encoder processes the input and the decoder generates the output.

End-to-End Learning: End-to-End Learning is an approach in machine learning where a model is trained to handle a complete task from start to finish, instead of dividing it into subprocesses.

Ensemble Averaging: Ensemble Averaging is an ensemble learning technique where predictions from multiple models are averaged to obtain a final prediction.

Ensemble Blending: Ensemble Blending is a technique in machine learning where predictions from various models are combined using statistical methods to improve accuracy.

Ensemble Diversity: Ensemble Diversity refers to the variety among individual models in an ensemble method, which is crucial for improving the overall model performance.

Ensemble Forecasting: Ensemble Forecasting is the use of multiple predictive models to obtain a better estimate or prediction than with a single model.

Ensemble Methods: Ensemble Methods are techniques that combine several machine learning algorithms to achieve better predictive performance than any of the individual algorithms.

Ensemble Pruning: Ensemble Pruning is the process of selecting a subset of models in an ensemble to improve efficiency and sometimes performance.

Ensemble Reduction: Ensemble Reduction is the technique of reducing the number of models in an ensemble to simplify the model without significantly sacrificing performance.

Ensemble Stacking: Ensemble Stacking is an ensemble learning technique where predictions from several models are used as input for a new model, which then makes the final prediction.

Ensemble Techniques: Ensemble Techniques are methods in machine learning that combine predictions from various base models to improve the stability and accuracy of predictions.

Ensemble Voting: Ensemble Voting is an ensemble learning technique where predictions from several models are combined based on a voting strategy.

Entity Extraction: Entity Extraction is the process of automatically identifying important terms such as names of people, places, and organizations in texts.

Entity Recognition: Entity Recognition is the process of identifying and classifying key words in a text into predefined categories, such as names of people, organizations, or places.

Entropy Coding: Entropy Coding is a data compression technique that assigns codes to symbols based on their frequency of occurrence.

Entropy: Entropy in the context of machine learning is a measure of impurity or uncertainty in a dataset, commonly used in algorithms like decision trees.

Environment in Reinforcement Learning: Environment in reinforcement learning is the space in which an agent makes decisions and receives feedback through rewards or penalties.

Epoch: Epoch is a complete iteration over the training dataset during the training process of a machine learning model.

Epochal Learning: Epochal Learning is a training method in machine learning where training is divided into epochs, allowing iterative adjustments in the model's learning.

Epoch-based Training: Epoch-based Training is a training strategy in which a model is exposed to the entire dataset for a determined number of times or epochs.

Epsilon-Greedy Algorithm: Epsilon-Greedy Algorithm is an action selection policy in reinforcement learning that balances exploration and exploitation by randomly selecting actions with an epsilon probability.

Error Backpropagation: Error Backpropagation is a method used in neural networks to efficiently adjust the weights of the network by propagating the error from the output to the previous layers.

Error Gradient: Error Gradient is a vector that indicates the direction in which a loss function increases most rapidly, used in the optimization process of machine learning models.

Error Rate: Error Rate is a measure of the number of errors made by a machine learning model, usually expressed as a percentage.

Euclidean Distance: Euclidean Distance is a measure of the "real" distance between two points in Euclidean space, used in various machine learning algorithms.

Evaluation Function: Evaluation Function is a function that provides a measure of the performance or quality of a solution in optimization algorithms and machine learning.

Evaluation Metrics: Evaluation Metrics are measures used to assess the performance of a machine learning model, such as accuracy, recall, and F1-score.

Event-Driven Architecture: Event-Driven Architecture is a software design pattern where the flow of the application is determined by events or state changes.

Evolutionary Algorithm: Evolutionary Algorithm is an optimization method that simulates biological evolution, such as natural selection and genetics, to solve complex problems.

Evolutionary Computation: Evolutionary Computation is a set of algorithms inspired by biological evolution, such as genetic algorithms, used to solve optimization problems.

Exception Handling: Exception Handling is a practice in programming that identifies, captures, and manages errors or exceptional conditions that occur during the execution of a program.

Exhaustive Search: Exhaustive Search is a problem-solving method that involves systematically testing all possible solutions until finding the correct or best one.

Experience Replay: Experience Replay is a technique in reinforcement learning that stores past experiences for reuse in training, improving the efficiency and stability of learning.

Expert Knowledge: Expert Knowledge refers to the use of information and expertise in a specific field within a machine learning model or AI system.

Expert System: Expert System is an application of Artificial Intelligence that simulates the judgment and behavior of a human expert in a specific field.

Explainable AI (XAI): Explainable AI refers to techniques and methods in Artificial Intelligence that make the results and functioning of AI models understandable by humans.

Explanatory Variable: Explanatory Variable is a variable that is believed to influence or determine another variable, often used in regression models.

Exploratory Analysis: Exploratory Analysis is an initial approach in data analysis to discover patterns, identify anomalies, test hypotheses, and verify assumptions.

Exploratory Data Analysis (EDA): Exploratory Data Analysis is an approach to analyzing datasets to summarize their main characteristics, often with visual methods.

Exponential Decay: Exponential Decay in the context of machine learning refers to a gradual decrease in a quantity, such as the learning rate, over time.

Exponential Smoothing: Exponential Smoothing is a time series analysis technique that uses exponentially decreasing weights to smooth data.

Extended Reality (XR): Extended Reality is a term that encompasses all forms of combined reality, including augmented reality (AR), virtual reality (VR), and mixed reality (MR).

External Data: External Data are data that do not originate within the system or model under study, but can be integrated to improve the analysis or performance of the model.

External Validity: External Validity refers to the extent to which the results of a study can be generalized to situations and populations outside the study environment.

Extreme Learning Machine (ELM): Extreme Learning Machine is a type of artificial neural network that trains its neurons quickly and efficiently, primarily used in classification and regression tasks.

Extreme Value Theory: Extreme Value Theory is an area of statistics concerned with the study of rare or extreme events and their impact on data modeling and analysis.

F

False Negative: A false negative is when a machine learning model incorrectly predicts the negative class for a case that is truly positive.

F1 Score: F1 Score is a measure of a classification model's accuracy, considering both precision and recall to provide a balance between these two metrics.

False Positive: A false positive is when a machine learning model incorrectly predicts the positive class for a case that is truly negative.

Fault Tolerance: Fault tolerance is the ability of a system, especially in networks and distributed systems, to continue functioning correctly in the event of failures of one or more of its components.

Feature Drift: Feature drift refers to changes in the statistical properties of a predictive model's variables over time, which can affect its performance.

Feature Fusion: Feature fusion is the process of combining multiple features or data sources to improve the performance of a machine learning model.

Feature Importance: Feature importance is a technique that identifies the most influential variables in a machine learning model's prediction.

Feature Normalization: Feature normalization is the process of adjusting the scale of input data features so that they have a common distribution, usually with a mean of zero and a standard deviation of one.

Feature Scaling: Feature scaling is the process of transforming input data features so they are within a specific range, such as between 0 and 1 or between -1 and 1.

Feature Space: Feature space is the multidimensional environment where each dimension represents a feature of the data, used to visualize and analyze relationships between data.

Feature Vector: A feature vector is a set of numerical attributes that represent some characteristic of an object, used in machine learning models.

Federated Database System: A federated database system is a type of database management system that coordinates and manages the query and access to data distributed across multiple databases, but treated as a single system.

Feedback Control: Feedback control refers to a system or process that adjusts its behavior based on the difference between the desired output and the measured output.

Feedback Loop: A feedback loop is a process or cycle where the output of a system is fed back as input, potentially influencing future output.

Feedback Network: A feedback network is a type of neural network where the outputs of one layer can re-enter as input, creating a feedback loop.

Feedforward Neural Network: A feedforward neural network is a type of artificial neural network where the connections between nodes do not form cycles, typically used in classification and regression tasks.

Field Programmable Gate Array (FPGA): A Field Programmable Gate Array is a semiconductor device that can be programmed after manufacturing to perform various processing and logical operations.

Filter Method: The filter method in feature selection is a technique that evaluates and selects input variables independently of the model, usually based on statistical measures.

Fine-Grained Classification: Fine-grained classification refers to the task of classifying within very specific and detailed categories, often within a larger general category.

Fine-Tuning: Fine-tuning is the process of making small adjustments to a pre-trained machine learning model to adapt it to a specific dataset or task.

Finite State Machine: A finite state machine is a computational model that represents a limited set of states and the transitions between these states, commonly used in software design and electronic systems.

First-Order Derivative: The first-order derivative in mathematics and data analysis refers to the instantaneous rate of change of a function at a specific point, useful in optimization and trend analysis.

First-Order Logic: First-order logic is a set of formal principles for deductive reasoning, where relationships and quantifications over objects can be expressed.

Fisher Score: Fisher Score is a statistical measure used to assess the importance of features in classification and variable selection.

Fisher's Linear Discriminant: Fisher's linear discriminant is a method used to find a linear combination of features that best separate two or more classes.

Fixed-Point Arithmetic: Fixed-point arithmetic is a method for representing numbers that have a fixed number of digits after the decimal point, used in systems where floating-point arithmetic is not practical.

Flatten Layer: A flatten layer in neural networks converts a multi-dimensional matrix of features into a one-dimensional vector.

Flatten: Flattening in data processing and machine learning refers to converting a multi-dimensional data structure into a one-dimensional structure, like converting a matrix into a vector.

Flip-Flop: A flip-flop is an electronic circuit that can maintain a binary state and is used in constructing memory and data processing systems.

Floating Point Operations Per Second (FLOPS): Floating point operations per second is a measure of a computer's performance, especially important in intensive calculations like those performed in deep learning.

Flood Fill Algorithm: The flood fill algorithm is a method used to determine connected areas in graphics or digital images.

Flood Fill: Flood filling is a technique in image processing and computer graphics to determine and modify areas with similar color or intensity.

Flowchart: A flowchart is a graphical representation of a process or algorithm, used for planning, documenting, and analyzing systems and programs.

Focal Loss: Focal loss is a loss function designed to address class imbalance in classification problems, giving more weight to difficult examples.

Fog Computing: Fog computing is a paradigm that extends cloud computing to the edge of the network, facilitating data processing closer to where it is generated.

Forward Propagation: Forward propagation is the process of passing inputs through a neural network to obtain an output, an essential part of training and using neural networks.

Fourier Transform: The Fourier transform is a mathematical tool that transforms a signal from the time domain to a frequency domain representation.

Frame of Reference: Frame of reference in data processing and machine learning refers to the context or set of assumptions under which a dataset is analyzed or interpreted.

Free Software: Free software refers to software that grants users the freedom to run, copy, distribute, study, change, and improve the software.

Fully Connected Layer: A fully connected layer in a neural network is one where each neuron is connected to all neurons in the previous and next layers.

Function Approximation: Function approximation is the process of finding a function that approximates as closely as possible to a set of data or a target function, common in regression problems.

Function Overloading: Function overloading in programming refers to the ability to have multiple functions with the same name but different implementations or arguments in a programming language.

Funnel Analysis: Funnel analysis is a methodology used to understand and visualize the flow and conversion of users through a series of steps or events, commonly used in data analysis and marketing.

Fuzzy Logic: Fuzzy logic is an approach to reasoning that supports degrees of truth, as opposed to traditional boolean logic that only supports true or false.

Fuzzy Matching: Fuzzy matching is a process that finds approximate or partial matches for a text string, useful in tasks like error correction.

Fuzzy Search: Fuzzy search is a search technique that finds matches that are approximate or partially similar to the search string, rather than exact matches.

Fuzzy Set: A fuzzy set is a mathematical concept that represents a set of elements with degrees of membership that are not necessarily entirely true or false, used in fuzzy logic.

Fuzzy System: A fuzzy system is a system that uses fuzzy logic to deal with approximate reasoning and ambiguity, applied in automatic control, decision making, and other intelligent systems.

G

Game Theory: Game theory is a field of study that focuses on the analysis of strategies and decisions in competitive or conflict situations, with applications in economics, social sciences, and decision theory.

Gated Recurrent Unit (GRU): Gated Recurrent Unit is a type of recurrent neural network that uses gating mechanisms to control the flow of information, being efficient in sequence modeling tasks such as natural language processing.

Gaussian Distribution: Gaussian distribution, also known as normal distribution, is a continuous probability distribution characterized by its Gaussian bell curve and is commonly used in statistics and machine learning.

Gaussian Mixture Model (GMM): Gaussian Mixture Model is a probabilistic technique for modeling subpopulations within a global data set, assuming that the data are distributed as a mixture of several Gaussian distributions.

Gaussian Process: Gaussian Process is an approach used in machine learning to predict the probability distribution of a phenomenon modeled as a series of Gaussian observations.

Generalization: Generalization is the ability of a machine learning model to perform well on new, unseen data, that is, data that were not part of the training set.

Generalized Linear Models (GLM): Generalized Linear Models are an extension of traditional linear regression models that allow the dependent variable to have a probability distribution different from the normal.

Generative Adversarial Network (GAN): Generative Adversarial Network is a type of neural network architecture consisting of a generator and a discriminator that compete with each other, used to generate realistic data.

Generative Model: Generative Model is a type of machine learning model that has the ability to generate new data resembling an existing data set.

Generative Pre-trained Transformer (GPT): Generative Pre-trained Transformer is a language model architecture based on transformers that has been pre-trained on large amounts of text for text generation tasks.

Generative Topographic Map (GTM): Generative Topographic Map is a probabilistic model used in the analysis and visualization of high-dimensional data, representing complex data in a low-dimensional space.

Genetic Algorithm: Genetic Algorithm is an optimization method inspired by biological evolution that uses concepts such as natural selection, mutation, and reproduction to find optimal solutions in complex problems.

Genetic Drift: Genetic Drift is a random process in the evolution of populations that can lead to changes in allele frequency in a population due to chance.

Genetic Programming: Genetic Programming is a technique of genetic algorithms where computer programs are the "individuals" that evolve. It is used to solve problems by optimizing and evolving programs.

Geometric Deep Learning: Geometric Deep Learning is a branch of deep learning that extends standard methods to analyze and process structured data in the form of graphs, meshes, and manifolds.

Geospatial Analysis: Geospatial Analysis refers to the use of analytical and data techniques to analyze geographic and spatial information.

Gibbs Sampling: Gibbs Sampling is a technique for generating samples from complex probability distributions, used especially in sampling Bayesian distributions.

Gini Impurity: Gini Impurity is a measure used in decision trees to quantify how often a randomly chosen element would be incorrectly labeled if it were labeled randomly according to the distribution of labels in the set.

Global Max Pooling: Global Max Pooling is an operation used in convolutional neural networks to extract the most relevant feature from a feature map.

Global Optimization: Global Optimization refers to the process of finding the best possible solution or a global optimum in the presence of multiple local optima in an optimization problem.

GloVe (Global Vectors for Word Representation): GloVe is an unsupervised learning model for obtaining vector representations of words, effectively capturing semantic and syntactic relationships.

Goodness of Fit: Goodness of Fit is a statistical measure that indicates how well a model fits the observed data.

GPU (Graphics Processing Unit): Graphics Processing Unit is specialized hardware used to accelerate calculations in machine learning applications and graphics processing.

Gradient Boosting: Gradient Boosting is a machine learning technique that combines multiple weak learning models to improve the accuracy of predictions.

Gradient Clipping: Gradient Clipping is a technique used to prevent the gradients of a neural network's parameters from becoming too large during training, which can help avoid gradient explosion problems.

Gradient Descent: Gradient Descent is an optimization algorithm used to adjust the parameters of a machine learning model by gradually minimizing a loss function.

Graph Convolutional Network (GCN): Graph Convolutional Network is a type of neural network designed to learn node representations in graphs by propagating information through close neighbors.

Graph Neural Network (GNN): Graph Neural Network is a type of neural network designed to process data represented in the form of graphs, capturing relationships between nodes and edges.

Graph Theory: Graph Theory is a field of mathematics and computer science that studies the properties and applications of graphs, structures composed of nodes (or vertices) connected by edges.

Gray Box Testing: Gray Box Testing is a software testing approach that combines elements of black box testing (where the internal structure is unknown) and white box testing (where the internal structure is known) to evaluate a program.

Grayscale: Grayscale refers to an image representation where shades of gray are used to represent intensity levels instead of colors.

Greedy Algorithm: Greedy Algorithm is a problem-solving approach that takes the best possible decision at each small step in the hope of finding the global optimum.

Greedy Layer-Wise Training: Greedy Layer-Wise Training is a technique for training deep neural networks in which each layer is trained independently and then stacked sequentially.

Green Computing: Green Computing refers to practices and technologies that seek to minimize the environmental impact of computing, including efficient energy use and reducing electronic waste.

Grid Search: Grid Search is an optimization technique that involves testing multiple combinations of a model's hyperparameters to find the best configuration.

Grid World: Grid World is a test environment used in the field of Artificial Intelligence and reinforcement learning to evaluate decision-making algorithms in a space of discrete actions.

Ground Truth: Ground Truth is the term used to refer to accurate information or actual data as compared to data inferred or predicted by a machine learning model.

Group Testing: Group Testing is a strategy for quickly identifying characteristics or elements in large populations using tests that group multiple samples.

H

Hadamard Product: Hadamard Product is an element-by-element operation between matrices or tensors, which is used in various operations in neural networks.

Hamming Distance: Hamming Distance is a measure of the difference between two sequences of equal length, counting the number of positions where the elements differ.

Hashing: Hashing is a technique that maps input data to a fixed value of fixed length, which can be useful for speeding up data search and comparison.

Heuristic: Heuristic is a general strategy or rule used to find approximate solutions in optimization problems when exhaustive search is not possible.

Hidden Layer: Hidden Layer is an intermediate layer of neurons in a neural network that is neither an input nor an output layer, used to learn more complex representations.

Hierarchical Clustering: Hierarchical Clustering is a clustering method that organizes data into a hierarchy of nested groups instead of assigning them to a single group.

Hinge Loss: Hinge Loss is a loss function used in classification problems, especially in support vector machines (SVMs), to measure the distance between predictions and targets.

HMM (Hidden Markov Model): Hidden Markov Model is a statistical model used to model data sequences, where it is assumed that there is a hidden process that generates the observations.

Hyperparameter: Hyperparameter is a configuration parameter of a machine learning model that is not automatically learned from the dataset and must be adjusted before training.

Hypothesis Testing: Hypothesis Testing is a statistical process used to determine whether a claim about a population is supported by evidence provided by a data sample.

Handling Missing Data: Handling Missing Data refers to the strategies and techniques used to deal with missing or incomplete values in a dataset during analysis and machine learning modeling.

Hard Margin SVM: Hard Margin SVM is a type of Support Vector Machine (SVM) that seeks to find a separation hyperplane that maximizes the margin between data classes and does not allow classification errors.

Hardware: Hardware is the physical part of a computer system, including components such as processors, memory, storage units, and input and output devices.

Hash Collision: Occurs when two different inputs generate the same hash value in a hash function, which can cause problems in data integrity.

Hash Function: Hash Function is an algorithm that takes an input (or 'message') and transforms it into a fixed-length character string, uniquely representing the original input.

Hashing: The transformation of data into a fixed-length character string using a hash function.
Heterogeneous Data: A dataset containing samples or examples with diverse and varied characteristics.

Heteroscedasticity: Heteroscedasticity refers to the property where the variance of errors in a statistical model is not constant across all levels of an independent variable, which can affect the quality of regression.

Heuristic: Heuristic is a general technique or rule used in decision making and problem solving, often as a quick approximation or practical approach when an exact solution is not available.

Hidden Layer: Hidden Layer is an intermediate layer in an artificial neural network located between the input layer and the output layer. Neurons in this layer perform calculations and transformations to learn more abstract representations of the input data.

Hierarchical Clustering: Hierarchical Clustering is a clustering approach that organizes data into a hierarchical tree structure.

Hierarchical Model: Hierarchical Model is an approach in statistics and machine learning that represents nested or hierarchical relationships between variables, allowing modeling of complex structures in the data.

Hierarchical Reinforcement Learning: Hierarchical Reinforcement Learning is an approach in reinforcement learning where multiple levels of control policies are organized to solve more complex problems hierarchically.

High Bias: High Bias is a situation where a machine learning model has high error in predicting training data due to excessive simplification.

High Variance: High Variance refers to a situation where a machine learning model is highly sensitive to small variations in training data and therefore does not generalize well to new data.

High-Dimensional Data: High-Dimensional Data refers to datasets that have a large number of features or dimensions, which can pose challenges in analysis and visualization.

Hinge Loss: Hinge Loss is a loss function used in machine learning algorithms, such as support vector machines (SVMs), that penalizes classification errors non-linearly.

Holdout Validation: A model validation approach where a dataset is split into a training set and a test set to evaluate model performance.

Homogeneous Data: Homogeneous Data refers to a dataset where all samples or examples have similar characteristics or belong to the same category.

Homoscedasticity: Homoscedasticity refers to the property where the variance of errors in a statistical model is constant across all levels of an independent variable, which is important in linear regression.

Human-AI Interaction: The interaction between humans and Artificial Intelligence systems, which can include collaboration, communication, and control tasks.

Human-in-the-Loop (HITL): Humans in the loop is an approach in machine learning where humans are involved to assist in decision making or error correction in the model training or inference process.

Hyperdimensional Computing: An approach to data processing that uses high-dimensional vectors to represent and operate on information.

Hyperparameter Grid Search: A hyperparameter optimization technique where a set of values is specified for each hyperparameter and the model's performance is evaluated for all possible combinations.

Hyperparameter Optimization: Hyperparameter Optimization is the process of searching for the best hyperparameter values for a machine learning model to maximize its predictive performance.

Hyperparameter Search: The process of exploring and adjusting the hyperparameters of a machine learning model to find the optimal configuration that maximizes model performance.

Hyperparameter Space: Hyperparameter Space is the set of all possible values that the hyperparameters of a machine learning model can take.

Hyperparameter Tuning: Hyperparameter Tuning is the process of finding the optimal values of the hyperparameters of a machine learning model to improve its performance.

Hyperparameter: Hyperparameter is a parameter of a machine learning model that is not learned directly from the data, but is adjusted before training the model and affects its performance.

Hyperplane: In the context of classification algorithms, it is a dimensional space one dimension less than the input space that is used to separate classes in linear classification problems.

Hypothesis: Hypothesis is a statement or assumption used in the hypothesis testing process to determine if it is supported by empirical evidence.

I

Image Recognition: Image recognition is the ability of an Artificial Intelligence system to identify and classify objects in images or videos.

Image Segmentation: Image segmentation is the process of dividing an image into regions or segments with similar characteristics.

Imbalanced Data: Imbalanced data refers to datasets where one class is overrepresented compared to others, which can affect the performance of the model.

Impact Analysis: Impact analysis is the evaluation of how a machine learning model will affect an existing system or process.

Imputation: Imputation is the process of filling in missing values in datasets, generally using statistics such as the mean or median.

Incremental Deployment: Incremental deployment is the practice of rolling out new versions of a machine learning model gradually, rather than replacing it completely.

Incremental Learning: Incremental learning is an approach in which a model is continuously updated as new data is received.

Inductive Learning: Inductive learning is a machine learning approach in which general rules are inferred from specific examples.

Inference Accuracy: Measure of how accurate a machine learning model's predictions are.

Inference API: Application programming interface that allows other systems to interact with a machine learning model to make predictions.

Inference Batch Size: Number of examples processed simultaneously during inference.

Inference Bias: Inference bias refers to the tendency of a machine learning model to make inaccurate or partial predictions due to lack of representation of certain data groups.

Inference Engine: Inference engine is a part of Artificial Intelligence systems that is responsible for reasoning and making decisions based on data and rules.

Inference Error: Inference error is the difference between the prediction made by a machine learning model and the actual value.

Inference Hardware: Devices designed to accelerate the inference process of machine learning models.

Inference Latency: Inference latency refers to the time it takes for an inference request to be processed and receive a response.

Inference Layer: A part of a neural network that performs calculations to make predictions.

Inference Mode: Inference mode is the setting in which a machine learning model is used to make predictions rather than being trained.

Inference Optimization: Process of improving the efficiency and speed of a machine learning model's predictions.

Inference Pipeline: Inference pipeline is a sequence of steps or processes that are applied to make predictions using a machine learning model.

Inference Server: Component that handles inference requests and coordinates the execution of machine learning models.

Inference Time: Inference time refers to the time it takes for a machine learning model to make predictions once it has been trained.

Inference Uncertainty: Inference uncertainty refers to the lack of confidence in the predictions made by a machine learning model.

Inference: Inference refers to the process of making predictions or conclusions based on data and machine learning models.

Inferential Statistics: Inferential statistics are statistical techniques used to draw conclusions or make predictions about a population based on data samples.

Information Retrieval: Process of finding and obtaining relevant data from a larger set of information.

In-memory Analytics: Data analysis performed directly in memory for faster performance.

In-memory Cache: Technique that stores data in memory for quick access and reduced latency.

In-Memory Computing: In-memory computing refers to the technique of storing and processing data in the main memory of a system rather than on disks or traditional storage.

In-Memory Database: In-memory database is a database management system that stores data in the main memory for quick access.

Innovative: Innovative refers to something that introduces new ideas, methods, or technologies.

Input Data: Data provided to a machine learning model for making predictions or training.

Input Layer: Input layer is the first layer of a neural network that receives the input data.

Instance Segmentation: Technique for identifying and delineating individual objects in an image.

Instance: Instance refers to an individual example or element in a dataset.

Instance-based Learning: Approach in which decisions are made based on specific examples rather than abstract rules.

Integrated Development Environment (IDE): Integrated development environment is a tool that provides a complete set of tools for developing, debugging, and testing software.

Interaction Design: Creation of user interfaces and intuitive and effective experiences.

Interactive Machine Learning: Interactive machine learning refers to an approach in which users can interact and provide feedback to the model during the training process.

Internet of Things (IoT): Internet of Things is the interconnection of physical devices with the ability to collect and transmit data over the Internet.

Interpretability Toolkit: Set of resources and tools to help understand and explain machine learning models.

Interpretability: Interpretability refers to the ability to understand and explain the workings of a machine learning model, especially in critical applications.

IoT Devices: IoT devices are physical objects that are connected to the network and can collect and transmit data.

IoT Edge Computing: IoT edge computing is the processing of data on IoT devices rather than sending it to the cloud, which allows for faster response and less bandwidth consumption.

Iteration: Repetitive cycle of training or processing data in a machine learning model.

Iterative Algorithm: Iterative algorithm is a method that solves a problem through repeated iterations until a stop condition is met.

J

J48 Algorithm: The J48 algorithm is a Java implementation of the C4.5 algorithm, which is a decision tree algorithm used in data mining and machine learning for data classification.

Jaccard Index: The Jaccard index, similar to Jaccard similarity, measures the similarity between sample sets and is used in classification and information retrieval, as well as in clustering analysis in machine learning.

Jaccard Similarity: Jaccard Similarity is a metric that measures the similarity between two sets by intersecting and uniting elements in the sets.

Jacobian Matrix: The Jacobian matrix is a matrix of all first partial derivatives of a vector-valued function. In machine learning, it is fundamental in gradient computation, especially in neural networks and optimization algorithms.

Jacobian Regularization: Jacobian regularization is a technique in deep learning to stabilize the training of neural networks by adjusting the model's complexity to avoid overfitting and improve generalization.

Jaro-Winkler Distance: The Jaro-Winkler distance is a similarity measure between two character strings, used in natural language processing tasks to measure the distance between words or phrases, important in AI applications like spell-checking and fuzzy search.

Java Database Connectivity (JDBC): JDBC is an API for the Java programming language, defining how a client can access a database. It is essential in AI applications for handling and analyzing large volumes of data.

Java Machine Learning Library (Java-ML): Java-ML is a collection of machine learning algorithms implemented in Java, designed to be easy to use and extensible, useful in AI applications requiring fast and efficient implementations of common algorithms.

Java Parallel Processing Framework: This framework in Java allows for parallel execution of processes, crucial in AI applications for efficiently handling computationally intensive tasks, like training machine learning models.

Java Virtual Machine (JVM): Java Virtual Machine is an engine that provides a runtime environment to run Java applications, relevant in Artificial Intelligence and machine learning for its ability to run Java-written programs efficiently and securely.

Java: Java is an object-oriented programming language widely used in software application development, including Artificial Intelligence and machine learning systems.

JavaBeans: JavaBeans are reusable software components in Java, used to encapsulate many objects into a single unit. In Artificial Intelligence, they can facilitate the integration and management of complex components.

JAX (Just Another Extension): JAX is a set of libraries and tools for differentiable programming and tensor calculus in Python, commonly used in machine learning projects and deep neural networks.

Jena Framework: The Jena framework is an open-source Java library for developing semantic web applications, including support for RDF, SPARQL, and OWL. It is useful in AI projects for handling semantic data and ontologies.

Jensen's Inequality: Jensen's inequality is a theorem in mathematics that relates the value of a convex function applied to the average of a set of points with the average of the function applied to those points, used in statistics and information theory.

Jensen-Shannon Distance: The Jensen-Shannon distance is a measure of the similarity between two probability distributions based on entropy. It is used in machine learning and data analysis to compare distributions and detect patterns.

JGraphT: JGraphT is a Java library for creating and manipulating graphs (data structures), useful in AI and machine learning for algorithms involving network analysis, graphs, and pathfinding.

JIT (Just-In-Time) Compilation: Just-In-Time compilation refers to a runtime optimization technique where code is compiled at the last moment to improve performance, often used in machine learning environments to speed up the execution of algorithms.

JIT Compilation for Neural Networks: JIT compilation for neural networks refers to the runtime optimization of neural networks, compiling parts of the model on the fly to improve performance and efficiency in AI applications.

JIT Compiler for Python: A JIT compiler for Python, like PyPy, increases the execution efficiency of Python scripts, which is beneficial in AI and machine learning projects that use Python as their primary programming language.

JIT Compiler: The JIT (Just-In-Time) compiler is a compilation approach that converts the code of a programming language to machine code at runtime to improve efficiency. It is relevant in AI environments to optimize the performance of algorithms.

JIT Learning: JIT (Just-In-Time) learning in Artificial Intelligence refers to systems that adapt and adjust their algorithms in real time, based on instant feedback or changes in input data, improving the efficiency and accuracy of machine learning.

JIT Optimization: JIT optimization refers to techniques that improve the performance of code by compiling it during execution, rather than beforehand. In AI, this can accelerate the execution of computationally intensive algorithms.

Job Queue: A job queue is a data structure used to manage and order jobs or tasks in computer systems. In AI environments, it facilitates the efficient management of machine learning tasks and data processing.

Job Scheduling: Job scheduling refers to the allocation of computational resources to execute jobs in computer systems, a crucial component in AI environments for efficiently managing machine learning workloads.

Johnson-Lindenstrauss Lemma: The Johnson-Lindenstrauss Lemma is a result in dimension theory that provides a way to reduce the dimensionality of data while preserving the distance structure, useful in machine learning algorithms handling large volumes of data.

Join Operation: The join operation in databases and data processing refers to combining rows from two or more tables based on a related column, an important concept in data preprocessing for machine learning applications.

Joint Entropy: Joint Entropy is a measure in information theory that quantifies the uncertainty associated with a set of random variables, important in the analysis of dependency and mutual information in machine learning models.

Joint Learning: Joint learning refers to training several models or parts of a model simultaneously in AI, which can improve the efficiency and effectiveness of learning by sharing representations or knowledge between related tasks.

Joint Probability Distribution: Joint probability distribution describes the joint probability of occurrence of multiple random variables in a statistical model.

JSON (JavaScript Object Notation): JSON is a lightweight data interchange format, easy for humans to read and write, and easy for machines to parse and generate, commonly used in Artificial Intelligence applications for data exchange.

JSON Schema: JSON Schema is a specification for defining the structure of JSON documents, useful in AI and machine learning projects to validate and document the data formats used in communication between systems and components.

JSON-LD (JSON for Linked Data): JSON-LD is a method for encoding linked data using JSON. In AI, it enables more efficient integration of data from various sources and is crucial for semantic web operations.

Julia Language: Julia is a high-level, high-performance programming language used in scientific computing, with growing popularity in fields such as Artificial Intelligence and machine learning, due to its speed and data handling capabilities.

Jump Diffusion Model: The jump-diffusion model is a mathematical model that represents a stochastic process, useful in quantitative finance and in certain types of predictive models in machine learning.

Jupyter Notebook: Jupyter Notebook is an interactive web application that allows the creation and execution of documents containing code, rich text, and visualizations.

K

Kaggle: Kaggle is an online platform that hosts data science and machine learning competitions, where researchers and enthusiasts can access datasets and solve complex problems.

Kappa Statistic: Kappa Statistic is a measure of agreement between two or more evaluators, used to assess the consistency of classification in machine learning tasks.

Keras: Keras is an open-source neural network library written in Python, designed to facilitate rapid experimentation with deep neural networks.

Kernel Density Estimation (KDE): Kernel Density Estimation is a non-parametric method for estimating the probability density function of a random variable, useful for data analysis and visualization.

Kernel Method: Kernel Method refers to a set of machine learning algorithms that use kernel functions to transform data into a higher dimensional space for easier classification or regression.

Kernel Regularization: Kernel Regularization in machine learning involves using techniques to prevent overfitting by adjusting the model's complexity, especially in methods that use kernels.

Kernel Trick: Kernel Trick is a technique used in support vector machines (SVM) to transform data into a higher dimensional space without explicitly calculating all features.

Kernel: A kernel is a function used in computation processes that transforms data before processing, especially in methods like SVM. It is essential for applying the "Kernel Trick."

Key Feature: Key Feature refers to a significant variable or attribute in a dataset that plays an important role in analysis and modeling in machine learning.

Key Point Detection: Key Point Detection in computer vision refers to the identification of specific points of interest within images, useful for tasks such as object recognition and motion tracking.

Key Value Store: Key Value Store is a type of non-relational database that uses a simple key-value method to store data, useful for certain big data and machine learning applications.

Keyframe: Keyframe in animation and video refers to a specific frame that defines a starting or ending point for a transition or animation. In computer vision, it is used to identify important frames in video sequences.

K-fold Cross Validation: k-fold Cross Validation is a technique in machine learning for evaluating a model's generalization ability, by dividing the data into 'K' groups and using each as a test set at some point.

k-Means Clustering: k-Means Clustering is an unsupervised machine learning algorithm that divides a dataset into clusters based on similarity.

k-means++: k-means++ is a variant of the k-means algorithm that improves the initialization phase to more effectively choose the initial cluster centers, reducing the likelihood of converging to a local optimum.

Knapsack Problem: The Knapsack Problem is a combinatorial optimization problem, where one must select a number of items with different weights and values to include in a knapsack, maximizing the total value without exceeding the maximum weight.

k-Nearest Neighbors (kNN): k-Nearest Neighbors is a supervised learning algorithm that classifies a new data point based on the majority votes of its 'K' nearest neighbors.

Knockout Experiment: Knockout Experiment is a method used in bioinformatics and computational genomics, where a gene is 'knocked out' to observe the effects on the phenotype, useful for understanding genetic functions.

Knowledge Base: Knowledge Base is a store of structured information, like facts and rules, that an Artificial Intelligence system can use to solve problems and make decisions.

Knowledge Discovery: Knowledge Discovery is the process of finding useful patterns, trends, and correlations in large data sets to aid in decision-making and forecasting.

Knowledge Engineering: Knowledge Engineering is the field that involves creating Artificial Intelligence systems that emulate human decision-making and reasoning, using knowledge bases and logical rules.

Knowledge Extraction: Knowledge Extraction is the process of discovering patterns and relationships in large data sets, often using techniques like data analysis and machine learning.

Knowledge Graph Embedding: Knowledge Graph Embedding is a technique for transforming nodes, edges, and relationships of a knowledge graph into low-dimensional vector representations, facilitating their use in machine learning tasks.

Knowledge Graph: Knowledge Graph is a structured database that uses a network of interconnected nodes to integrate dispersed data, enabling more effective analysis and knowledge extraction.

Knowledge Representation: Knowledge Representation refers to methods for structuring and organizing information in a way that machines can process, understand, and simulate human reasoning.

Knowledge Transfer: Knowledge Transfer in machine learning refers to the process of improving learning in a new task through the transfer of knowledge from a previously learned related task.

Knowledge-Based System: Knowledge-Based System is a program that reasons and uses a knowledge base to solve specific domain problems, applying rules and logic to simulate human judgment.

Kolmogorov Complexity: Kolmogorov Complexity measures the amount of information required to describe an object, such as a text string, and is used in information theory and compression algorithms.

Krylov Subspace: Krylov Subspace is a mathematical concept used in iterative methods to solve systems of linear equations, and has applications in numerical algorithms in machine learning.

Kullback-Leibler Divergence: Kullback-Leibler Divergence is a measure of the difference between two probability distributions, used in training generative models.

Kurtosis Risk: Kurtosis Risk refers to the risk arising from the non-normal shape of the return distribution in finance, particularly the presence of heavy tails in the distribution.

Kurtosis: Kurtosis is a statistical measure that describes the shape of the data distribution, particularly the degree of peakedness or flatness in the distribution.

L

L1 Regularization: L1 regularization is similar to L2, but it penalizes the absolute sum of the model weights, which can lead to sparser models.

L2 Regularization: L2 regularization is a technique used to reduce the complexity of the model and prevent overfitting by penalizing weights with large magnitudes.

Label Encoding: Label encoding is a process of converting categorical labels into numbers, which facilitates their use in machine learning algorithms.

Label Propagation: Label Propagation is a semi-supervised learning method that uses the structure of unlabeled data to propagate labels throughout the dataset.

Label Smoothing: Label Smoothing is a technique used in the training of classification models that involves smoothing the true labels to make the model more robust to classification errors.

Label: Label is a term used in supervised learning to refer to the correct or desired output value for an input instance during training.

Lambda Architecture: Lambda Architecture is a framework for processing large amounts of data that combines real-time processing with batch processing.

Latent Dirichlet Allocation (LDA): Latent Dirichlet Allocation is a topic model used in natural language processing to discover hidden topics in a set of documents.

Latent Factor Model: Latent Factor Model is a type of predictive model that tries to explain observations through the inference of unobserved latent variables, commonly used in recommendation systems.

Latent Semantic Analysis (LSA): Latent Semantic Analysis is a technique in natural language processing for analyzing the relationships between a set of documents and the terms they contain, identifying patterns in the use of words.

Latent Variable: Latent Variable is an unobserved variable in a statistical model that is used to capture hidden information in the data.

Layer: Layer refers to a collection of neurons in an artificial neural network. Each layer can have a specific function and contribute differently to data processing.

Lazy Learning: Lazy Learning refers to machine learning algorithms that delay data processing until a prediction is made, unlike eager learning that builds a general model from the dataset before making predictions.

L-BFGS (Limited-memory Broyden–Fletcher–Goldfarb–Shanno): L-BFGS is an optimization algorithm for solving nonlinear optimization problems with a large number of variables, used in machine learning model training methods.

Lead Scoring: Lead Scoring is a technique in marketing and sales that uses machine learning algorithms to predict the likelihood that a potential customer will become a real customer.

Leaky ReLU: Leaky ReLU is an activation function in neural networks that allows a small amount of negative value to pass when the input is less than zero, helping to mitigate the problem of inactive neurons.

Learning Curve: Learning Curve represents the progress of a model's learning in terms of performance on the training set and validation set as the amount of training data increases.

Learning Rate: Learning Rate is a hyperparameter that controls how much the model adjusts in response to the estimated error each time the model weights are updated.

Leave-One-Out Cross-Validation: Leave-One-Out Cross-Validation is a cross-validation method where a single data point is used as the test set and the rest as the training set, repeating the process for each data point in the set.

Levenshtein Distance: Levenshtein Distance is a metric used to measure the difference between two sequences, such as the minimum number of edits needed to transform one sequence into another.

Lift: Lift is a measure in data mining and predictive analysis that indicates how much better a classification model is at predicting a class compared to a random prediction.

LightGBM: LightGBM is an efficient machine learning framework based on gradient boosting that uses tree-based algorithms and is effective for large datasets.

Linear Discriminant Analysis (LDA): Linear Discriminant Analysis is a statistical method used to find a linear combination of features that best separates two or more classes of objects or events.

Linear Regression: Linear regression is a statistical approach to modeling the relationship between a dependent variable and one or more independent variables, assuming that the relationship is linear.

Linearly Separable: Linearly Separable is a property of a set of points that indicates that there is a hyperplane that can separate two classes of points without errors.

Link Analysis: Link Analysis is the study of how elements in a network are connected to each other, commonly used in social network analysis, web page classification, etc.

Local Outlier Factor (LOF): Local Outlier Factor is an algorithm for anomaly detection that calculates the local deviation of a point's density relative to its neighbors.

Locally Weighted Learning: Locally Weighted Learning is a machine learning technique that weights data points according to their distance from a query point, focusing more on nearby points for making predictions.

Logistic Regression: Logistic Regression is a classification algorithm used to predict the probability that an instance belongs to a specific class.

Logit Function: Logit Function is a function used to transform probabilities into a range of values that can extend from negative infinity to infinity, commonly used in logistic regression.

Log-Loss (Logarithmic Loss): Log-Loss is a metric used to evaluate the quality of predictions of classification models.

Lookahead Optimizer: Lookahead Optimizer is an optimization method in the training of neural networks that anticipates the future direction of the gradient to make more informed adjustments in the model weights.

Loss Function: Loss Function is a function used in machine learning to measure the difference between the output predicted by the model and the actual output. It serves to guide the model training process.

LSTM (Long Short-Term Memory): Long Short-Term Memory is a type of recurrent neural network designed to remember information over extended periods, making it useful for tasks involving temporal sequences.

M

Machine Learning (ML): Machine learning is a branch of Artificial Intelligence that focuses on the development of algorithms that allow computers to learn and improve their performance in specific tasks based on data.

Manifold Learning: Manifold learning is an approach to dimensionality reduction that assumes that data lies in a low-dimensional manifold embedded in a high-dimensional space.

Marginal Probability: Marginal probability is the probability of an event or set of events, without considering the effects of other variables. It is important in statistical analysis and machine learning.

Markov Decision Process (MDP): Markov Decision Process is a mathematical approach to modeling decision making in situations where outcomes are partially random and partially under the control of a decision maker.

Matrix Factorization: Matrix factorization is a technique used to decompose a matrix into products of matrices. It is widely used in recommendation systems and for dimensionality reduction.

Maximum Likelihood Estimation (MLE): Maximum likelihood estimation is a method for estimating the parameters of a statistical model by maximizing the likelihood that the model produces the observed data.

Mean Squared Error (MSE): Mean squared error is a common metric for evaluating the accuracy of a regression model, calculating the average of the squares of the differences between the predicted values and the actual values.

Message Passing Interface (MPI): Message Passing Interface is a specification for communication between nodes in a distributed computing system, commonly used in high-performance computing and in large-scale machine learning applications.

Meta-Learning: Meta-learning refers to the process of improving the learning of a machine learning algorithm. It implies that the algorithm learns from previous experiences to perform future tasks more efficiently.

Mining Data Streams: Mining data streams is the process of extracting useful patterns from continuous and rapid data streams, such as real-time sensor data or financial transactions.

Mixture Models: Mixture models are statistical models that assume that data comes from a combination of several probability distributions. They are useful in the analysis of heterogeneous data.

Model Aggregation: Model aggregation is a process in federated learning and other distributed approaches where multiple independently trained models are combined to improve performance or robustness.

Model Calibration: Model calibration involves adjusting the outputs of a classification model so that the predicted probabilities better reflect reality, which is crucial in applications where the interpretation of probabilities is important.

Model Checkpointing: Model checkpointing is a technique used during the training of machine learning models to periodically save the state of the model, allowing training to resume from that point in case of interruptions.

Model Compression: Model compression is the technique of reducing the size of a machine learning model without significantly losing accuracy, which is crucial for implementation on devices with limited resources.

Model Consistency: Model consistency refers to the ability of a machine learning model to produce coherent and stable results over time or on different subsets of data.

Model Deployment: Model deployment refers to the process of taking a machine learning model from the development environment to a production environment.

Model Distillation: Model distillation is a technique for transferring knowledge from a large and complex model (teacher) to a smaller and more efficient model (student), preserving accuracy as much as possible.

Model Drift: Model drift occurs when the machine learning model is no longer representative of the current data due to changes in the underlying environment, which can lead to a decrease in model performance.

Model Ensemble: Model ensemble refers to the method of combining multiple machine learning models to improve the accuracy and robustness of predictions.

Model Evaluation: Model evaluation is the process of measuring the performance of a machine learning model using metrics such as accuracy, recall, F1-score, among others.

Model Explainability: Model explainability is the study of how to make the processes and decisions of a machine learning model understandable to humans, which is crucial for trust and adoption in sensitive applications.

Model Fidelity: Model fidelity refers to the accuracy with which a simplified or explanatory model represents the behavior of the original model, being important in the interpretation of complex models.

Model Fine-Tuning: Model fine-tuning is the process of making small adjustments to a pre-trained model to better adapt it to a specific task or dataset.

Model Generalization: Model generalization refers to the ability of a machine learning model to make accurate predictions on unseen data, in addition to the training data.

Model Governance: Model governance is the set of practices and policies aimed at ensuring that machine learning models are developed and used responsibly, ethically, and in compliance with regulations.

Model Inference: Model inference is the process of using a trained model to make predictions, usually on new data not seen during training.

Model Interpretability: Model interpretability refers to the ability to understand and explain how a machine learning model makes its decisions, which is crucial for reliability and transparency in critical applications.

Model Monitoring: Model monitoring is the continuous process of tracking and evaluating the performance of a machine learning model in production, to detect and address issues such as model drift or changes in data patterns.

Model Optimization: Model optimization is the process of adjusting and improving a machine learning model to achieve the best possible performance, often by modifying hyperparameters or the model structure.

Model Overfitting: Refers to a machine learning model that learns too well the details and noise in the training data to the point that it impairs its performance on new data.

Model Personalization: Model personalization is the adjustment of a machine learning model to better suit the preferences or individual characteristics of a user or group of users.

Model Pruning: Model pruning is a technique for simplifying machine learning models, eliminating weights or neurons that have little impact on predictions, to improve efficiency and reduce complexity.

Model Registry: Model registry is a system for managing and tracking different versions and configurations of machine learning models throughout the development lifecycle.

Model Robustness: Model robustness describes the ability of a machine learning model to maintain its performance when faced with new or perturbed data, which is important for the reliability and safety of AI systems.

Model Selection: Model selection is the process of choosing between different models or configurations of models in machine learning, based on their performance on a validation dataset.

Model Serving Framework: Model serving framework is a platform or set of tools that facilitate the implementation, hosting, and management of machine learning models in production environments.

Model Serving: Model serving refers to the implementation and operation of machine learning models in a production environment, allowing their use in real applications.

Model Tracking: Model tracking is the process of recording and documenting the different stages of development of a machine learning model, including experiments, tests, and modifications.

Model Tuning: Model tuning is the process of optimizing the parameters of a machine learning model to improve its performance on a specific dataset.

Model Underfitting: Occurs when a machine learning model cannot capture the underlying structure of the data and therefore cannot make accurate predictions.

Model Validation: Model validation is the process of evaluating and confirming that a machine learning model works correctly and generalizes well to new data.

Moment Matching: Moment matching is a statistical technique used to estimate the parameters of a probability distribution by matching the statistical moments of the distribution with those of the data.

Monte Carlo Methods: Monte Carlo methods are a set of algorithms that rely on the repetition of random sampling to obtain numerical results and are used in various applications such as optimization and simulation.

Monte Carlo Tree Search (MCTS): Monte Carlo Tree Search is an algorithm for making optimal decisions in some environments, especially in strategy games like Go and chess.

Multi-Class Classification: Multi-class classification is a machine learning problem where instances are classified into three or more classes. The model must predict a single label from a set of categories.

Multi-Layer Perceptron (MLP): Multi-layer perceptron is an artificial neural network composed of at least three layers of nodes: an input layer, one or more hidden layers, and an output layer. It is useful for complex classification and regression problems.

Multi-Task Learning: Multi-task learning is an approach in machine learning where a model is simultaneously trained on multiple related tasks, which can improve performance on individual tasks.

Mutual Information: Mutual information is a measure of the amount of information that one random variable contains about another and is used in feature analysis and model selection.

N

Naive Bayes Classifier: A naive Bayes classifier is a simple probabilistic model based on applying Bayes' theorem with assumptions of independence among predictors.

Named Entity Recognition (NER): Named entity recognition is a natural language processing task that seeks to identify and classify key elements in text, such as names of people, organizations, locations, etc.

Narrow AI: Narrow AI refers to artificial intelligence systems designed and trained to perform a specific task or a limited set of tasks, unlike general AI which would mimic human intelligence in a broader sense.

Nash Equilibrium: Nash equilibrium, from game theory, is a concept that can be applied in AI to model and analyze decision-making situations among multiple agents.

Natural Deduction: Natural deduction is an approach in formal logic that attempts to reflect the ordinary process of logical reasoning, and can be used in AI systems for logical inferences.

Natural Language Annotation: Natural language annotation is the process of tagging elements in text with linguistic information, such as parts of speech or named entities, used in natural language processing.

Natural Language Generation (NLG): Natural language generation is the process of automatically generating human language text from data or information.

Natural Language Generation Template: A natural language generation template is a method used in NLG to generate text based on predefined templates, which are filled with specific data or information.

Natural Language Interaction: Natural language interaction is the communication between humans and computer systems using spoken or written human language.

Natural Language Processing (NLP): A field of artificial intelligence that focuses on the interaction between computers and human language, aiming to make computers understand, interpret, and manipulate human language.

Natural Language Query: Natural language query refers to a system's ability to interpret and process questions or commands formulated in natural human language.

Natural Language Understanding (NLU): Natural language understanding is the ability of a machine to understand and extract meaning from human language.

Negative Reinforcement: Negative reinforcement in machine learning and artificial intelligence refers to a training method where a negative or unwanted response is reduced to increase the frequency of a desired behavior.

Negative Sampling: Negative sampling is a technique to improve the efficiency of training models on large datasets by selecting only a small sample of negative examples.

Nested Cross-Validation: Nested cross-validation is a model evaluation technique involving multiple rounds of cross-validation for a more robust estimation of model performance.

Nesterov Accelerated Gradient: Nesterov accelerated gradient is an optimization technique for neural networks that speeds up the gradient descent method, improving convergence in model training.

Network Topology: Network topology refers to the arrangement or structure of a network, especially in the context of neural networks and computer systems.

Neural Architecture Search: Neural architecture search is an automated process to find the best neural network architecture for a specific task.

Neural Network Pruning: Neural network pruning is the process of removing unnecessary units or connections in a neural network to reduce its complexity and improve efficiency without sacrificing performance.

Neural Network Weight Initialization: Neural network weight initialization is the process of assigning initial values to the weights in a neural network before starting training, which can significantly affect its convergence and performance.

Neural Network: A neural network is a computational model designed to mimic the way the human brain analyzes and processes information. It is used in machine learning and in brain and nervous system research.

Neural Style Transfer: Neural style transfer is a technique that uses neural networks to apply the artistic style of one image to another while maintaining the content of the second image.

Neuroevolution: Neuroevolution is a methodology in machine learning that uses evolutionary algorithms to optimize neural networks, particularly their architecture and weights.

Neuro-Fuzzy Systems: Neuro-fuzzy systems combine techniques from neural networks and fuzzy logic to model complex systems, leveraging the learning capability of neural networks and fuzzy reasoning to handle uncertainty.

Neuroinformatics: Neuroinformatics is the discipline that combines informatics with neuroscience, focusing on the development of tools and algorithms to analyze and model neural data.

Neuro-Linguistic Programming: Neuro-linguistic programming is a pseudoscientific approach that relates language patterns and behavior to model and change human behaviors, although its application in AI is limited and controversial.

Neuro-Symbolic AI: Neuro-symbolic AI combines elements of neural networks (deep learning) with symbolic representations of knowledge, seeking to leverage the advantages of both approaches.

N-Gram: An N-gram is a contiguous sequence of n items from a given text or speech. It is used in language models and text analysis.

NLP Pipeline: An NLP pipeline is a series of sequential steps or processes in natural language processing, including tasks such as tokenization, syntactic analysis, entity recognition, among others.

Node Embedding: Node embedding in graphs and networks refers to the representation of nodes in a low-dimensional vector space, facilitating tasks such as node classification and link prediction.

Node: In the context of neural networks, a node refers to a basic processing unit, similar to neurons in the human brain.

Noise Reduction: Noise reduction is the process of eliminating unnecessary noise or interference from data to improve the quality of machine learning models or signal processing.

Noise: In the context of AI and machine learning, noise refers to random or irrelevant variations in data that can affect the performance and accuracy of models.

Nominal Data: Nominal data are data that represent categories without an inherent order or hierarchy, such as color names or class labels.

Non-Convex Optimization: Non-convex optimization deals with optimization problems where the objective function is not convex, presenting additional challenges in terms of finding the global optimum.

Non-Deterministic Algorithm: A non-deterministic algorithm is a type of algorithm in which multiple possible outcomes can exist for the same input, often used in contexts where chance or probability plays a role.

Nonlinear Dynamics: Nonlinear dynamics in AI refers to the study of systems that do not follow a linear relationship, which is important in modeling complex phenomena.

Non-Linear Regression: Non-linear regression refers to regression models that establish a non-linear relationship between independent variables and the dependent variable.

Non-Parametric Models: Non-parametric models refer to models that do not assume a fixed or predefined form for the relationship between variables, allowing greater flexibility in data analysis.

Non-Uniform Memory Access (NUMA): Non-uniform memory access is a computer architecture that allows a processor to access local memory faster than non-local memory, which can be relevant in high-performance AI systems.

Normalization: Normalization is the process of adjusting and scaling data to have a common range, often necessary in data preprocessing for machine learning techniques.

O

Object Detection: Object detection is the ability of an Artificial Intelligence system to identify and locate specific objects in images or videos.

Objective Function: Objective function is the function that an automatic learning algorithm tries to optimize during training. It can be a loss, gain, or cost function, depending on the specific context.

Objective Optimization: Objective optimization is the process of finding the best solution or parameter configuration for a specific objective function in automatic learning and optimization.

Occam's Razor: Occam's Razor in AI refers to the principle that suggests that, among two models with similar performance, the simpler one should be preferred.

Offline Learning: Offline learning is an automatic learning method where the model is trained with a fixed data set and is not updated with new data as it arrives.

One-Class Classification: One-class classification is a type of problem in automatic learning where the goal is to identify whether an instance belongs to a specific class or not, without having comparison classes.

One-Hot Encoding: One-hot encoding is a data representation technique in which each category is represented as a binary vector in which only one position is active.

One-vs-All Classification: One-vs-all classification is a strategy used to address multi-class classification problems, where a classifier is trained for each class against all others.

Online Algorithm: Online algorithm refers to a type of algorithm that processes input data in the order they arrive, without access to the entire data set beforehand.

Online Experimentation: Online experimentation is the process of testing and validating AI models in a real-time environment, where data and interactions are continuous and dynamic.

Online Feature Selection: Online feature selection is a method where the relevant features for an automatic learning model are selected continuously as new data is received.

Online Learning: Online learning is an automatic learning method where the model is continuously updated as it receives new data.

Ontology: Ontology in the context of AI refers to a structured representation of knowledge that defines the relationships between different concepts and entities.

Open Set Recognition: Open set recognition is a task in which the system must identify whether an input belongs to a known or unknown category.

Operationalization: Operationalization is the process of defining a modeling task clearly and in detail, including the specification of data, metrics, and objectives.

Operator Overloading: Operator overloading is a programming technique in which common operators are redefined or given additional functionality, which can be relevant in the creation of automatic learning algorithms.

Opportunistic Learning: Opportunistic learning is an approach in which the automatic learning model adapts and learns from any available data source, taking advantage of learning opportunities as they arise.

Optimal Policy: Optimal policy refers to the strategy or set of decisions that maximizes reward or minimizes cost in reinforcement learning problems.

Optimal Transport: Optimal transport is a mathematical concept used in automatic learning to measure the distance or discrepancy between different probability distributions.

Optimization Landscape: Optimization landscape is a representation of the solution space of an optimization problem, showing how the model's performance varies based on different parameter configurations.

Optimization: Optimization refers to the process of making a system or model more effective, efficient, or suitable by adjusting its parameters and structures.

Oracle Complexity: Oracle complexity refers to the amount of information or advice needed from an oracle in theoretical automatic learning algorithms to achieve optimal performance.

Oracle Learning: Oracle learning is a theoretical approach in automatic learning where an "oracle" (an idealized source of perfect information) is used to guide or improve the learning process.

Ordinal Encoding: Ordinal encoding is a technique for converting categorical variables with an inherent order into numerical representations that maintain that order relationship.

Ordinal Regression: Ordinal regression is an automatic learning technique used to predict a dependent variable with inherent order, but without a continuous scale.

Orthogonal Learning: Orthogonal learning is an approach that seeks to learn features or representations that are statistically independent or uncorrelated.

Orthogonalization: Orthogonalization in automatic learning refers to the process of making different components or functions of a model statistically independent or uncorrelated.

Oscillation Reduction: Oscillation reduction refers to techniques used to stabilize the learning process in automatic learning algorithms, especially in neural networks.

Outlier Analysis: Outlier analysis is the process of identifying and examining data that significantly deviates from general behavior or trends in a data set.

Outlier Detection: Outlier detection is the identification of rare or suspicious observations in data that may result from errors or unusual events.

Out-of-Bag Error: Out-of-bag error is an estimate of prediction error in ensemble methods, such as random forests, calculated using data that was not selected for the training of a specific sub-model.

Out-of-Core Learning: Out-of-core learning refers to automatic learning techniques that handle data too large to fit in the main memory of a computer.

Out-of-Distribution Detection: Out-of-distribution detection is the identification of data that is significantly different from the training data of the model.

Out-of-Sample Prediction: Out-of-sample prediction refers to the evaluation of an automatic learning model's performance on a data set that was not used during its training.

Output Encoding: Output encoding is the process of transforming the output of an automatic learning model into a specific format, suitable for the task at hand, such as classification or regression.

Output Layer: Output layer is the last layer of a neural network that provides the final result of the network's processing.

Output Regularization: Output regularization is a technique for imposing restrictions on the output layer of a model, in order to reduce the model's complexity or improve its generalization.

Overfitting Avoidance: Overfitting avoidance is the set of techniques used to prevent an automatic learning model from excessively fitting to training data, which could impair its performance on new data.

Overfitting Correction: Overfitting correction is the set of techniques aimed at adjusting an automatic learning model that has excessively fitted to training data, thereby improving its generalization capability.

Overfitting: Overfitting is a phenomenon in automatic learning where a model fits too closely to training data and performs poorly on new data.

Overlap Coefficient: Overlap coefficient is a statistical measure indicating the degree to which two samples or sets overlap or coincide.

Overlap Score: Overlap score is a metric used to evaluate the degree to which two data sets or classifications overlap or coincide.

Overlapping Classes: Overlapping classes refer to situations in automatic learning where several classes have similar characteristics, making their separation a challenge.

Overparameterization: Overparameterization refers to an automatic learning model that has more parameters than necessary, which can lead to overfitting.

Overparameterized Model: Overparameterized model is a model that has an excessive number of parameters compared to the amount of available data, which can lead to overfitting issues.

Ownership Learning: Ownership learning is an approach in automatic learning that focuses on identifying and attributing the ownership or source of learned data or patterns.

P

Parallel Computing: Parallel computing refers to the simultaneous use of multiple computational resources to solve complex problems more efficiently.

Parameter Tuning: Parameter tuning refers to the process of selecting the optimal values for the parameters of a machine learning model to improve its performance.

Partial Dependence Plot: A partial dependence plot is a visualization tool to show the relationship between a specific feature and the outcome predicted by the model, keeping other features constant.

Particle Swarm Optimization: Particle swarm optimization is a swarm intelligence-based optimization algorithm that simulates the social behavior of animals, such as birds and fish, to find optimal solutions.

Part-of-Speech Tagging: Part-of-speech tagging is the process of assigning tags to words in a text, such as noun, verb, adjective, etc., typically used in natural language processing.

Pathfinding: Pathfinding is an Artificial Intelligence algorithm used to find the shortest or most efficient route between two points.

Pattern Recognition: Pattern recognition refers to a system's ability to identify patterns and regularities in data.

Perceptron: Perceptron is a type of artificial neural network and supervised learning algorithm that can be used to classify inputs.

Performance Metric: Performance metric is a quantitative measure used to assess the effectiveness and quality of a machine learning model.

Permutation Feature Importance: Permutation feature importance is a method for evaluating the importance of different features in a predictive model based on the change in model performance when the values of a feature are randomly permuted.

Permutation Testing: Permutation testing is a non-parametric statistical technique used to determine the statistical significance of a result.

Persistent Homology: Persistent homology is a data topology method used in data analysis to detect structures and patterns at different scales.

Personalization: Personalization refers to the use of machine learning algorithms to tailor products, services, or content to individual users' preferences.

Pipeline: Pipeline in machine learning refers to a series of data processing and modeling steps, organized sequentially, used to automate workflows.

Platt Scaling: Platt scaling is a probability calibration technique in classification models to produce more accurate probability estimates.

Point Estimation: Point estimation is a type of statistical estimation that uses a single value to estimate an unknown parameter of a population.

Poisson Distribution: Poisson distribution is a probability distribution that describes the number of events occurring in a fixed interval of time or space, under certain conditions.

Policy Gradient: Policy gradient in reinforcement learning is a technique that adjusts an agent's decision policy directly, to maximize a long-term performance measure.

Polynomial Regression: Polynomial regression is a type of regression analysis in which the relationship between the independent variable and the dependent variable is modeled as a polynomial.

Pooling Layer: Pooling layer is a part of the convolutional neural network that reduces the data's dimensionality and highlights the most important features.

Positive Predictive Value: Positive predictive value is a metric that measures the proportion of true positives among all the positive predictions made by a model.

Posterior Probability: Posterior probability is the revised probability of a given event, after taking into account new information or evidence.

Precision: Precision in machine learning is a metric that measures the proportion of true positive identifications among all positive identifications (true and false).

Precision-Recall Curve: The precision-recall curve is a graphical representation of the relationship between precision and recall in classification problems.

Precision-Recall Trade-off: The trade-off between precision and recall refers to the balance between a classification model's precision and its ability to retrieve all relevant samples.

Predictive Analytics: Predictive analytics uses data, statistics, and machine learning algorithms to identify the likelihood of future outcomes based on historical data.

Predictive Modelling: Predictive modeling refers to the use of statistics and machine learning algorithms to predict future outcomes based on historical data.

Predictor Variable: A predictor variable is an independent variable in a statistical or machine learning model, used to predict the value of the dependent variable.

Preprocessing: Preprocessing in machine learning refers to the process of preparing and cleaning data before feeding it into a learning algorithm.

Pre-trained Model: A pre-trained model refers to a machine learning model that has been previously trained on a large dataset and can be used or adapted for specific tasks.

Principal Component Analysis (PCA): Principal component analysis is a dimensionality reduction technique that finds the main directions of variability in a dataset.

Probabilistic Graphical Model: A probabilistic graphical model is a framework that represents variables and their conditional dependencies using a graph, used in statistics and machine learning.

Probabilistic Model: A probabilistic model is a type of statistical model that uses probabilities to make predictions and decisions.

Processing Unit: A processing unit refers to a hardware component, such as a CPU or GPU, used to perform calculations and process data in Artificial Intelligence applications.

Product Recommendation System: A product recommendation system is a type of recommendation system that suggests products to users based on their previous preferences and behaviors.

Programmatic AI: Programmatic AI refers to AI systems designed to perform specific tasks based on programmed rules and logic.

Projection: Projection in machine learning refers to the process of transforming data into a lower-dimensional space, often to simplify analysis.

Prototype Model: A prototype model in Artificial Intelligence refers to an initial or preliminary version of a system or algorithm, used to test and refine concepts.

Proximity Measure: Proximity measure is a metric used to determine the similarity or distance between two entities or data points.

Pruning: Pruning is a technique used in decision trees and neural networks to eliminate unnecessary nodes or connections and simplify the model.

Pseudocode: Pseudocode is a high-level, human-readable description of a programming algorithm, using structural conventions of real programming languages, but easier to read.

P-value: P-value in statistics is a measure that indicates the probability of obtaining a result at least as extreme as the observed one, assuming the null hypothesis is true.

Python: Python is a high-level programming language, widely used in developing Artificial Intelligence and machine learning algorithms due to its simplicity and flexibility.

PyTorch: PyTorch is a deep learning and tensor computing framework, popular for research and development in Artificial Intelligence.

Q

Quadratic Discriminant Analysis: Quadratic Discriminant Analysis is a statistical method used to classify and separate data sets into different categories based on their characteristics.

Quadratic Programming: Quadratic Programming is a type of mathematical optimization problem where the objective function is quadratic and the constraints are linear, used in optimization and machine learning.

Qualitative Analysis: Qualitative Analysis is the evaluation of non-numerical elements such as text, images, and sounds, used in natural language processing and sentiment analysis.

Quality Assurance: Quality Assurance refers to the practices and processes used to ensure that products or services meet quality standards.

Quality Function Deployment (QFD): Quality Function Deployment is a technique used to transform user needs into design specifications, relevant in software development and intelligent systems.

Quality Metric: Quality Metric is a quantitative measure used to assess the quality of a model or process in Artificial Intelligence and machine learning.

Quality of Service (QoS): Quality of Service is a set of technologies and policies to manage network traffic and ensure optimal performance of different applications and services.

Quantile Regression: Quantile Regression is a type of statistical regression that estimates the median or quantiles of a distribution, useful in data analysis and predictions.

Quantitative Analysis: Quantitative Analysis is the process of examining numerical data and performing statistical calculations to gain insights and make decisions.

Quantitative Research: Quantitative Research refers to the systematic analysis of phenomena through the collection and analysis of numerical data, common in machine learning and statistical studies.

Quantization: Quantization in signal processing and machine learning refers to reducing the number of bits representing a signal, often used in data compression and deep neural networks.

Quantum Annealing: Quantum Annealing is a method for finding the global minimum of an objective function, used in quantum computing to solve complex optimization problems.

Quantum Computing: Quantum Computing is a computing paradigm that uses principles of quantum mechanics to perform advanced computations.

Quantum Machine Learning: Quantum Machine Learning combines the principles of quantum computing with machine learning algorithms to process and analyze data at a greater scale and speed.

Quantum Neural Network: Quantum Neural Network is a neural network model that uses concepts of quantum computing, aiming to improve performance and efficiency in data processing.

Quartic Polynomial: Quartic Polynomial is a fourth-degree polynomial equation, relevant in regression algorithms and mathematical analysis in AI.

Quasi-Experiment: Quasi-Experiment is a research design that does not use random assignment, common in social and behavioral sciences research, and applicable in AI for impact studies.

Quasi-Newton Methods: Quasi-Newton Methods are optimization techniques for finding minima or maxima of functions, widely used in machine learning algorithms.

Quasi-Real-Time Processing: Quasi-Real-Time Processing refers to systems that process data with minimal latency, important in applications where quick response is crucial but not instantaneous.

Quaternion Neural Network: Quaternion Neural Network is a network that uses quaternion numbers in its operations, providing advantages in signal processing and 3D graphics.

Query Expansion: Query Expansion is the process of modifying and expanding search queries to improve information retrieval in databases and search engines.

Query Language: Query Language is a programming language used to make queries in databases and information systems.

Query Optimization: Query Optimization is the process of improving the performance of queries in databases and information retrieval systems.

Query Processing: Query Processing is the set of operations that a database system performs to execute queries and retrieve the requested data.

Query Understanding: Query Understanding refers to a system's ability to interpret and process user queries, crucial in search engines and recommendation systems.

Queue Management System: Queue Management System is used to control the flow and waiting in queues, important in the optimization of systems and in the modeling of network traffic.

Queue Theory: Queue Theory is the mathematical study of waiting lines or queues, which is fundamental in modeling service processes and computer systems.

Queueing Network: Queueing Network is a mathematical model that represents a network of interconnected queues, important in the study of the performance of computer and telecommunications systems.

Quick Response Code (QR Code): Quick Response Code (QR Code) is a type of two-dimensional barcode that can store information and is widely used in augmented reality applications and marketing.

Quiescent State: Quiescent State in computer systems and networks refers to a state in which the system is inactive or at a low level of activity, important in performance and security analysis.

Quine: Quine is a computer program that takes no input and produces a copy of its own source code as output, interesting in the study of computation theory and Artificial Intelligence.

R

Random Forest: Random Forest is an ensemble machine learning algorithm that combines multiple decision trees to improve performance and generalization.

Random Initialization: Random Initialization refers to the process of setting the initial weights and biases of a neural network randomly, which is a critical step to begin the network's training.

Random Variable: Random Variable is a statistical concept used in machine learning to denote a variable whose values depend on the outcomes of a random phenomenon.

Randomized Algorithms: Algorithms that incorporate an element of randomness in their logic or process, used in various machine learning applications to improve performance and efficiency.

Ranking Algorithms: Ranking Algorithms are used in machine learning to order or classify a set of items in a list based on certain criteria or characteristics.

Ranking Loss: Ranking Loss in machine learning models, used to measure the effectiveness of a model in classifying and ordering sets of items.

RapidMiner: A software platform for data analysis, machine learning, and data mining, widely used for predictive analysis and modeling tasks.

Rate of Learning: Rate of Learning in the context of machine learning refers to the speed at which a machine learning model adjusts its parameters during training.

Ray Tracing: Rendering technique that simulates the path of light to generate realistic images, used in computer graphics and in Artificial Intelligence simulations.

Real-Time Processing: Real-Time Processing is the analysis and instantaneous decision-making on data as it is received, essential in Artificial Intelligence applications that require quick responses.

Recall (in Machine Learning): Recall in machine learning is a metric that measures the ability of a model to correctly identify all relevant instances within a dataset.

Recommendation System: Recommendation System is a type of information system that provides personalized suggestions to users, commonly used in streaming platforms, e-commerce, etc.

Recurrent Convolutional Neural Network: Neural network that combines the features of recurrent and convolutional neural networks, suitable for processing sequential data with a spatial component.

Recurrent Layer: Recurrent Layer refers to a layer in a recurrent neural network where the connections between neurons form cycles, allowing the processing and learning of data sequences.

Recurrent Neural Network (RNN): A class of neural networks where connections between nodes form a cycle. This allows them to exhibit dynamic temporal behavior and are suitable for tasks like voice recognition or time series analysis.

Redundant Features: Redundant Features refer to those attributes in a dataset that do not provide additional or useful information for the machine learning model.

Regression Analysis: Regression Analysis is a statistical technique used in machine learning to model and analyze the relationship between variables, especially to predict the value of one variable based on others.

Regression Coefficient: Regression Coefficient is a value that represents the relationship between the dependent variable and one of the independent variables in regression analysis.

Regularization: Regularization is a technique used in machine learning to reduce overfitting by adding penalty terms to the cost function.

Reinforcement Learning Agent: Reinforcement Learning Agent is an entity that takes actions in an environment to maximize a specific reward or goal.

Reinforcement Learning Environment: Reinforcement Learning Environment is the context or space in which a reinforcement learning agent operates and interacts to learn and make decisions.

Reinforcement Learning Policy: Reinforcement Learning Policy is a strategy that determines how a reinforcement learning agent makes decisions in an environment.

Reinforcement Learning: Reinforcement Learning is a Machine Learning approach where an agent learns to make optimal decisions through interaction with an environment.

Relational Database: Relational Database is a type of database that uses a relational model to organize and store data, important in Artificial Intelligence applications involving large volumes of data handling.

Relational Machine Learning: Relational Machine Learning focuses on models that can learn from data structured in a relational form, like databases.

ReLU (Rectified Linear Unit): Rectified Linear Unit is a commonly used activation function in neural networks, introducing non-linearity and improving training by accelerating convergence.

Representation Learning: Representation Learning is the process in machine learning where a system automatically learns to identify and represent the important features or attributes of data.

Reservoir Computing: An approach for processing temporal and spatial signals in neural networks, particularly useful in prediction and classification tasks.

Residual Networks (ResNets): Residual Networks are a deep neural network architecture that uses skip connections to avoid the gradient vanishing problem, thereby improving performance in deep learning tasks.

Resource Allocation: Process of optimally allocating resources in Artificial Intelligence systems, especially in environments with limited resources or constraints.

Restricted Boltzmann Machine (RBM): Restricted Boltzmann Machine is a type of stochastic neural network used to learn the probability distribution of a set of inputs.

Robot Operating System (ROS): Robot Operating System is a flexible framework for writing robot software, providing abstract hardware services, device drivers, libraries, visualizers, messaging tools, etc.

Robotics: The field of engineering that focuses on the design, construction, operation, and use of robots, often incorporating Artificial Intelligence systems to enhance autonomy and capabilities of robots.

Robust Machine Learning: Robust Machine Learning focuses on creating models that are resistant to errors, disturbances, or variations in input data.

Root Mean Square Error (RMSE): Root Mean Square Error is a commonly used measure to evaluate the difference between predicted values and observed values in regression models and other predictive models.

S

Self-Organizing Maps (SOMs): Self-organizing maps are an unsupervised learning technique that produces a low-dimensional representation of the input data, preserving topological properties.

Self-Supervised Learning: Self-supervised learning is a machine learning technique where the system generates its own labels from the data for training.

Semi-Parametric Models: Semi-parametric models are statistical models that combine parametric and non-parametric components, offering flexibility in data modeling.

Semi-Supervised Learning: Semi-supervised learning is an approach that combines labeled and unlabeled data to train machine learning models.

Sensitivity Analysis: Sensitivity analysis is the study of how variations in the outputs of a model can be attributed to variations in its inputs.

Sentiment Analysis: Sentiment analysis is the process of determining the attitude or emotion expressed in a text, such as positive, negative, or neutral.

Sequence-to-Sequence Models (Seq2Seq): Sequence-to-sequence models are neural networks that convert input sequences into output sequences, used in tasks such as automatic translation.

Sequential Decision Making: Sequential decision making refers to making decisions in situations where successive decisions must consider the changing state of the system or environment.

Sequential Model: A sequential model is a type of deep learning model that is built layer by layer, where each layer receives information only from the previous layer.

Shallow Learning: Shallow learning refers to machine learning techniques that do not involve deep neural networks and usually have one or a few layers of processing.

Siamese Networks: Siamese networks are a special type of neural networks used to compare the similarity between two different inputs.

Signal Processing: Signal processing refers to the analysis, modification, and synthesis of signals such as sound, images, and biological data.

Simulated Annealing: Simulated annealing is a probabilistic optimization technique that tries to avoid getting trapped in local minima by simulating the heating and cooling process of materials.

Simulated Reality: Simulated reality is the use of computer-based simulations to create realistic virtual environments for training, education, or entertainment.

Single-Shot Multibox Detector (SSD): Single-shot multibox detector is a method for object detection in images that allows identifying and locating multiple objects in a single pass of the network.

Skip-gram Model: The skip-gram model is an approach in natural language processing used to predict the context of a word in a sentence.

Sliding Window Technique: The sliding window technique is used in signal processing and time-series analysis to divide data into overlapping segments for analysis.

Social Network Analysis: Social network analysis is the process of investigating social structures using networks and graph theory.

Soft Computing: Soft computing is an approach to computing that tolerates imprecision and uncertainty, using techniques such as neural networks, fuzzy logic, and genetic algorithms.

Softmax Function: The softmax function is used in multiclass classification in machine learning to convert the values of a vector into probabilities.

Sparse Autoencoders: Sparse autoencoders are a variant of autoencoders that are trained to learn efficient representations of data, where most activations are zero.

Sparse Coding: Sparse coding is a method in machine learning to find a sparse representation of input data.

Sparse Data: Sparse data refers to data sets where most of the elements are zero or do not present relevant information, common in areas such as natural language processing.

Spatial Analysis: Spatial analysis is the study and analysis of data that have a geographical component, applied in fields such as geolocation and cartography.

Spectral Analysis: Spectral analysis is the analysis of how different frequencies contribute to a signal, commonly used in signal processing.

Spectral Clustering: Spectral clustering is a machine learning clustering technique that uses the properties of spectra (eigenvalues) of matrices to group data.

Spiking Neural Networks (SNNs): Spiking neural networks are a type of artificial neural networks that more closely mimic the behavior of biological neurons, where information is transmitted through discrete pulses.

Stacked Autoencoders: Stacked autoencoders are a network of autoencoders in which the output of each layer is used as input for the next, to learn more complex features.

Standardization: Standardization in data processing involves rescaling features to have a mean of zero and a standard deviation of one.

State Space Models: State space models are mathematical models that describe a dynamic system in terms of its state variables and inputs.

Statistical Learning Theory: Statistical learning theory is a theoretical framework for machine learning that focuses on understanding and improving the performance of learning algorithms from a statistical perspective.

Stochastic Gradient Descent (SGD): Stochastic gradient descent is a variant of the gradient descent algorithm that uses random samples to update the parameters of a model.

Stochastic Processes: Stochastic processes are processes that evolve over time in a random manner, and are fundamental in statistical modeling and probability theory.

Stream Processing: Stream processing refers to the technology used to process and analyze data streams in real time.

Structured Data: Structured data are those that are organized in a defined format, facilitating their storage, search, and analysis, such as in databases.

Structured Prediction: Structured prediction is a type of problem in machine learning where the predictions involve complex structures such as trees or graphs, instead of simple values or labels.

Structured Query Language (SQL): Structured Query Language is a programming language used to manage and manipulate relational databases.

Subset Selection: Subset selection is a process in data analysis and statistics to select a subset of relevant variables or features for a model.

Subspace Learning: Subspace learning is an approach in machine learning that seeks to find a lower-dimensional subspace within the feature space where data can be more easily analyzed and classified.

Supervised Learning: A type of machine learning where a model is trained from data that already contain the answers, i.e., the input data are labeled with the correct response.

Support Vector Machine (SVM): Support vector machine is a machine learning algorithm used for classification and regression problems by finding an optimal hyperplane that separates the classes.

Swarm Intelligence: Swarm intelligence refers to systems that mimic the collective behavior of groups of organisms, such as ant colonies or fish schools, to solve complex problems.

Symbolic AI: Symbolic AI is an approach to AI that uses the manipulation of symbols and logical rules to simulate human reasoning, in contrast to data-based and machine learning approaches.

Synthetic Data: Synthetic data are artificially generated data, often by algorithms, that can be used to train machine learning models in situations where real data are scarce or confidential.

System Identification: System identification is a method in automatic control and signal processing to construct mathematical models of dynamic systems based on observed data.

T

Tanh (Hyperbolic Tangent): The hyperbolic tangent is an activation function used in neural networks. It transforms input values into a range between -1 and 1, helping to manage the problem of vanishing gradients in deep network training.

T-distributed Stochastic Neighbor Embedding (t-SNE): t-SNE is a dimensionality reduction technique that is particularly effective for visualizing high-dimensional datasets. It helps to interpret and visualize data by grouping them in a lower-dimensional space.

Tensor: In the context of Artificial Intelligence, a tensor is a data structure that generally represents a multi-dimensional array. They are fundamental in deep learning, as neural networks work with tensors to process data and information.

TensorFlow: TensorFlow is an open-source software library for numerical computations using data flow graphs. It is widely used in deep learning and other Artificial Intelligence applications.

Text Classification: Text classification is the process of assigning labels or categories to texts based on their content. It is used in applications such as spam filtering, sentiment analysis, and document categorization.

Text Generation: Text generation is the automatic creation of coherent and legible text by machines. It is used in chatbots, automatic content generation, and virtual assistants.

Text Mining: Text mining is the process of extracting relevant information and patterns from large text data sets. It uses natural language processing techniques, statistics, and machine learning.

Text Summarization: Text summarization is the process of creating a concise and coherent summary of a longer text. It is used to extract key information from documents, articles, and books.

Text-to-Speech (TTS): Text-to-speech is a technology that converts text into speech. It uses natural language processing and machine learning models to generate naturally sounding voice from written text.

Thompson Sampling: Thompson Sampling is a technique in reinforcement learning and process optimization. It is used to balance exploration and exploitation when making decisions based on a probabilistic understanding of rewards.

Thresholding: Thresholding is a technique in image processing and computer vision where pixels are selected based on an intensity range. It is used to simplify visual representation and facilitate further analysis.

Time Complexity: Time complexity refers to the amount of time it takes for an algorithm to run as a function of the size of the input. It is crucial for evaluating the efficiency of algorithms in Artificial Intelligence.

Time Series Analysis: Time series analysis is the study of sequential data over time to identify patterns and trends.

Time Series Forecasting: Time series forecasting is the process of predicting future values in a data sequence based on its temporal history.

TinyML: Machine learning in small devices is a technology that enables running machine learning models on devices with limited resources, such as microcontrollers.

Tokenization: Tokenization is the process of breaking text into smaller parts, called tokens. It is a crucial step in natural language processing for data preparation, analysis, and modeling.

Topic Extraction: Topic extraction is the process of identifying and extracting key themes or concepts from a text. It is fundamental in natural language processing for content analysis and information discovery.

Topic Modeling: Topic modeling is a type of statistical analysis that identifies recurring patterns and themes in a text data set. It is common in natural language processing to uncover hidden structures in collections of documents.

Topological Data Analysis: Topological data analysis is an approach that studies the shape of data using topological techniques. It helps to understand the structure and intrinsic characteristics of complex data sets.

Training Epoch: A training epoch is a term in machine learning that refers to a complete iteration of the learning algorithm over the entire training data set. Epochs are important for tuning and improving the performance of models.

Training Set: A training set is a subset of data used to train models in machine learning. Models learn to make predictions or decisions based on this data set.

Transfer Entropy: Transfer entropy is a measure in information theory that quantifies the amount of information transferred from one time series to another. It is used in time series analysis and complex systems to understand interactions and dependencies.

Transfer Learning: An approach in machine learning where a model developed for one task is reused as a starting point for a model on a second task. It is especially popular in the field of deep learning due to the amount of time and resources required to train a deep model from scratch.

Transformer Models: Transformer models are a type of deep learning architecture primarily used in natural language processing. They are known for their ability to handle data sequences, such as text, more effectively than previous architectures.

Transformer Networks: Transformer networks are an advanced architecture in deep learning, particularly effective in sequence processing, as in automatic translation and text generation.

Tree-Based Models: Tree-based models are supervised learning methods that use tree structures for decision-making. They include decision trees, random forests, and tree boosting, and are widely used for their ease of interpretation and effectiveness in many tasks.

True Positive, True Negative, False Positive, False Negative: True positive, true negative, false positive, and false negative are terms used in classification to describe the outcomes of a model. They indicate the accuracy of the model's predictions compared to actual values.

Truncated SVD (Singular Value Decomposition): Truncated singular value decomposition is a dimensionality reduction technique. It is similar to PCA, but is designed to work with sparse matrices and is common in text analysis and natural language processing.

Trustworthy AI: Trustworthy Artificial Intelligence refers to AI systems designed to be ethical, transparent, and fair. This concept encompasses the creation of AI that is safe, respects privacy, and is accountable in its decisions and actions.

Tuple: In programming, a tuple is a collection of elements that is immutable (cannot be modified once created) and can contain elements of different types. In Python, tuples are common for grouping data and results.

Turing Test: The Turing Test is a criterion proposed by Alan Turing to evaluate a machine's intelligence. If a human interacts with the machine and cannot distinguish whether they are speaking with a human or a machine, the machine is said to have passed the test.

Two-Stage Learning: Two-stage learning is an approach in machine learning where the learning process is divided into two distinct phases, such as pre-training and fine-tuning, to improve the efficiency and efficacy of the model.

Type Inference: Type inference is the process of automatically determining data types in programming languages, which is useful in the development of Artificial Intelligence and machine learning tools to ensure code correctness.

U

Ubiquitous Computing: Ubiquitous computing in AI refers to the integration of Artificial Intelligence into everyday devices and environments, enabling more natural and contextual interactions.

Ultra-Low Power AI: Ultra-low power AI refers to the development and use of Artificial Intelligence systems that require very little energy, suitable for mobile devices or Internet of Things (IoT).

Unbiased Estimator: An unbiased estimator is a term in statistics and machine learning that describes an estimator whose expected value is equal to the actual parameter it tries to estimate.

Uncertainty Principle: The uncertainty principle in AI is a concept that reflects the idea that it is not always possible to have total certainty in the predictions or results generated by an Artificial Intelligence model.

Uncertainty Quantification: Uncertainty quantification in AI is the practice of assessing and expressing the uncertainty associated with the outcomes and predictions of Artificial Intelligence models.

Underfitting: Underfitting is a problem in machine learning where a model is too simple to adequately represent the data and fails to achieve good performance.

Under-specification: Under-specification in model design refers to the situation where a machine learning model is not sufficiently defined or constrained, leading to ambiguous or unstable results.

U-Net Architecture: U-Net architecture in deep learning is a type of convolutional neural network specifically designed for image segmentation tasks.

Unified Modeling Language (UML): Unified Modeling Language (UML) in AI is a standard methodology for modeling software systems, including those incorporating Artificial Intelligence and machine learning components.

Unified Threat Management (UTM): Unified Threat Management (UTM) in AI is the integration of multiple security functions, such as antivirus, firewall, and intrusion prevention, using intelligent systems to enhance information security.

Uniform Distribution: Uniform distribution in AI refers to a probability distribution where all events have the same likelihood of occurring, commonly used in the initialization of parameters of machine learning models.

Unimodal Distribution: Unimodal distribution in data analysis refers to a distribution that has a single peak or mode, commonly analyzed in statistics and machine learning.

Unit Testing: Unit testing in AI refers to the practice of individually testing the components or modules of an Artificial Intelligence system to ensure they function correctly.

Univariate Analysis: Univariate analysis is the analysis of data focusing on a single variable to describe its distribution, centrality, and dispersion.

Universal Approximation Theorem: The Universal Approximation Theorem refers to the ability of single hidden layer neural networks to approximate any continuous function, given enough neurons in the hidden layer.

Unlabeled Data: Unlabeled data in machine learning are data that do not have labels or annotations assigned, used in unsupervised learning methods.

Unstructured Data: Unstructured data are data that do not follow a predefined structure, such as plain text, images, or audio.

Unsupervised Anomaly Detection: Unsupervised anomaly detection is a process of identifying unusual or rare patterns in unlabeled data, using unsupervised machine learning techniques.

Unsupervised Clustering Algorithms: Unsupervised clustering algorithms are methods used in machine learning to automatically group data into sets or clusters based on similarities, without the need for prior labels.

Unsupervised Data Reduction: Unsupervised data reduction is a machine learning technique for simplifying and reducing the amount of data, while retaining as much relevant information as possible, without using labels or external supervision.

Unsupervised Feature Learning: Unsupervised feature learning is a technique where a model learns to identify useful features or patterns in unlabeled data.

Unsupervised Learning: Unsupervised learning is a machine learning approach where a model is trained on unlabeled data to discover patterns and structures.

Unsupervised Time Series Analysis: Unsupervised time series analysis refers to the study of patterns and structures in time series without the use of labels or supervision, using machine learning techniques.

Update Rule: An update rule in machine learning is a formula or method used to adjust the parameters of a model during training.

Uplift Analysis: Uplift analysis in marketing and AI is a technique that evaluates the impact of a marketing campaign or specific action using machine learning algorithms to predict changes in customer behavior.

Uplift Modeling: Uplift modeling in Customer Relationship Management (CRM) refers to the application of predictive modeling techniques to estimate the impact of CRM strategies on customer behavior.

Upsampling: Upsampling in machine learning is a technique to increase the size of data samples, commonly used in image and signal processing.

User Behavior Modeling: User behavior modeling in AI involves using algorithms to predict or understand how users interact with systems or products, based on historical data and behavior patterns.

User Experience (UX): User Experience (UX) design in AI involves designing Artificial Intelligence products focusing on ease of use, accessibility, and a pleasing user experience.

User Interface (UI): User Interface (UI) design in AI involves creating interfaces for Artificial Intelligence applications that are intuitive and easy to use.

User Profiling: User profiling in AI is the practice of using machine learning algorithms to analyze and predict users' characteristics and behaviors.

User Segmentation: User segmentation in AI is the process of dividing a user base into smaller groups based on similar characteristics, commonly used in marketing and data analysis.

User-Generated Content Analysis: User-generated content analysis in AI involves using natural language processing and machine learning techniques to analyze and extract information from texts, images, or videos created by users.

UTF-8 Encoding: UTF-8 encoding in data processing is a method for encoding text strings in formats that are compatible and efficient for storage and processing by AI systems.

Utility Function: A utility function in reinforcement learning describes a function that measures the value or reward of different states or actions in the context of reinforcement learning.

Utility Maximization: Utility maximization in decision making is an approach where AI agents make decisions to maximize a specific utility function, reflecting their preferences or goals.

Utility Theory: Utility theory in AI decision making is an approach that models how intelligent agents should make rational decisions based on the maximization of expected utility.

Utility-Based Feature Selection: Utility-based feature selection is an approach in machine learning that chooses features based on their ability to improve a model's performance according to a utility function.

Utility-based Learning: Utility-based learning is a machine learning approach where decisions are made to maximize a specific utility function.

Utility-based Ranking: Utility-based ranking in AI is a method for ordering or classifying items based on a utility function, which may include multiple criteria or preferences.

UUID (Universally Unique Identifier): UUID (Universally Unique Identifier) in data management is a standard identifier used to ensure the uniqueness of elements in databases and information systems.

V

Validation Set: A validation set is a subset of data used to evaluate the performance of a machine learning model during training.

Validation: Validation refers to the process of evaluating the performance of a machine learning model using a dataset that was not used during training.

Value Decomposition: Value decomposition is a concept in data analysis and machine learning that involves breaking down a matrix or dataset into components that capture significant aspects of the data.

Value Function: A value function in reinforcement learning is a function that estimates how much benefit can be obtained from a particular state or action.

Value Iteration: Value iteration is a dynamic programming method used in reinforcement learning to find the optimal policy.

Value-Based Learning: Value-based learning is an approach in reinforcement learning where the goal is to maximize a value function that represents the expected return from actions or states.

Vanishing Gradient Problem: The vanishing gradient problem is a challenge in deep neural networks where gradients tend to disappear, making effective training difficult.

Variable Encoding: Variable encoding is the process of transforming categorical variables into a format that can be more easily processed by machine learning algorithms.

Variable Importance Plot: A variable importance plot is a visualization used in machine learning to show the relative importance of different input variables in a predictive model.

Variable Selection: Variable selection is the process of identifying and selecting the most relevant variables for a machine learning model.

Variance Reduction: Variance reduction refers to techniques in statistics and machine learning that seek to decrease the variance of estimates to improve the accuracy of the model.

Variance: Variance is a measure of the dispersion of a model's predictions, indicating how sensitive the model is to variations in the training set.

Variational Autoencoder (VAE): A variational autoencoder is a type of generative model used to generate synthetic data and learn latent representations.

Variational Bayesian Methods: Variational Bayesian methods are techniques in Bayesian statistics that use approximations to solve complex inference problems.

Variational Inference: Variational inference is a method in Bayesian statistics that approximates complex probability distributions with simpler distributions to facilitate computation.

Variogram: A variogram is a tool in spatial statistics used to describe the spatial dependence of data, applicable in machine learning for geospatial analysis.

Vector Autoregressive Model (VAR): A vector autoregressive model is a type of statistical model used to predict multivariate time series systems, applicable in various AI contexts.

Vector Field: A vector field in AI can refer to the use of vector fields to represent and analyze directional data in various applications, such as robotics and image processing.

Vector Quantization: Vector quantization is a data compression and reduction technique that converts large sets of vectors into a smaller number of representative vectors.

Vector Space Model: A vector space model is a mathematical representation of text documents as vectors in a multidimensional space, commonly used in natural language processing and information retrieval.

Vectorization: Vectorization is the conversion of non-numeric data into numeric vectors so that they can be processed by machine learning algorithms.

Version Space: Version space is a concept in machine learning that represents the set of all hypotheses consistent with the observed training examples.

VGGNet: VGGNet is a deeply developed convolutional neural network architecture for image recognition, known for its simplicity and effectiveness in computer vision competitions.

Virtual Agent: A virtual agent is a software program that uses AI to automate tasks, answer questions, and assist users, commonly in the form of chatbots or personal assistants.

Virtual Environment: A virtual environment in the context of AI refers to a simulated space where machine learning models can be trained and tested under controlled conditions.

Virtual Reality (VR): Virtual reality is a technology that creates simulated environments and can be used to train AI models in controlled settings.

Virtual Sensor: A virtual sensor refers to a software model that simulates the readings of a physical sensor, used in contexts where physical sensors are not available or impractical.

Vision Processing Unit (VPU): A vision processing unit is a type of microprocessor or specialized hardware designed to accelerate image processing and computer vision tasks.

Vision Transformer (ViT): A vision transformer is a type of model based on the Transformer architecture, specifically designed for image processing tasks.

Vision-Based Model: A vision-based model refers to AI systems that process and analyze images or videos to perform tasks such as object recognition, motion tracking, and scene analysis.

Visual Analytics: Visual analytics is the study of how visual representations and interactive techniques can help analyze and understand complex data, often in the context of AI and big data.

Visual Feature Extraction: Visual feature extraction is the process of identifying and selecting significant features in images or videos for use in recognition and classification tasks.

Visual Recognition: Visual recognition is the process by which AI systems identify and classify objects in images and videos.

Visual SLAM (Simultaneous Localization and Mapping): Visual SLAM is a technique used in robotics and autonomous systems to build a map of an unknown environment while simultaneously estimating the location of the device in that environment.

Viterbi Algorithm: The Viterbi algorithm is a dynamic algorithm used to find the most probable sequence of hidden states in Markov models, especially in signal processing and natural language.

Vocal Emotion Recognition: Vocal emotion recognition is the ability of an AI system to identify and classify human emotions from voice characteristics.

Voice Recognition: Voice recognition is the ability of a system to identify and process spoken language.

Volume Integration: Volume integration is a concept in computer graphics and simulations that can be used in AI to understand and process three-dimensional structures.

Volumetric Analysis: Volumetric analysis in the context of AI refers to the study and processing of three-dimensional data, such as in medical image reconstruction or 3D modeling.

Voting Classifier: A voting classifier is an ensemble approach that combines the predictions of multiple machine learning models to make a final prediction.

Vowpal Wabbit: Vowpal Wabbit is an open-source machine learning library for regression, classification, and other problems, known for its efficiency in processing large datasets.

W

Word Embedding: Word embedding is a technique that assigns words to numeric vectors in a high-dimensional space for processing in natural language models.

Walk-Forward Optimization: Walk-forward optimization is a technique in quantitative analysis and algorithmic trading that involves adjusting and testing a trading model on a data set, and then testing it on a future data set.

Walk-Through: Walk-through is a software or system review method where developers or analysts review code or design with colleagues to detect errors or improve quality.

Wasserstein Distance: Wasserstein distance is a measure in optimal transport theory that quantifies the distance between two probability distributions, used in areas such as machine learning to compare distributions.

Wavelet Transform: Wavelet transform is a mathematical technique used to decompose signals into components of different frequencies, useful in signal processing and data analysis.

Weak AI: Weak AI refers to AI systems designed and trained to perform specific tasks, unlike Strong AI which would have general cognitive abilities.

Weak Learner: A weak learner in machine learning refers to a model that is slightly better than chance, often used in ensemble methods such as boosting to build stronger models.

Weak Supervision: Weak supervision is an approach in machine learning where noisy or approximate labels are used instead of precisely labeled data, reducing the need for manual annotation.

Web Mining: Web mining is the use of data mining techniques and machine learning to discover and extract useful information from web data, which includes web content, link structure, and usage data.

Web Ontology Language (OWL): Web Ontology Language is a language used to create complex and detailed ontologies on the web, allowing for the representation of knowledge and its use in AI for semantic understanding.

Web Scraping: Web scraping is a technique used to extract data from websites, often used to collect large data sets from the Internet for analysis or machine learning.

Weight Clipping: Weight clipping is a technique used in neural network training to prevent gradient explosion, limiting the value of weights to a defined range.

Weight Decay: Weight decay is a regularization technique in machine learning aimed at preventing overfitting by adding a penalty term to the cost function based on the magnitude of the network's weights.

Weight Initialization: Weight initialization refers to the process of assigning initial values to the weights in a neural network before starting training.

Weight Matrix: Weight matrix in neural networks and machine learning is a matrix that stores the weights between neurons of adjacent layers, playing a crucial role in determining the model's output.

Weight Pruning: Weight pruning is a neural network optimization technique that involves removing small-magnitude weights to reduce model complexity and improve computational efficiency.

Weight Regularization: Weight regularization is a technique used in machine learning to reduce overfitting by penalizing models with extreme weights, typically by adding a penalty term to the loss function.

Weight Sharing: Weight sharing is a technique in convolutional neural networks where the same weight is used for multiple neural connections, reducing model complexity and improving efficiency.

Weighted Average: Weighted average in machine learning is a calculation that gives different weights to different elements, allowing some to contribute more to the final outcome than others.

Weighted Decision Tree: A weighted decision tree is a decision tree in which different weights are assigned to different nodes or branches, allowing for more effective handling of inequalities in data sets.

Weighted Graph: A weighted graph is a data structure where edges have assigned weights, fundamental in shortest path algorithms and other graph optimization problems.

Weighted k-Nearest-Neighbors (W-k-N-N): Weighted k-Nearest Neighbors is a variant of the k-N-N algorithm where a different weight is assigned to each of the neighbors, based on their distance, for classification or regression.

Weighted Least Squares: Weighted least squares is a statistical method in which different weights are assigned to different observations, commonly used in regression to handle unequal variances in data.

Weighted Loss Function: Weighted loss function in machine learning is a function that assigns different weights to different classes or examples, to account for variable importance or unequal frequency of classes.

Weighted Majority Algorithm: Weighted majority algorithm is a method in machine learning that combines predictions of multiple models, assigning more weight to models that have proven to be more accurate.

Weighted Random Forest: Weighted random forest is a variant of the random forest algorithm in machine learning where different weights are assigned to trees based on their performance, improving prediction accuracy.

Weighted Sampling: Weighted sampling is a technique in statistics and machine learning where samples are selected with a probability proportional to their importance or weight, used to create more representative data sets or to handle unbalanced classes.

Weighted Support Vector Machine (WSVM): Weighted support vector machine is a variation of SVM that assigns different weights to different classes or examples, to address imbalances in data sets.

Weka: Weka is a set of software tools for data analysis and machine learning, providing a collection of algorithms and tools for data mining.

Whale Optimization Algorithm: Whale optimization algorithm is an optimization algorithm inspired by the hunting behavior of humpback whales, used to solve complex optimization problems in various fields.

Whisker Plot: Whisker plot is a visual representation of statistical data that shows the distribution of data, including the median, quartiles, and outliers, useful in data analysis and machine learning.

Whitelisting: Whitelisting in computer security systems refers to the practice of explicitly allowing certain entities (such as applications or IP addresses) to access a system, while blocking all others.

Whitening Transformation: Whitening transformation is a statistical process in principal component analysis (PCA) and other methods, which transforms a set of correlated variables into a set of uncorrelated variables.

Wide & Deep Learning: Wide and deep learning is an approach in machine learning that combines wide models for memorization and deep models for generalization, particularly used in recommendation systems.

Wide Learning: Wide learning is a machine learning approach that uses models with a large number of features but shallow depth, in contrast to deep learning.

Wildcard Matching: Wildcard matching in data processing and pattern searching refers to the use of special symbols to represent one or several characters in text strings, facilitating the search and filtering of data.

Window Function: Window function in signal processing and machine learning refers to the use of a mathematical function to select a subset of data within a larger time series.

Window Sliding Technique: Window sliding technique in signal processing and machine learning involves moving a 'window' along the data to analyze data segments sequentially or temporally.

Word Association: Word association is a process in natural language processing (NLP) where relationships between words are identified and analyzed, which can aid in tasks like language understanding and text generation.

Word Frequency Analysis: Word frequency analysis is a technique in natural language processing to study the frequency and distribution of words in a text, useful for tasks such as sentiment analysis or text classification.

Word Sense Disambiguation: Word sense disambiguation is a problem in natural language processing that involves determining the sense of a word in a specific context, crucial for natural language understanding.

Word Tokenization: Word tokenization is a process in natural language processing where text is divided into smaller units, such as words or phrases.

Word2Vec: Word2Vec is a group of models in NLP for producing word embeddings, where words with similar meanings have similar vector representations, used in a variety of NLP applications.

WordNet: WordNet is a lexical database for English, used in natural language processing and groups words into sets of synonyms, providing brief definitions and relationships between them.

Workflow Automation: Workflow automation refers to the use of technology to automate complex business processes, often using Artificial Intelligence to improve efficiency and reduce human errors.

Workflow Mining: Workflow mining is the process of extracting useful patterns and models from an organization's workflow data, which can help improve process efficiency and automation.

Workflow Optimization: Workflow optimization in the context of AI refers to improving business processes using algorithms to increase efficiency and effectiveness.

Workflow Scheduling: Workflow scheduling in the context of AI and cloud computing involves assigning and managing computing tasks and resources to execute workflows efficiently and effectively.

Workload Balancing: Workload balancing in AI systems refers to the optimal distribution of computational tasks to maximize efficiency and minimize processing time.

Wrapper Feature Selection: Wrapper feature selection is a feature selection technique that uses a machine learning algorithm to evaluate the performance of different feature subsets and select the best.

Wrapper Method: Wrapper method is a feature selection technique in machine learning where a predictive model is used to evaluate the combination of features, selecting the most relevant.

X

XAI (Explainable Artificial Intelligence): XAI refers to methods and techniques in the field of Artificial Intelligence that make the outcomes of AI more understandable to humans.

XAI for Decision Support: XAI for decision support systems refers to the integration of explainable AI techniques in systems that help users make informed decisions, especially in contexts where understanding AI recommendations is crucial.

XAI Frameworks: XAI frameworks provide tools and methods for implementing explainable AI techniques. These frameworks facilitate the interpretation and understanding of AI models.

XAI in Autonomous Vehicles: The application of XAI in autonomous vehicles focuses on making the AI systems that control these vehicles more transparent and understandable, which is vital for safety and user trust.

XAI in Finance: The use of XAI in finance involves applying explainable AI techniques to improve the transparency and understanding of AI models used in financial analysis, risk management, and investment decisions.

XAI in Healthcare: The application of XAI in healthcare involves using explainable AI techniques to enhance the transparency and reliability of AI systems in medical diagnostics, treatment, and patient management.

XAI in Robotics: XAI in robotics focuses on making AI-driven robotic systems more comprehensible and transparent to humans, thereby improving human-robot interaction and the adoption of robots in various environments.

XAI Methodologies: XAI methodologies refer to the approaches and systematic processes used to implement and evaluate explainability in AI systems.

XAI Models Evaluation: Evaluating XAI models involves measuring the effectiveness of explainable AI techniques in terms of their ability to provide comprehensible and useful interpretations of AI models.

XAI Techniques: Refers to the various techniques used in explainable Artificial Intelligence, such as LIME (Local Interpretable Model-agnostic Explanations) and SHAP (SHapley Additive exPlanations), which help to interpret and explain AI models.

Xavier Initialization: It is a technique for initializing weights in neural networks, named after Xavier Glorot, aimed at maintaining the variance of activations and gradients across layers to improve training.

XCS (eXtended Classifier System): XCS is a classification system based on genetic algorithms and reinforcement learning. It is used for solving classification and modeling problems in AI.

X-Entropy Loss: In machine learning, X-Entropy Loss, or cross-entropy loss, is a loss function used to measure the performance of a classification model whose output is a probability value between 0 and 1.

XGBoost Algorithm Variants: Variants of the XGBoost algorithm include modified or extended versions of the original algorithm to enhance its performance or adapt it to specific use cases.

XGBoost Feature Importance: Feature importance in XGBoost is a technique for evaluating which variables in the input data are most significant for the predictions made by an XGBoost model.

XGBoost for Time Series: The use of XGBoost for time series involves applying the XGBoost algorithm to analyze and predict data that is sequentially ordered in time, such as in financial or weather forecasts.

XGBoost Hyperparameter Optimization: Hyperparameter optimization of XGBoost refers to the process of tuning and selecting the best hyperparameters for an XGBoost model, in order to maximize its performance in classification or regression tasks.

XGBoost in Natural Language Processing: The application of XGBoost in natural language processing (NLP) involves using the algorithm for tasks like text classification, sentiment analysis, and named entity recognition.

XGBoost Model Interpretation: Interpreting XGBoost models involves using techniques to understand how and why an XGBoost model makes certain decisions or predictions, which is important for validating and trusting the model's results.

XGBoost Tuning: Refers to the process of tuning the hyperparameters of the XGBoost model to improve its performance. This can include adjusting the learning rate, maximum tree depth, and other parameters.

XGBoost with Big Data: The use of XGBoost with large volumes of data involves adapting and scaling the algorithm to work efficiently with massive datasets, maintaining its performance and accuracy.

XGBoost: XGBoost is a machine learning library commonly used for classification and regression problems.

XML (eXtensible Markup Language): XML is a markup language that defines a set of rules for encoding documents in a way that is both human-readable and machine-readable. It is often used in data exchange on the web and in software configuration and documentation.

XML Data Integration: Integrating XML data involves combining data from different sources that are in XML format, which is a crucial aspect in managing large volumes of data and in integrating enterprise systems.

XML Parsing: XML parsing refers to the process of reading and manipulating data in XML documents. It is fundamental in data processing and in systems integration where XML is used as a data exchange format.

XOR (Exclusive OR): XOR is a logical operation between two operands that results in a true value only if the operands are different. In the context of neural networks, XOR is a classic problem to test a system's ability to model non-linear relationships.

XOR Problem in Neural Networks: The XOR problem in neural networks refers to the difficulty of using simple perceptrons to model the XOR logical function, which led to the development of multilayer neural networks and deep learning algorithms.

XPath: XPath is a language that allows developers to navigate through elements and attributes in an XML document. It is commonly used to locate information in XML documents.

XSS (Cross-Site Scripting): Although more related to web security than to AI directly, XSS is a type of computer security vulnerability that allows an attacker to inject malicious code into web pages viewed by other users. It is relevant in the context of AI for the security of intelligent web applications.

XSS Prevention in AI Systems: XSS (Cross-Site Scripting) prevention in AI systems refers to security measures implemented to protect intelligent web applications from script injection attacks.

X-Validation: X-Validation, or cross-validation, is a technique in statistics and machine learning for evaluating a model's ability to predict new data. It involves dividing a data set into subsets, training the model on one subset, and validating the model on another.

Y

Y Combinator: Famous startup accelerator that has funded companies using Artificial Intelligence and machine learning.

YAGNI Principle (You Aren't Gonna Need It): Software development principle that promotes simplicity, avoiding adding features until they are really necessary, applicable in the development of AI solutions.

Yahoo Labs: Yahoo's research department that has contributed to the advancement of machine learning and Artificial Intelligence.

Yale Face Database: Database of faces from Yale University, used in research and applications of facial recognition in Artificial Intelligence.

YAML (YAML Ain't Markup Language): Data serialization language used in the configuration of systems and applications, including tools and platforms of AI.

YARN (Yet Another Resource Negotiator): Resource management and job scheduling system in distributed computing clusters, commonly used with Hadoop and Spark in big data processing.

Y-axis in Plots: Y axis in graphs. In machine learning data visualization, it represents one of the data dimensions, such as features or prediction values.

Y-axis Interception: Y-axis interception, in graphs and data visualizations, is the point where a trend line crosses the Y axis, useful in regression analysis in machine learning.

YCbCr Color Space: Color space used in image and video processing, relevant in AI tasks such as computer vision.

Y-Combinator Networks: Networks that follow the Y-Combinator model, a structure in functional programming, applicable in some AI algorithm architectures.

Year-on-Year Analysis: Year-to-year analysis, in data science and machine learning, refers to the comparison of data from a specific period with the same period in previous years to detect trends or changes.

Year-over-Year Growth: Year-over-year growth. In data analysis and machine learning, it refers to the comparison of performance or results of a period with respect to the same period in previous years.

Yellow Box: In the context of AI, it may refer to tools or visual interfaces used in the development of Artificial Intelligence applications.

Yield Algorithm: Yield algorithm, in machine learning refers to algorithms designed to maximize or optimize performance in various applications, such as in neural networks.

Yield Curve Analysis: Yield curve analysis, in the context of AI refers to the use of algorithms to analyze and predict behaviors in financial markets.

Yield Enhancement: Yield enhancement, in machine learning refers to techniques that seek to optimize the performance of AI models.

Yield Farming: In the context of decentralized finance (DeFi) and blockchain, it refers to automated investment strategies that can be optimized using machine learning algorithms.

Yield Management: Yield management, in AI is used to optimize prices and availability in industries such as hospitality and aviation, using predictive algorithms.

Yield Optimization: Yield optimization. In machine learning, it refers to improving the performance of a model to obtain better results or greater efficiency.

Yield Prediction: Yield prediction, in the context of machine learning, refers to the estimation of future results or yields based on historical data.

Yield Rate Optimization: Yield rate optimization, in machine learning is applied to the improvement of success rates or performance in different systems, such as in classification or prediction.

Yoctosecond Processing: Yoctosecond processing, hypothetically refers to extremely fast computing systems, relevant in the context of future advances in AI.

YOLO (You Only Look Once): Real-time object detection algorithm that divides the image into a grid and predicts object classes and object locations simultaneously.

Yottabyte Processing: Yottabyte processing, referring to systems capable of handling huge volumes of data, an important capacity for big data applications in AI.

Yottabyte: Unit of digital storage measurement equivalent to 10^24 bytes. It is relevant in the context of big data and the storage of large volumes of data.

Yottaflops: Unit of measure for computing performance, especially relevant in large-scale data processing and intensive AI operations.

Yottascale Computing: Yottabyte-scale computing, a term referring to data processing systems of extremely large sizes, relevant for big data and AI applications.

Young's Modulus Prediction: Prediction of Young's modulus, in AI applies to the prediction of mechanical properties of materials using machine learning algorithms.

YouTube-8M: A large and diverse benchmark dataset composed of millions of YouTube videos tagged, useful for video classification tasks and machine learning.

YUV Color Space: Color space used in video and image processing, important in computer vision tasks and image analysis with AI.

Z

Z-Buffer Algorithm: Method in computer graphics for handling the problem of surface visibility in 3D images.

Z-Buffering: Rendering technique used in computer graphics to manage the depth of elements in a 3D scene, relevant in advanced visualization and virtual reality.

Zendesk Benchmark: Zendesk data analysis tool that allows comparing customer service performance with industry data, useful in predictive analysis and AI applied to business.

Zero-Day Attack: Refers to a type of cyber threat that exploits an unknown software vulnerability to the manufacturer or that has no patch available.

Zero-Knowledge Proof: Concept in cryptography and computer security where one party proves to another that a statement is true, without revealing any additional information.

Zero-Order Hold: Technique in signal processing used to keep the values of a discrete signal constant between sampling intervals.

Zero-Shot Learning: Refers to the ability of a model to identify and classify objects or situations it has never seen during its training.

Zeroth-Order Optimization: Method in machine learning and optimization that does not require gradient calculation, and is based on estimates from function evaluations.

Zeta Function: In mathematics, a complex function that is significant in number theory, complex analysis, and physics. In AI, it may be relevant in algorithms involving advanced calculations.

Zettabyte: Unit of measure used in computing to describe quantities of data. Equivalent to a billion terabytes.

ZigBee: Low-power wireless communication technology, used in home automation and IoT, which can interact with Artificial Intelligence systems.

Zigzag Learning: Machine learning strategy that alternates between different types of tasks or data to improve generalization and avoid overfitting.

Zigzag Search: A search or exploration method that follows a zigzag pattern, useful in certain optimization algorithms and in pattern searching.

Zonal Statistics: Technique in image processing and computer vision involving the statistical analysis of regions or zones in an image.

Zone Mapping: Technique in computer vision and image analysis where images are divided into zones for processing and detailed analysis.

Z-Score Normalization: Method for standardizing data, rescaling them so that their average is 0 and their standard deviation is 1.

Z-Score: Statistical measure that describes the position of a value in terms of standard deviations from the mean. Used in data normalization in machine learning.

Z-Statistics: In statistics, it refers to the number of standard deviations that a data point is from the population average.

Z-Test: Type of statistical test used to determine if there are significant differences between the means of two groups, which can be applied in AI data analysis.

Z-Transform: Mathematical tool used in the analysis and processing of digital signals, relevant in the field of Artificial Intelligence to understand and process temporal sequences.

Z-Wave: Wireless communication protocol mainly used in home automation, similar to ZigBee, and that can also be integrated into AI systems for device control.

www.ingramcontent.com/pod-product-compliance
Lightning Source LLC
Chambersburg PA
CBHW080934240926
51849CB00003BA/451
9783912099041